The Tibetan
Book of the Dead

The Tibetan Book of the Dead

OR

The After-Death Experiences
on the *Bardo* Plane, according
to Lāma Kazi Dawa-Samdup's
English Rendering

Compiled and edited by
W. Y. EVANS-WENTZ

OXFORD   NEW YORK
OXFORD   UNIVERSITY   PRESS

Oxford University Press, Walton Street, Oxford OX2 6DP

London Glasgow New York Toronto
Delhi Bombay Calcutta Madras Karachi
Kuala Lumpur Singapore Hong Kong Tokyo
Nairobi Dar es Salaam Cape Town
Melbourne Auckland

and associated companies in
Beirut Berlin Ibadan Mexico City Nicosia

Oxford is a trade mark of Oxford University Press

© W. Y. Evans-Wentz 1960

First published 1927
Second edition 1949
Third edition 1957
First published as an Oxford University Press paperback 1960
Re-issued 1980
Reprinted 1984

All rights reserved. No part of this publication may be reproduced,
stored in a retrieval system, or transmitted, in any form or by any means,
electronic, mechanical, photocopying, recording, or otherwise, without
the prior permission of Oxford University Press

This book is sold subject to the condition that it shall not, by way of
trade or otherwise, be lent, re-sold, hired out, or otherwise circulated
without the publisher's prior consent in any form of binding or cover
other than that in which it is published and without a similar condition
including this condition being imposed on the subsequent purchaser

British Library Cataloguing in Publication Data

The Tibetan book of the dead. — 3rd ed., revised and expanded.
I. Evans-Wentz, Walter Yeeling
294.3'82 BQ1652.E5 60-13909

ISBN 0-19-281302.1

Printed in Great Britain by
The Guernsey Press Co. Ltd.
Guernsey, Channel Islands.

IN MEMORY OF
MY DECEASED FATHER AND MOTHER
I DEDICATE
THIS BOOK TO MY TEACHERS
BOTH SECULAR AND RELIGIOUS
IN EUROPE AND AMERICA
AND THROUGHOUT
THE ORIENT

'Thou shalt understand that it is a science most profitable, and passing all other sciences, for to learn to die. For a man to know that he shall die, that is common to all men; as much as there is no man that may ever live or he hath hope or trust thereof; but thou shalt find full few that have this cunning to learn to die. . . . I shall give thee the mystery of this doctrine; the which shall profit thee greatly to the beginning of ghostly health, and to a stable fundament of all virtues.'—*Orologium Sapientiae.*

'Against his will he dieth that hath not learned to die. Learn to die and thou shalt learn to live, for there shall none learn to live that hath not learned to die.'—*Toure of all Toures: and Teacheth a Man for to Die.*

The Book of the Craft of Dying (Comper's Edition).

'Whatever is here, that is there; what is there, the same is here. He who seeth here as different, meeteth death after death.
'By mind alone this is to be realized, and [then] there is no difference here. From death to death he goeth, who seeth as if there is difference here.'—*Katha Upanishad,* iv. 10-11 (Swami Sharvananda's Translation).

PREFACE

The following is an abridgement of the preface to the 1960 impression

That the living do come from the dead, as Socrates intuitively perceived as he was about to drink the hemlock and experience death, this treatise maintains, not in virtue of tradition or belief, but on the sound basis of the unequivocal testimony of yogins who claim to have died and re-entered the human womb consciously.

If this treatise, bequeathed to the West by Sages of the Snowy Ranges, be as it thus purports to be, it undoubtedly offers trustworthy guidance at the time of death and in the after-death state into which every one of human kind must inevitably pass, but of which very few of them have enlightened understanding. It is, therefore, of inestimable value.

The exploration of Man the Unknown in a manner truly scientific and yogic such as this book suggests is incomparably more important than the exploration of outer space. To stand in the physical body on the Moon, or on Venus, or on any of the celestial spheres, will add to human knowledge, but only to knowledge of things transitory. Man's ultimate goal is, as the Sages herein teach, transcendence over the transitory.

Today, as during the European Renaissance when Oriental influences inspired a number of remarkable treatises on the Art of Dying (to which reference is hereinafter made), there is an ever-increasing desire to know more of man's origin and destiny. As the recently deceased Great Teacher Bhagavan Sri Ramana Maharshi, of Tiruvannamalai, South India, admonished me when I sojourned in his ashram, each of us should ask ourself, 'Who, or what, am I? Why am I here incarnate? Whither am I destined? Why is there birth and why is there death?'

These are for mankind the supreme questions; and in any attempt to answer them this book offers aid, which the editor is glad to be able to report has been universally acknowledged, not only by representatives of various faiths, inclusive of both Catholic and Protestant Christians, but by scientists as well. Dr. C. G.

Jung, the eminent dean of psychologists, has himself recognized the unique value of the book and in his lengthy Psychological Commentary to it, herein contained, says, 'For years, ever since it was first published [in 1927], the *Bardo Thödol* has been my constant companion, and to it I owe not only many stimulating ideas and discoveries, but also many fundamental insights.'

May the book continue to fulfil the hopes of its Translator and editor, by assisting to bring about not only better understanding between the peoples of the East and West, but also in correcting, especially throughout the West, the lack of Right Knowledge concerning humanity's paramount problem, the problem of birth and death.

The editor accepts the opportunity to thank those who more recently have given expression, in journals and in lectures, as well as by letters, of their appreciation of the book, as already he has thanked those who previously did so. It is owing to these appreciative journalists, lecturers, and readers, in all parts of the world, that the book's marked success has been made possible.

And in conveying good wishes to all those who have read or shall hereafter read this book, particularly students, the editor has the high privilege of here directing their attention to the significant words contained in the farewell teachings of Milarepa, one of his most beloved Tibetan Gurus:

'Combine, in a single whole, the goal of aspiration, the meditation, and the practice, and so attain Understanding by Experimentation.

'Regard, as one, this life, the next life, and the life between, in the *Bardo*, and accustom thyself to them thus, as one.'

By practically applying these teachings, so the Gurus assure us, the supramundane goal revealed by this book will be, as it was for Milarepa, realizable.

W. Y. E.-W.

San Diego, California,
  Midsummer Day, 1959.

PREFACE TO THE THIRD EDITION

It is with a consciousness of the deepest gratitude that I write this Preface. No greater honour could be shown by the Western World to this Tibetan treatise on the Science of Death and Rebirth than that shown by the most illustrious of the West's psychologists, Dr. Carl G. Jung, in his Psychological Commentary to it, first published in the Swiss edition of *The Tibetan Book of the Dead, Das Tibetanische Totenbuch*, by Rascher Verlag, Zürich, 1938, and herein presented in English translation for the first time. And no exposition of the arcane significance of the book's teachings could have been written more knowledgeably than that set forth in the Introductory Foreword hereto, in its original English form, by the learned Lāma Anagarika Govinda.

The Editor and all who read this book are indebted to Dr. Jung and to Lāma Govinda for having made this enlarged and greatly enriched edition possible, and to Mr. R. F. C. Hull, also, for his able translation from the German of Dr. Jung's Psychological Commentary. Grateful acknowledgement, too, is here made to the Bollingen Foundation for the granting of permission to publish the English translation of the Psychological Commentary.

To each member of the One Human Family, now incarnate here, on the planet Earth, this book bears the greatest of all great messages. It reveals to the peoples of the Occident a science of death and rebirth such as only the peoples of the Orient have heretofore known.

Inasmuch as all mankind must relinquish their fleshly bodies and experience death, it is supremely profitable that they should know how rightly to meet death when it comes. Lāma Govinda makes comprehensible, as the Ancient Mysteries did, and as the *Upanishads* declare, that the unenlightened meet death after death unceasingly.

According to the Avatāra Krishna, in the *Bhagavad-Gītā*, only the Awakened Ones remember their many deaths and births. The Buddha sets forth the *yogic* method whereby all who doubt these teachings, concerning a plurality of births and deaths, can prove them to be true, as He did, by self-realization.

The argument of the unenlightened man, that, merely because he himself has no conscious memory of his many births and deaths, the teachings are untrue, is scientifically untenable. The field of the normal man's sense perceptions is, as can be demonstrated, narrowly circumscribed and extremely limited. There are objects and colours he cannot see, sounds he cannot hear, odours he cannot smell, tastes he cannot taste, and feelings he cannot feel. And beyond his work-a-day consciousness, which he assumes to be his only consciousness, there are other consciousnesses, of which *yogins* and saints have cognizance, and of which psychologists are beginning to glean some, but as yet very little, understanding. As Lāma Govinda concisely explains, there exists, in completeness, in a potentially realizable consciousness, the memory of a forgotten past, in which each of us now incarnate shares.

In his Psychological Commentary, Dr. Jung points out that although Freud's 'is the first attempt made by the West to investigate, as if from below, from the animal sphere of instinct, the psychic territory that corresponds in Tantric Lāmaism, to the *Sidpa Bardo*', or state of reincarnating, 'a very justifiable fear of metaphysics prevented Freud from penetrating into the sphere of the " occult " '. In this, Freud was typically non-Oriental, and fettered by his own self-imposed limitations. But such self-imposed limitations of Western Science, which are very much like those that Western Theology imposed upon itself by refusing to take into proper account the esoteric in Christian tradition, cannot always hold back psychological research. Dr. Jung himself has, indeed, gone far beyond these limitations of Freud, his predecessor. ' It is therefore not possible ', Dr. Jung states, ' for Freudian theory to reach anything except an essentially negative valuation of the unconscious '—wherein are stored, apparently imperishably, as Dr. Jung holds, the records, in completeness, of mankind's past. At a conclusion parallel to this of Western Science, Lāma Govinda arrived by means of Eastern Science.

Dr. Jung reports that ' psychoanalysts even claim to have probed back to memories of intra-uterine origin '; and that had Freudian psychoanalysis succeeded in pursuing these so-called intra-uterine experiences still further back, ' it would surely have come out beyond the *Sidpa Bardo* and penetrated from behind into the lower reaches of the *Chönyid Bardo*.' But, as he points out, ' with the equipment of our existing biological ideas such a venture would not have been crowned with success; it would have needed a wholly different kind of philosophical preparation from that based on current scientific assumptions. But, had the journey back been consistently pursued, it would undoubtedly have led to the postulate of a pre-uterine existence, a true *Bardo* life, if only it had been possible to find at least some trace of an experiencing subject.'

Western psychologists have, therefore, advanced appreciably beyond Freud in the study of the psychic life of man, and will advance much further when they no longer allow the Freudian fear of metaphysics to bar their entrance into the realm of the occult. This finds ample support in Dr. Jung's further pronouncement:

' I think, then, we can state it as a fact that with the aid of psychoanalysis the rationalizing mind of the West has pushed forward into what one might call the neuroticism of the *Sidpa* [or Rebirth] state, and has there been brought to an inevitable standstill by the uncritical assumption that everything psychological is subjective and personal. Even so, this advance has been a great gain, inasmuch as it has enabled us to take one more step behind our conscious lives.'

Thus it is of far-reaching historical importance that the profound doctrine of pre-existence and rebirth, which many of the most enlightened men in all known epochs have taught as being realizable, is now under investigation by our own scientists of the West. And some of these scientists seem to be approaching that place, on the path of scientific progress, where, as with respect also to other findings by the Sages of Asia long before the rise of Western Science, East and West appear to be destined to meet in mutual understanding.

Apparently, however, before this much-desired understanding can be attained, there must be, as Dr. Jung observes, ' a wholly different kind of philosophical preparation ' from that based upon the West's ' existing biological ideas '. May it not be that ' heretical ' Western psychologists who are prepared to blaze a new path of research will eventually find the lacking complement to their at present inadequate methods in the psychological techniques of oriental *yoga*, such as those referred to in Lāma Govinda's Foreword? At least the writer believes that they will. According to his view, that much sought-after higher understanding of the human psyche will be won not by these admittedly inadequate Freudian methods, now in vogue, of ' psychoanalyzing' a subject, but by meditation and an integrating self-analysis, such as the master *yogins* employ and the Buddha prescribes. He believes, too, that thereby Western Science and Eastern Science will, at last, attain at-one-ment.

Then, when that long-awaited at-one-ment shall have been consummated, there will no longer be doubt, nor fallacious argumentation, nor unwise and unscientific Church-Council anathematizations directed against that paramount doctrine of pre-existence and re-birth, upon which the *Bardo Thödol* is based. Then, too, not only will Pythagoras and Plato and Plotinus, and the Gnostic Christians, and Krishna and the Buddha be vindicated in their advocacy of the doctrine, but, equally, the Hierophants of the Ancient Mysteries of Egypt and Greece and Rome, and the Druids of the Celtic World. And Western man will awaken from that slumber of Ignorance which has been hypnotically induced by a mistaken Orthodoxy. He will greet with wide-opened eyes his long unheeded brethren, the Wise Men of the East.

As set forth in my first important work, *The Fairy-Faith in Celtic Countries*, forty-four years ago, the postulate of rebirth implies a scientific extension and correction of Darwin's conception of evolutionary law,—that alone through traversing the Cycle of Death and Birth, as taught by our revered ancestors, the Druids of Europe, twenty-five and more centuries ago, man attains in the spiritual and psychic sphere that destined perfection which all life's processes and all living things exhibit at the end of their evolutionary course, and from which at present man is so far removed.

May this third edition of the first volume of the Oxford Tibetan Series bear to all who read it the good wishes of its compilers, not only of those of them who dwell in far-away Tibet and Hindustan, but, also, of those of them who dwell in the Western World. And may we heed the solemn admonition set forth in this book—not to fritter away in the worthless doings of this world the supreme opportunity afforded by human birth, lest by our spiritual improvidence we depart from this life spiritually empty-handed.

W. Y. E-W.

San Diego, California,

Easter, 1955

SRI KRISHNA'S REMEMBERING

' Many lives, Arjuna, you and I have lived,
I remember them all, but thou dost not.'
Bhagavad-Gītā, iv, 5.

BONDAGE TO REBIRTH

' As a man's desire is, so is his destiny. For as his desire is, so is his will; and as his will is, so is his deed; and as his deed is, so is his reward, whether good or bad.

' A man acteth according to the desires to which he clingeth. After death he goeth to the next world bearing in his mind the subtle impressions of his deeds; and, after reaping there the harvest of his deeds, he returneth again to this world of action. Thus he who hath desire continueth subject to rebirth.'

Brihadaranyaka Upanishad.

FREEDOM FROM REBIRTH

' He who lacketh discrimination, whose mind is unsteady and whose heart is impure, never reacheth the goal, but is born again and again. But he who hath discrimination, whose mind is steady and whose heart is pure, reacheth the goal, and having reached it is born no more.'

Katha Upanishad.

(Swami Prabhavananda's and Frederick
Manchester's Translations).

PREFACE TO THE SECOND EDITION

THE MESSAGE OF THIS BOOK

As this, the second, edition of *The Tibetan Book of the Dead* was about to be published, its editor was invited to explain, by means of an additional Preface, what the essential message is that the book holds for peoples so enamoured of this world's utilitarianism and physical existence and so fettered to bodily sensuousness as are the peoples of the Occident.

The message is, that the Art of Dying is quite as important as the Art of Living (or of Coming into Birth), of which it is the complement and summation; that the future of being is dependent, perhaps entirely, upon a rightly controlled death, as the second part of this volume, setting forth the Art of Reincarnating, emphasizes.

The Art of Dying, as indicated by the death-rite associated with initiation into the Mysteries of Antiquity, and referred to by Apuleius,[1] the Platonic philosopher, himself an initiate,

[1] Of this pre-mortem experiencing of death, presumably while out of the body, Apuleius states, in his *Metamorphoses* (XI, 23): 'I drew nigh to the confines of death. I trod the threshold of Proserpine [in the realm of the dead]. I was borne through all the elements, and I returned to Earth again.' Cf. translation by H. E. Butler (Oxford, Clarendon Press, 1910).

The art of going out from the body, or of transferring the consciousness from the earth-plane to the after-death plane, or to any other plane, is still practised, in Tibet, where it is known as *Pho-wa*. See W. Y. Evans-Wentz, *Tibetan Yoga and Secret Doctrines* (Oxford University Press, London, 1935), pages 169-70, 246-76.

and by many other illustrious initiates, and as *The Egyptian Book of the Dead* suggests, appears to have been far better known to the ancient peoples inhabiting the Mediterranean countries than it is now by their descendants in Europe and the Americas.

To those who had passed through the secret experiencing of pre-mortem death, right dying is initiation, conferring, as does the initiatory death-rite, the power to control consciously the process of death and regeneration. Throughout the Middle Ages, and during the Renaissance that followed, Europe still retained enough of the Mystery teachings concerning death to understand the paramount importance of knowing how to die; and many treatises, hereinafter referred to, on the Art of Dying were then current there. Various primitive Churches of Christendom, notably the Roman, Greek, Anglican, Syrian, Armenian, and Coptic, and other of the Churches dating from Reformation days, wisely incorporated into their rituals and observances many principles of this pre-Christian Art of Dying. And to-day, in their efforts thus to aid the dying, these Churches are in outstanding contrast, sociologically and culturally, to an Earth-limited medical science which has no word of guidance to convey to the dying concerning the after-death state, but which, on the contrary, frequently augments rather than ameliorates, by its questionable practices, the unfounded fears and often extreme unwillingness to die of its death-bed patients, to whom it is likely to have administered stupefying drugs and injections.

As *The Tibetan Book of the Dead* teaches, the dying should face death not only calmly and clear-mindedly and heroically,

[1]Among these illustrious initiates, who, in their various extant writings, make reference similar to that by Apuleius to this death-rite, but usually in language more veiled than his, may be mentioned Aeschylus, the founder of Greek drama, Pindar, the Greek poet, Plato, the disciple of Pythagoras, Plutarch, the Greek biographer, Cicero, the Roman orator and statesman, Plotinus, the Neo-Platonist, and his disciples Porphyry and Iamblichus. Cicero, rejoicing in his initiation-acquired enlightment, writes: ' We at last possess reasons why we should live; and we are not only eager to live, but we cherish a better hope in death ' (*De Legibus*, II, 14; translation by A. Moret, in his *Kings and Gods of Egypt*, New York and London, 1912, page 194). In the same context, A. Moret states: ' The same sentiment is found in the inscription of an Eleusinian initiate: " Behold! it is a fair mystery that comes unto us from the Blessed; for mortals, death is no more an evil, but a bliss " '. And Plutarch, in his *Immortality of the Soul*, refers to ' the crowd of the folk who are not initiated and purified, and who throng to the mud-pit [of sensuality] and flounder in the darkness, and through fear of death cling to their woes, not trusting in the bliss of the hereafter ' (Cf. A. Moret, *op. cit.*, page 195[1]).

but with an intellect rightly trained and rightly directed, mentally transcending, if need be, bodily suffering and infirmities, as they would be able to do had they practised efficiently during their active lifetime the Art of Living, and, when about to die, the Art of Dying. When Milarepa, Tibet's saintly master of Yoga, was preparing to die, he chose not only a favourable external environment, in the Cave of Brilche, in Chubar, Tibet, but an inner state of mental equilibrium in keeping with his approaching *Nirvāṇa*. Indomitably controlling his body, which, having been poisoned by an enemy, was disease-weakened and pain-wracked, he welcomed death with song, as being natural and inevitable. After having delivered his final testamentary teachings and parting admonitions to his assembled disciples, he composed, extemporaneously, a remarkable hymn in grateful praise of his Guru Marpa, which is yet preserved in his *Biography*. Then, when Milarepa had completed the singing of the hymn, he entered the quiescent state of *Samādhi*, and relinquished his fleshly form. Thus did Milarepa die triumphantly, as do the saints and sages of all saving faiths throughout the ages.[1]

But in the Occident, where the Art of Dying is little known and rarely practised, there is, contrastingly, the common unwillingness to die, which, as the *Bardo* ritual suggests, produces unfavourable results. As here in America, every effort is apt to be made by a materialistically inclined medical science to postpone, and thereby to interfere with, the death-process. Very often the dying is not permitted to die in his or her own home, or in a normal, unperturbed mental condition when the hospital has been reached. To die in a hospital, probably while under the mind-benumbing influence of some opiate, or else under the stimulation of some drug injected into the body to enable the dying to cling to life as long as possible, cannot but be productive of a very undesirable death, as undesirable as that of a shell-shocked soldier on a battle-field. Even as the normal result of the birth-process may be aborted by malpractices, so, similarly, may the normal result of the death-process be aborted.

The oriental Sages believe that, despite these unfortunate circumstances which now encompass him when dying, occidental

[1] See W. Y. Evans-Wentz, *Tibet's Great Yogi Milarepa* (Oxford University Press, London, 1928), pages 244-304.

man will, as he grows in right understanding, recognize that everywhere throughout the all-embracing universe, whose immensities
he measures in millions of light years, there is the reign of uner-
ring Law. The Cycle of Necessity, the Circle of Existence of the
old Druidic faith, the Round of Life and Death, he will know to be
universal, that worlds and suns, no less than he himself and every
living thing, repeatedly come into the illusory manifestation of
embodiment, and that each of these many manifestations is
rounded by what the Lāmas of Tibet call the *Bardo*, the state
intervening between death and rebirth.

If the suggestive observations herein presented in this new
Preface, which are born of the doctrines contained in the translated texts of this book, aid in any small degree to awaken the
Occident to the extreme dangers into which it has been led, in
large measure by a medical science ignorant for the most part of
the Art of Dying, they will have furthered the prayers of the
Lāmas by helping to dissipate that Darkness of Ignorance which,
as the Buddha realized, enshrouds the world. As the Fully
Enlightened One and all the Supreme Guides of Humanity have
taught, it is only by the inner Light of Wisdom, ' the true Light,
which lighteth every man that cometh into the world,'[1] that the
Darkness of Ignorance can be dispersed.

The Egyptian Book of the Dead, correctly entitled, is *The Coming
Forth from Day*, with reference to the sacred Egyptian art of the
coming forth from this life into another life, or, in the language
of Pharaonic Egypt, the *Per em hru*.[2] Similarly, *The Tibetan
Book of the Dead*, in the original Tibetan, is the *Bardo Thödol*,
meaning ' Liberation by Hearing on the After-Death Plane ',
and implying a *yogic* method of coming forth into *Nirvāṇic*
Liberation, beyond the Cycle of Birth and Death. Each of these
two books concerning death thus inculcates, by its own peculiar
method, an Art of Dying and Coming Forth into a New Life,
but in a more symbolic and esoterically profound manner than
do the treatises of medieval Christian Europe on the Art of Dying,
among which the *Ars Moriendo* (' Craft of Dying ') may be taken
as being typical and illustrative of this contrasting difference.

It was the fervent hope of the late Lāma Kazi Dawa-Samdup,

[1] Cf. *St. John*, I, 9.
[2] Cf. H. M. Tirard, *The Book of the Dead* (London, 1910), pages 48-9.

the translator, and of other of the learned Lāmas who directed the editor's Tibetan research—a hope in which the editor, too, shares—that, aided by the Mystery teachings and its own Christianized versions of many principles of them, the Occident might reformulate and practise an Art of Dying, and, also, an Art of Living. For the peoples of the Occident, as it was for the initiates of antiquity and still is for the peoples of the Orient, the transition from the human plane of consciousness, in the process called death, can be and should be accompanied by solemn joyousness. Eventually, as the master *yogins* declare, when humanity shall have grown spiritually strong, death will be experienced ecstatically, in that state known to them as *Samādhi*. By right practising of a trustworthy Art of Dying, death will then, indeed, have lost its sting and been swallowed up in victory.

Whilst this Preface is being written it is Easter, in California. As was the custom in many great civilizations of yore, so here to-day, from hilltop and mountain, with prayer and joyous singing, obeisance is being paid to the new-born Sun at dawn, amidst the fresh and glistening greenery of renascent leaves and the fragrance of blossoms and the joy of Spring. It is, truly, the ever-recurrent Resurrection, the coming forth into a new life of things that had died; and, in like manner, are those who have fallen asleep in the *Christos* to be empowered to rise from their tombs. Over the bosom of the Earth-Mother, in pulsating vibrations, radiant and energizing, flows the perennial Stream of Life; and whosoever has the power of right-seeing sees that for unemancipated beings death is but the necessary and Law-directed prelude to birth.

W. Y. E-W.

San Diego, California,

   Easter 1948.

Buddhists and Hindus alike believe that the last thought at the moment of death determines .the character of the next incarnation. As the *Bardo Thödol* teaches, so have the Sages of India long taught, that the thought-process of a dying person should be rightly directed, preferably by the dying person if he or she has been initiated or psychically trained to meet death, or, otherwise, by a *guru* or a friend or relative versed in the science of death.

Sri Krishna, in the *Bhagavad Gītā* (viii, 6), says to Arjuna, ' One attaineth whatever state [of being] one thinketh about at the last when relinquishing the body, being ever absorbed in the thought thereof.'

Our past thinking has determined our present status, and our present thinking will determine our future status; for man is what man thinks. In the words of the opening verse of the *Dhammapāda*, ' All that we are is the result of what we have thought: it is founded on our thoughts, it is made up of our thoughts.'

Likewise did the Hebrew Sages teach, as in *Proverbs* xxiii, 7, ' As a man thinketh in his heart, so is he '.

PREFACE TO THE FIRST EDITION

In this book I am seeking—so far as possible—to suppress my own views and to act simply as the mouthpiece of a Tibetan sage, of whom I was a recognized disciple.

He was quite willing that I should make known his interpretation of the higher *lāmaic* teachings and of the subtle esotericism underlying the *Bardo Thödol*, following the private and orally transmitted instructions which he as a young man had received when living the life of an ascetic with his late hermit-*guru* in Bhutan. Being himself a man who possessed a considerable amount of Western learning, he took great trouble to enable me to reproduce Oriental ideas in a form which would be intelligible to the European mind. If, in amplification, I have frequently referred to Occidental parallels of various mystic or occult doctrines current in the Orient, I have done so largely because in my wanderings there, chiefly in the high Himalayas and on the Tibetan frontiers of Kashmir, Garhwal, and Sikkim, I had come across learned philosophers and holy men who have found or thought they had found beliefs and religious practices—some recorded in books, some preserved by oral tradition alone—not only analogous to their own, but so closely akin to those of the Occident as to imply some historical connexion therewith. Whether the supposed influence passed from East to West or from West to East, was not so clear to their minds. A certain similarity does, however, seem to attach to the culture of these geographically divided provinces.

I have spent more than five years in such research, wandering from the palm-wreathed shores of Ceylon, and thence through the wonder-land of the Hindus, to the glacier-clad heights of the Himalayan Ranges, seeking out the Wise Men of the East. Sometimes I lived among city dwellers, sometimes in jungle and mountain solitudes among *yogīs*, sometimes in monasteries with monks; sometimes I went on pilgrimages, as one of the salvation-seeking multitude. The Introduction —which in its unusual lengthiness is intended to serve as a very necessary commentary to the translation—and the annotations to the text record the more important results of this research, more especially in relation to Northern or Mahāyāna Buddhism.

Nevertheless, I have been really little more than a compiler and editor of 'The Tibetan Book of the Dead'. To the deceased translator—who combined in himself a greater knowledge of the Occult Sciences of Tibet and of Western Science than any Tibetan scholar of this epoch—the chief credit for its production very naturally belongs.

In addition to that greatest of all debts which the student ever owes to his preceptor, I acknowledge my indebtedness to each of my many good friends and helpers who have personally aided me herewith. Some of them are of one Faith, some of another; some are far away in Japan and in China, some in the land of my birth, America; many are in Ceylon and in India; a few are in Tibet.

Here in England I think first of all of Dr. R. R. Marett, Reader in Social Anthropology in the University of Oxford, and Fellow of Exeter College, who ever since I first came up to Oxford, in the year 1907, has faithfully guided my anthropological research. Sir John Woodroffe, late a Judge of the High Court, Calcutta, now Reader in Indian Law in the University of Oxford, and the foremost authority in the West on the *Tantras*, has read through our translation, chiefly in relation to the character of the work as a ritual more or less Tantric, and offered important advice. I am also very grateful to him for the Foreword.

To Sj. Atal Bihari Ghosh, of Calcutta, Joint Honorary Secretary with Sir John Woodroffe of the *Āgamānusandhāna Samiti*, as to Sir E. Denison Ross, Director of the School of Oriental Studies, London Institution, and to Dr. F. W. Thomas, Librarian of the India Office, London, I am under a special obligation for important constructive criticism on the book as a whole. To Major W. L. Campbell, British Political Representative in Tibet, Bhutan, and Sikkim during my sojourn in Gangtok, I am indebted for much encouragement and scholarly aid, and for the gift of two valuable paintings prepared by his orders in the chief monastery of Gyantse, Tibet, to illustrate the symbolism of the *Bardo Thödol* text, and herein reproduced. To his predecessor and successor in the same post, Sir Charles Bell, I am also a debtor for important advice at the outset of my Tibetan research, when in Darjeeling. To Mr. E. S. Bouchier, M.A. (Oxon.), F. R. Hist. S., author of *Syria as a Roman Province*, *A Short History of Antioch*, &c., my heartiest thanks are due for the assistance which he has so kindly rendered in reading the whole of this book when in proof.

Sardar Bahadur S.W. Laden La, Chief of Police, Darjeeling, who sent me to Gangtok with a letter of introduction to the late Lāma Kazi Dawa-Samdup, the translator of the *Bardo Thödol*; Dr. Johan Van Manen, Secretary of the Asiatic Society, Calcutta, who lent me Tibetan books which proved very helpful while the translation was taking shape, and who afterwards contributed advice concerning translations; and Dr. Cassius A. Pereira, of Colombo, Ceylon, who criticized parts of the Introduction in the light of Theravāda Buddhism, are among many others to whom my thanks are due.

Thus, under the best of auspices, this book is sent forth to the world, in the hope that it may contribute something to the sum total of Right Knowledge, and serve as one more spiritual strand in an unbreakable bond of good will and universal peace, binding East and West together in mutual respect and understanding, and in love such as overleaps every barrier of creed and caste and race.

W. Y. E-W.

JESUS COLLEGE, OXFORD,
Easter, 1927.

I. RENUNCIATION

'Get thee away from life-lust, from conceit,
  From ignorance, and from distraction's craze;
  Sunder the bonds; so only shalt thou come
  To utter end of Ill. Throw off the Chain
  Of birth and death—thou knowest what they mean.
  So, free from craving, in this life on earth,
  Thou shalt go on thy way calm and serene.'—The Buddha.

Psalms of the Early Buddhists, I. lvi
(Mrs. Rhys Davids' Translation).

II. VICTORY

'But anguish crept upon me, even me,
  Whenas I pondered in my little cell:
  Ah me! how have I come into this evil road.
  Into the power of Craving have I strayed!
  Brief is the span of life yet left to me;
  Old age, disease, hang imminent to crush.
  Now ere this body perish and dissolve,
  Swift let me be; no time have I for sloth.
  And contemplating, as they really are,
  The Aggregates of Life that come and go,
  I rose and stood with mind emancipate!
  For me the Buddha's words had come to pass'.—

Mittakalī, a Brāhmin *Bhikkhunī.*

Psalms of the Early Buddhists, I. xliii
(Mrs. Rhys Davids' Translation).

CONTENTS

BOOK I

THE *CHIKHAI BARDO* AND THE *CHÖNYID BARDO*

PART I

THE *BARDO* OF THE MOMENTS OF DEATH

PART II

THE *BARDO* OF THE EXPERIENCING OF REALITY

BOOK II

THE *SIDPA BARDO*

PART I

THE AFTER-DEATH WORLD

PART II

THE PROCESS OF REBIRTH

THE APPENDIX

ADDENDA

ILLUSTRATIONS

I. THE TRANSLATOR AND THE EDITOR . *Plate 1*

From a photograph of the Translator and the Editor in Tibetan dress, taken in Gangtok, Sikkim, during the year 1919.

II. FOLIOS 35a AND 67a OF THE *BARDO THÖDOL* MS.

Plate 2

A photographic reproduction (about two-thirds of the original size). In the original the illuminations are in colour (now much faded) painted on the folios (cf. p. 68).

The painting on the upper folio illustrates, with the colours, emblems, and orientation in strict accord with the traditions of Tibetan monastic art, the description in the text of the united *maṇḍalas*, or divine conclaves, of the Peaceful Deities of the First to the Sixth Day of the *Bardo* that dawn thus in one complete conclave on the Sixth Day (cf. pp. 118-26). In the central circle (Centre) is the Dhyānī Buddha Vairochana, embraced by his *shakti*, or divine spouse, the Mother of Infinite Space. In the next circle, each likewise embraced by his *shakti*, are the four Dhyānī Buddhas, who, with Vairochana, constitute the *maṇḍala* of the Five Dhyānī Buddhas. In the outermost circle are typical Bodhisattvas and other deities who accompany the Five Dhyānī Buddhas (cf. pp. 118-20); and in the four small outer circles the four female Door-Keepers of the complete conclave (cf. p. 120).

The painting on the lower folio similarly illustrates, in colours, emblems, and orientation, the united *maṇḍalas* of the Wrathful Deities of the Eighth to the Fourteenth Day that dawn thus in one complete conclave on the Fourteenth Day (cf. pp. 143-6). In the cruciform design at the centre are the three-headed Herukas of the Buddha, Vajra, Ratna, Padma, and Karma Order, each with his *shakti*, that dawn, *maṇḍala* by *maṇḍala*, from the Eighth to the Twelfth Day (cf. pp. 136-41). The outer circle contains representations of the various animal-headed deities that dawn on the Thirteenth and the Fourteenth Day (cf. pp. 141-6). In the four small outer circles are the Four Yoginīs of the Door (cf. pp. 145-6).

The translation of the text on the two folios is indicated by special markings on pages 120 and 144.

III. EFFIGY OF THE DEAD PERSON . . . . p. 21

A reproduction (slightly reduced) of a copy of a Tibetan printed *Chang-ku* paper.

IV. THE GREAT *MAṆḌALA* OF THE PEACEFUL DEITIES

Plate 3

This and the companion illustration, number V, following, are photographic reproductions (about one-fourth of the original size) of two paintings in colour, on heavy cotton cloth, made in the chief monastery of Gyantse, Tibet, on the instructions of Major W. L. Campbell, to illustrate our *Bardo Thödol* translation (see Preface, p. xi). The colours, emblems, and orientations, as in the two manuscript illuminations described above, are in accord with the strict conventions of the religious art of Tibet. The correlations, too, between the text and the deities depicted, as brought out in the description of the two manuscript illuminations, also apply to these two more elaborate paintings.

Innermost circle (representing the Centre of the orientation): at the centre, Vairochana (white) and *shakti*, on lion throne (cf. pp. 105–6); at the top, Samanta-Bhadra (blue) and *shakti*; in subordinate circle on the left, Chenrazee (above), Mañjushrī (below, on left), Vajra-Pāni (below, on right); in subordinate circle on the right, Tsoṅ Khapa, a famous Tibetan *guru* (above), and his two chief *shishyas* (or disciples), Gendundub (below, on left), and Gyltshabje (below, on right).

Lower circle (East): at the centre, Vajra-Sattva (blue), the reflex of Akṣhobhya, and *shakti*, on elephant throne; Pushpā (above); Lāsyā (below); and Bodhisattvas (on left and right). Cf. pp. 108–9.

Left circle (South): at the centre, Ratna-Sambhava (yellow) and *shakti*, on horse throne; Dhūpa (above); Mālā (below); and Bodhisattvas (on left and right). Cf. pp. 110–11.

Upper circle (West): at the centre, Amitābha (red) and *shakti*, on peacock throne; Āloka (above); Gīta (below); and Bodhisattvas (on left and right). Cf. p. 113.

Right circle (North): at the centre, Amogha-Siddhi (green) and *shakti*, on harpy throne; Naivedya (above); Gandha (below); and Bodhisattvas (on left and right). Cf. pp. 115–6.

Occupying the four corners of the great circle are the four chief Door-Keepers (cf. p. 120) of the *Maṇḍala*, each pair on a fire-enhaloed lotus throne: upper left, Yamāntaka (yellow) and *shakti*, the Door-Keepers of the South; upper right, Hayagrīva (red) and *shakti*, the Door-Keepers of the West; lower right, Amṛitā-Dhāra (white) and *shakti*, the Door-Keepers of the North; lower left, Vijaya (green) and *shakti*, the Door-Keepers of the East. At the bottom, in the centre, Padma Sambhava, the Great Human *Guru* of the *Bardo Thödol* Doctrine, in royal robes and pandit head-dress, holding a skull filled with blood, symbolical of renunciation of life, in his left hand, and a *dorje*, symbolical of mastery over life, in his right. At his feet lie offerings: (1) the *Tri-Ratna* or Three Jewels of the Buddhist Faith, (2) a pair of elephant tusks, and (3) a branch of red coral. To the right of the *Guru* stands the Buddha of the Human *Loka* (yellow), Shakya Muni, holding a *bhikkhu*-staff and a begging-bowl; to the right, the Buddha of the Brute *Loka* (blue) holding a book, symbolizing language and expression, or divine wisdom, which brute creatures lack.

In the four corners are the four other Buddhas of the Six *Lokas* (cf. p. 121): upper left, the Buddha of the *Deva Loka* (white), holding a guitar, symbolizing excellence in arts and sciences and the harmony of existence in the world of the *devas*; upper right, the Buddha of the *Asura Loka* (green), holding a sword symbolizing the warlike nature of *asuras*; lower left, the Buddha of the *Preta Loka* (red), holding a box filled with all desirable objects to satisfy the cravings of the *pretas*; lower right, the Buddha of Hell (smoke-coloured), holding fire for consuming and water for purifying.

Among other embellishments added by the artist are a sacred mirror (symbolizing form or body, which it reflects) near the trees on the left, and a sacred conch-shell trumpet of victory over the *Sangsāra* (symbolizing sound) near the tree on the right; and, between the two Buddhas at the bottom, in two caves, *yogīs*, or holy men, in the Tibetan wilderness.

At the top, in the centre, presiding over the whole *maṇḍala*, Buddha Amitābha (red), on an enhaloed lotus and lunar throne holding a begging-bowl, with lotuses and the moon (white) on the left and lotuses and the sun (gold) on the right.

V. THE GREAT *MAṆḌALA* OF THE KNOWLEDGE-HOLDING AND WRATHFUL DEITIES . . . . .   *Plate 4*

Innermost circle: upper centre, Samanta-Bhadra (blue) and *shakti*, in wrathful aspect; lower centre (Centre), the Buddha Heruka (dark brown) and *shakti* (cf. p. 137); lower left (East), the Vajra Heruka (dark blue) and *shakti* (cf. p. 138); upper left (South), the Ratna Heruka (yellow) and *shakti* (cf. pp. 138-9); upper right (West), the Padma Heruka (reddish-brown) and *shakti* (cf. pp. 139-40); lower right (North), the Karma Heruka (dark green) and *shakti* (cf. pp. 140-1). Each pair of these deities are on a lotus and solar throne, enhaloed by flames of wisdom, and treading under foot *mārā* beings (i. e. human beings, whose existence, being purely phenomenal, or *karmic*, is illusion, or *māyā*), symbolizing the treading under foot of *sangsāric* (i. e. worldly) existence. At the bottom are offerings of the five *sangsāric* senses, symbolized by (1) two eyes, (2) two ears, (3) a tongue, (4) a heart (in the centre), and (5) a nose (above the heart); also of three blood-filled human skull-cups, held in position by small human skulls, all of which symbolize renunciation of the world.

Second circle: the Eight Kerimas (cf. pp. 142-3).

Third circle: the Eight Htamenmas (cf. p. 143) and the Four Female Door-Keepers (cf. pp. 143-4).

Outermost circle: the Twenty-Eight Various-Headed Mighty Goddesses (cf. pp. 144-5), four of whom are the Four Yoginīs of the Door (cf. pp. 145-6).

At the bottom, in the centre (Centre) the supreme Knowledge-Holding Deity, the Lotus Lord of Dance (red, for the five colours of text) and *shakti*. In the four corners, his four companion deities: lower left (East), the Earth-Abiding Knowledge-Holder (white) and *shakti*; upper left (South), the Knowledge-Holder Having Power Over Duration of Life (yellow) and *shakti*; upper right (West), the Knowledge-Holding Deity of the Great Symbol (red) and *shakti*; lower right (North), the Self-Evolved Knowledge-Holder (green) and *shakti*. Each pair of deities of this *maṇḍala*, that dawns intermediately (i.e. between the *maṇḍalas* of the Peaceful Deities and the *maṇḍalas* of the Wrathful Deities) on the Seventh Day (cf. pp. 126-8), are in peaceful aspect, on an enhaloed lotus and lunar throne, performing a mystic dance which is Tantric.

At the top, in the centre, presiding over the whole greater *maṇḍala*, is Samanta-Bhadra (dark blue), the Ādi-Buddha, and *shakti* (white), in peaceful aspect, on a lotus and lunar throne, enhaloed in rainbow colours, with lotuses and the moon (white) on his right and lotuses and the sun (gold) on his left.

VI. THE TIBETAN JUDGEMENT . . . . *Plate 5*

A photographic reproduction (about one-fourth of the original size) of a monastic painting in colour, on heavy cotton cloth, made on the instructions of the editor, in Gangtok, Sikkim, by a Tibetan artist named Lharipa-Pempa-Tendup-La, to illustrate the Judgement (see p. 37).

Occupying the central position is Dharma-Rāja, the King of Truth, or Administrator of Truth and Justice, otherwise called Yama-Rāja, the King and Judge of the Dead. He is the wrathful aspect of Chenrazee, the National Divine Protector of Tibet. The third eye of spiritual insight is in his forehead. He stands enhaloed in flames of wisdom, on a solar throne supported by a lotus throne, treading under foot a *mārā* form, symbolic of the *māyā* (i.e. illusionary) nature of human existence. His head-dress is adorned with human skulls, and a serpent forms his necklace. His necklet is a human hide, the head of which protrudes from behind his right side, and a hand and foot hang down over the centre of his breast. A girdle of human heads surrounds his waist. His pavilion and the walls of his Court are adorned with the skull-symbols of death. His sword is the sword of spiritual power. The mirror in his left hand is the Mirror of *Karma*, in which are reflected every good and evil act (cf. p. 166) of each of the dead who are being judged, one by one. There is written on the mirror, in Tibetan, '*Hri*,' the *bij*, or chief, *mantra* of Chenrazee.

Directly in front of Dharma-Rāja is the Monkey-Headed One, Sprehu-gochan (Tib. *Spre-hu-mgo-chan*), otherwise called Shinje (cf. pp. 36–7), holding the scales, on one side of which are heaped-up black pebbles, the evil deeds, and, on the other, heaped-up white pebbles, the good deeds. On the right of Shinje stands the Little White God, emptying a sack of white pebbles; on the other side, the Little Black God, emptying a sack of black pebbles (cf. p. 166).

Guarding the weighing are the Bull-Headed One, Wang-gochan (Tib. *Glang-mgo-chan*), holding another mirror of *karma*, and the Serpent-Headed One, Dul-gochan (Tib. *Sbrul-mgo-chan*), holding a scourge and a noose.

A yellow deity, on the right of Dharma-Rāja, holding a writing-tablet and a stilus, and a brown deity, on the left, holding a sword and a noose, are the two Advocates. The yellow advocate is the defender, the brown advocate is the accuser. The six deities, five of whom are animal-headed, sitting in the Court of Judgement, three on either side, like a jury of subordinate judges, supervise the proceedings in order to ensure regularity of procedure and impartial justice (cf. pp. 35–7). The first above on the right holds a mirror of *karma* and a skull-cup of blood, the second a battle-axe and a skull-cup of blood, the third a noose. The first above on the left holds a battle-axe and skull-cup of blood, the second a small vase of blossoms in his right hand, the third a *dorje* and a skull-cup of blood.

Near the gate on the left and the gate on the right stands one of the avenging furies who act as warders. There are ten Tibetans in the foreground of the Court awaiting judgement. The one with a conical head-dress (in red) is a red-cap *lāma*; the one with a round head-dress (in yellow) is a government official. The others are ordinary people. The three gates, through which the condemned enter the Hells below, are guarded by three animal-headed porters, each holding a noose.

Issuing from the Court, at either side of the Judge, are the Six *Karmic* Pathways, leading to the Six Buddhas of the Six *Lokas*, in whom the Pathways end, each Pathway and Buddha in appropriate colour (cf. p. 124 and Illustration IV). Traversing the Pathways are twelve of the dead who have recently been judged. The highest one, upon the left, on the white light-path approaching the Buddha of the *Deva Loka*, is a yellow-cap *lāma*; next to him is a government official on the yellow light-path approaching the Buddha of the Human *Loka*; the highest upon the right, on the green light-path approaching the Buddha of the *Asura Loka*, is a red-cap *lāma*.

In the Lower World, at the bottom of the painting, typical punishments in various Hells are depicted, none of which, however, are everlasting. On the left, in the upper corner, where two sinners are immersed in a glacial region, the Eight Cold Hells are suggested. Near the edge of the painting, on the opposite side, a sinner amidst flames suggests the Eight Hot Hells. The commission of any of the ten impious acts, deliberately and from selfish motives, leads to purgation in the Cold Hells; any of the same acts done through anger lead to purgation in the Hot Hells.

Just below the Cold Hells is the Hell of the 'Spiked Tree' or 'Hill of Spikes' (Tib. *Shal-ma-li*), in which an evil-doer has been quartered and affixed to the spikes. Beside it, in charge of a hell-fury, is 'The Doorless Iron House' (Tib. *Lchags-khang-sgo-med*). Next to this there are four *lāmas* held under the mountainous weight of an enormous Tibetan sacred book; they are being punished thus for having in their earth-life hurried through and skipped passages when reading religious texts. The triangle, in which an evil-doer is fixed, symbolizes the terrible Avitchi Hell, wherein one guilty of a heinous sin, such as using sorcery to destroy enemies or deliberate failure to fulfil Tantric vows, endures punishment for ages which are almost immeasurable. Close to the triangle, a hell-fury is pouring spoonfuls of molten metal into a woman condemned for prostitution. The person next to her, bowed under the weight of a heavy rock tied to his back, is being punished in that manner for having killed small living creatures like vermin or other insects. The sinner whom a hell-fury is holding stretched out on a floor of spiked iron while another hell-fury is preparing to hack him to pieces (cf. p. 166) has been found guilty of another of the ten impious acts. So also has been the woman who is about to be sawn in two lengthwise; her sin has been murder. As in Dante's *Inferno*, other evil-doers, incapable, as our text explains, of succumbing to the process (cf. p. 166), are being cooked in the iron cauldron at the lower right-hand corner. Three hell-furies (one brown, one yellow, one blue in the original) are to be seen holding by the end of nooses and leading and dragging along (cf. p. 166) to appropriate punishments three of the dead who have just been cast into Hell.

At the top of the picture, in the centre, on an enhaloed lotus and lunar throne, with the moon (white) at his right and the sun (gold) at his left, presiding over all, is Dorje Chang (blue), the Divine *Guru* of the Red-Hat School of Padma Sambhava; for he is held to be the Ever-living and Spiritual Source whence continue to emanate, as in the days of the Buddha Shakya Muni, all the Esoteric Doctrines underlying the *Bardo Thödol*, which are referred to on pages 133 to 134 of our translation.[1]

EMBLEMS

1. THE INDIAN WHEEL OF THE LAW (*Dharma-Chakra*)

Plate 6

From designs sculptured on the Sanchi Topes, dating from about 500 B.C. to 100 A.D.

2. THE *LĀMAIC* CROSSED DORJE . . *Plate 6*

Symbolical of equilibrium, immutability, and almighty power. (Cf. pp. 63, 116[1].)

3. THE TIBETAN WHEEL OF THE LAW (*Ch'os-'k'or-bskor*)

Plate 7

The Eight-Spoked Wheel (cf. p. 106), on a lotus throne and enhaloed by Flames of Wisdom, is representative of the Thousand-Spoked Wheel of the Good Law of the Buddha, symbol of the symmetry and completeness of the Sacred Law of the *Dharma*, or Scriptures. The design at the centre, called in Tibetan *rgyan-'k'yil*, composed of three whirling segments, symbolizes—as does the *svastika* at the centre of the Indian Wheel of the Law—the *Sangsāra*, or ceaseless change or 'becoming'.

4. THE *DORJE*, THE *LĀMAIC* SCEPTRE . . *Plate 8*

A type of the Thunderbolt of Indra, the Indian Jupiter, used in most *lāmaic* rituals (cf. pp. 10, 108[2], 137-8, 142-5), symbolical of dominion over *sangsāric* (or worldly) existence.

[1] It should be noted that each of the dead possesses a body suited to the paradise realm or hell-world in which *karma* brings about birth; and that when any of the after-human-death states of existence ends there is again a death process and a casting off of a body (cf. pp. 155-8, and Book II *passim*). The *Bardo* is the intermediate state whence one may be reborn in this world in a human body, or in the ghost-world in a ghost body, or in one of the paradise realms, such as the *deva-loka*, in a god body, or in the *asura-loka* in an *asura* body, or in one of the hells in a body capable of enduring suffering and incapable of dying there until the purgation is complete. Following death in a hell, or in any other of the after-human-death states, the normal process is to be reborn on earth as a human being. The True Goal, as the *Bardo Thödol* repeatedly explains, is beyond all states of embodiment, beyond all hells, worlds, and heavens, beyond the *Sangsāra*, beyond Nature; it is called *Nirvāṇa* (Tib. *Myang-hdas*). See Addenda, V, pp. 224-32.

5. THE *MANTRA* OF CHENRAZEE (Avalokiteshvara)

Plate 7

In *Ranja* or *Lantsa* Indian characters of about the seventh century A.D. *Lantsa* characters, slightly modified, are used in Tibetan manuscripts, commonly on title-pages. In Tibetan characters the sacred *Mantra* is ཨོཾ་མ་ཎི་པ་དྨེ་ཧཱུྃ, which means literally: 'Ōm! The Jewel in the Lotus! Hūm!' (Cf. pp. 134², 149¹, 206.)

THE TIBETAN BOOK OF THE DEAD

PSYCHOLOGICAL COMMENTARY
By Dr. C. G. Jung[1]

Translated by R. F. C. Hull from *Das Tibetanische Totenbuch*

Before embarking upon the psychological commentary, I should like to say a few words about the text itself. *The Tibetan Book of the Dead*, or the *Bardo Thödol*, is a book of instructions for the dead and dying. Like *The Egyptian Book of the Dead*, it is meant to be a guide for the dead man during the period of his *Bardo* existence, symbolically described as an intermediate state of forty-nine days' duration between death and rebirth. The text

[1] To one of Dr. Jung's most successful disciples, Dr. James Kirsch, Analytical Psychologist, of Los Angeles, California, who has discussed this Psychological Commentary with Dr. Jung in Zürich and aided in its English translation, the Editor is indebted for the important prefatory admonition which follows, addressed to the Oriental reader:—

'This book addresses itself, primarily, to the Occidental reader, and attempts to describe important Oriental experiences and conceptions in Occidental terms. Dr. Jung seeks to facilitate this difficult undertaking by his Psychological Commentary. It is, therefore, unavoidable that, in so doing, he employs terms which are familiar to the Occidental mind but which are, in some instances, objectionable to the Oriental mind.

'One such objectionable term is " soul ". According to Buddhistic belief, the " soul " is ephemeral, is an illusion, and, therefore, has no real existence. The Germanic word " *Seele* ", as employed in the original German version of this Psychological Commentary, is not synonymous with the English word " Soul ", although commonly so translated. " *Seele* " is an ancient word, sanctioned by Germanic tradition and used, by outstanding German mystics like Eckhart and great German poets like Goethe, to signify the Ultimate Reality, symbolized in feminine, or *shakti*, aspect. Herein, Dr. Jung uses it poetically with reference to the " Psyche ", as the Collective Psyche. In psychological language it represents the Collective Unconscious, as being the matrix of everything. It is the womb of everything, even of the *Dharma-Kāya*; it is the *Dharma-Kāya* itself.

'Accordingly, Oriental readers are invited to put aside, for the time being, their understanding of " soul " and to accept Dr. Jung's use of the word, in order to be able to follow him with an open mind into the depths where he seeks to build a bridge from the Shore of the Orient to the Shore of the Occident, and to tell of the various paths leading to the Great Liberation, the *Una Salus*.'

falls into three parts. The first part, called *Chikhai Bardo*, describes the psychic happenings at the moment of death. The second part, or *Chönyid Bardo*, deals with the dream-state which supervenes immediately after death, and with what are called ' *karmic* illusions '. The third part, or *Sidpa Bardo*, concerns the onset of the birth-instinct and of prenatal events. It is characteristic that supreme insight and illumination, and hence the greatest possibility of attaining liberation, are vouchsafed during the actual process of dying. Soon afterward, the ' illusions ' begin which lead eventually to reincarnation, the illuminative lights growing ever fainter and more multifarious, and the visions more and more terrifying. This descent illustrates the estrangement of consciousness from the liberating truth as it approaches nearer and nearer to physical rebirth. The purpose of the instruction is to fix the attention of the dead man, at each successive stage of delusion and entanglement, on the ever-present possibility of liberation, and to explain to him the nature of his visions. The text of the *Bardo Thödol* is recited by the *lāma* in the presence of the corpse.

I do not think I could better discharge my debt of thanks to the two previous translators of the *Bardo Thödol*, the late Lāma Kazi Dawa-Samdup and Dr. Evans-Wentz, than by attempting, with the aid of a psychological commentary, to make the magnificent world of ideas and the problems contained in this treatise a little more intelligible to the Western mind. I am sure that all who read this book with open eyes, and who allow it to impress itself upon them without prejudice, will reap a rich reward.

The *Bardo Thödol*, fitly named by its editor, Dr. W. Y. Evans-Wentz, ' The Tibetan Book of the Dead ', caused a considerable stir in English-speaking countries at the time of its first appearance in 1927. It belongs to that class of writings which are not only of interest to specialists in Mahāyāna Buddhism, but which also, because of their deep humanity and their still deeper insight into the secrets of the human psyche, make an especial appeal to the layman who is seeking to broaden his knowledge of life. For years, ever since it was first published, the *Bardo Thödol* has been my constant companion, and to it I owe not only many stimulating ideas and discoveries, but also many fundamental insights. Unlike *The Egyptian Book of the Dead*, which always prompts one to say too much or too little, the *Bardo Thödol* offers one an intelligible philosophy addressed to human beings rather than to gods or primitive savages. Its philosophy contains the quintessence of Buddhist psychological criticism; and, as such, one can truly say that it is of an unexampled superiority. Not only the ' wrathful ' but also the ' peaceful ' deities are conceived as *sangsāric* projections of the human psyche, an idea that seems all too obvious to the enlightened European, because it reminds him of his own banal simplifications. But though the European can easily explain away these deities as projections, he would be quite incapable of positing them at the same time as real. The *Bardo Thödol* can do that, because, in certain of its most essential metaphysical premises, it has the enlightened as well as the unenlightened European at a disadvantage. The ever-present, unspoken assumption of the *Bardo Thödol* is the antinominal character of all metaphysical assertions, and also the idea of the qualitative difference of the various levels of consciousness and of the metaphysical realities conditioned by them. The background of this unusual book is not the niggardly European ' either-or ', but a magnificently affirmative ' both-and '. This statement may appear objectionable to the Western philosopher, for the West loves clarity and unambiguity; consequently, one philosopher clings to the position, ' God is ', while another clings equally fervently to the negation. ' God is not '. What would these hostile brethren make of an assertion like the following:

' Recognizing the voidness of thine own intellect to be Buddhahood, and knowing it at the same time to be thine own consciousness, thou shalt abide in the state of the divine mind of the Buddha.'

Such an assertion is, I fear, as unwelcome to our Western philosophy as it is to our theology. The *Bardo Thödol* is in the highest degree psychological in its outlook; but, with us, philosophy and theology are still in the mediaeval, pre-psychological stage where only the assertions are listened to, explained, defended, criticized and disputed, while the authority that makes them has, by general consent, been deposed as outside the scope of discussion.

Metaphysical assertions, however, are *statements of the psyche*, and are therefore psychological. To the Western mind, which compensates its well-known feelings of resentment by a slavish regard for 'rational' explanations, this obvious truth seems all too obvious, or else it is seen as an inadmissible negation of metaphysical 'truth'. Whenever the Westerner hears the word 'psychological', it always sounds to him like ' *only* psychological'. For him the 'soul' is something pitifully small, unworthy, personal, subjective, and a lot more besides. He therefore prefers to use the word 'mind' instead, though he likes to pretend at the same time that a statement which may in fact be very subjective indeed is made by the 'mind', naturally by the 'Universal Mind', or even—at a pinch—by the 'Absolute' itself. This rather ridiculous presumption is probably a compensation for the regrettable smallness of the soul. It almost seems as if Anatole France had uttered a truth which were valid for the whole Western world when, in his *Penguin Island*, Cathérine d'Alexandrie offers this advice to God: ' *Donnez leur une ame, mais une petite* '! [' Give them a soul, but a little one!']

It is the soul which, by the divine creative power inherent in it, makes the metaphysical assertion; it posits the distinctions between metaphysical entities. Not only is it the condition of all metaphysical reality, it *is* that reality.[1]

With this great psychological truth the *Bardo Thödol* opens. The book is not a ceremonial of burial, but a set of instructions for the dead, a guide through the changing phenomena of the *Bardo* realm, that state of existence which continues for 49 days after death until the next incarnation. If we disregard for the moment the supra-temporality of the soul—which the East accepts as a self-evident fact—we, as readers of the *Bardo Thödol*, shall be able to put ourselves without difficulty in the position of the dead man, and shall consider attentively the teaching set forth in the opening section, which is outlined in the quotation above. At this point, the following words are spoken, not presumptuously, but in a courteous manner:—

' O nobly-born (so and so), listen. Now thou art experiencing
the Radiance of the Clear Light of Pure Reality. Recognize it.
O nobly-born, thy present intellect, in real nature void, not

---

[1]This paragraph makes apparent the interpretative importance of the annotation set forth above, page xxxv, concerning the difference in meaning of the term ' soul ' of the English rendering and of the term ' *Seele* ' of the original German; and, at this point, readers would benefit by re-reading the annotation.

formed into anything as regards characteristics or colour, naturally void, is the very Reality, the All-Good.

' Thine own intellect, which is now voidness, yet not to be regarded as of the voidness of nothingness, but as being the intellect itself, unobstruced, shining, thrilling, and blissful, is the very consciousness, the All-good Buddha.'

This realization is the *Dharma-Kāya* state of perfect enlightenment; or, as we should express it in our own language, the creative ground of all metaphysical assertion is consciousness, as the invisible, intangible manifestation of the soul. The ' Voidness ' is the state transcendent over all assertion and all predication. The fulness of its discriminative manifestations still lies latent in the soul.

The text continues:—
' Thine own consciousness, shining, void, and inseparable from the Great Body of Radiance, hath no birth, nor deatlı, and is the Immutable Light—Buddha Amitābha.'

The soul [or, as here, one's own consciousness] is assuredly not small, but the radiant Godhead itself. The West finds this statement either very dangerous, if not downright blasphemous, or else accepts it unthinkingly and then suffers from a theosophical inflation. Somehow we always have a wrong attitude to these things. But if we can master ourselves far enough to refrain from our chief error of always wanting to *do* something with things and put them to practical use, we may perhaps succeed in learning an important lesson from these teachings, or at least in appreciating the greatness of the *Bardo Thödol*, which vouchsafes to the dead man the ultimate and highest truth, that even the gods are the radiance and reflection of our own souls. No sun is thereby eclipsed for the Oriental as it would be for the Christian, who would feel robbed of his God; on the contrary, his soul is the light of the Godhead, and the Godhead is the soul. The East can sustain this paradox better than the unfortunate Angelus Silesius, who even today would be psychologically far in advance of his time.

It is highly sensible of the *Bardo Thödol* to make clear to the dead man the primacy of the soul, for that is the one thing which life does not make clear to us. We are so hemmed in by things which jostle and oppress that we never get a chance, in the midst of all these ' given ' things, to wonder by whom they are ' given '. It is from this world of ' given ' things that the dead man liberates himself; and the purpose of the instruction is to help him towards this liberation. We, if we put ourselves in his place, shall derive no lesser reward from it, since we learn from the very first paragraphs that the ' giver ' of all ' given ' things dwells within us. This is a truth which in the face of all evidence, in the greatest things as in the smallest, is never known, although it is often so very necessary, indeed vital, for us to know it. Such knowledge, to be sure, is suitable only for contemplatives who are minded to understand the purpose of existence, for those who are Gnostics by temperament and therefore believe in a saviour who, like the saviour of the Mandaeans, calls himself ' gnosis of life ' (*manda d'hajie*). Perhaps it is not granted to many of us to see the world as something ' given '. A great reversal of standpoint, calling for much sacrifice, is needed before we can see the world as ' given' by the very nature of the soul. It is so much more straight-forward, more dramatic, impressive, and therefore more convincing, to see that all the things happen to me than to observe how I make them happen. Indeed, the animal nature of man makes him resist seeing himself as the maker of his circumstances. That is why attempts of this kind were always the object of secret initiations, culminating as a rule in a figurative death which symbolized the total character of this reversal. And, in point of fact, the instruction given in the *Bardo Thödol* serves to recall to the dead man the experiences of his initiation and the teachings of his *guru*, for the instruction is, at bottom, nothing less than an initiation of the dead into the *Bardo* life, just as the initiation of the living was a preparation for the Beyond. Such was the case, at least, with all the mystery cults in ancient civilizations from the time of the Egyptian and Eleusinian mysteries. In the initiation of the living, however, this ' Beyond ' is not a world beyond death, but a reversal of the mind's intentions and outlook, a psychological ' Beyond ' or, in Christian terms, a ' redemption ' from the trammels of the world and of sin. Redemption is a separation and deliverance from an earlier condition of darkness and unconsciousness, and leads to a condition of illumination and releasedness, to victory and transcendence over everything ' given '.

Thus far the *Bardo Thödol* is, as Dr. Evans-Wentz also feels, an initiation process whose purpose it is to restore to the soul the divinity it lost at birth. Now it is a charactertistic of Oriental religious literature that the teaching invariably begins with the most important item, with the ultimate and highest principles which, with us, would come last—as for instance in Apuleius, where Lucius is worshipped as Helios only right at the end. Accordingly, in the *Bardo Thödol*, the initiation is a series of diminishing climaxes ending with rebirth in the womb. The only ' initiation process ' that is still alive and practised today in the West is the analysis of the unconscious as used by doctors for therapeutic purposes. This penetration into the ground-layers of consciousness is a kind of rational maieutics in the Socratic sense, a bringing forth of psychic contents that are still germinal, subliminal, and as yet unborn. Originally, this therapy took the form of Freudian psychoanalysis and was mainly concerned with sexual fantasies. This is the realm that corresponds to the last and lowest region of the *Bardo*, known as the *Sidpa Bardo*, where the dead man, unable to profit by the teachings of the *Chikhai* and *Chönyid Bardo*, begins to fall a prey to sexual fantasies and is attracted by the vision of mating couples. Eventually he is caught by a womb and born into the earthly world again. Meanwhile, as one might expect, the Oedipus complex starts functioning. If his *karma* destines him to be reborn as a man, he will fall in love with his mother-to-be and will find his father hateful and digusting. Conversely, the future daughter will be highly attracted by her father-to-be and repelled by her mother. The European passes through this specifically Freudian domain when his unconscious contents are brought to light under analysis, but he goes in the reverse direction. He journeys back through the world of infantile-sexual fantasy to the womb. It has even been suggested in psychoanalytical circles that the trauma par excellence is the birth-experience itself—nay more, psychoanalysts even claim to have probed back to memories of intra-uterine origin. Here Western reason reaches its limit, unfortunately. I say ' unfortunately ', because one rather wishes that Freudian psychoanalysis could have happily pursued these so-called intra-uterine experiences still further back; had it succeeded in this bold undertaking, it would surely have come out beyond the *Sidpa Bardo* and penetrated from behind into the lower reaches of the *Chönyid Bardo*. It is true that with the equipment of our existing biological ideas such a venture would not have been crowned with success; it would have needed a wholly different kind of philosophical preparation from that based on current scientific assumptions. But, had the journey back been consistently pursued, it would undoubtedly have led to the postulate of a pre-uterine existence, a true *Bardo* life, if only it had been possible to find at least some trace of an experiencing subject. As it was, the psychoanalysts never got beyond purely conjectural traces of intra-uterine experiences, and even the famous ' birth trauma ' has remained such an obvious truism that it can no longer explain anything, any more than can the hypothesis that life is a disease with a bad prognosis because its outcome is always fatal.

Freudian psychoanalysis, in all essential aspects, never went beyond the experiences of the *Sidpa Bardo;* that is, it was unable to extricate itself from sexual fantasies and similar ' incompatible ' tendencies which cause anxiety and other affective states. Nevertheless, Freud's theory is the first attempt made by the West to investigate, as if from below, from the animal sphere of instinct, the psychic territory that corresponds in Tantric Lāmaism to the *Sidpa Bardo*. A very justifiable fear of metaphysics prevented Freud from penetrating into the sphere of the ' occult '. In addition to this, the *Sidpa* state, if we are to accept the psychology of the *Sidpa Bardo*, is characterized by the fierce wind of *karma*, which whirls the dead man along until he comes to the ' womb-door '. In other words, the *Sidpa* state permits of no going back, because it is sealed off against the *Chönyid* state by an intense striving downwards, towards the animal sphere of instinct and physical rebirth. That is to say, anyone who penetrates into the unconscious with purely biological assumptions will become stuck in the instinctual sphere and be unable to advance beyond it, for he will be pulled back again and again into physical existence. It is therefore not possible for Freudian theory to reach anything except an essentially negative valuation of the unconscious. It is a ' nothing but '. At the same time, it must be admitted that this view of the psyche is typically Western, only it is expressed more blatantly, more plainly, and more ruthlessly than others would have dared to express it, though at bottom they think no differently. As to what ' mind ' means in this connection, we can only cherish the hope that it will carry conviction. But, as even Max Scheler noted with regret, the power of this ' mind ' is, to say the least of it, doubtful.

I think, then, we can state it as a fact that with the aid of psychoanalysis the rationalizing mind of the West has pushed forward into what one might call the neuroticism of the *Sidpa* state, and has there been brought to an inevitable standstill by the uncritical assumption that everything psychological is subjective and personal. Even so, this advance has been a great gain, inasmuch as it has enabled us to take one more step behind our conscious lives. This knowledge also gives us a hint of how we ought to read the *Bardo Thödol*—that is, backwards. If, with the help of our Western science, we have to some extent succeeded in understanding the psychological character of the *Sidpa Bardo*, our next task is to see if we can make anything of the preceding *Chönyid Bardo*.

The *Chönyid* state is one of *karmic* illusion—that is to say, illusions which result from the psychic residua of previous existences. According to the Eastern view, *karma* implies a sort of psychic theory of heredity based on the hypothesis of reincarnation, which in the last resort is an hypothesis of the supratemporality of the soul. Neither our scientific knowledge nor our reason can keep in step with this idea. There are too many if's and but's. Above all, we know desperately little about the possibilities of continued existence of the individual soul after death, so little that we cannot even conceive how anyone could prove anything at all in this respect. Moreover, we know only too well, on epistemological grounds, that such a proof would be just as impossible as the proof of God. Hence we may cautiously accept the idea of *karma* only if we understand it as *psychic heredity* in the very widest sense of the word. Psychic heredity does exist—that is to say, there is inheritance of psychic characteristics such as predisposition to disease, traits of character, special gifts, and so forth. It does no violence to the psychic nature of these complex facts if natural science reduces them to what appear to be physical aspects (nuclear structures in cells, and so on). They are essential phenomena of life which express themselves, in the main, psychically, just as there are other inherited characteristics which express themselves, in the main, physiologically, on the physical level. Among these inherited psychic factors there is a special class which is not confined either to family or to race. These are the universal dispositions of the mind, and they are to be understood as analogous to Plato's forms (*eidola*), in accordance with which the mind organizes its contents. One could also describe these forms as *categories* analogous to the logical categories which are always and everywhere present as the basic postulates of reason. Only, in the case of our ' forms ', we are not dealing with categories of reason but with categories of the *imagination*. As the products of imagination are always in essence visual, their forms must, from the outset, have the character of images and moreover of *typical* images, which is why, following St. Augustine, I call them ' archetypes '. Comparative religion and mythology are rich mines of archetypes, and so is the psychology of dreams and psychoses. The astonishing parallelism between these images and the ideas they serve to express has frequently given rise to the wildest migration theories, although it would have been far more natural to think of the remarkable similarity of the human psyche at all times and in all places. Archetypal fantasy-forms are, in fact, reproduced spontaneously anytime and any-where, without there being any conceivable trace of direct trans-mission. The original structural components of the psyche are of no less surprising a uniformity than are those of the visible body. The archetypes are, so to speak, organs of the pre-rational psyche. They are eternally inherited forms and ideas which have at first no specific content. Their specific content only appears in the course of the individual's life, when personal experience is taken up in precisely these forms. If the archetypes were not pre-existent in identical form everywhere, how could one explain the fact, pos-tulated at almost every turn by the *Bardo Thödol*, that the dead do not know that they are dead, and that this assertion is to be met with just as often in the dreary, half-baked literature of Euro-pean and American Spiritualism? Although we find the same assertion in Swedenborg, knowledge of his writings can hardly be sufficiently widespread for this little bit of information to have been picked up by every small-town 'medium'. And a connection between Swendenborg and the *Bardo Thödol* is completely unthinkable. It is a primordial, universal idea that the dead simply continue their earthly existence and do not know that they are disembodied spirits—an archetypal idea which enters into immediate, visible manifestation whenever anyone sees a ghost. It is significant, too, that ghosts all over the world have certain features in common. I am naturally aware of the unverifiable spiritualistic hypothesis, though I have no wish to make it my own. I must content myself with the hypothesis of an omnipresent, but differentiated, psychic structure which is inherited and which necessarily gives a certain form and direction to all experience. For, just as the organs of the body are not mere lumps of indifferent, passive matter, but are dynamic, functional complexes which assert themselves with imperious urgency, so also the archetypes, as organs of the psyche, are dynamic, instinctual complexes which determine psychic life to an extraordinary degree. That is why I also call them *dominants* of the unconscious. The layer of unconscious psyche which is made up of these universal dynamic forms I have termed the *collective unconscious*.

So far as I know, there is no inheritance of individual prenatal, or pre-uterine, memories, but there are undoubtedly inherited archetypes which are, however, devoid of content, because, to begin with, they contain no personal experiences. They only emerge into consciousness when personal experiences have rendered them visible. As we have seen, *Sidpa* psychology consists in wanting to live and to be born. (The *Sidpa Bardo* is the '*Bardo* of Seeking Rebirth'.) Such a state, therefore, precludes any experience of transubjective psychic realities, unless the individual refuses categorically to be born back again into the world of consciousness. According to the teachings of the *Bardo Thödol*, it is still possible for him, in each of the *Bardo* states, to reach the *Dharma-Kāya* by transcending the four-faced Mount Meru, provided that he does not yield to his desire to follow the 'dim lights'. This is as much as to say that the dead man must desperately resist the dictates of reason, as we understand it, and give up the supremacy of egohood, regarded by reason as sacrosanct. What this means in practice is complete capitulation to the objective powers of the psyche, with all that this entails; a kind of symbolical death, corresponding to the Judgement of the Dead in the *Sidpa Bardo*. It means the end of all conscious, rational, morally responsible conduct of life, and a voluntary surrender to what the *Bardo Thödol* calls ' *karmic* illusion '. *Karmic* illusion springs from belief in a visionary world of an extremely irrational nature, which neither accords with nor derives from our rational judgements but is the exclusive product of uninhibited imagination. It is sheer dream or ' fantasy ', and every well-meaning person will instantly caution us against it; nor indeed can one see at first sight what is the difference between fantasies of this kind and the phantasmagoria of a lunatic. Very often only a slight *abaissement du niveau mental* is needed to unleash this world of illusion. The terror and darkness of this moment has its equivalent in the experiences described in the opening sections of the *Sidpa Bardo*. But the contents of this *Bardo* also reveal the archetypes, the *karmic* images which appear first in their terrifying form. The *Chönyid* state is equivalent to a deliberately induced psychosis.

One often hears and reads about the dangers of *yoga*, particularly of the ill-reputed *Kuṇḍalinī yoga*. The deliberately induced psychotic state, which in certain unstable individuals might easily lead to a real psychosis, is a danger that needs to be taken very seriously indeed. These things really are dangerous and ought not to be meddled with in our typically Western way. It is a meddling with fate, which strikes at the very roots of human existence and can let loose a flood of sufferings of which no sane person ever dreamed. These sufferings correspond to the hellish torments of the *Chönyid* state, described in the text as follows:—

> ' Then the Lord of Death will place round thy neck a rope and drag thee along; he will cut off thy head, tear out thy heart, pull out thy intestines, lick up thy brain, drink thy blood, eat thy flesh, and gnaw thy bones; but thou wilt be incapable of dying. Even when thy body is hacked to pieces, it will revive again. The repeated hacking will cause intense pain and torture.'

These tortures aptly describe the real nature of the danger: it is a disintegration of the wholeness of the *Bardo* body, which is a kind of 'subtle body' constituting the visible envelope of the psychic self in the after-death state. The psychological equivalent of this dismemberment is psychic dissociation. In its deleterious form it would be schizophrenia (split mind). This most common of all mental illnesses consists essentially in a marked *abaissement du niveau mental* which abolishes the normal checks imposed by the conscious mind and thus gives unlimited scope to the play of the unconscious 'dominants'.

The transition, then, from the *Sidpa* state to the *Chönyid* state is a dangerous reversal of the aims and intentions of the conscious mind. It is a sacrifice of the ego's stability and a surrender to the extreme uncertainty of what must seem like a chaotic riot of phantasmal forms. When Freud coined the phrase that the ego was 'the true seat of anxiety', he was giving voice to a very true and profound intuition. Fear of self-sacrifice lurks deep in every ego, and this fear is often only the precariously controlled demand of the unconscious forces to burst out in full strength. No one who strives for selfhood (individuation) is spared this dangerous passage, for that which is feared also belongs to the wholeness of the self—the sub-human, or supra-human, world of psychic 'dominants' from which the ego originally emancipated itself with enormous effort, and then only partially, for the sake of a more or less illusory freedom. This liberation is certainly a very necessary and very heroic undertaking, but it represents nothing final: it is merely the creation of a *subject*, who, in order to find fulfilment, has still to be confronted by an *object*. This, at first sight, would appear to be the world, which is swelled out with projections for that very purpose. Here we seek and find our difficulties, here we seek and find our enemy, here we seek and find what is dear and precious to us; and it is comforting to know that all evil and all good is to be found out there, in the visible object, where it can be conquered, punished, destroyed or enjoyed. But nature herself does not allow this paradisal state of innocence to continue for ever. There are, and always have been, those who cannot help but see that the world and its experiences are in the nature of a symbol, and that it really reflects something that lies hidden in the subject himself, in his own transubjective reality. It is from this profound intuition, according to *lāmaist* doctrine, that the *Chönyid* state derives its true meaning, which is why the *Chönyid Bardo* is entitled 'The *Bardo* of the Experiencing of Reality'.

The reality experienced in the *Chönyid* state is, as the last section of the corresponding *Bardo* teaches, the reality of thought. The 'thought-forms' appear as realities, fantasy takes on real form, and the terrifying dream evoked by *karma* and played out by the unconscious 'dominants' begins. The first to appear (if we read the text backwards) is the all-destroying God of Death, the epitome of all terrors; he is followed by the 28 'power-holding' and sinister goddesses and the 58 'blood-drinking' goddesses. In spite of their daemonic aspect, which appears as a confusing chaos of terrifying attributes and monstrosities, a certain order is already discernible. We find that there are companies of gods and goddesses who are arranged according to the four directions and are distinguished by typical mystic colours. It gradually becomes clearer that all these deities are organized into *maṇḍalas*, or circles, containing a cross of the four colours. The colours are co-ordinated with the four aspects of wisdom:

(1)   White=the light-path of the mirror-like wisdom;
(2)   Yellow=the light-path of the wisdom of equality;
(3)   Red=the light-path of the discriminative wisdom;
(4)   Green=the light-path of the all-performing wisdom.

On a higher level of insight, the dead man knows that the real thought-forms all emanate from himself, and that the four light-paths of wisdom which appear before him are the radiations of his own psychic faculties. This takes us straight to the psychology of the *lāmaistic maṇḍala*, which I have already discussed in the book I brought out with the late Richard Wilhelm, *The Secret of the Golden Flower*.

Continuing our ascent backwards through the region of the *Chönyid Bardo*, we come finally to the vision of the Four Great Ones: the green Amogha-Siddhi, the red Amitābha, the yellow Ratna-Sambhava, and the white Vajra-Sattva. The ascent ends with the effulgent blue light of the *Dharma-Dhātu*, the Buddha-body, which glows in the midst of the *maṇḍala* from the heart of Vairochana.

With this final vision the *karmic* illusions cease; consciousness, weaned away from all form and from all attachment to objects, returns to the timeless, inchoate state of the *Dharma-Kāya*. Thus (reading backwards) the *Chikhai* state, which appeared at the moment if death, is reached.

I think these few hints will suffice to give the attentive reader some idea of the psychology of the *Bardo Thödol*. The book describes a way of initiation in reverse, which, unlike the eschatological expectations of Christianity, prepares the soul for a descent into physical being. The thoroughly intellectualistic and rationalistic worldly-mindedness of the European makes it advisable for us to reverse the sequence of the *Bardo Thödol* and to regard it as an account of Eastern initiation experiences, though one is perfectly free, if one chooses, to substitute Christian symbols for the gods of the *Chönyid Bardo*. At any rate, the sequence of events as I have described it offers a close parallel to the phenomenology of the European unconscious when it is undergoing an ' initiation process ', that is to say, when it is being analyzed. The transformation of the unconscious that occurs under analysis makes it the natural analogue of the religious initiation ceremonies, which do, however, differ in principle from the natural process in that they forestall the natural course of development and substitute for the spontaneous production of symbols a deliberately selected set of symbols prescribed by tradition. We can see this in the *Exercitia* of Ignatius Loyola, or in the *yoga* meditations of the Buddhists and Tantrists.

The reversal of the order of the chapters, which I have suggested here as an aid to understanding, in no way accords with the original intention of the *Bardo Thödol*. Nor is the psychological use we make of it anything but a secondary intention, though one that is possibly sanctioned by *lāmaist* custom. The real purpose of this singular book is the attempt, which must seem very strange to the educated European of the twentieth century, to enlighten the dead on their journey through the regions of the *Bardo*. The Catholic Church is the only place in the world of the white man where any provision is made for the souls of the departed. Inside the Protestant camp, with its world-affirming optimism, we only find a few mediumistic ' rescue circles ', whose main concern is to make the dead aware of the fact that they *are* dead. But, generally speaking, we have nothing in the West that is in any way comparable to the *Bardo Thödol*, except for certain secret writings which are inaccessible to the wider public and to the ordinary scientist. According to tradition, the *Bardo Thödol*, too, seems to have been included among the ' hidden ' books, as Dr. Evans-Wentz makes clear in his Introduction. As such, it forms a special chapter in the magical ' cure of the soul ' which extends even beyond death. This cult of the dead is rationally based on the belief in the supra-temporality of the soul, but its irrational basis is to be found in the psychological need of the living to do something for the departed. This is an elementary need which forces itself upon even the most ' enlightened ' individuals when faced by the death of relatives and friends. That is why, enlightenment or no enlightenment, we still have all manner of ceremonies for the dead. If Lenin had to submit to being embalmed and put on show in a sumptuous mausoleum like an Egyptian pharaoh, we may be quite sure it was not because his followers believed in the resurrection of the body. Apart, however, from the Masses said for the soul in the Catholic Church, the provisions we make for the dead are rudimentary and on the lowest level, not because we cannot convince ourselves of the soul's immortality, but because we have rationalized the above-mentioned psychological need out of existence. We behave as if we did not have this need, and because we cannot believe in a life after death we prefer to do nothing about it. Simpler-minded people follow their own feelings, and, as in Italy, build themselves funeral monuments of gruesome beauty. The Catholic Masses for the soul are on a level considerably above this, because they are expressly intended for the psychic welfare of the deceased and are not a mere gratification of lachrymose sentiments. But the highest application of spiritual effort on behalf of the departed is surely to be found in the instructions of the *Bardo Thödol*. They are so detailed and thoroughly adapted to the apparent changes in the dead man's condition that every serious-minded reader must ask himself whether these wise old *lāmas* might not, after all, have caught a glimpse of the fourth dimension and twitched the veil from the greatest of life's secrets.

If the truth is always doomed to be a disappointment, one almost feels tempted to concede at least that much reality to the vision of life in the *Bardo*. At any rate, it is unexpectedly original, if nothing else, to find the after-death state, of which our religious imagination has formed the most grandiose conceptions, painted in lurid colours as a terrifying dream-state of a progressively degenerative character. The supreme vision comes not at the end of the *Bardo*, but right at the beginning, in the moment of death; what happens afterward is an ever-deepening descent into illusion and obscuration, down to the ultimate degradation of new physical birth. The spiritual climax is reached at the moment when life ends. Human life, therefore, is the vehicle of the highest perfection it is possible to attain; it alone gener-ates the *karma* that makes it possible for the dead man to abide in the perpetual light of the Voidness without clinging to any object, and thus to rest on the hub of the wheel of rebirth, freed from all illusion of genesis and decay. Life in the *Bardo* brings no eternal rewards or punishments, but merely a descent into a new life which shall bear the individual nearer to his final goal. But this eschatological goal is what he himself brings to birth as the last and highest fruit of the labours and aspirations of earthly existence. This view is not only lofty, it is manly and heroic.

The degenerative character of *Bardo* life is corroborated by the spiritualistic literature of the West, which again and again gives one a sickening impression of the utter inanity and banality of communications from the ' spirit world '. The scientific mind does not hesitate to explain these reports as emanations from the unconscious of the ' mediums ' and of those taking part in the séance, and even to extend this explanation to the description of the Hereafter given in *The Tibetan Book of the Dead*. And it is an undeniable fact that the whole book is created out of the archetypal contents of the unconscious. Behind these there lie— and in this our Western reason is quite right—no physical or metaphysical realities, but ' merely ' the reality of psychic facts, the data of psychic experience. Now whether a thing is ' given ' subjectively or objectively, the fact remains that it *is*. The *Bardo Thödol* says no more than this, for its five Dhyāni Buddhas are themselves no more than psychic data. That is just what the dead man has to recognize, if it has not already become clear to him during life that his own psychic self and the giver of all data are one and the same. The world of gods and spirits is truly

' nothing but ' the collective unconscious inside me. To turn this sentence round so that it reads: The collective unconscious is the world of gods and spirits outside me, no intellectual acrobatics are needed, but a whole human lifetime, perhaps even many lifetimes of increasing *completeness*. Notice that I do not say ' of increasing perfection ', because those who are ' perfect ' make another kind cf discovery altogether.

*   *   *

The *Bardo Thödol* began by being a ' closed ' book, and so it has remained, no matter what kind of commentaries may be written upon it. For it is a book that will only open itself to spiritual understanding, and this is a capacity which no man is born with, but which he can only acquire through special training and special experience. It is good that such to all intents and purposes ' useless ' books exist. They are meant for those ' queer folk ' who no longer set much store by the uses, aims, and meaning of present-day ' civilisation '.

INTRODUCTORY FOREWORD
By Lāma Anagarika Govinda

It may be argued that nobody can talk about death with authority who has not died; and since nobody, apparently, has ever returned from death, how can anybody know what death is, or what happens after it?

The Tibetan will answer: ' There is not *one* person, indeed, not *one* living being, that has *not* returned from death. In fact, we all have died many deaths, before we came into this incarnation. And what we call birth is merely the reverse side of death, like one of the two sides of a coin, or like a door which we call " entrance " from outside and " exit " from inside a room.'

It is much more astonishing that not everybody remembers his or her previous death; and, because of this lack of remembering, most persons do not believe there was a previous death. But, likewise, they do not remember their recent birth—and yet they do not doubt that they were recently born. They forget that active memory is only a small part of our normal consciousness, and that our subconscious memory registers and preserves every past impression and experience which our waking mind fails to recall.

There are those who, in virtue of concentration and other *yogic* practices, are able to bring the subconscious into the realm of discriminative consciousness and, thereby, to draw upon the unrestricted treasury of subconscious memory, wherein are stored the records not only of our past lives but the records of the past of our race, the past of humanity, and of all pre-human forms of life, if not of the very consciousness that makes life possible in this universe.

If, through some trick of nature, the gates of an individual's subconsciousness were suddenly to spring open, the unprepared mind would be overwhelmed and crushed. Therefore, the gates of the subconscious are guarded, by all initiates, and hidden behind the veil of mysteries and symbols.

For this reason, the *Bardo Thödol*, the Tibetan book vouchsafing liberation from the intermediate state between life and re-birth,—which state men call death,—has been couched in symbolical language. It is a book which is sealed with the seven seals of silence,—not because its knowledge should be withheld from the uninitiated, but because its knowledge would be mis-understood, and, therefore, would tend to mislead and harm those who are unfitted to receive it. But the time has come to break the seals of silence; for the human race has come to the juncture where it must decide whether to be content with the sub-jugation of the material world, or to strive after the conquest of the spiritual world, by subjugating selfish desires and transcending self-imposed limitations.

According to Tibetan tradition, the *Bardo Thödol* is one of those works of Padma-Sambhava which were secretly hidden in order to preserve them for later generations, and which were to be revealed to the world when the time was ripe. However this may be, it is a fact that during the persecution of Buddhism by Langdarma, at the beginning of the ninth century, A.D., innum-erable books of the earliest period of Tibetan Buddhism were concealed under rocks, in caves, and other places, to prevent their destruction. Since all members of the Buddhist Order and their supporters were either killed or driven out of Tibet, most of these buried scriptures remained where they had been hidden. Many of them were recovered during the succeeding centuries and designated *Termas*, a term derived from the Tibetan word *Gter*, pronounced *Ter*, meaning ' Treasure '. Those who discovered these spiritual treasures and propagated their teachings were called *Tertöns*, from Tibetan *Gter-bston*, pronounced *Tertön*, meaning ' Revealer of Treasure '.

This seems to me a far more reasonable explanation for the tradition of the *Tertöns*, which, significantly, is held in the oldest Schools of Tibetan Buddhism, like the Nyingmapa and Kargyütpa, than the theory advanced by certain Western critics, that these scriptures had been ' faked ' by people who wanted to pass off their own ideas under the guise of ancient revelations. Such critics underestimate the religious sincerity and the deep respect for the sanctity of spiritual tradition which is engrained in every Tibetan, layman and *lāma* alike. To add to or omit from the Sacred Scriptures a single word or letter has ever been looked upon by Tibetans as a heinous sin, which even the most impious would fear to commit.

Furthermore, these same critics underestimate the difficulties of forging and issuing such scriptures, for the forging would require a technical and critical knowledge of history and linguistics such as was not only unknown in Tibet, but such as would have required a master-mind for its execution. Had a genius of that sort existed in Tibet, he would have had no need to resort to the subterfuge of forgery, for he could have stood on his own feet, as did many scholarly geniuses who wrote and taught in their own name. Nor is it likely that men who could create and propagate such profound thoughts and lofty ideals as the *Termas* contain would stoop so low as to deceive their fellow-men. And when we consider that the literature in question is not a matter of a few isolated treatises but of about a hundred big volumes (according to tradition 108 volumes), running into tens of thousands of folios, then the theory of wilful deception becomes not only improbable, but absurd.

In considering the influences on the *Bardo Thödol* of the pre-Buddhistic religion of Tibet, namely that of the Bön-pos, there must be taken into account the fact that all of those *Termas* attributed to Padma-Sambhava declare, in no uncertain terms, their adherence to him, the very personage who opposed and defeated the Bön-pos. These recovered scriptures cannot, therefore, be regarded as propagating Bön ideas.

Even though Padma-Sambhava did adopt into the Buddhist system some of the local Tibetan deities, to serve as guardians of the Faith, in doing so he did not give up one inch of Buddhist ground to the Bön-pos, but acted in perfect conformity with the principles of orthodox Buddhism, wherein, in all Buddhist countries, the deities of the Earth and of space have always been honoured and propitiated, as being protectors of the *Dharma*. Thus, the following Pāli verses are still recited, in the course of the regular *pūjā* (or ceremony of worship), by the followers of Theravāda Buddhism, in Ceylon, Burma, Siam, Cambodia, and elsewhere:—

' *Ākāsaṭṭhā ca bhummaṭṭhā, devā nāgā mahiddhikā,*
    Puññantaṃ anumoditvā, ciraṃ rakkhantu sāsanaṃ.'

These verses may be rendered into English as follows:—

' May the beings of the sky [or of space] and of the Earth,
    Devas and *Nāgas* [i.e., gods and serpent-spirits] of great
    power,
    After having shared in the merit [of this *pūjā*],
    Long protect the Sacred Doctrine.'

Any cultural influence, as between Buddhism and Bönism, was more in the nature of a one-way traffic than a mutual exchange of ideas; for the Bön-pos, who had no literature of their own, took over Buddhist concepts and symbols on a vast scale, and thereby created a literature and an iconography which so greatly resemble those of the Buddhists as to be almost indistinguishable to the casual observer.

There is also current the wholly arbitrary assertion that it was the Bön influence which encouraged laxity in the observance of Buddhist monastic rules in Tibet and led to a general decline in the standard of Tibetan learning and morality. Whoever has had the opportunity to stay for even a short time in one of the still existing Bön monasteries of Tibet, will have noticed, with surprise, that the rules of celibacy and monastic discipline are stricter there than in most Buddhist monasteries, and that for many of the major scriptures of the Tibetan Buddhist Canon a parallel can be found in the scriptures of the Bön-pos. They have their ' *Prajñāpāramitā Sūtras*,' their ' *Pratīyasamutpāda* ' (represented in a Wheel of Life of thirteen divisions), their *Tantras* and *Mantras;* and their deities more or less correspond to the various Buddhas, Bodhisattvas, Devatas, and Dharmapālas of Buddhism.

It may seem paradoxical, but it is a fact, that whereas the older Schools of Tibetan Buddhism, despite their tolerance of local deities, succeeded in breaking the power of Bönism, it was the Gelugpas, the youngest and most vigorously reformed School, which re-introduced one of the most influential institutions of the Bön-pos, namely, State Oracles in Oracle-Temples, in all important monasteries of the Yellow Sect. The deities who are invoked in these Oracle-Temples are exclusively of Bön origin. Among the older Buddhist sects, and especially among the Kargyütpas, no such Oracle-Temples exist. This shows that the Old Schools, contrary to common belief, are less under the influence of Bönism than the Gelugpas, in spite of the Gelugpas' reforms and stricter monastic discipline. This stricter monastic discipline of the Gelugpas really brings them nearer to the above-mentioned puritanism of the Bön-pos.

We must, therefore, beware of sweeping statements, as to what can be attributed to the influence of Bönism and what not. Especially is this so because we do not know of what the teachings of Bön consisted before the advent of Buddhism, although we can safely assume that they were animistic, the spiritualised forces of man and nature being worshipped, chiefly in their awe-inspiring and terrifying aspects; and certain rituals were performed for the benefit and the guidance of the dead. Such religious practices as these are commonly found in almost all early civilizations; and they prevailed in India as much as they did in Tibet. This ' animism ' permeates all Buddhistic texts, wherein every tree and grove, and every locality, is held to have its own peculiar deities; and the Buddha is represented as discoursing with gods and other spiritual beings, inhabiting the Earth and the realms beyond, as if that were a most natural procedure. Only a completely intellectualized and Westernized Buddhism, which attempts to separate the rational thought-content of Buddhism from its equally profound mythological elements, can deny this animistic background and with it the metaphysical foundations of Buddhism.

The Buddhist universe is alive through and through; it has no room for inert matter and mere mechanism. And what is more, the Buddhist is alert to all possibilities of existence and to all aspects of reality. If we have read of the fearful apparitions which surrounded the Buddha during the night preceding His Enlightenment, we need not search for Bön influences in relation to the animal-headed monsters that appear from the abyss of the subconscious mind in the hour of death, or in the visions of meditation. Wrathful deities, demons in animal form, and gods in demonical guise are as much at home in Indian as in Tibetan tradition. Despite the popular usages to which the *Bardo Thödol* has been put in connection with the death rituals—and herein, probably, is discernible the only trace of Bön influence worth considering—the central idea and the profound symbolism of the *Bardo Thödol* are genuinely Buddhistic.

The Tibetans themselves have put forth considerable effort

to free their Scriptures from errors and non-Buddhistic accretions, and to ensure the correctness and reliability of their traditions. After the rules for the translation of Sanskrit texts and the necessary corresponding Tibetan terminology had been established by the early Tibetan translators and pioneers of the *Dharma*, ' translators were explicitly forbidden to coin new terms. When this was unavoidable, they were directed to report the matter to a special Tribunal, called " the Tribunal of the Doctrine of the Blessed One," attached to the royal palace. The translation of Tantric works could be undertaken with the king's permission only. These rules were promulgated by King Ti-de Song-tsen (Ral-pa-can, 817-36 A.D.) and have been followed by all Tibetan translators ever since.'[1]

With the advent of wooden block-prints, similar precautions were taken, not only with regard to translations, but with regard to all religious literature. Thus it became a rule that no religious book could be published without the sanction of the highest spiritual authorities, who appointed qualified proof-readers and scholars to prevent faulty renderings or unwarranted interpolations. This, however, did not interfere with the diversity of interpretations by the various acknowledged Schools and their Teachers. The chief purpose was to prevent the degeneration of established traditions either through carelessness or ignorance of unqualified copyists and interpreters.

It is for this reason that the authorized block-prints contain the most reliable versions of the generally accepted traditional sacred texts. But hand-written books, although sometimes suffering from mistakes in spelling and from other errors of the copyist, who often shows lack of understanding of the archaic or classical language of the text, are, nevertheless, valuable, especially if they go back to originals of greater antiquity than those of the current block-prints, or if they represent some lesser known tradition handed down from *guru* to *chela* through many generations.

If, therefore, I direct the reader's attention to certain differences between the officially accepted version of the block-print and that of the manuscript, which formed the basis of Lāma Kazi Dawa

---

[1]Cf. Dr. George Roerich, *Introduction of Buddhism into Tibet*, in *Stepping Stones* (Kalimpong, 1951), Vol. II., No. 5, p. 135.

Samdup's translation, I do not wish to question the value of the manuscript, but merely to throw light upon some important points of Buddhist tradition, which may lead to a deeper understanding, not only from the historical, but, likewise, from a spiritual point of view.

Indeed, it is the spiritual point of view that makes this book so important for the majority of its readers. If the *Bardo Thödol* were to be regarded as being based merely upon folklore, or as consisting of religious speculation about death and a hypothetical after-death state, it would be of interest only to anthropologists and students of religion. But the *Bardo Thödol* is far more. It is a key to the innermost recesses of the human mind, and a guide for initiates, and for those who are seeking the spiritual path of liberation.

Although the *Bardo Thödol* is at the present time widely used in Tibet as a breviary, and read or recited on the occasion of death, —for which reason it has been aptly called ' The Tibetan Book of the Dead'—one should not forget that it was originally conceived to serve as a guide not only for the dying and the dead, but for the living as well. And herein lies the justification for having made *The Tibetan Book of the Dead* accessible to a wider public.

Notwithstanding the popular customs and beliefs which, under the influence of age-old traditions of pre-Buddhist origin, have grown around the profound revelations of the *Bardo Thödol*, it has value only for those who practise and realize its teaching during their life-time.

There are two things which have caused misunderstanding. One is that the teachings seem to be addressed to the dead or the dying; the other, that the title contains the expression " Liberation through Hearing " (in Tibetan, *Thos-grol*). As a result, there has arisen the belief that it is sufficient to read or to recite the *Bardo Thödol* in the presence of a dying person, or even of a person who has just died, in order to effect his or her liberation.

Such misunderstanding could only have arisen among those who do not know that it is one of the oldest and most universal practices for the initiate to go through the experience of death before he can be spiritually reborn. Symbolically he must die to his past, and to his old ego, before he can take his place in the new spiritual life into which he has been initiated.

The dead or the dying person is addressed in the *Bardo Thödol* mainly for three reasons: (1) the earnest practitioner of these teachings should regard every moment of his or her life as if it were the last; (2) when a follower of these teachings is actually dying, he or she should be reminded of the experiences at the time of initiation, or of the words (or *mantra*) of the *guru,* especially if the dying one's mind lacks alertness during the critical moments; and (3) one who is still incarnate should try to surround the person dying, or just dead, with loving and helpful thoughts during the first stages of the new, or after-death, state of existence, without allowing emotional attachment to interfere or to give rise to a state of morbid mental depression. Accordingly, one function of the *Bardo Thödol* appears to be more to help those who have been left behind to adopt the right attitude towards the dead and towards the fact of death than to assist the dead, who, according to Buddhist belief, will not deviate from their own *karmic* path.

In applying the *Bardo Thödol* teachings, it is ever a matter of remembering the right thing at the right moment. But in order so to remember, one must prepare oneself mentally during one's life-time; one must create, build up, and cultivate those faculties which one desires to be of deciding influence at death and in the after-death state,—in order never to be taken unawares, and to be able to react, spontaneously, in the right way, when the critical moment of death has come.

This is clearly expressed in the Root Verses of the *Bardo Thödol* as rendered in *The Tibetan Book of the Dead*:—

[' O] procrastinating one, who thinketh not of the coming of death,
   Devoting thyself to the useless doings of this life,
   Improvident art thou in dissipating thy great opportunity;
   Mistaken, indeed, will thy purpose be now if thou returnest
                                empty-handed [from this life].
Since the Holy Dharma is known to be thy true need,
   Wilt thou not devote [thyself] to the Holy Dharma even now?'

It is recognized by all who are acquainted with Buddhist philosophy that birth and death are not phenomena which happen only once in any given human life; they occur uninterruptedly. At every moment something within us dies and something is reborn. The different *bardos*, therefore, represent different states of consciousness of our life: the state of waking consciousness, the normal consciousness of a being born into our human world, known in Tibetan as the *skyes-nas bardo;* the state of dream-consciousness (*rmi-lam bar-do*); the state of *dhyāna*, or trance-consciousness, in profound meditation (*bsam-gtan bar-do*); the state of the experiencing of death (*hchhi-kha bar-do*); the state of experiencing of Reality (*chhos-nyid bar-do*); the state of rebirth-consciousness (*srid-pa bar-do*).

All this is clearly described in *The Root-Verses of the Six Bardos*, which, together with *The Paths of Good Wishes*, form the authentic and original nucleus of the *Bardo Thödol*, around which the prose parts crystallized as commentaries. This proves that we have to do here with life itself and not merely with a mass for the dead, to which the *Bardo Thödol* was reduced in later times.

The *Bardo Thödol* is addressed not only to those who see the end of their life approaching, or who are very near death, but to those who still have years of incarnate life before them, and who, for the first time, realize the full meaning of their existence as human beings. To be born as a human being is a privilege, according to the Buddha's teaching, because it offers the rare opportunity of liberation through one's own decisive effort, through a ' turning-about in the deepest seat of consciousness,' as the *Lankāvatāra Sūtra* puts it.

Accordingly, *The Root Verses of the Six Bardos* open with the words:

' O that now, when the *Bardo of Life*[1] is dawning upon me,
—After having given up indolence, since there is no time to
                                                    waste in life—
May I undistractedly enter the path of listening, reflecting,
                                                    and meditating,
So that, . . . once having attained human embodiment,
No time may be squandered through useless distractions.'

[1]Lāma Kazi Dawa-Samdup has here ' Birthplace Bardo '. Apparently his manuscript has ' *skyes-gnas* ' instead of ' *skyes-nas* ', which is found in the block-print. The latter means, literally, ' having been born ', that is, having been born into the state men call life. ' *Skyes-gnas* ' refers to the womb, the ' place ' (*gnas*) of birth; and this is the subject of the sixth verse, dealing with the *bardo* of rebirth, which, therefore, cannot be meant here, for otherwise there would be only five *bardos* instead of six.

Listening, reflecting, and meditating are the three stages of discipleship. The Tibetan word for ' listening ', or ' hearing ', *thos* in this connection, as well as in the expression ' *Thödol* ' (*thos-grol*), cannot be confused with the mere physical sense-awareness of hearing, as may be seen from the Tibetan term ' *nyan-thos,*' the equivalent of the Sanskrit word ' *sravaka,*' referring to a ' disciple,' and, more particularly, to a personal disciple of the Buddha, and not merely to one who by chance happened to hear the Buddha's teaching. It refers to one who has accepted this teaching in his heart and has made it his own. Thus the word ' listening,' in this connection, implies ' hearing with one's heart,' that is, with sincere faith (*śraddha*). This represents the first stage of discipleship. In the second stage, this intuitive attitude is transformed into understanding through reason; while, in the third stage, the disciple's intuitive feeling, as well as intellectual understanding, are transformed into living reality through direct experience. Thus intellectual conviction grows into spiritual certainty, into a knowing in which the knower is *one* with the known.

This is the high spiritual state vouchsafed by the teachings set forth in the *Bardo Thödol*. Thereby the initiated disciple attains dominion over the realm of death, and, being able to perceive death's illusory nature, is freed from fear. This illusoriness of death comes from the identification of the individual with his temporal, transitory form, whether physical, emotional, or mental, whence arise the mistaken notion that there exists a personal, separate egohood of one's own, and the fear of losing it. If, however, the disciple has learned, as the *Bardo Thödol* directs, to identify himself with the Eternal, the *Dharma*, the Imperishable Light of Buddahood within, then the fears of death are dissipated like a cloud before the rising sun. Then he knows that whatever he may see, hear, or feel, in the hour of his departure from this life, is but a reflection of his own conscious and subconscious mental content; and no mind-created illusion can then have power over him if he knows its origin and is able to recognize it. The illusory *Bardo* visions vary, in keeping with the religious or cultural tradition in which the percipient has grown up, but their underlying motive-power is the same in all human beings. Thus it is that the profound psychology set forth by the *Bardo Thödol* constitutes an important contribution to our knowledge of the human mind and of the path that leads beyond it. Under the guise of a science of death, the *Bardo Thödol* reveals the secret of life; and therein lies its spiritual value and its universal appeal.

The *Bardo Thödol* is a treatise which needs more than philological knowledge for its translation and interpretation, namely, a thorough knowledge of its traditional background and of the religious experience of one who either has grown up in the tradition or who has imbibed its tradition from a competent living *guru*. In times of old ' it was not considered that the mere knowledge of language sufficed to make a man a " translator" in any serious sense of the word; no one would have undertaken to translate a text who had not studied it for long years at the feet of a traditional and authoritative exponent of its teaching, and much less would anyone have thought himself qualified to translate a book in the teachings of which he did not believe.'[1]

Our modern attitude, unfortunately, is a complete reversal of this: a scholar is regarded as being all the more competent (' scholarly ') the less he believes in the teachings which he has undertaken to interpret. The sorry results are only too apparent, especially in the realm of Tibetology, which such scholars have approached with an air of their own superiority, thus defeating the very purpose of their endeavours.

Lāma Kazi Dawa-Samdup and Dr. Evans-Wentz were the first to re-establish the ancient method of *Lotsavas* (as the translators of sacred texts are called in Tibet). They approached their work in the spirit of true devotion and humility, as a sacred trust that had come into their hands through generations of initiates, a trust which had to be handled with the utmost respect for even the smallest detail. At the same time, they did not regard their translation as final, or infallible, but rather like the pioneer translations of the *Bible*, that is, as being a starting-point for ever deeper and more perfect renderings in accordance with our growing acquaintance with the sources of Tibetan tradition.

[1] *Cf.* Ananda K. Coomaraswami, *Hinduism and Buddhism* (Philosophical Library, New York, n.d.), p. 49; and Marco Pallis, *Peaks and Lamas* (Cassell & Co., London, 1946), pp. 79-81. The latter is probably the best and most readable introduction to Tibetan Buddhism which so far has been written.

Such an attitude is not only the hall-mark of spiritual under-standing and true scholarship, but it makes even the reader feel that he is treading on sacred ground. This explains the deep impression which *The Tibetan Book of the Dead*, as well as the other complementary volumes of the Oxford Tibetan Series, have made upon thoughtful readers all over the world. The outstanding success of these works was due to their convincing sincerity and seriousness of purpose. Indeed, the world owes a great debt of gratitude to these two devoted scholars. '*Sabbadānaṃ dhammadānaṃ jināti*': 'The best of all gifts is the gift of Truth.'[1]

THE BUDDA'S REMEMBERING

'In recollection all former births passed before His eyes. Born in such a place, of such a name, and downwards to His present birth, so through hundreds, thousands, myriads, all His births and deaths He knew.'

Ashvaghosha's Life of the Buddha
(Samuel Beal's Translation).

---

[1] Cf. *Dhammapāda*, xxiv, 21.

FOREWORD

BY SIR JOHN WOODROFFE

THE SCIENCE OF DEATH [1]

'Strive after the Good before thou art in danger, before pain masters thee and thy mind loses its keenness.'—*Kulārnava Tantra*, I. 27.

THE thought of death suggests two questions. The first is: 'How may one avoid death, except when death is desired as in "Death-at-will" (*Ichchhāmrityu*)?' The avoidance of death is the aim when *Hathayoga* is used to prolong present life in the flesh. This is not, in the Western sense, a 'yea-saying' to 'life', but, for the time being, to a particular form of life. Dr. Evans-Wentz tells us that according to popular Tibetan belief no death is natural. This is the notion of most, if not of all, primitive peoples. Moreover, physiology also questions whether there is any 'natural death', in the sense of death through mere age without lesion or malady. This Text, however, in the language of the renouncer of fleshly life the world over, tells the nobly-born that Death comes to all, that human kind are not to cling to life on earth with its ceaseless wandering in the Worlds of birth and death (*Sangsāra*). Rather should they implore the aid of the Divine Mother for a safe passing through the fearful state following the body's dissolution, and that they may at length attain all-perfect Buddhahood.

The second question then is: 'How to accept Death and die?' It is with this that we are now concerned. Here the technique of dying makes Death the entrance to good future lives, at first out of, and then again in, the flesh, unless and until liberation (*Nirvāna*) from the wandering (*Sangsāra*) is attained.

[1] As to the title of this Foreword, 'The Science of Death', see *Thanatology*, by Dr. Roswell Parks, in *The Journal of the American Medical Association* April 27, 1912.

This Book, which is of extraordinary interest, both as regards Text and Introduction, deals with the period (longer or shorter according to the circumstances) which, commencing immediately after death, ends with 'rebirth'. In the Buddhists' view, Life consists of a series of successive states of consciousness. The first state is the Birth-Consciousness; the last is the consciousness existing at the moment of death, or the Death-Consciousness. The interval between the two states of Consciousness, during which the transformation from the 'old' to a 'new' being is effected, is called the *Bardo* or intermediate state (*Antarābhāva*), divided into three stages, called the *Chikhai*, *Chönyid*, and *Sidpa Bardo* respectively.

This Manual, common in various versions throughout Tibet, is one of a class amongst which Dr. Evans-Wentz includes the Egyptian Book of the Dead, a guide for the use of the *Ka* or so-called 'Double', the *De Arte Moriendi* and other similar medieval treatises on the craft of dying, to which may be added the Orphic Manual called *The Descent into Hades* (cf. 'He descended into Hell') and other like guide-books for the use of the dead, the *Pretakhanda* of the Hindu *Garuda Purāna*, Swedenborg's *De Coelo et de Inferno*, Rusca's *De Inferno*, and several other eschatological works both ancient and modern. Thus, the *Garuda Purāna* deals with the rites used over the dying, the death-moment, the funeral ceremonies, the building up, by means of the *Pretashrāddha* rite, of a new body for the *Preta* or deceased in lieu of that destroyed by fire, the Judgement, and thereafter (ch. V) the various states through which the deceased passes until he is reborn again on earth.

Both the original text and Dr. Evans-Wentz's Introduction form a very valuable contribution to the Science of Death from the standpoint of the Tibetan Mahāyāna Buddhism of the so-called 'Tantrik' type. The book is welcome not merely in virtue of its particular subject-matter, but because the ritual works of any religion enable us more fully to comprehend the philosophy and psychology of the system to which they belong.

The Text has three characteristics. It is, firstly, a work on the Art of Dying ; for Death, as well as Life, is an Art, though both are often enough muddled through. There is a Bengali saying, 'Of what use are *Japa* and *Tapas* (two forms of devotion) if one knoweth not how to die?' Secondly, it is a manual of religious therapeutic for the last moments, and a psychurgy exorcising, instructing, consoling, and fortifying by the rites of the dying, him who is about to pass on to another life. Thirdly, it describes the experiences of the deceased during the intermediate period, and instructs him in regard thereto. It is thus also a Traveller's Guide to Other Worlds.

The doctrine of 'Reincarnation' on the one hand and of 'Resurrection' on the other is the chief difference between the four leading Religions—Brahmanism, Buddhism, Christianity, and Islam. Christianity, in its orthodox form, rejects the most ancient and widespread belief of the *Kúklos geneseōn*, or *Sangsāra*, or 'Reincarnation', and admits one universe only—this, the first and last—and two lives, one here in the natural body and one hereafter in the body of Resurrection.

It has been succinctly said that as Metempsychosis makes the same soul, so Resurrection makes the same body serve for more than one Life. But the latter doctrine limits man's lives to two in number, of which the first or present determines for ever the character of the second or future.

Brahmanism and Buddhism would accept the doctrine that 'as a tree falls so shall it lie', but they deny that it so lies for ever. To the adherents of these two kindred beliefs this present universe is not the first and last. It is but one of an infinite series, without absolute beginning or end, though each universe of the series appears and disappears. They also teach a series of successive existences therein until morality, devotion, and knowledge produce that high form of detachment which is the cause of Liberation from the cycle of birth and death called 'The Wandering' (or *Sangsāra*). Freedom is the attainment of the Supreme State called the Void, *Nirvāṇa*, and by other names. They deny that there is only one universe, with one life for each of its human units, and then a division of men for all eternity into those who are saved in Heaven or are in Limbo and those who are lost in

Hell. Whilst they agree in holding that there is a suitable body for enjoyment or suffering in Heaven and Hell, it is not a resurrected body, for the fleshly body on death is dissolved for ever.

The need of some body always exists, except for the non-dualist who believes in a bodiless (*Videha*) Liberation (*Mukti*); and each of the four religions affirms that there is a subtle and death-surviving element—vital and psychical—in the physical body of flesh and blood, whether it be a permanent entity or Self, such as the Brahmanic *Ātmā*, the Moslem *Ruh*, and the Christian 'Soul', or whether it be only a complex of activities (or *Skandha*), psychical and physical, with life as their function—a complex in continual change, and, therefore, a series of physical and psychical momentary states, successively generated the one from the other, a continuous transformation, as the Buddhists are said to hold. Thus to none of these Faiths is death an absolute ending, but to all it is only the separation of the *Psyche* from the gross body. The former then enters on a new life, whilst the latter, having lost its principle of animation, decays. As Dr. Evans-Wentz so concisely says, Death disincarnates the 'soul-complex', as Birth incarnates it. In other words, Death is itself only an initiation into another form of life than that of which it is the ending.

On the subject of the physical aspect of Death, the attention of the reader is drawn to the remarkable analysis here given of symptoms which precede it. These are stated because it is necessary for the dying man and his helpers to be prepared for the final and decisive moment when it comes.[1] Noteworthy, too, is the description of sounds heard as (to use Dr. Evans-Wentz's language) 'the psychic resultants of the disintegrating process called death'. They call to mind the humming, rolling, and crackling noises heard before and up to fifteen hours after death, which, recognized by Greunwaldi in 1618 and referred to by later writers, were in 1862 made the subject of special study by Dr. Collingues.

[1] Cf. *Tantrarāja*, ch. xxvii, vv. 83–100, dealing with signs of approaching death, *Tantrik Texts*, edited by Arthur Avalon, vol. xii.

But it is said that the chain of conscious states is not always broken by death, since there is *Phowa,* or power to project consciousness and enter the body of another.[1] Indian occultism speaks of the same power of leaving one's body (*Svechchhotkrānti*), which, according to the *Tantrarāja* (ch. XXVII, vv. 45–7, 72–80), is accomplished through the operation (*Vāyudhārana*) of the vital activity (or *Vāyu*) in thirty-eight points, or junctions (*Marma*), of the body. How, it may be asked, does this practice work in with the general doctrine or 'reincarnation'? We should have been glad if Dr. Evans-Wentz had elucidated this point. On principle, it would seem that in the case of entry into an unborn body such entry may be made into the *Matrix* in the same way as if it had occurred after a break of consciousness in death. But in the case of entry into beings already born the operation of the power or *Siddhi* would appear to be by the way of possession (*Āvesha*) by one consciousness of the consciousness and body of another, differing from the more ordinary case by the fact that the possessing consciousness does not return to its body, which *ex hypothesi* is about to die when the consciousness leaves it.

If transference of consciousness is effected, there is, of course, no *Bardo,* which involves the break of consciousness by death. Otherwise, the Text is read.

Then, as the breathing is about to cease, instruction is given and the arteries are pressed. This is done to keep the dying person conscious with a consciousness rightly directed. For the nature of the Death-consciousness determines the future state of the 'soul-complex', existence being the continuous transformation of one conscious state into another. Both in Catholic and Hindu ritual for the dying there is constant prayer and repetition of the sacred names.

The pressing of the arteries regulates the path to be taken by the outgoing vital current (*Prāna*). The proper path is that which passes through the *Brāhmarandhra,* or Foramen of Monro. This notion appears to have been widely held (to quote an instance) even in so remote and primitive a spot as San Cristoval in the Solomon Islands (see *Threshold of the*

---

[1] Cf. *Tantrik Texts,* vol. vii, p. 23, the Buddhist *Shrīchakra-sambhāra Tantra.*

Pacific, by C. E. Fox). The function of a holed-stone in a Dolmen found there (reminiscent of the Dolmen *à dalle percée* common in the Marne district of Western Europe, in South Russia, and in Southern India) is 'to allow the free passage to its natural seat, the head, of the dead man's *adaro*, or "double" '.

According to Hindu belief (see *Pretakhanda* of *Garuda Purāna*) there are nine apertures of the body which are the means of experience, and which, in the divine aspect, are the Lords (*Nātha*) or *Gurus*.[1] A good exit is one which is above the navel. Of such exits the best is through the fissure on the top of the cranium called *Brāhmarandhra*. This is above the physical *cerebrum* and the *Yoga* centre called 'Lotus of the Thousand Petals' (*Sahasrāra Padma*), wherein Spirit is most manifest, since it is the seat of Consciousness. Because of this, the orthodox Hindu wears a crest-lock (*Shikhā*) at this spot; not, as some have absurdly supposed, so that he may thereby be gripped and taken to Heaven or Hell, but because the *Shikhā* is, as it were, a flag and its staff, raised before and in honour of the abode of the Supreme Lord, Who is Pure Consciousness itself. (The fancy-picture in a recent work by C. Lancelin, *La Vie posthume*, p. 96, does not show the aperture of exit, which is given in Plate 8 of the second edition of Arthur Avalon's *Serpent Power*, p. 93.)

Whatever be the ground for the belief and practice of primitive peoples, according to *Yoga* doctrine, the head is the chief centre of consciousness, regulating other subordinate centres in the spinal column. By withdrawal of the vital current through the central or *Sushumnā* 'nerve' (*nādī*), the lower parts of the body are devitalized, and there is vivid concentrated functioning at the cerebral centre.

Exotericism speaks of the 'Book of Judgement'. This is an objective symbol of the 'Book' of Memory. The 'reading' of that 'Book' is the recalling to mind by the dying man of the whole of his past life on earth before he passes from it.[2]

---

[1] Cf. A. Avalon's *Tantrik Texts*, vol. viii, p. 2.

[2] That such a review of earth-life is experienced by the dying has been frequently attested by persons who had begun to die, as, for example, in drowning, and then been resuscitated.—W. Y. E-W.

The vital current at length escapes from the place where it last functioned. In *Yoga*, thought and breathing being inter-dependent, exit through the *Brāhmarandhra* connotes previous activity at the highest centre. Before such exit, and whilst self-consciousness lasts, the mental contents are supplied by the ritual, which is so designed as to secure a good death, and, therefore (later on), birth-consciousness.

At the moment of death the empiric consciousness, or con-sciousness of objects, is lost. There is what is popularly called a 'swoon', which is, however, the corollary of super-conscious-ness itself, or the Clear Light of the Void; for the swoon is in, and of, the Consciousness as knower of objects (*Vijñāna Skandha*). This empiric consciousness disappears, unveiling Pure Consciousness, which is ever ready to be 'discovered' by those who have the will to seek and the power to find It.

That clear, colourless Light is a sense-symbol of the form-less Void, 'beyond the Light of Sun, Moon, and Fire', to use the words of the Indian *Gītā*. It is clear and colourless, but *māyik* (or 'form') bodies are coloured in various ways. For colour implies and denotes form. The Formless is colourless. The use of psycho-physical chromatism is common to the Hindu and Buddhist *Tantras*, and may be found in some Islamic mystical systems also.

What then is this Void? It is not absolutely 'nothingness'. It is the Alogical, to which no categories drawn from the world of name and form apply. But whatever may have been held by the Mādhyamika Bauddha, a Vedāntist would say that 'Being', or 'Is-ness', is applicable even in the case of the Void, which is experienced as 'is' (*asti*). The Void is thus, in this view, the negation of all determinations, but not of 'Is-ness' as such, as has been supposed in accounts given of Buddhist 'Nihilism'; but it is nothing known to finite ex-perience in form, and, therefore, for those who have had no other experience, it is no-thing.

A description of Buddhist *Mahāyāna* teaching which is at once more succinct and clear than, to my knowledge, any other, is given in the Tibetan work, *The Path of Good Wishes of Samanta Bhadra*, which I have published in the seventh volume of *Tantrik Texts* (p. xxi *et seq.*) and here summarize and explain.

All is either *Sangsāra* or *Nirvāṇa*. The first is finite experience in the 'Six Worlds' or *Loka*—a word which means 'that which is experienced' (*Lokyante*). The second, or *Nirvāṇa*, is, negatively speaking, release from such experience, that is from the worlds of Birth and Death and their pains. The Void cannot even be strictly called *Nirvāṇa*, for this is a term relative to the world, and the Void is beyond all relations. Positively, and concomitantly with such release, it is the Perfect Experience which is Buddhahood, which, again, from the cognitive aspect, is Consciousness unobscured by the darkness of Unconsciousness, that is to say, Consciousness freed of all limitation. From the emotional aspect, it is pure Bliss unaffected by sorrow; and from the volitional aspect, it is freedom of action and almighty power (*Amogha-Siddhi*). Perfect Experience is an eternal or, more strictly speaking, a timeless state. Imperfect Experience is also eternal in the sense that the series of universes in which it is undergone is infinite. The religious, that is practical, problem is then how from the lesser experience to pass into that which is complete, called by the *Upanishads* 'the Whole' or *Pūrna*. This is done by the removal of obscuration. At base, the two are one—the Void, uncreated, independent, uncompounded, and beyond mind and speech. If this were not so, Liberation would not be possible. Man is in fact liberated, but does not know it. When he realizes it, he is freed. The great saying of the Buddhist work the *Prajñā-Pāramitā* runs thus : 'Form (*Rūpa*) is the Void and the Void is Form.'[1] Realization of the Void is to be a Buddha, or 'Knower', and not to realize it is to be an 'ignorant being' in the *Sangsāra*. The two paths, then, are Knowledge and Ignorance. The first path leads to—and, as actual realization, is—*Nirvāṇa*. The second means continuance of fleshly life as man or brute, or as a denizen of the other four *Lokas*. Ignorance in the individual is in its cosmic aspect *Māyā*, which in Tibetan (*sGyuma*) means a magical show. In its most generic form,

[1] See *Tantrik Texts*, vol. vii, p. 33.

the former is that which produces the pragmatic, but, in a transcendental sense, the 'unreal' notion of self and otherness. This is the root cause of error (whether in knowing, feeling, or action) which becomes manifest as the 'Six Poisons' (which Hindus call the 'Six Enemies') of the Six *Lokas* of *Sangsāra* (of which the Text gives five only)—pride, jealousy, sloth (or ignorance), anger, greed, and lust. The Text constantly urges upon the dying or 'dead' man to recognize in the apparitions, which he is about to see or sees, the creatures of his own *māyā*-governed mind, veiling from him the Clear Light of the Void. If he does so, he is liberated at any stage.

This philosophical scheme has so obvious a resemblance to the Indian *Māyāvāda Vedānta* that the Vaishnava *Padma Purāna* dubs that system 'a bad scripture and covert Buddhism' (*māyāvādam asachchāstram prachchhannam bauddham*). Nevertheless, its great scholastic, 'the incomparable Shangkarāchāryya', as Sir William Jones calls him, combated the Buddhists in their denial of a permanent Self (*Ātmā*), as also their subjectivism, at the same time holding that the notion of an individual self and that of a world of objects were pragmatic truths only, superseded by and on the attainment of a state of Liberation which has little, if anything, to distinguish it from the Buddhist Void. The difference between the two systems, though real, is less than is generally supposed. This is a matter, however, which it would be out of place to discuss further here.

However this may be, the after-death apparitions are 'real' enough for the deceased who does not, as and when they appear, recognize their unsubstantiality and cleave his way through them to the Void. The Clear Light is spoken of in the *Bardo Thödol* as such a Dazzlement as is produced by an infinitely vibrant landscape in the springtide. This joyous picture is not, of course, a statement of what It is in itself, for It is not an object, but is a translation in terms of objective vision of a great, but, in itself, indescribable joyful inner experience. My attention was drawn, in this connexion, to a passage in a paper on the *Avatamsaka Sūtra* (ch. xv), by Mr. Hsu, a Chinese scholar, which says, 'The

Bodhisattva emits the light called " Seeing the Buddha " in order to make the dying think about the Tathāgata and so enable them to go to the pure realms of the latter after death '.

The dying or deceased man is adjured to recognize the Clear Light and thus liberate himself. If he does so, it is because he is himself ripe for the liberated state which is thus presented to him. If he does not (as is commonly the case), it is because the pull of worldly tendency (*Sangskāra*) draws him away. He is then presented with the secondary Clear Light, which is the first, somewhat dimmed to him by the general *Māyā*. If the mind does not find its resting-place here, the first or *Chikhai Bardo*, which may last for several days, or 'for the time that it takes to snap a finger' (according to the state of the deceased), comes to an end.

In the next stage (*Chönyid Bardo*) there is a recovery of the Death-Consciousness of objects. In one sense, that is compared with a swoon, it is a rewakening. But it is not a waking-state such as existed before death. The 'soul-complex' emerges from its experience of the Void into a state like that of dream. This continues until it attains a new fleshly body and thus really awakes to earth-life again. For this world-experience is life in such a body.

When I first read the account of the fifteen days following recovery from the 'swoon', I thought it was meant to be a scheme of gradual arising of limited consciousness, ana-logous to that described in the thirty-six *Tattvas* by the Northern *Shaivāgama* and its *Tantras*, a process which is given in its ritual form in the Tantrik *Bhūtashuddhi* rite and in *Laya* or *Kuṇḍalinī Yoga*. But on closer examination I found that this was not so. After the ending of the first *Bardo* the scheme commences with the complete recovery, without inter-mediate stages, of the Death-Consciousness. The psychic life is taken up and continued from that point, that is from the stage immediately prior to the 'swoon'.[1] Life im-mediately after death is, according to this view, as Spiritists assert, similar to, and a continuation of, the life preceding it.

[1] Cf. *Yogavāshishṭha*, CLX, v. 41.

As in Swedenborg's account, and in the recent play *Outward Bound*, the deceased does not at first know that he is 'dead'. Swedenborg, who also speaks of an intermediate state, says that, except for those immediately translated to Heaven or Hell, the first state of man after death is like his state in the world, so that he knows no other, believing that he is still in the world notwithstanding his death.[1]

Two illustrations may be given of the doctrine of the continuity and the similarity of experience before and immediately after death. In India, on the one hand, there are reports of hauntings by unhappy ghosts or *Pretas*, which hauntings are said to be allayed by the performance of the *Preta Shrāddha* rite at the sacred town of Gaya. On the other hand, I have heard of a case in England where it was alleged that a haunting ceased on the saying of a *Requiem* Mass. In this case, it was supposed that a Catholic soul in Purgatory felt in need of a rite which in its earth-life it had been taught to regard as bringing peace to the dead. The Hindu ghost craves for the Hindu rite which gives to it a new body in lieu of that destroyed on the funeral pyre. These souls do not (in an Indian view) cease to be Hindu or Catholic, or lose their respective beliefs because of their death. Nor (in this view) do those who have passed on necessarily and at once lose any habit, even though it be drinking and smoking. But in the after-death state the 'whisky and cigars' of which we have heard are not gross, material things. Just as a dream reproduces waking experiences, so in the after-death state a man who was wont to drink and smoke imagines that he still does so. We have here to deal with 'dream-whisky' and 'dream-cigars' which, though imaginary, are, for the dreamer, as real as the substances he drank and smoked in his waking state.[2]

---

[1] *De Coelo*, ed. 1868, 493–7.

[2] The editor has heard of a European planter who, having died in the jungles of the Malabar country of South-west India, was buried there by the people. Some years afterwards, a friend of the planter found the grave carefully fenced in and covered with empty whisky and beer bottles. At a loss to understand such an unusual sight, he asked for an explanation, and was told that the dead *sahib's* ghost had caused much trouble and that no way had been

Subsequently, the deceased becomes aware that he *is* ' dead '. But as he carries over with him the recollection of his past life, he, at first, still thinks that he has such a physical body as he had before. It is, in fact, a dream-body, such as that of persons seen in dreams. It is an imagined body, which, as the Text says, is neither reflected in a mirror nor casts a shadow, and which can do such wonders as passing through mountains and the like, since Imagination is the greatest of magicians. Even in life on earth a man may imagine that he has a limb where he has none. Long after a man's leg has been amputated above the knee he can ' feel his toes ', or is convinced that the soles of his feet (buried days before) are tickling. In the after-death state the deceased imagines that he has a physical body, though he has been severed therefrom by the high surgery of death. In such a body the deceased goes through the experiences next described.

In the First *Bardo* the deceased glimpses the Clear Light, as the *Dharma-Kāya*, called by Professor Sylvain Lévy the ' Essential Body '. This, which is beyond form (*Arūpa*), is the *Dharma-Dhātu*, or *Matrix* of *Dharma*-substance, whence all the Blessed Ones, or *Tathāgatas*, issue. This is the body of a Buddha in *Nirvāna*. The second body, or *Sambhoga-Kāya*, has such subtle form (*Rūpavān*) as is visible to the *Bodhisattvas*, and is an intermediate manifestation of the *Dharma-Dhātu*. In the third body, or *Nirmāna-Kāya*, the Void, or State of Buddha-hood, is exteriorized into multiple individual appearances more material, and, therefore, visible to the gross senses of men, such as the forms in which the manifested Buddhas (for there are many and not, as some think, only one, or Gautama) have appeared on earth. If the deceased recognizes the Clear Light of the First *Bardo*, he is liberated in the

---

discovered to lay the ghost until an old witch-doctor declared that the ghost craved whisky and beer, to which it had long been habituated when in the flesh and which were the real cause of its separation from the fleshly body. The people, although religiously opposed to intoxicants, began purchasing bottled whisky and beer of the same brands which the *sahib* was well known to have used, and, with a regular ritual for the dead, began sacrificing them to the ghost by pouring them out upon the grave. Finding that this kept the ghost quiet they kept up the practice in self-defence.—W. Y. E-W.

Dharma-Kāya. In the Second *Bardo* Liberation is into the *Sambhoga-Kāya* (the passage touching the Paradise Realms is not, I think, meant to conflict with this); and in the Third *Bardo* Liberation is experienced in the *Nirmāṇa-Kāya.*

During the Second and Third *Bardo* the deceased is in the *Māyik*-world (or world of forms), and if Liberation is then attained it is with form (*Rūpavān*). The deceased being thus in the world of duality, we find that from this point onwards there is a double parallel presentation to his consciousness. There is firstly a *Nirvāṇic* line, comprising the Five Dhyānī Buddhas of the *Sambhoga-Kāya*, symbolized by various dazzling colours, with certain Divinities, peaceful and wrathful, emanating from them; and, secondly, a *Sangsāric* line, consisting of the Six *Lokas*. These latter, with one exception (if it be one and not due to corruption of text, viz. the association of the smoky or black light of Hell with the blue *Vajra-Sattva*), have the same colour as their *Nirvāṇic* counterparts, but of a dull hue. With the *Lokas* are given their 'Poisons', or the sinful characteristics of their inhabitants. The 'soul-complex' is then adjured, on the one hand, to seek Liberation through the compassionate grace of the *Nirvāṇic* line of *Buddhas* and *Devatās* (Divinities), and, on the other hand, to shun the particular *Loka* (World) which is concomitantly presented to his mental vision. With these *Buddhas*, *Devatās*, and *Lokas* are associated certain *Nidānas* (Causal Connexions), *Skandhas* (Constituent Factors), material elements, and the colours of the latter. This account appears to have suffered from corruption of the Text. Thus the *Nidānas* and *Skandhas* are not complete. Logically, *Vijñāna Skandha* should go first with *Vairochana*, and *Nāma-rūpa* with *Vajra-Sattva*. Only four out of the five elements are mentioned. Ether, which is omitted, should be associated with *Vairochana* and *Vijñāna*. The colours of the elements accord with those given in the Hindu *Tantras* except as regards 'air', to which is assigned a green colour, appropriate for *Asuric* jealousy, though it is not that of the Hindu colouration, which is smoky grey. Again, the order of the Six *Lokas* is not the usual one, viz. first the better *Lokas*, of *Devas*, *Asuras*, and Men, and then the *Lokas* of Ghosts (*Pretas*), Brutes, and Hell. Each *Loka* is characterized by its 'poison' or besetting sin, but, of these, five only are mentioned. The editor has, however, referred to corruption in the Text in some of these matters, and others I have noted on a careful analysis of the translated Text.

The peaceful *Devatās* follow on the sixth and seventh day, and the wrathful *Devatās* on the eighth and subsequent days. The latter are of the terrific type, characteristic both of the Buddhist and Hindu *Shākta Tantras*, with their *Bhairavas*, *Bhairavīs*, *Dākinīs*, *Yoginīs*, and so on. Hinduism also makes this distinction in the nature of Divinities and interprets the wrathful orders as representative of the so-called 'destructive' power of the Supreme Lord and of his lesser manifestations; though, in truth, 'God never destroys' (*na devo nāshakah kvachit*), but withdraws the Universe to Himself.

But Power, which thus dissolves the world, is ever terrible to those who are attached to the world. All bad action (*Adharma*), too, is dissolvent; and, according to the Text, the deceased's evil *Karma* in the *Sangsāra* is reflected in the *Nirvāṇic* line in its forms as Divinities of the Lower *Bardo*, who so terrify the deceased that he flees from them and sinks therefore more and more into such a state as will eventually bring him birth in one or other of the *Lokas*.

The Peaceful *Devatās* are said to issue from the heart, and the Wrathful from the head. I do not, however, think that this statement necessarily lets in the *Yoga* doctrine of the 'Serpent Power' and the Six Centres, which the editor has shortly set out in Part II of the Addenda, assuming (a matter of which I have no personal knowledge) that the Tibetans both practise this *Yoga* and teach it in its Indian form. I myself think that the mention of the heart and head does not refer to these places as *Yoga*-centres, but possibly to the fact that the Peaceful Deities reflect, as stated in the Text, the love of the deceased which springs from his heart.

I make a reservation also as regards the subject of *Mantras*, dealt with in Part III of the Addenda. No doubt the Tibetans employ Sanskrit *Mantras*, but such *Mantras* are often found in a sadly corrupt form in their books—a fact which suggests that the Tibetans feel little appreciation of the supposed sound-value of *Mantras*. But whether their theory on this subject is the same in all respects as that of the Hindus I cannot say.[1] The Hindu theory, which I have elsewhere endeavoured to elucidate (cf. *Garland of Letters*), is still on several points obscure; the subject being perhaps the most difficult of any in Hinduism. Even though Tibetan Buddhism may have *Mantra-Sādhanā*, the presentment of it is likely to differ as much as does the general substance of these two Faiths.

About the fifteenth day, passage is made into the Third *Bardo*, in which the deceased, if not previously liberated, seeks 'Rebirth'. His past life has now become dim. That of the future is indicated by certain premonitory signs which represent the first movements of desire towards fulfilment. The 'soul-complex' takes on the colour of the *Loka* in which it is destined to be born. If the deceased's *Karma* leads him to Hell, thither he goes after the Judgement, in a subtle body which cannot be injured or destroyed, but in which he may suffer atrocious pain. Or he may go to the Heaven-world or other *Loka*, to return at length and in all cases (for neither punishment nor reward are eternal) to earth, whereon only can new *Karma* be made. Such return takes place after expiation of his sins in Hell, or the expiration of the term of enjoyment in Heaven which his *Karma* has gained for him. If, however, the lot of the deceased is immediate rebirth on earth, he sees visions of mating men and women. He, at this final stage towards the awakening to earth-life, now knows that he has not a gross

---

[1] Just as the Tibetans took over *Tantricism* from India, so, as the well-known Tibetan *Biography of Jetsün Milarepa* (Tibet's most famous *Yogī* and Saint), for example, makes clear, they appear also to have derived various systems of *Yoga* from India, including *Laya* or *Kuṇḍalinī Yoga*. While it is undoubtedly true that many *Mantras* likewise derived from India have grown hopelessly corrupt in the Tibetan language itself, the practice of *Laya* or *Kuṇḍalinī Yoga* by Tibetans seems to have been kept fairly pure, largely through oral trans-mission from *guru* to *guru* rather than through written records, except for Tibetanized terminologies and methods of application. Certain Tibetan treatises on *Yoga* which the editor possesses, both in the original and in English translation, suggest this. —W. Y. E-W.

body of flesh and blood. He urgently desires to have one, in order that he may again enjoy physical life on the earth-world.

The Freudian psycho-analyst will find herein a remarkable passage supporting his doctrine of the aversion of the son for the father. The passage says that, if the deceased is to be born as a male, the feeling of its being a male comes upon the knower, and a feeling of intense aversion for the father and attraction for the mother is begotten, and vice versa as regards birth as a female. This is, however, an old Buddhist doctrine found elsewhere. Professor De la Vallée Poussin cites the following passage: 'L'esprit troublé par désir d'amour, il va au lieu de sa destinée. Même très éloigné, il voit, par l'œil né de la force de l'acte, le lieu de sa naissance; voyant là son père et sa mère unis, il conçoit désir pour la mère quand il est mâle, désir pour le père quand il est femelle, et, inversement, haine' (*Bouddhisme: Études et Matériaux, Abhidharmakosha*, iii. 15, p. 25). The work cited also contains other interesting details concerning the embryo. (See, too, the same author's *La Théorie de douze causes*.)

At length the deceased passes out of the *Bardo* dream-world into a womb of flesh and blood, issuing thence once more into the waking state of earth-experience. This is what in English is called Re-incarnation, or Re-birth in the flesh. The Sanskrit term is *Sangsāra*, that is, 'rising and rising again' (*Punarutpatti*) in the worlds of birth and death. Nothing is permanent, but all is transitory. In life, the 'soul-complex' is never for two consecutive moments the same, but is, like the body, in constant change. There is thus a series (*Santāna*) of successive, and, in one sense, different states, which are in themselves but momentary. There is still a unifying bond in that each momentary state is a present transformation representative of all those which are past, as it will be the generator of all future transformations potentially involved in it.

This process is not interrupted by death. Change continues in the *Skandhas* (or constituents of the organism) other than the gross body which has been cast off and which undergoes changes of its own. But there is this difference: the after-death change is merely the result of the action of accumulated past *Karma* and does not, as in earthly life, create new *Karma*, for which a physical body is necessary. (Buddhism, Hinduism, and Christianity are in agreement in holding that man's destiny is decided on Earth, though the last differs from the first two, as explained above, on the question whether there is more than one life on Earth.) There is no breach (*Uchchheda*) of consciousness, but a continuity of transformation. The Death-Consciousness is the starting-point, followed by the other states of consciousness already described. *Karma* at length generates a fully-formed desire or mental action. This last is followed by the consciousness taking up its abode in a suitable *matrix*, whence it is born again as a Birth-Consciousness. What is so born is not altogether different from what has gone before, because it is the present trans-formation of it; and has no other independent existence.

There are thus successive births of (to use Professor de la Vallée Poussin's term) a 'fluid soul-complex', because the series of psychic states continues at intervals of time to enter the physical womb of living beings. It has been said by the authority cited (*Way to Nirvāṇa*, p. 85) that the birth-consciousness of a new celestial or infernal being makes for itself and by itself, out of unorganized matter, the body it is to inhabit. Therefore the birth of such beings will follow immediately after the death of the being which is to be reborn as an infernal or celestial being. But the case is said to be different, as a rule, where there is to be 'reincarnation', that is 'rebirth' in the flesh. Conception and birth then presuppose physical circumstances that may not be realized at the moment of the death of the being to be 're-incarnated'. In these cases and others it is alleged that the dying consciousness cannot be continued at once into the birth-consciousness of a new being. The Professor says that this difficulty is solved by those Schools which, maintaining the intermediary existence (*Antarābhāva*), hold that the dying consciousness is continued into a short-lived being called *Gandharva*, which lasts for seven days, or seven times seven days (cf. the forty-nine days of the *Bardo*). This *Gandharva* creates, with the help of the conceptional elements, an embryo as soon as it can find opportunity. This doctrine, if it has been rightly understood, is apparently another and cruder version of the *Bardo* doctrine. There cannot, in any philosophic view of the doctrine of *Karma*, be any ' hold up ' of what is a continuous life-process. Such process does not consist of independent sections waiting upon one another. And so a ' soul-complex ' cannot be ready to reincarnate before the circumstances are fit for it. The law which determines that a being shall incarnate is the same as that which provides the means and conditions by, and under, which the incarnation is to take place. Nor is the body of the infernal or celestial being gross matter. This is clear from the present Text.

Dr. Evans-Wentz raises again the debated question of the transmigration of human ' souls ' into sub-human bodies, a process which this Text, exoterically viewed, seems to assume, and which is, as he points out, the general Hindu and Buddhist belief. It seems to be an irrational, though it may be a popular, belief that a human ' soul ' can permanently inhabit a sub-human body as its own. For the body cannot exist in such disagreement with its occupant. The right doctrine appears to be that, as man has evolved through the lowest forms of being (Hinduism speaks of 8,400,000 graded kinds of births culminating in man),[1] so by misconduct and neglect to use the opportunity of manhood there can, equally, be a descent along the ' downward path ' to the same low forms of being from which humanity has, with difficulty, emerged. The Sanskrit term *Durlabham*, meaning ' difficult to get ', refers to this difficulty of securing human birth. But such descent involves (as Dr. Evans-Wentz says) the loss of the human nature and the enormous lengths of time of a creation epoch.

If the series (*Santāna*) of conscious states are determined

---

[1] As plants, aquatic animals, reptiles, birds, quadrupeds, simian forms, and man. See *Brihad Vishnu Purāna*.

by the past *Karma*, it may be asked how that liberty of choice exists which the whole Text assumes by its injunctions to the deceased to do this or to avoid that. No doubt even in one individual there are diverse tendencies (*Sangskāra*). But the question still remains. If the *Karma* ready to ripen determines the action, then advice to the accused is useless. If the 'soul' is free to choose, there is no determination by *Karma*. Hinduism holds that, notwithstanding the influence of *Karma*, the *Ātmā* is essentially free. Here the answer appears to be twofold. Apart from what is next stated, the instructions given may, by their suggestions, call up that one of several latent tendencies which tends towards the action counselled. Further, this system allows that one 'soul' can help another. And so there are prayers for, and application of merits to, the deceased, just as we find in Hinduism the *Pretashrāddha*, in Catholicism the *Requiem* Mass, and in Islam the Moslem's *Fatiha*. In this and other matters one mind can, it is alleged, influence another otherwise than through the ordinary sense channels whether before or after death. There is also a tendency to overlook collective *Karma* and its effects. An individual is not only affected by his own *Karma*, but by that of the community to which he belongs. A wider question arises as to the meaning of the Re-incarnation Doctrine itself, but this is not the place to discuss it.

There are many other points of interest in this remarkable Book, but I must now stop and let the reader discover them for himself. I would like, however, to add a word as to the manner of its making. The Text has been fortunate in finding as its editor Dr. Evans-Wentz, whose knowledge of, and sympathy with, his subject has enabled him to give us a very comprehensible account of it. He, in his turn, was fortunate in his teacher, the translator, the late Lāma Kazi Dawa-Samdup (Tib. *Zla-va-bsam-hgrub*), who, when I first met him, was Chief Interpreter on the staff of His Excellency Lonchen Satra, the Tibetan Plenipotentiary to the Government of India. He was also attached to the Political Staff of His Holiness the Dalai Lāma on the latter's visit to India. At the time of his premature and greatly regretted death Lāma Kazi Dawa-Samdup was Lecturer in Tibetan to the University of Calcutta. These, and the other appointments which the translator held, and to which Dr. Evans-Wentz has referred, sufficiently establish his high competency both in Tibetan and English. He had also, I may add, some knowledge of Sanskrit, which I found of much use in discussing with him the meaning of terms used in Tibetan-Buddhist doctrine and ritual. I can, then, speak personally of his attainments, for I saw a good deal of him when he was preparing for me a translation of the Tibetan *Shrīchakrasambhāra Tantra*, which I have published as the seventh volume of the series of *Tantrik Texts* (Luzac & Co.). I can, likewise, from my own knowledge, associate myself with what Dr. Evans-Wentz has said as to this remarkable man. May their joint work have the success it deserves, and so encourage Dr. Evans-Wentz to publish some at least of the other Texts which he tells me he has in store.

JOHN WOODROFFE.

OXFORD,
October 3, 1925.

INTRODUCTION [1]

'The phenomena of life may be likened unto a dream, a phantasm, a bubble, a shadow, the glistening dew, or lightning flash; and thus they ought to be contemplated.'—The Buddha, in *The Immutable Sutra*.

I. THE IMPORTANCE OF THE *BARDO THÖDOL*

As a contribution to the science of death and of the existence after death, and of rebirth, *The Tibetan Book of the Dead*,

[1] This Introduction is—for the most part—based upon and suggested by explanatory notes which the late Lāma Kazi Dawa-Samdup, the translator of the *Bardo Thödol*, dictated to the editor while the translation was taking shape, in Gangtok, Sikkim. The Lāma was of opinion that his English rendering of the *Bardo Thödol* ought not to be published without his exegetical comments on the more abstruse and figurative parts of the text. This, he thought, would not only help to justify his translation, but, moreover, would accord with the wishes of his late *guru* (see p. 80) with respect to all translations into a European tongue of works expository of the esoteric lore of the Great Perfectionist School into which that *guru* had initiated him. To this end, the translator's exegesis, based upon that of the translator's *guru*, was transmitted to the editor and recorded by the editor herein.

The editor's task is to correlate and systematize and sometimes to expand the notes thus dictated, by incorporating such congenial matter, from widely separated sources, as in his judgement tends to make the exegèsis more intelligible to the Occidental, for whom this part of the book is chiefly intended.

The translator felt, too, that, without such safeguarding as this Introduction is intended to afford, the *Bardo Thödol* translation would be peculiarly liable to misinterpretation and consequent misuse, more especially by those who are inclined to be, for one reason or another, inimical to Buddhistic doctrines, or to the doctrines of his particular Sect of Northern Buddhism. He also realized how such an Introduction as is here presented might itself be subject to adverse criticism, perhaps on the ground that it appears to be the outcome of a philosophical eclecticism. However this may be, the editor can do no more than state here, as he has stated in other words in the Preface, that his aim, both herein and in the closely related annotations to the text itself, has been to present the psychology and the teachings peculiar to and related to the *Bardo Thödol* as he has been taught them by qualified initiated exponents of them, who alone have the unquestioned right to explain them.

If it should be said by critics that the editor has expounded the *Bardo Thödol* doctrines from the standpoint of the Northern Buddhist who believes in them rather than from the standpoint of the Christian who perhaps would disbelieve at least some of them, the editor has no apology to offer; for he holds that there is no sound reason adducible why he should expound them in any other manner. Anthropology is concerned with things as they are; and the hope of

called, in its own language, *Bardo Thödol* ('Liberation by Hearing on the After-Death Plane'),[1] is, among the sacred books of the world, unique. As an epitomized exposition of the cardinal doctrines of the *Mahāyāna* School of Buddhism, it is of very great importance, religiously, philosophically, and historically. As a treatise based essentially upon the Occult Sciences of the *Yoga* Philosophy, which were fundamental in the curriculum of the great Buddhist University of Nālanda, the Oxford of ancient India, it is, perhaps, one of the most remarkable works the West has ever received from the East. As a mystic manual for guidance through the Otherworld of many illusions and realms, whose frontiers are death and birth, it resembles *The Egyptian Book of the Dead* sufficiently to suggest some ultimate cultural relationship between the two; although we only know with certainty that the germ of the teachings, as herein made accessible to English readers, has been preserved for us by a long succession of saints and seers of the God-protected Land of the Snowy Ranges, Tibet.

II. THE SYMBOLISM

The *Bardo Thödol* is unique in that it purports to treat rationally of the whole cycle of *sangsāric* (i. e. phenomenal) existence intervening between death and birth;—the ancient doctrine of *karma*, or consequences (taught by Emerson as compensation), and of rebirth being accepted as the most essential laws of nature affecting human life. Often, however, its teaching appears to be quite the antithesis of rational, because much of it is recorded in an occult cipher. Dr. L. A. Waddell has declared, after careful research, that 'the *lāmas*

all sincere researchers into comparative religion devoid of any religious bias ought always to be to accumulate such scientific data as will some day enable future generations of mankind to discover Truth itself—that Universal Truth in which all religions and all sects of all religions may ultimately recognize the Essence of Religion and the Catholicity of Faith.

[1] Mr. Talbot Mundy, in his interesting Tibetan romance *Om*, in making reference to this title, *The Tibetan Book of the Dead*, has taken it to be a very free translation of *Bardo Thödol*. It should not, however, so be taken; it has been adopted because it seems to be the most appropriate short title for conveying to the English reader the true character of the book as a whole.

have the keys to unlock the meaning of much of Buddha's doctrine which has been almost inaccessible to Europeans.' [1]

Some of the more learned *lāmas*, including the late Lāma Kazi Dawa-Samdup, have believed that since very early times there has been a secret international symbol-code in common use among the initiates, which affords a key to the meaning of such occult doctrines as are still jealously guarded by religious fraternities in India, as in Tibet, and in China, Mongolia, and Japan.

In like manner, Occidental occultists have contended that the hieroglyphical writings of ancient Egypt and of Mexico seem to have been, in some degree, a popularized or exoteric outgrowth of a secret language. They argue, too, that a symbol-code was sometimes used by Plato and other Greek philosophers, in relation to Pythagorean and Orphic lore; that throughout the Celtic world the Druids conveyed all their esoteric teachings symbolically; that the use of parables, as in the sermons of Jesus and of the Buddha, and of other Great Teachers, illustrates the same tendency; and that through works like *Aesop's Fables*, and the miracle and mystery plays of medieval Europe, many of the old Oriental symbols have been introduced into the modern literatures of the West. [2]

---

[1] L. A. Waddell, *The Buddhism of Tibet or Lāmaism* (London, 1895), p. 17.

[2] There is some sound evidence for supposing that one source of the moral philosophy underlying certain of the *Aesop's Fables* (and, also, by way of comparison, of the Indian *Panchatantra* and *Hitopadesha*) may yet be shown to have been such primitive Oriental folk-tales about animals and animal symbols as scholars now think helped to shape the *Jātaka Tales* concerning the various births of the Buddha (cf. *The Jātaka*, ed. by E. B. Cowell, Cambridge, 1895–1907). Similarly, the Christian mystery plays contain symbolism so much akin to that found in mystery plays still flourishing under ecclesiastical patronage throughout Tibet and the neighbouring territories of Northern Buddhism as to point to another stream of Orientalism having come into Europe (cf. *Three Tibetan Mysteries*, ed. by H. I. Woolf, London, n.d.). The apparent Romanist canonization of the Buddha, under the medieval character of St. Jehoshaphat, is an additional instance of how things Eastern seem to have become things Western (cf. *Baralâm and Yêwâsêf*, ed. by E. A. W. Budge, Cambridge, 1923). Furthermore, the once very popular medieval work *De Arte Moriendi* (cf. *The Book of the Craft of Dying*, ed. by F. M. M. Comper, London, 1917), of which there are many versions and variants in Latin, English, French, and other European languages, seems to suggest a still further infiltration of Oriental ideas, concerning death and existence after death, such as underlie both the Tibetan *Bardo*

Be this as it may, it is certain that none of the great systems
of ancient thought, nor even vernacular literatures, have
always found the ordinary work-a-day language of the world
adequate to express transcendental doctrines or even to bring
out the full significance of moral maxims.

The lamb, the dragon (or serpent), the dove above the altar,
the triangle enclosing the all-seeing eye (common to Free-
masonry as well), the sacred fish-symbol, the ever-burning
fire, or the image of the risen sun upon the receptacle for the
consecrated wafer in the Roman Mass, the architectural symbols and the orientation of church and cathedral, the cross
itself, and even the colours and designs of the robes of priest
and bishop and pope, are a few of the silent witnesses of the
survival in the modern Christian churches of the symbolism of
paganism. But the key to the interpretation of the inner
significance of almost all such Christianized symbols was
unconsciously thrown away: uninitiated ecclesiastics, gathered
together in heresy-seeking councils, having regarded that
primitive Christianity, so deeply involved in symbolism, called
Gnosticism, as 'Oriental imagery gone mad', repudiated it as
being 'heretical', whereas from its own point of view it was
merely esoteric.

Similarly, Northern Buddhism, to which symbolism is so
vital, has been condemned by Buddhists of the Southern
School for claiming to be the custodian of an esoteric doctrine,
for the most part orally transmitted by recognized initiates,
generation by generation, direct from the Buddha—as well as
for teaching (as, for example, in the *Saddharma-Pandarīka*)
recorded doctrines not in agreement with doctrines contained

Thödol and the Egyptian *Book of the Dead*; and, in order to show this, a few of
the most striking passages, found in the *De Arte Moriendi* cycle, which parallel
textually certain parts of the *Bardo Thödol*, have been added in foot-notes to the
Bardo Thödol translation from Mr. Comper's excellent edition in *The Book of
the Craft of Dying*.

Buddhist and Christian Gospels (Philadelphia, 1908), a pioneer study of the
remarkable parallelism which exists between the texts of the *New Testament*
and the texts of the Buddhist Canon, by Mr. A. J. Edmunds, suggests, likewise,
that one of the most promising fields of research, as yet almost virgin, lies in
a study of just such correspondences between Eastern and Western thought and
literature as is suggested in this note.

in the *Ti-Pitaka* (Skt. *Tri-Pitaka*), the Pali Canon. And yet, though the Southern Buddhist commonly assumes that there cannot be any but a literal interpretation of the Buddha's teachings, the Pali Scriptures contain many parables and metaphorical expressions, some of which the *lāmas* regard as symbolical and confirmatory of their own esoteric tradition, and to which they thus claim to hold—perhaps not without good reason—the initiate's key.

The *lāmas* grant that the *Ti-Pitaka* ('Three *Pitakas*, or Baskets' [of the Law]) are, as the Southern Buddhist holds, the recorded Word (or Doctrine) of the Ancients, the *Theravāda*; but they claim that the *Pitakas* do not contain all the Word, that the *Pitakas* lack much of the Buddha's *yogīc* teachings, and that it is chiefly these teachings which, in many instances, have been handed down esoterically to the present day. 'Esoteric Buddhism', as it has come to be called— rightly or wrongly—seems to depend in large measure upon 'ear-whispered' doctrines of this character, conveyed according to long-established and inviolable rule, from *guru* to *shishya*, by word of mouth alone.

The Pali Canon records that the Buddha held no doctrine secretly 'in a closed fist' (cf. *Mahā Parinibbāṇa Sūttanta, Dīgha Nikāya II*), that is to say, withheld no essential doctrine from the members of the *Saṅgha* (Priesthood), just as no *guru* nowadays withholds a doctrine necessary for the spiritual enlightenment of his initiated or accepted disciples. This, however, is far from implying that all such teachings were intended to be set down in writing for the uninitiated and worldly multitude, or that they ever were so recorded in any of the Canons. The Buddha Himself wrote down nothing of His teachings, and His disciples who after His death compiled the Buddhist Scriptures may not have recorded therein all that their Master taught them. If they did not, and there are, therefore, as the *lāmas* contend, certain un-written teachings of the Buddha which have never been taught to those who were not of the *Saṅgha*, then there is, un-doubtedly, an extra-canonical, or esoteric, Buddhism. An esoteric Buddhism thus conceived is not, however, to be regarded as in any wise in disagreement with canonical, or exoteric, Buddhism, but as being related to it as higher mathematics are to lower mathematics, or as being the apex of the pyramid of the whole of Buddhism.

In short, the evidence adducible gives much substantial support to the claim of the *lāmas*, to whom we refer, that there is—as the *Bardo Thödol* appears to suggest—an unrecorded body of orally transmitted Buddhistic teachings complementary to canonical Buddhism.[1]

III. THE ESOTERIC SIGNIFICANCE OF THE FORTY-NINE DAYS OF THE *BARDO*

Turning now to our text itself, we find that structurally it is founded upon the symbolical number Forty-nine, the square of the sacred number Seven; for, according to occult teachings common to Northern Buddhism and to that Higher Hinduism which the Hindu-born Bodhisattva Who became the Buddha Gautama, the Reformer of the Lower Hinduism and the Codifier of the Secret Lore, never repudiated, there are seven worlds or seven degrees of *Māyā*[2] within the *Sangsāra*,[3] constituted as seven globes of a planetary chain. On each globe there are seven rounds of evolution, making the forty-nine (seven times seven) stations of active existence. As in the

---

[1] It is probably unnecessary for the editor to remind his friends who profess the Theravāda Buddhism of the Southern School that, in preparing this Introduction, his aim has necessarily been to present Buddhism chiefly from the standpoint of the Northern Buddhism of the Kargyutpa Sect (see page 79), by which the *Bardo Thödol* is accepted as a sacred book and to which the translator belonged. Although the Southern Buddhist may not agree with the *Bardo Thödol* teachings in their entirety, he will, nevertheless, be very apt to find them, in most essentials, based upon doctrines common to all Schools and Sects of Buddhism; and he may even find those of them with which he disagrees interesting and possibly provocative of a reconsideration of certain of his own antagonistic beliefs.

[2] *Māyā*, the Sanskrit equivalent of the Tibetan *Gyūma* (*Sgyūma*), means a magical or illusory show, with direct reference to the phenomena of Nature. In a higher sense, in Brāhmanism, it refers to the *Shakti* of Brāhman (the Supreme Spirit, the Ain Soph of Judaism).

[3] The Sanskrit term *Sangsāra* (or *Saṁsāra*), Tibetan *Khorva* (*Hkhorva*), refers to the phenomenal universe itself, its antithesis being *Nirvāṇa* (Tib. *Myang-hdas*), which is beyond phenomena (cf. pp. 67–8).

embryonic state in the human species the foetus passes through every form of organic structure from the amoeba to man, the highest mammal, so in the after-death state, the embryonic state of the psychic world, the Knower or principle of consciousness, anterior to its re-emergence in gross matter, analogously experiences purely psychic conditions. In other words, in both these interdependent embryonic processes—the one physical, the other psychical—the evolutionary and the involutionary attainments, corresponding to the forty-nine stations of existence, are passed through.

Similarly, the forty-nine days of the *Bardo* may also be symbolical of the Forty and Nine Powers of the Mystery of the Seven Vowels. In Hindu mythology, whence much of the *Bardo* symbolism originated, these Vowels were the Mystery of the Seven Fires and their forty-nine subdivisional fires or aspects. They are also represented by the *Svastika* signs upon the crowns of the seven heads of the Serpent of Eternity of the Northern Buddhist Mysteries, originating in ancient India. In Hermetic writings they are the seven zones of after-death, or *Bardo*, experiences, each symbolizing the eruption in the Intermediate State of a particular sevenfold element of the complex principle of consciousness, thus giving the consciousness-principle forty-nine aspects, or fires, or fields of manifestation [1].

The number seven has long been a sacred number among Aryan and other races. Its use in the *Revelation* of John illustrates this, as does the conception of the seventh day being regarded as holy. In Nature, the number seven governs the periodicity and phenomena of life, as, for example, in the series of chemical elements, in the physics of sound and colour, and it is upon the number forty-nine, or seven times seven, that the *Bardo Thödol* is thus scientifically based.

[1] As regards the esoteric meaning of the Forty-nine Days of the *Bardo*, compare H. P. Blavatsky, *The Secret Doctrine* (London, 1888), i. 238, 411; ii. 617, 627-8. The late Lāma Kazi Dawa-Samdup was of opinion that, despite the adverse criticisms directed against H. P. Blavatsky's works, there is adequate internal evidence in them of their author's intimate acquaintance with the higher *lāmaistic* teachings, into which she claimed to have been initiated.

IV. THE ESOTERIC SIGNIFICANCE OF THE FIVE ELEMENTS

Likewise, in a very striking manner, the esoteric teachings concerning the Five Elements, as symbolically expounded in the *Bardo Thödol*, parallel, for the most part, certain of the teachings of Western Science, as the following interpretation, based upon that made by the translator himself, indicates:

In the First Round of our Planet, one element alone—Fire—was evolved. In the fire-mist, which, in accordance with the *karmic* law governing the *Sangsāra*, or cosmos, assumed a rotary motion and became a blazing globular body of undifferentiated primeval forces, all the other elements lay in embryo. Life first manifested itself clothed in robes of fire; and man, if we conceive him as then existing, was incarnate—as the Salamanders of medieval occultism were believed to be—in a body of fire. In the Second Round, as the Element Fire assumed definite form, the Element Air separated from it and enwrapped the embryonic Planet as a shell covers an egg. The body of man, and of all organic creatures, thereupon became a compound of fire and air. In the Third Round, as the Planet, bathed in the Element Air and fanned by it, abated its fiery nature, the Element Water came forth from the vaporous air. In the Fourth Round, in which the Planet still is, air and water neutralized the activities of their Parent Fire; and the Fire, bringing forth the Element Earth, became encrusted with it. Esoterically, the same teachings are said to be conveyed by the old Hindu myth of the churning of the Sea of Milk, which was the Fire-Mist, whence came, like butter, the solid earth. Upon the earth, so formed, the gods are credited with having fed; or, in other words, they, hankering after existence in gross physical bodies, became incarnated on this Planet and so became the Divine Progenitors of the human race.

In the *Bardo*, on the first four days these Four Elements manifest themselves, or dawn upon the deceased, in their primordial form, although not in their true occult order.[1]

[1] It is held, too, that whereas from the Five Dhyānī Buddhas, as in our text,

The Fifth Element, Ether, in its primal form, symbolized as 'the green light-path of the Wisdom of Perfected Actions', does not dawn, for, as the text explains, the Wisdom (or *Bodhic*) Faculty of the consciousness of the deceased has not been perfectly developed.

The Ether Element, like the aggregate of matter (symbolical of the fire-mist), is personified in Vairochana, He Who in Shapes makes visible all things. The psychical attribute of the Ether Element is—to render the *lāmaic* conception in the language of the psychology of the West—that of the subconsciousness; and the subconsciousness, as a transcendental consciousness higher than the normal consciousness in mankind, and as yet normally undeveloped, is—as the vehicle for the manifestation of the *Bodhic* Faculty—believed to be destined to become the active consciousness of the humanity of the Fifth Round. The memory-records of all past experiences throughout the many states of *sangsāric* existence being latent in the subconsciousness, as the Buddha's own teachings imply (see pp. 40–41), the Fifth Round races in whom it becomes active will thus be able to recall all their past existences. In place of faith or mere belief, Man will then possess Knowledge, will come to know himself in the sense implied by the Mysteries of ancient Greece; he will realize the unreality of *sangsāric* existence, attaining Enlightenment and Emancipation from the *Sangsāra*, from all the Elements; and this will come as a normal process of human evolution. It is, however, the aim in all schools of Indian and Tibetan *Yoga* alike—as in the *Bardo Thödol*—to outstrip this tedious process of normal evolution and win Freedom even now.

In the body of man as he is—in our present Fourth

emanate the five elements—ether, or aggregate of matter (Vairochana), air, or aggregate of volition (Amogha-Siddhi), fire, or aggregate of feelings (Amitābha), water, or aggregate of consciousness (Vajra-Sattva, esoterically as a reflex of Akṣhobhya), and earth, or aggregate of touch (Ratna-Sambhava)—from the Ādi-Buddha (from whom, according to the Ādi-Buddha School, the Five Dhyānī Buddhas themselves emanate) emanates the sixth element, which is mind (*manas*). Vajra-Sattva, as an esoteric deity, sometimes occupies (as does Vairochana)—according to the School and ritual—the place of the Ādi-Buddha, and is then synonymous with him.

Round—there are four kingdoms of living creatures: (1) those of the Element Fire, (2) those of the Element Air, (3) those of the Element Water, and (4) those of the Element Earth. Over this collective life of innumerable myriads of lives man is king. If he be a Great King, filled with the transcendent consciousness of the triumphant *Yogī* (or Saint), to him the countless multitude of his elemental subjects severally reveal themselves in their true nature and place in his hand the Sceptre (symbolized by the Tibetan *dorje*, or thunderbolt) of Universal Dominion over Matter. Then, indeed, is he Lord of Nature, becoming in his turn Ruler by Divine Right, a *Chakravartin*, or Universal Emperor, God and Creator.[1]

V. THE WISDOM TEACHINGS

Also involved in symbolical language there are, as fundamental occult doctrines of the *Bardo Thödol*, what the translator called The Wisdom Teachings; and these—which are essential *Mahāyāna* doctrines—may be outlined as follows:

The Voidness.—In all Tibetan systems of *yoga*, realization of the Voidness (Tib. *Stong-pa-ñid*—pron. *Tong-pa-ñid*: Skt. *Shūnyatā*) is the one great aim; for to realize it is to attain the unconditioned *Dharma-Kāya*, or 'Divine Body of Truth' (Tib. *Chos-sku*—pron. *Chö-Ku*), the primordial state of un-createdness, of the supramundane *Bodhic* All-Consciousness— Buddhahood. Realization of the Voidness (Pali, *Suññata*) is the aim of Theravādists too.

The Three Bodies.—The *Dharma-Kāya* is the highest of the Three Bodies (Tib. *Sku-gsum*—pron. *Kū-sum*: Skt. *Tri-Kāya*) of the Buddha and of all Buddhas and beings who have Perfect Enlightenment. The other two bodies are the *Sambhoga-Kāya* or 'Divine Body of Perfect Endowment' (Tib. *Longs-spyod-rzogs-sku*—pron. *Long-chöd-zo-ku*) and the *Nirmāna-Kāya* or

---

[1] Manu, in *The Laws* (xii. 10–11), says: 'He, whose firm understanding obtains a command over his words, a command over his thoughts, and a command over his whole body, may justly be called a Triple-Commander.

'The man who exerts this triple self-command with respect to all animated creatures, wholly subduing both lust and wrath, shall by those means attain Beatitude.'—(Cf. trans. by Sir William Jones.)

'Divine Body of Incarnation' (Tib. *Sprul-pahi-sku*—pron. *Tül-pai-ku*).

The *Dharma-Kāya* is symbolized—for all human word-concepts are inadequate to describe the Qualityless—as an infinite ocean, calm and without a wave, whence arise mist-clouds and rainbow, which symbolize the *Sambhoga-Kāya*; and the clouds, enhaloed in the glory of the rainbow, condensing and falling as rain, symbolize the *Nirmāna-Kāya*.[1]

The *Dharma-Kāya* is the primordial, formless *Bohdi*, which is true experience freed from all error or inherent or accidental obscuration. In it lies the essence of the Universe, including both *Sangsāra* and *Nirvāna*, which, as states or conditions of the two poles of consciousness, are, in the last analysis, in the realm of the pure intellect, identical.[2]

In other words, the *Dharma-Kāya* (lit. 'Law Body') being Essential Wisdom (*Bodhi*) unmodified, the *Sambhoga-Kāya* (lit. 'Compensation Body', or 'Adorned Body') embodies, as in the Five Dhyānī Buddhas, Reflected or Modified Wisdom, and the *Nirmāna-Kāya* (lit. 'Changeable Body', or 'Transformed Body') embodies, as in the Human Buddhas, Practical or Incarnate Wisdom.[3]

[1] Sj. Atal Bihari Ghosh (see our Preface, p. x) has added here the following comment: 'The word *Dharma* is derived from the verb-root *Dhri*, meaning 'to Support' or 'to Uphold'. *Dharma* is that which upholds or supports the Universe, as also the individual. *Dharma* is in mankind Right Conduct, the result of True Knowledge. Truth according to Brāhmanism is the Brāhman, is Liberation—*Moksha*, *Nirvāna*. *Sambhoga* is the Life of Enjoyment. *Nirmāna* is the Process of Building. In the Brāhmanic scheme, *Dharma* is the first thing needed. Then comes *Artha* (i.e. Wealth, or Possessions), which corresponds with *Nirmāna*. After this comes *Sambhoga*; and the last is *Moksha*, or Liberation.'

[2] 'Whatever is visible and invisible, whether *Sangsāra* or *Nirvāna*, is at base one [that is, *Shūnyatā*], with two Paths [*Avidyā*, Ignorance, and *Vidyā*, Knowledge] and two ends [*Sangsāra* and *Nirvāna*].' . . . 'The Foundation of all is uncreated and independent, uncompounded and beyond mind and speech. Of It neither the word *Nirvāna* nor *Sangsāra* may be said'—*The Good Wishes of the Ādi-Buddha*, 1-2 (cf. the late Lāma Kazi Dawa-Samdup's translation, *Tantrik Texts*, vol. vii, London, 1919). The *Shūnyatā*, the Void, synonymous with the *Dharma-Kāya*, is thus beyond all mental concepts, beyond the finite mind with all its imaginings and use of such ultimate terms of the dualistic world as *Nirvāna* and *Sangsāra*.

[3] Cf. Waddell, op. cit., pp. 127, 347.

Ashvaghosha, the great philosopher of Mahāyāna Buddhism (see pp. 225-6),

The Uncreated, the Unshaped, the Unmodified is the *Dharma-Kāya*. The Offspring, the Modification of the Unmodified, the manifestation of all perfect attributes in one body, is the *Sambhoga-Kāya*: 'The embodiment of all that is wise, merciful and loving in the *Dharma-Kāya*— as clouds on the surface of the heavens or a rainbow on the surface of the clouds—is said to be *Sambhoga-Kāya*'.[1] The condensation and differentiation of the One Body as many is the *Nirmāṇa-Kāya*, or the Divine Incarnations among sentient beings, that is to say, among beings immersed in the Illusion called *Sangsāra*, in phenomena, in worldly existence. All enlightened beings who are reborn in this or in any other world with full consciousness, as workers for the betterment of their fellow creatures, are said to be *Nirmāṇa-Kāya* incarnates.

With the *Dharma-Kāya* Tantric Buddhism associates the Primordial Buddha Samanta-Bhadra (Tib. *Kün-tu-bzang-po*— pron. *Kün-tu-zang-po*), Who is without Beginning or End, the

has explained the *Tri-Kāya* Doctrine in *The Awakening of Faith*, translation by T. Suzuki (Chicago, 1900, pp. 99–103), as follows :

'Because All Tathāgatas are the *Dharmakāya* itself, are the highest truth (*paramārthasatya*) itself, and have nothing to do with conditionality (*samvrittisatya*) and compulsory actions; whereas the seeing, hearing, &c. [i.e. the particularizing senses], of the sentient being diversify [on its own account] the activity of the Tathāgatas.

'Now this activity [in another word, the *Dharmakāya*] has a twofold aspect. The first one depends on the phenomena-particularizing-consciousness, by means of which the activity is conceived by the minds of common people (*prithagjana*), Crāvakas, and Pratyekabuddhas. This aspect is called the Body of Transformation (*Nirmāṇakāya*).

'But as the beings of this class do not know that the Body of Transformation is merely the shadow [or reflection] of their own evolving-consciousness (*pravritti-vijñāna*), they imagine that it comes from some external sources, and so they give it a corporeal limitation. But the Body of Transformation [or what amounts to the same thing, the *Dharmakāya*] has nothing to do with limitation and measurement.

'The second aspect [of the *Dharmakāya*] depends on the activity-consciousness (*karma-vijñāna*) by means of which the activity is conceived by the minds of Bodhisattvas while passing from their first aspiration (*cittotpāda*) stage up to the height of Bodhisattvahood. This is called the Body of Bliss (*Sambhogakāya*). . . .

'The *Dharmakāya* can manifest itself in various corporeal forms just because it is the real essence of them' (cf. p. 228[2]).

[1] Cf. A. Avalon, *Tantrik Texts*, vii (London and Calcutta, 1919), pp. 36 n., 41 n.

Source of all Truth, the All-Good Father of the Lāmaistic Faith. In this same highest Buddha realm Lāmaism places Vajra-Dhāra (Tib. *Rdorje-Chang*—pron. *Dorje-Chang*), 'The Holder of the *Dorje* (or Thunderbolt)', 'the Divine Expounder of the Mystic Doctrine called *Vajra Yāna* (Tib. *Rdorje Theg-pa*—pron. *Dorje Theg-pa*) or *Mantra Yāna*'; and also the Buddha Amitābha (Tib. *Hod-dpag-med*—pron. *Wod-pag-med*; or, as in the text, page 113[1]), the Buddha of Boundless Light, Who is the Source of Life Eternal. In the *Sambhoga-Kāya* are placed the Five Dhyānī Buddhas (or Buddhas of Meditation), the Lotus Herukas, and the Peaceful and Wrathful Deities, all of whom will appear in the *Bardo* visions. With the *Nirmāṇa-Kāya* is associated Padma Sambhava, who, being the first teacher in Tibet to expound the *Bardo Thödol*, is the Great *Guru* for all devotees who follow the *Bardo* teachings.

The opinion commonly held by men not initiated into the higher *lāmaic* teachings, that Northern Buddhism recognizes in the Primordial or Ādi-Buddha a Supreme Deity, is apparently erroneous. The translator held that the Ādi-Buddha, and all deities associated with the *Dharma-Kāya*, are not to be regarded as personal deities, but as Personifications of primordial and universal forces, laws, or spiritual influences, which sustain—as the sun sustains the earth's physical life—the divine nature of all sentient creatures in all worlds, and make man's emancipation from all *sangsāric* existences possible:

'In the boundless panorama of the existing and visible universe, whatever shapes appear, whatever sounds vibrate, whatever radiances illuminate, or whatever consciousnesses cognize, all are the play or manifestation of the *Tri-Kāya*, the Three-fold Principle of the Cause of All Causes, the Primordial Trinity. Impenetrating all, is the All-Pervading Essence of Spirit, which is Mind. It is uncreated, impersonal, self-existing, immaterial, and indestructible.'

(Lāma Kazi Dawa-Samdup.)

Thus, the *Tri-Kāya* symbolizes the Esoteric Trinity of

the higher Buddhism of the Northern School; the Exoteric Trinity being, as in the Southern School, the *Buddha*, the *Dharma* (or Scriptures), the *Saṅgha* (or Priesthood). Regarded in this way—the one trinitarian doctrine as esoteric, the other as exoteric—there are direct correspondences between the two Trinities. Detailed and comprehensive understanding of the *Tri-Kāya* Doctrine, so the *lāmas* teach, is the privilege of initiates, who, alone, are fitted to grasp and to realize it.

The translator himself regarded the *Tri-Kāya* Doctrine as having been transmitted by a long and unbroken line of initiates, some Indian, some Tibetan, direct from the days of the Buddha. He considered that the Buddha, having re-discovered it, was merely its Transmitter from preceding Buddhas; that it was handed on orally, from *guru* to *guru*, and not committed to writing until comparatively recent times, when Buddhism began to decay, and there were not always sufficient living *gurus* to transmit it in the old way. The theory of Western scholars, that simply because a doctrine is not found recorded before a certain time it consequently did not exist previously, he—as an initiate—laughed at; and the rather strenuous efforts of Christian apologists to claim for the *Tri-Kāya* Doctrine a Christian origin he held, likewise, to be wholly untenable. He had been a close and sympathetic student of Christianity; and, as a young man, he had been much sought after by Christian missionaries, who looked upon him, with his remarkable learning and superior social standing, as an unusually desirable subject for conversion. He carefully examined their claims, and then rejected them, on the ground that, in his opinion, Christianity, as presented by them, is but an imperfect Buddhism, that the Aṣokan Buddhist missionaries to Asia Minor and Syria, as to Alexandria,[1] must have profoundly influenced Christianity through some such probable connecting link as the Essenes, that, if Jesus were an historical character, He, being—as the Lāma interpreted the Jesus of the *New Testament* clearly to be—a Bodhisattva (i.e. a Candidate for Buddhahood), was, undoubtedly, well acquainted with

[1] Cf. V. A. Smith, *Early History of India* (Oxford, 1914), p. 184.

Buddhist ethics, and taught them, as in the Sermon on the Mount.

The Doctrine of the Three Bodies conveys the esoteric teachings concerning the Path of the Teachers, their descent from the Higher to the Lower, from the threshold of *Nirvāṇa* to the *Sangsāra*; and progression from the Lower to the Higher, from the *Sangsāra* to *Nirvāṇa*, is symbolized by the Five Dhyānī Buddhas, each personifying a universal divine attribute. Contained in the Five Dhyānī Buddhas lies the Sacred Way leading to At-one-ment in the *Dharma-Kāya*, to Buddhahood, to Perfect Enlightenment, to *Nirvāṇa*— which is spiritual emancipation through Desirelessness.

The Five Wisdoms.—As the All-Pervading Voidness, the *Dharma-Kāya* is the shape (which is shapelessness) of the Body of Truth; the Thatness constituting it is the *Dharma-Dhātu* (Tib. *Chös-kyi-dvyings*—pron. *Chö-kyi-ing*), the Seed or Potentiality of Truth; and this dawns on the First Day of the *Bardo* as the glorious blue light of the Dhyānī Buddha Vairochana, the Manifester, 'He Who in Shapes Makes Visible' [the universe of matter]. The *Dharma-Dhātu* is symbolized as the Aggregate of Matter. From the Aggregate of Matter arise the creatures of this world, as of all worlds, in which animal stupidity is the dominant characteristic; and the *mārā* (or illusion of shape) constitutes in all realms of the *Sangsāra* —as in the human kingdom where *manas* (or mind) begins to operate—the Bondage, emancipation from which is *Nirvāṇa*. When in man, made as perfect as human life can make him, the stupidity of his animal nature and the illusion of shape, or personality, are transmuted into Right Knowledge, into Divine Wisdom, there shines forth in his consciousness the All-Pervading Wisdom of the *Dharma-Dhātu*, or the Wisdom born of the Voidness, which is all-pervading.

As the Aggregate of Matter, dawning in the *Bardo* of the First Day, produces physical bodies, so the Water-Element, dawning on the Second Day, produces the life-stream, the blood; Anger is the obscuring passion, consciousness is the aggregate, and these, when transmuted, become the Mirror-like Wisdom, personified in Vajra-Sattva (the *Sambhoga-Kāya* reflex of the Dhyānī Buddha Akṣhobhya), the 'Triumphant One of Divine Heroic Mind'.

The Earth-Element of the Third Day, producing the chief solid constituents of the human form, and of all physical forms, gives rise to the passion of Egoism, and the aggregate is Touch; and these, when divinely transmuted, become the Wisdom of Equality, personified in Ratna-Sambhava, the 'Gem-born One', the Beautifier.

The Fire-Element of the Fourth Day, producing the animal-heat of embodied human and animal beings, gives rise to the passion of Attachment, or Lust, and the Aggregate of Feelings. Herein the transmutation gives birth to the All-Discriminating Wisdom, which enables the devotee to know each thing separately, yet all things as one; personified in the Dhyānī Buddha Amitābha, 'He of Boundless Light', the Illuminator, or Enlightener.

The Element Air, of the Fifth Day, produces the breath of life. Its quality, or passions, in man is Envy, or Jealousy. Its aggregate is Volition. The transmutation is into the All-Performing Wisdom, which gives perseverance and un-erring action in things spiritual, personified in Amogha-Siddhi, the 'Almighty Conqueror', the Giver of Divine Power.

As explained above, in Section IV, the last Element, Ether, which produces the mind, or Knower, and the desire-body of the dwellers in the Intermediate State, does not dawn for the deceased, because—as the text tells us—the Wisdom Faculty of the Consciousness, that is to say, the supramundane Buddha (or *Bodhic*) consciousness, has not been developed in the ordinary humanity. To it is related—as in our text—Vajra-Sattva and the Mirror-like Wisdom and the Aggregate of *Bodhic* Wisdom, Vajra-Sattva being then synonymous, eso-terically, with Samanta-Bhadra (who, in turn, is often personi-fied in Vairochana, the Chief of the Five Dhyānī Buddhas), the Ādi-Buddha, the Primordial, the Unborn, Unshaped, Un-modified *Dharma-Kāya*.

When the perfection of the Divine Body-Aggregate is attained by man, it becomes the unchanging, immutable Vajra-Sattva. When the perfection of the Divine Speech-

Principle is attained, with it comes the power of divine speech, symbolized by Amitābha. The perfection of the Divine Thought-Principle brings divine infallibility, symbolized by Vairochana. The perfection of the Divine Qualities of Goodness and Beauty is the realization of Ratna-Sambhava, their producer. With the perfection of Divine Actions comes the realization of Amogha-Siddhi, the Omnipotent Conqueror.

To one after another of these divine attributes, or principles, innate in every human being, the deceased is introduced, as though in a symbolic drama of initiation, to test him and discover whether or not any part of his divine (or *bodhic*) nature has been developed. Full development in all the *bodhic* powers of the Five Dhyānī Buddhas, who are the personifications of them, leads to Liberation, to Buddhahood. Partial development leads to birth in one of the happier states: *deva-loka*, the world of the *devas* or gods; *asura-loka*, the world of the *asuras* or titans; *nara-loka*, the world of mankind.

After the Fifth Day the *Bardo* visions become less and less divine; the deceased sinks deeper and deeper into the morass of *sangsāric* hallucinations; the radiances of the higher nature fade into the lights of the lower nature. Then—the after-death dream ending as the Intermediate State exhausts itself for the percipient, the thought-forms of his mental-content all having shown themselves to him like ghostly spectres in a nightmare—he passes on from the Intermediate State into the equally illusionary state called waking, or living, either in the human world or in one of the many mansions of existence, by being born there. And thus revolves the Wheel of Life, until the one who is bound on it breaks his own bonds through Enlightenment, and there comes, as the Buddha proclaims, the Ending of Sorrow.

In Sections I to V, above, the more prominent occult teachings underlying the *Bardo Thödol* have been briefly expounded. In Sections VI to XII, which are to follow, the chief *Bardo* rites and ceremonies, the *Bardo* psychology, and other of the *Bardo* doctrines will be explained and interpreted. The last Sections, XIII to XV, will be devoted to a consideration of our manuscript, its history, the origin of the *Bardo Thödol* texts, and our translating and editing.

In addition to these fifteen sections, there are, as Addenda (see pp. 211–41), six complementary sections, addressed chiefly to the student, who, more than the ordinary reader, will be interested in certain of the more abstruse doctrines and problems which arise from a careful study of the translation and its annotations.

VI. THE DEATH CEREMONIES

When the death-symptoms, as described in the first sections of our text, are completed, a white cloth is thrown over the face of the corpse ; and no person then touches the corpse, in order that the culminating process of death, which ends only upon the complete separation of the *Bardo* body from its earth-plane counterpart, shall not be interfered with. It is commonly held that normally the process takes from three and one-half to four days, unless assisted by a priest called the *hpho-bo* (pron. *pho-o*) or 'extractor of the consciousness-principle' ; and that, even if the priest be successful in the extracting, the deceased ordinarily does not wake up to the fact of being separated from the human body until the said period of time has expired.

The *hpho-bo*, upon his arrival, takes a seat on a mat or chair at the head of the corpse ; he dismisses all lament-making relatives from the death-chamber and orders its doors and windows to be closed, so as to secure the silence necessary for the right performance of the *hpho-bo* service. This consists of a mystic chant containing directions for the spirit of the deceased to find its way to the Western Paradise of Amitābha, and thus escape—if *karma* permits—the undesirable Inter-mediate State. After commanding the spirit to quit the body and its attachment to living relatives and goods, the *lāma* examines the crown of the head of the corpse at the line of the sagittal suture, where the two parietal bones articulate, called the 'Aperture of Brahma' (Skt. *Brāhma-randhra*), to determine if the spirit has departed thence, as it should have done ; and, if the scalp be not bald, he pulls out a few of the hairs directly over the aperture. If through accident or otherwise there be no corpse, the *lāma* mentally concentrates upon the deceased, and, visualizing the body of the deceased, imagines it to be present; and, calling the spirit of the deceased, performs the ceremony, which usually lasts about one hour.

Meanwhile, the *tsi-pa*, or astrologer-*lāma*, has been engaged to cast a death-horoscope, based upon the moment of death of the deceased, to determine what persons may approach and touch the corpse, the proper method of disposing of the corpse, the time and manner of the funeral, and the sort of rites to be performed for the benefit of the departed. Then the corpse is tied up in a sitting posture, much the same as that in which mummies and skeletons have been found in ancient graves or tombs in various parts of the world, and sometimes called the embryonic posture, symbolical of being born out of this life into the life beyond death. The corpse, so postured, is then placed in one of the corners of the death-chamber which has not been assigned to the household daemon.

Relatives and friends, having been notified of the death, gather together at the house of the deceased; and there they are fed and lodged until the corpse is disposed of. If doubt exists concerning the complete separation of the consciousness-principle (or spirit) of the deceased from the body, there is not likely to be any disposal of the corpse until three and one-half to four days after the time of the death. So long as the entertaining of the mourners continues—usually for not less than two, but more often for three days—the spirit of the deceased is offered a part of all food, both solid and liquid, of each meal. This food is placed in a bowl in front of the corpse; and then, after the spirit of the deceased has extracted from the food thus offered the subtle invisible essences, the food is thrown away. After the corpse has been removed from the house for final disposal, an effigy of the deceased is put in the corner of the room which the corpse had occupied; and before this effigy food continues thus to be offered until the forty-nine days of the *Bardo* have expired.

Whilst the funeral rites—including the reading of the *Bardo Thödol*—are being performed, in the house of the deceased or at the place of death, other *lāmas* chant by relays, all day and night, the service for assisting the spirit of the deceased to reach the Western Paradise of Amitābha. In Tibetan, this service (which the *hpho-bo* also chants) is called *De-wa-chan-kyi-mon-lam*. If the family be well-to-do, another service of like nature may be performed at the temple wherein the deceased used to worship, by all of the monks of the temple assembled.

After the funeral, the *lāmas* who read the *Bardo Thödol* return to the house of death once a week until the forty-ninth day of the Intermediate State has ended. It is not uncommon, however, for them to intermit one day of the first week and of each of the succeeding periods in order to shorten the service, so that they return after six, five, four, three, two, and one day respectively, thereby concluding the reading in about three weeks.

From the First to the Fourteenth Day, as the arrangement of Book One of our text suggests, the *Chönyid Bardo* is to be read and re-read, and from the Fifteenth Day onwards the *Sidpa Bardo*. In poorer families the rites may cease after the Fourteenth Day; for families in better circumstances it is usual in Sikkim to continue the rites at least until the expiration of the twenty-one-day period and sometimes during the whole period of the Forty-nine Days of the *Bardo*. On the first day of the funeral rites, if the deceased were a man of wealth or position, as many as one hundred *lāmas* may assist; at the funeral of a poor man only one or two *lāmas* are likely to be present. After the Fourteenth Day, as a rule for all alike, only one *lāma* is retained to complete the reading.

The effigy of the body of the deceased is made by dressing a stool, block of wood, or other suitable object in the clothes of the deceased; and where the face should be there is inserted a printed paper called the *mtshan-spyang* or *spyang-pu* (pronounced *chang-ku*), of which the following reproduction of a specimen is typical:[1]

[1] Our reproduction, made by special permission given to the editor by Dr. L. A. Waddell, is from pl. xxi, *Gazetteer of Sikhim*, edited by H. H. Risley (Calcutta, 1894), section on *Lamaism in Sikhim* by L. A. Waddell.

THE EFFIGY OF THE DEAD PERSON

(1. Mirror. 2. Conch. 3. Lyre. 4. Vase with flowers. 5. Holy Cake.)

In this *spyang-pu*, the central figure represents the deceased with legs bound and in an attitude of adoration, surrounded by symbols of 'the five excellent sensuous things': (1) a mirror (the first of the three objects on the left and numbered 1), symbolical of the body, which reflects all phenomena or sensations, and of sight as well; (2) a conch (numbered 2) and a lyre (numbered 3), symbolical of sound; (3) a vase of flowers (numbered 4), symbolical of smell; (4) holy cakes in a receptacle like that employed at the Roman Catholic Eucharist (numbered 5), symbolical of essence or nutriment, and of taste; (5) the silk clothes of the central figure and the over-hanging royal canopy, symbolical of dress and ornamental art, and of the sense of touch. It is before such a paper figure, inserted in the effigy as a head and face, that the food offerings to the spirit of the deceased continue to be made, and to which, when visualized by the *lāma* as the deceased in person, the *Bardo Thödol* is read.

Having begun my Tibetan researches fresh from three years of research in the ancient funeral lore of the Nile Valley, I realized as soon as I gained knowledge of the Tibetan funeral rites—which are very largely pre-Buddhistic—that the effigy of the dead, as now used in Tibet and Sikkim, is so definitely akin to the effigy of the deceased called 'the statue of the Osiris (or deceased one)', as used in the funeral rites of ancient Egypt, as to suggest a common origin. Furthermore, the *spyang-pu* taken by itself alone, as the head-piece for the effigy, has its Egyptian parallel in the images made for the *Ka* or spirit. These sometimes were merely heads, complete in themselves, to replace or duplicate the head of the mummy and to furnish additional assistance to the *Ka* when seeking—as the Knower in the *Bardo* seeks—a body to rest in, or that which our text calls a prop for the body (see p. 182). And even as to 'the statue of the Osiris' the ancient priests of Egypt read their *Book of the Dead*, so to the Tibetan effigy the *lāmas* now read the *Bardo Thödol*—both treatises alike being nothing more than guide-books for the traveller in the realm beyond death.

Again, the preliminary rituals of the Egyptian funeral were

designed to confer upon the deceased the magic power of
rising up in the ghost-body or *Ka* possessed of all sense
faculties, the service having consisted of ' the opening of the
mouth and eyes ' and the restoration of the use of all other
parts of the body.   Likewise, the *lāmas'* aim, at the outset, is
to restore complete consciousness to the deceased after the
swoon-state immediately following death, and to accustom
him to the unfamiliar environment of the Otherworld, assuming that he be, like the multitude, one of the unenlightened,
and thus incapable of immediate emancipation.

In conformity with our own view, that that part of the
Tibetan funeral rites directly concerned with the effigy and the
spyang-pu has come down to our day as a survival from
pre-Buddhist, probably very ancient, times, Dr. L. A. Waddell
writes of it as follows: ' This is essentially a Bön rite, and is
referred to as such in the histories of *Guru* Padma Sambhava,
as being practised by the Bön [i. e. the religion prevalent in
Tibet before the advent of Buddhism, and, in its transcen-
dentalism, much like Taoism], and as having incurred the
displeasure of the *Guru* Padma Sambhava, the founder of
Lāmaism.'

Of the *spyang-pu* itself, Dr. Waddell adds: ' Its inscription [as in our copy above] usually runs :

' I, the world-departing One, . . . (and here is inserted the
name of the deceased), adore and take refuge in my *lāma*-
confessor, and all the deities, both mild [translated by us as
"peaceful"] and wrathful; [1] and [may] "the Great Pitier" [2]
forgive my accumulated sins and impurities of former lives,
and show me the way to another good world !' [3]

At the left shoulder of the central figure of the *spyang-pu*,
as in our copy, and sometimes down the middle in other

[1] 'Of the hundred superior deities, forty-two are supposed to be *mild*, and
fifty-eight of an angry nature.'—L. A. Waddell.

[2] 'An aboriginal or Chinese deity now identified with *Avalokita*, with whom
he has much in common.'—L. A. Waddell.

[3] Our translation is based upon that made by Dr. Waddell; cf. *Gazetteer of
Sikhim*, pp. 387-8.

copies, are inscribed phonetic symbols referring to the six worlds of *sangsāric* existence, translated as follows :

S = *sura*, or god, referring to the *deva*-world ;

A = *asura*, or titan, referring to the *asura*-world ;

Na = *nara*, or man, referring to the human-world ;

Tri = *trisan*, or brute animal, referring to the brute-world ;

Pre = *preta*, or unhappy ghost, referring to the *preta*-world ;

and *Hung* (from *hunu*, meaning ' fallen ') = hell, referring to the hell-world.[1]

At the termination of the funeral rites the *spyang-pu* or face-paper is ceremoniously burned in the flame of a butter-lamp, and the spirit of the deceased given a final farewell. By the colour of the flame and the way in which the flame acts the after-death fate which the deceased has met with is determined.

The ashes of the cremated *spyang-pu* are collected in a plate, and then, upon being mixed with clay, are made into miniature stupas called *sa-tschha*, usually in moulds leaving impressions either of symbolical ornamentation or of sacred letters. One is kept for the family altar in the home of the deceased, and the rest are deposited in a sheltered place at a cross-roads or on a hill-top, usually under a projecting ledge of rock, or in a cave if there happens to be a cave.

With the burning of the paper, the rest of the effigy of the deceased is taken apart, the clothes going to the *lāmas*, who carry them off and sell them to the first purchaser, keeping the proceeds as part of their fee. When one year has elapsed after the death, a feast in honour of the deceased is usually given and the service of the Medical Buddhas is performed.[2] Thereafter, a widow of the deceased is free to remarry.[3]

Connected with the Tibetan funeral itself there is much interesting ritual. Thus, when the officiating *lāma* is pre-paring to assist at the removal of the corpse from the house,

---

[1] Cf. Waddell, *Gazetteer of Sikhim*, p. 388.

[2] ' In Ceylon, death-feasts are given, to the *Bhikkhus*, seven days, one month, and one year after the death. These feasts are given " in the name of " the dead, to whom also the merit is offered. This, under certain circumstances, helps the dead to attain higher rebirth.'—Cassius A. Pereira.

[3] Cf. Waddell, *Gazetteer of Sikhim*, pp. 391 and 383.

he presents a 'scarf of honour' to the corpse and, addressing the corpse as the deceased, advises it to partake freely of the food offered, warns it that it is dead and that its ghost must not haunt the place or trouble living relatives, saying in conclusion, 'Remember the name of thy spiritual *lāma*-teacher, which is . . . [so and so], and by his aid take the right path— the white one. Come this way!'[1]

Then, as the *lāma* begins to lead the funeral procession, he takes hold of one end of the long scarf, the other end having been tied to the corpse, and begins to chant a liturgy to the accompaniment of a miniature hand-drum (having loose-hanging knotted cords attached, which, striking the drum as it is twirled by the hand of the *lāma*, cause it to sound) and of a trumpet made of a human thigh-bone. When there are a number of priests, the chief priest, going before the rest, rings a handbell (as the Breton priest does in a Breton peasant funeral procession), and the other priests assist with the chanting and the music, one blowing at intervals the sacred conch-shell, another clashing brass cymbals, and perhaps another twirling the small drum, or blowing the thigh-bone trumpet. From time to time the chief *lāma* looks back to invite the spirit to accompany the body and to assure it that the route is in the right direction. After the corpse-bearers come the main body of mourners, some bearing refreshments (to be in part cast on the funeral-pyre for the benefit of the deceased and in part partaken of by the priests and mourners), and last of all the weeping and wailing relatives. Such priestly guiding of the deceased's spirit is for the laity alone, for the spirits of deceased *lāmas*, having been trained in the doctrines of the *Bardo Thödol*, know the right path and need no guidance.

In Tibet itself all known religious methods of disposing of a corpse are in vogue; but, owing to lack of fuel for purposes of cremation, ordinarily the corpse, after having been carried to a hill-top or rocky eminence, is chopped to pieces and, much after the Parsee custom in Persia and Bombay, given to the birds and beasts of prey. If the corpse be that of a nobleman, whose family can well afford

[1] Cf. Waddell, *Gazetteer of Sikhim*, pp. 391 and 383.

a funeral pyre, it may be cremated. In some remote districts earth burial is customary; and it is commonly employed everywhere when death has been caused by a very contagious and dangerous disease, like small-pox for example. Otherwise, Tibetans generally object to earth burial, for they believe that when a corpse is interred the spirit of the deceased, upon seeing it, attempts to re-enter it, and that if the attempt be successful a vampire results, whereas cremation, or other methods of quickly dissipating the elements of the dead body, prevent vampirism. Sometimes, too, as among the Hindus, corpses are cast into rivers or other bodies of water. In the case of the Dalai Lāma and the Tashi Lāma, and of some very great man or saint, embalming is practised; and the corpse, in a way somewhat resembling the ancient Egyptian embalming process, is packed in a box of marsh salt, usually for about three months, or until the salt has absorbed all the watery parts of the corpse. Then, after the corpse is well cured, it is coated with a cement-like substance made of clay, pulverized sandal-wood, spices, and drugs. This adheres and hardens; and all the sunken or shrivelled parts of the body, such as the eyes, cheeks, and stomach, having been rounded out by it to their natural proportions, a very Egyptian-like mummy is produced. Finally, when thoroughly dried and then covered with a paint made of dissolved gold, the mummy is set up like an image in a sort of Tibetan Westminster Abbey.

At Shigatze, the seat of the Tashi Lāma, there are five such funereal temples. With their double roofs, resplendent with gold, they resemble the palaces or royal shrines of China. In size and embellishment they differ, in accordance with the rank and wealth of the mummies occupying them, some being inlaid with gold, some with silver.[1] Before these enshrined mummies prayer is offered up, incense burnt, and elaborate rituals are performed, as in the ancestral cults of the Chinese and Japanese.

The four Northern Buddhist methods of disposing of a corpse correspond to those mentioned in various of the sacred

1 Cf. Ekai Kawaguchi, *Three Years in Tibet* (Madras, 1909), p. 394.

books of the Hindus : a human body is said to consist of four elements,—earth, water, air, and fire,—and it should be returned to these elements as quickly as possible. Cremation is considered the best method to adopt. Earth-burial, as among Christians also, is the returning of the body to the element Earth ; water-burial is the returning of the body to the element Water, air-burial, to the element Air—the birds which devour the corpse being the denizens of the air ; and fire-burial, or cremation, the returning of the body to the element Fire.

When air-burial is adopted in Tibet, even the bones of the corpse, after the birds have stripped them of flesh, are disposed of by being hammered to bits in small cavities in the rocks of the funeral hill, then mixed with flour and formed into a dough and given to the birds to devour.[1] The Tibetan air-burial is thus more thorough than that of the Parsees, who allow the bones of their dead to remain in the air and slowly decompose.

In a Tibetan funeral of the ordinary sort, neither a coffin nor any corpse-receptacle is used. The corpse after being laid upon its back on a sheet or piece of cloth spread over a framework, commonly made of a light material like wicker affixed to two poles, is covered with a pure white cloth. Two men, inserting their heads between the projecting ends of the two poles, act as pall-bearers. In Sikkim, however, the corpse is carried thus sitting, in the embryonic posture described above.

Both in Sikkim and in Tibet every funeral is conducted in strict accordance with the directions which have been given by the astrologer who cast the death-horoscope, indicating who shall touch or handle the corpse, who shall carry it, and the form of the burial. The astrologer also declares what kind of evil spirit caused the death, for in popular belief—as also among the Celtic peoples of Europe— no death is natural, but is always owing to interference by one of the innumerable death-demons. The astrologer announces, too, what ceremonies are necessary to exorcize the death-demon

---

[1] The men who perform this part of the burial belong to a special caste, and, being regarded as unclean, are ordinarily shunned by other Tibetans.

from the house of death, what special rituals need to be read for the benefit of the spirit of the deceased, the precautions necessary to secure for the deceased a good rebirth, and the country and sort of family in which the rebirth will occur.

In Sikkim, on the space of ground levelled for the funeral-pyre, a mystic diagram, symbolical of the Happy Realm of Sukhavati, or the Red Western Realm of Happiness (see text, p. 113), is outlined with flour and divided into com-partments, the central space (upon which the funeral-pyre is built) being dedicated to the Dhyānī Buddha Amitābha. At the beginning of the cremation ceremonies the chief *lāma* visualizes the funeral-pyre as being the *maṇḍala* of Amitābha, and the fire as being Amitābha, who, as in our text (see p. 113), personifies the element Fire. Then the corpse itself, when laid upon the pyre, is visualized as the *maṇḍala* of Amitābha and its heart as the dwelling-place of Amitābha. As the fire begins to grow in volume, sweet-smelling oils and spices and sandal-wood and incense-sticks are cast into it in sacrifice, as in the Hindu ritual of *Homa*, or sacrifice to fire. Finally, as the cremation ceremonies end, the priests and the mourners visualize the spirit of the departed as being purged of all *karmic* obscurations by the fire which is Amitābha, the Incomprehensible Light.

Such, in brief, is the mysticism underlying the beautiful rites performed for the dead at the place of cremation in Sikkim.

In all other forms of burial, throughout Tibet or territories under Tibetan influence, a parallel or corresponding funeral service, based on the same symbolical rituals, is performed, with variations according to sect and province.

VII. THE *BARDO*[1] OR AFTER-DEATH STATE

From the moment of death and for three and one-half or sometimes four days afterwards, the Knower, or principle of

---

[1] *Bar-do* literally means 'between (*Bar*) two (*do*)', i.e. 'between two [states]'—the state between death and rebirth—and, therefore, 'Intermediate' or 'Transitional [State]'. The translator, in certain instances, favoured 'Un-certain [State]' as its English rendering. It might also be rendered as 'Twilight [State]'.

consciousness, in the case of the ordinary person deceased, is believed to be thus in a sleep or trance-state, unaware, as a rule, that it has been separated from the human-plane body. This period is the First *Bardo*, called the *Chikhai Bardo* (Tib. *Hchi-khahi Bar-do*), or ' Transitional State of the Moment of Death', wherein dawns the Clear Light, first in primordial purity, then the percipient, being unable to recognize it, that is to say, to hold on to and remain in the transcendental state of the unmodified mind concomitant with it, perceives it *karmically* obscured, which is its secondary aspect. When the First *Bardo* ends, the Knower, awakening to the fact that death has occurred, begins to experience the Second *Bardo*, called the *Chönyid Bardo* (Tib. *Chös-nyid Bar-do*), or ' Transitional State of [the Experiencing or Glimpsing of] Reality ' ; and this merges into the Third *Bardo*, called the *Sidpa* (or *Sidpai*) *Bardo* (Tib. *Srid-pahi Bar-do*), or ' Transitional State of [or while seeking] Rebirth ', which ends when the principle of consciousness has taken rebirth in the human or some other world, or in one of the paradise realms.

As explained in Section III, above, the passing from one *Bardo* to another is analogous to the process of birth ; the Knower wakes up out of one swoon or trance state and then another, until the Third *Bardo* ends. On his awakening in the Second *Bardo*, there dawn upon him in symbolic visions, one by one, the hallucinations created by the *karmic* reflexes of actions done by him in the earth-plane body. What he has thought and what he has done become objective : thought-forms, having been consciously visualized and allowed to take root and grow and blossom and produce, now pass in a solemn and mighty panorama, as the consciousness-content of his personality.[1]

In the Second *Bardo*, the deceased is, unless otherwise enlightened, more or less under the delusion that although

---

[1] Some of the more learned *lāmas*—chiefly of the Gelugpa, or Yellow-Hat Sect—believe that the highly symbolic visions of the one hundred and ten principal deities of the *Chönyid Bardo* are seen only by devotees of some spiritual advancement who have studied Tantricism; and that the ordinary person when deceased will have visions more like those described in the *Sidpa Bardo*.

he is deceased he still possesses a body like the body of flesh and blood. When he comes to realize that really he has no such body, he begins to develop an overmastering desire to possess one; and, seeking for one, the *karmic* predilection for *sangsāric* existence naturally becoming all-determining, he enters into the Third *Bardo* of seeking Rebirth, and eventually, with his rebirth in this or some other world, the after-death state comes to an end.

For the commonalty, this is the normal process; but for those very exceptional minds, possessed of great *yogīc* knowledge and enlightenment, only the more spiritual stages of the *Bardo* of the first few days will be experienced; the most enlightened of *yogīs* may escape all of the *Bardo*, passing into a paradise realm, or else reincarnating in this world as soon as the human body has been discarded, maintaining all the while unbroken continuity of consciousness.[1] As men think, so are they, both here and hereafter, thoughts being things, the parents of all actions, good and bad alike; and, as the sowing has been, so will the harvest be.

If escape from the Intermediate State is not achieved, through rebirth into some other state—that of Hell being possible for the very exceptional evil-doer, though not for the ordinary person, who expiates normal moral delinquencies upon being reborn as a human being—within the symbolic period of Forty-nine Days, a period whose actual duration is determined by *karma*, the deceased remains subject to all the *karmic* illusions of the *Bardo*, blissful or miserable as the case may be, and progress is impossible. Apart from liberation by gaining *Nirvāṇa* after death—thus cutting asunder for ever the *karmic* bonds of worldly or *sangsāric* existence in an illusionary body of propensities—the only hope for the ordinary person of reaching Buddhahood lies in being reborn as a human being; for birth in any other than the human world causes delay for one desirous of reaching the Final Goal.

---

[1] 'This is borne out in the Pali *Ti-Pitaka*, which records several instances of high *deva* rebirth immediately after death on the human plane.'—Cassius A. Pereira.

VIII. THE PSYCHOLOGY OF THE *BARDO* VISIONS

Definite psychological significance attaches to each of the deities appearing in the *Bardo Thödol*; but, in order to grasp it, the student must bear in mind that—as suggested above— the apparitional visions seen by the deceased in the Inter- mediate State are not visions of reality, but nothing more than the hallucinatory embodiments of the thought-forms born of the mental-content of the percipient; or, in other words, they are the intellectual impulses which have assumed personified form in the after-death dream-state.

Accordingly, the Peaceful Deities (Tib. *Z'i-wa*) are the personified forms of the sublimest human sentiments, which proceed from the psychic heart-centre. As such, they are represented as the first to dawn, because, psychologically speaking, the heart-born impulses precede the brain-born impulses. They come in peaceful aspect to control and to influence the deceased whose connexion with the human world has just been severed; the deceased has left relatives and friends behind, works unaccomplished, desires unsatisfied, and, in most cases, he possesses a strong yearning to recover the lost opportunity afforded by human embodiment for spiritual enlightenment. But, in all his impulses and yearn- ings, *karma* is all-masterful; and, unless it be his *karmic* lot to gain liberation in the first stages, he wanders downwards into the stages wherein the heart-impulses give way to brain- impulses.

Whereas the Peaceful Deities are the personifications of the feelings, the Wrathful Deities (Tib. *T'o-wo*) are the personi- fications of the reasonings and proceed from the psychic brain-centre. Yet, just as impulses arising in the heart-centre may transform themselves into the reasonings of the brain- centre, so the Wrathful Deities are the Peaceful Deities in a changed aspect.

As the intellect comes into activity, after the sublime heart- born impulses subside, the deceased begins to realize more and more the state in which he is; and with the supernormal faculties of the *Bardo*-body which he begins to make use of—

in much the same manner as an infant new-born in the human world begins to employ the human plane sense-faculties—he is enabled to think how he may win this or that state of existence. *Karma* is, however, still his master, and defines his limitations. As on the human plane the sentimental impulses are most active in youth and often lost in mature life, wherein reason commonly takes the place of them, so on the after-death plane, called the *Bardo*, the first experiences are happier than the later experiences.

From another aspect, the chief deities themselves are the embodiments of universal divine forces, with which the deceased is inseparably related, for through him, as being the microcosm of the macrocosm, penetrate all impulses and forces, good and bad alike. Samanta-Bhadra, the All-Good, thus personifies Reality, the Primordial Clear Light of the Unborn, Unshaped *Dharma-Kāya* (cf. p. 95). Vairochana is the Originator of all phenomena, the Cause of all Causes. As the Universal Father, Vairochana manifests or spreads forth as seed, or semen, all things; his *shakti*, the Mother of Great Space, is the Universal Womb into which the seed falls and evolves as the world-systems. Vajra-Sattva symbolizes Immutability. Ratna-Sambhava is the Beautifier, the Source of all Beauty in the Universe. Amitābha is Infinite Compassion and Love Divine, the *Christos*. Amogha-Siddhi is the personification of Almighty Power or Omnipotence. And the minor deities, heroes, *ḍākinīs* (or 'fairies'), goddesses, lords of death, *rākṣhasas*, demons, spirits, and all others, correspond to definite human thoughts, passions, and impulses, high and low, human and sub-human and superhuman, in *karmic* form, as they take shape from the seeds of thought forming the percipient's consciousness-content (cf. p. 219).

As the *Bardo Thödol* text makes very clear by repeated assertions, none of all these deities or spiritual beings has any real individual existence any more than have human beings: 'It is quite sufficient for thee [i.e. the deceased percipient] to know that these apparitions are [the reflections of] thine own thought-forms' (p. 104). They are merely the consciousness-content visualized, by *karmic* agency, as apparitional appearances in the Intermediate State—airy nothings woven into dreams.

The complete recognition of this psychology by the deceased sets him free into Reality. Therefore is it that the *Bardo Thödol*, as the name implies, is The Great Doctrine of Liberation by Hearing and by Seeing.

The deceased human being becomes the sole spectator of a marvellous panorama of hallucinatory visions; each seed of thought in his consciousness-content *karmically* revives; and he, like a wonder-struck child watching moving pictures cast upon a screen, looks on, unaware, unless previously an adept in *yoga*, of the non-reality of what he sees dawn and set.

At first, the happy and glorious visions born of the seeds of the impulses and aspirations of the higher or divine nature awe the uninitiated; then, as they merge into the visions born of the corresponding mental elements of the lower or animal nature, they terrify him, and he wishes to flee from them; but, alas, as the text explains, they are inseparable from himself, and to whatsoever place he may wish to flee they will follow him.

It is not necessary to suppose that all the dead in the Intermediate State experience the same phenomena, any more than all the living do in the human world, or in dreams. The *Bardo Thödol* is merely typical and suggestive of all after-death experiences. It merely describes in detail what is assumed will be the *Bardo* visualizations of the consciousness-content of the ordinary devotee of the Red Hat School of Padma Sambhava. As a man is taught, so he believes. Thoughts being things, they may be planted like seeds in the mind of the child and completely dominate his mental content. Given the favourable soil of the will to believe, whether the seed-thoughts be sound or unsound, whether they be of pure superstition or of realizable truth, they take root and flourish, and make the man what he is mentally.

Accordingly, for a Buddhist of some other School, as for a Hindu, or a Moslem, or a Christian, the *Bardo* experiences would be appropriately different: the Buddhist's or the Hindu's thought-forms, as in a dream state, would give rise to corresponding visions of the deities of the Buddhist or Hindu pantheon; a Moslem's, to visions of the Moslem Paradise; a Christian's, to visions of the Christian Heaven, or an American Indian's to visions of the Happy Hunting Ground. And, similarly, the materialist will experience after-death visions as negative and as empty and as deityless as any he ever dreamt while in the human body. Rationally considered, each person's after-death experiences, as the *Bardo Thödol* teaching implies, are entirely dependent upon his or her own mental content. In other words, as explained above, the after-death state is very much like a dream state, and its dreams are the children of the mentality of the dreamer. This psychology scientifically explains why devout Christians, for example, have had—if we are to accept the testimony of Christian saints and seers—visions (in a trance or dream state, or in the after-death state) of God the Father seated on a throne in the New Jerusalem, and of the Son at His side, and of all the Biblical scenery and attributes of Heaven, or of the Virgin and Saints and Archangels, or of Purgatory and Hell.

In other words, the *Bardo Thödol* seems to be based upon verifiable data of human physiological and psychological experiences; and it views the problem of the after-death state as being purely a psycho-physical problem; and is, therefore, in the main, scientific. It asserts repeatedly that what the percipient on the *Bardo* plane sees is due entirely to his own mental-content; that there are no visions of gods or of demons, of heavens or of hells, other than those born of the hallucinatory *karmic* thought-forms constituting his personality, which is an impermanent product arising from the thirst for existence and from the will to live and to believe.

From day to day the *Bardo* visions change, concomitant with the eruption of the thought-forms of the percipient, until their *karmic* driving force exhausts itself; or, in other words, the thought-forms, born of habitual propensities, being mental records comparable as has already been suggested to records on a cinema-film, their reel running to its end, the after-death state ends, and the Dreamer, emerging from the womb, begins to experience anew the phenomena of the human world.

The *Bible* of the Christians, like the *Koran* of the Moslems, never seems to consider that the spiritual experiences in the form of hallucinatory visions by prophet or devotee, reported therein, may, in the last analysis, not be real. But the *Bardo Thödol* is so sweeping in its assertions that it leaves its reader with the clear-cut impression that every vision, without any exception whatsoever, in which spiritual beings, gods or demons, or paradises or places of torment and purgation play a part, in a *Bardo* or any *Bardo*-like dream or ecstasy, is purely illusionary, being based upon *sangsāric* phenomena.

The whole aim of the *Bardo Thödol* teaching, as otherwise stated elsewhere, is to cause the Dreamer to awaken into Reality, freed from all the obscurations of *karmic* or *sangsāric* illusions, in a supramundane or *Nirvānic* state, beyond all phenomenal paradises, heavens, hells, purgatories, or worlds of embodiment. In this way, then, it is purely Buddhistic and unlike any non-Buddhist book in the world, secular or religious.

IX. THE JUDGEMENT

The Judgement Scene as described in our text and that described in the Egyptian *Book of the Dead* seem so much alike in essentials as to suggest that common origin, at present unknown, to which we have already made reference. In the Tibetan version, Dharma-Rāja (Tib. *Shinje-chho-gyal*) King of the Dead (commonly known to Theravādists as Yama-Rāja), the Buddhist and Hindu Pluto, as a Judge of the Dead, corresponds to Osiris in the Egyptian version. In both versions alike there is the symbolical weighing: before Dharma-Rāja there are placed on one side of the balance black pebbles and on the other side white pebbles, symbolizing evil and good deeds; and similarly, before Osiris, the heart and the feather (or else in place of the feather an image of the Goddess of Truth which it symbolizes) are weighed one against the other, the heart representing the conduct or conscience of the deceased and the feather righteousness or truth.

In the Egyptian *Book of the Dead*, the deceased, addressing his heart, says: ' Raise not thyself in evidence against me.

Be not mine adversary before the Divine Circle; let there be no fall of the scale against me in the presence of the great god, Lord of Amenta.' In the Egyptian Judgement Scene it is the ape-headed (less commonly the ibis-headed) Thoth, god of wisdom, who supervises the weighing; in the Tibetan Judgement Scene it is the monkey-headed Shinje; and in both scenes there is the jury of deities looking on, some animal-headed, some human-headed.[1] In the Egyptian version there is a monstrous creature waiting to devour the deceased should the deceased be condemned, whilst in the Tibetan version devils wait to conduct the evil-doer to the hell-world of purgation; and the record-board which Thoth is sometimes depicted as holding corresponds to the Mirror of *Karma* held by Dharma-Rāja or, as in some versions, by one of the divine jury. Furthermore, in both Books of the Dead, the deceased when first addressing the Judge pleads that he has done no evil. Before Osiris, this plea seems to be accepted in all the texts now known; before Dharma-Rāja it is subject to the test of the Mirror of *Karma*, and this seems to be distinctly an Indian and Buddhist addition to the hypothetical pre-historic version, whence arose the Egyptian and the Tibetan versions, the Egyptian being the less affected.

Plato, too, in recording the other-world adventures of Er, in the tenth book of the *Republic*, describes a similar Judgement, in which there are judges and *karmic* record-boards (affixed to the souls judged) and paths—one for the good, leading to Heaven, one for the evil, leading to Hell—and demons waiting to take the condemned souls to the place of punishment, quite as in the *Bardo Thödol* (see p. 49).[2]

---

[1] Such animal-headed deities as appear in the *Bardo Thödol* are, for the most part, derived from the pre-Buddhistic religion of Tibet called Bön, and, therefore, probably of very great antiquity. Like their Egyptian parallels, they seem to be more or less totemistic; and, through their impersonation by masked priests, as in the Ancient Egyptian Mysteries and surviving Tibetan mystery plays, may be—as our text also suggests—symbolic of definite attributes, passions, and propensities of *sangsāric*, or embodied, beings—human, sub-human, and superhuman. (See p. 140[1].)

[2] The student is here referred to Section VII of our Addenda (pp. 238–41), concerning the Christianized version of the Judgement contained in the curious medieval treatise entitled *The Lamentation of the Dying Creature*.

The purgatorial lore now Christianized and associated with St. Patrick in the originally pagan St. Patrick's Purgatory in Ireland, the whole cycle of Otherworld and Rebirth legends of the Celtic peoples connected with their Fairy-Faith, and similar Proserpine lore recorded in the Sacred Books of mankind the world over, as well as the Semitic doctrines of heaven and hell and judgement, and of resurrection as the Christianized corruption of a pre-Christian and Jewish rebirth doctrine, as also the passage in Plato, all testify to beliefs universal among mankind, probably far older than the oldest of ancient records from Babylon or from Egypt.[1]

The painting of the Tibetan Judgement Scene as reproduced herein (see opposite p. 166) was made, in strict accord with monastic tradition, in Gangtok, Sikkim, during the year 1919, by Lharipa-Pempa-Tendup-La, a Tibetan artist then sojourning there. An early prototype of it was, until quite recently, preserved as one of the old frescoes contained within the pictorial Wheel of Life of the Tashiding temple-picture in Sikkim, which Dr. L. A. Waddell has described as follows: 'The judgement is in every case meted out by the impartial *Shinje-chho-gyal* or "Religious King of the Dead" [*Dharma-Rāja*], a form of *Yama*, the Hindu god of the dead, who holds a mirror in which the naked soul is reflected, while his servant *Shinje* weighs out in scales the good as opposed to the bad deeds; the former being represented by white pebbles, and the latter by black.'[2] And Dr. Waddell has traced back

---

[1] In my *Fairy-Faith in Celtic Countries* (Oxford, 1911), Chapter X, I have suggested how very probable it is that the purgatorial lore which centred about the cavern for mystic pagan initiations formerly existing on an island in Loch Derg, Ireland, at what is now the famous place of Catholic pilgrimage called St. Patrick's Purgatory, gave rise to the doctrine of Purgatory in the Roman Church. The original purgatorial cavern was demolished, by order of the English Government in Ireland, to destroy, as was said, pagan superstition.

Furthermore, the subterranean places of worship and initiation, dedicated to the Sun-God Mithras, still preserved as ancient remains throughout the Southern European countries, bear such close resemblance to the original Irish Purgatory—as to other underground places of initiation in Celtic countries like New Grange in Ireland and Gavrinis in Brittany—as to indicate a common prehistoric origin, essentially religious and connected with a cult of the *Bardo*-world and its inhabitants.

[2] Cf. *The Gazetteer of Sikhim*, ed. by H. H. Risley, p. 269.

the origin of the picture to a similar Wheel of Life, commonly, though incorrectly, known as ' the Zodiac' in the verandah of the Ajaṇṭā Cave No. XVII, India. (See p. 56.) This, then, establishes the antiquity of the Judgement Scene, of which our text contains one version.

Throughout the canonical and apocryphal literature of Northern Buddhism other versions are numerous. In the Pali canon of Southern Buddhism there are parallel versions, for example in the *Devadūta Vagga* of the *Anguttara Nikāya*, and in the *Devadūta Sūttam* of the *Majjhima Nikāya*. The latter version may be summarized as follows: The Exalted One, the Buddha, while sojourning at the Jetavana Monastery, addresses the monks assembled therein concerning the after-death state of existence. Like a man of clear vision, sitting between two houses, each with six doors, He beholds all who come and go; the one house symbolizing the *Bardo* or state of disembodied existence, the other the embodied state of existence, and the twelve doors the six entrances and the six exits of the six *lokas*. Then, after explaining the manner in which *karma* governs all states of existence, the Buddha describes how the evil-doer is brought before the King of Death and questioned about the Five Messengers of Death.

The first messenger is symbolized by a new-born babe lying on its back; and the message is that even for it, as for all living creatures, old age and death are inevitable. The second messenger comes in the guise of an aged person, eighty, ninety, or a hundred years of age, decrepit, crooked as the curved rafter of a gabled roof, leaning on a staff, trembling as he walks, pathetically miserable, with youth entirely gone, broken-toothed, grey-haired and nearly bald, and with wrinkled brow; and his message is that the babe but grows up and matures and decays to become a victim of Death. The third messenger, a person confined by illness, rolling in his own filth, unable to rise or to lie down without the aid of an attendant, brings the message that disease, too, is inevitable, even as death. The fourth messenger, a thief undergoing most terrible punishment, bears the message that the punishment for evil-doing in this world is as nothing compared to the punishment which *karma* inflicts after death. The fifth messenger, to emphasize the same message of death and the corruptibility of the body, is a corpse, swollen, discoloured, and putrid.

In each instance, King Yama asks the deceased if he had seen the messenger and receives the reply, ' No '. Then the King explains to him who the messenger was and the meaning of the messages ; and the deceased, thereby remembering, is obliged to confess that, not having done good deeds, he had not acted upon the messages, but had done evil instead, for-getting the inevitability of death. Thereupon, Yama pro-nounces the judgement, that since the deceased had failed to do good he must suffer the *karmic* consequences. Accordingly, the hell-furies take the deceased and cause him to suffer five sorts of purgatorial punishments ; and, though he suffers most unbearable pains, he is, as the *Bardo Thödol* makes clear, incapable of dying

In the *Anguttara Nikāya* version, wherein there are but three messengers, the aged person, the man or woman over-come with disease, and the corpse, the Buddha concludes the discourse thus :

' If men who have been warned by heavenly messengers have been indifferent as regards religion they suffer long, being born in a low condition.

' If virtuous men have been warned by heavenly messengers in this world, they do not neglect to profess the holy doctrines. Seeing the danger of attachment, which is the cause of birth and death, they have in this life extinguished the miseries of existence by arriving at a condition free from fear, happy and free from passions and sins.' [1]

X. THE REBIRTH DOCTRINE

In examining the Rebirth Doctrine, more particularly as it presents itself in our text, two interpretations must be taken into account : the literal or exoteric interpretation,

---

[1] Cf. translation by E. R. J. Gooneratne, *Anguttara Nikāya, Eka Duka and Tika Nipāta* (Galle, Ceylon, 1913), pp. 160-5.

which is the popular interpretation; and the symbolical or esoteric interpretation, which is held to be correct by the initiated few, who claim not scriptural authority or belief, but knowledge. With respect to Tibet, these few are chiefly learned *lāmas* who are said to have made successful application of methods like those which the Buddha expounded for remembering past incarnations, and for acquiring the *yogīc* power of seeing what really takes place in the natural process of death and rebirth. To the devotee, seeking thus to know rather than merely to believe on the authority of priests or books, the Buddha has offered the following guidance:

'If he desireth to be able to call to mind his various temporary states in days gone by, such as one birth, two births, three, four, five, ten, twenty, thirty, forty, fifty, a hundred, a thousand, or a hundred thousand births, his births in many an aeon of destruction, in many an aeon of renovation, in many an aeon of both destruction and renovation [so as to be able to say]: "In that place such was my name, such my family, such my caste, such my subsistence, such my experience of comfort or of pain, and such the limit of my life; and when I passed from thence I took form again in that other place, where my name was so and so, such my family, such my caste, such my subsistence, such my experience of comfort or of pain, and such my term of life; and from thence I was born here—thus I am able to call to mind my various temporary states of existence in days gone by"—in that state of self-concentration, if the mind be fixed on the acquirement of any object, that object will be attained.

'If he desireth to see with pure and heavenly vision, surpassing that of men, beings as they pass from one state of existence and take form in others—beings base or noble, good-looking or ill-favoured, happy or miserable, according to the *karma* they inherit—in that state of self-concentration, if the mind be fixed on the acquirement of any object, that object will be attained' (*Lonaphala Vagga, Anguttara Nikāya*).

Again in the *Brāhmaṇa Vagga, Anguttara Nikāya*, where the *yogīc* method of recovering from the content of the subconsciousness (which—in confirmation of the Buddha's psychology—the science of the West has now proven 'is the abode of everything that is latent'[1]) is likewise described, there is this additional passage: 'Thus he calleth to mind the various appearances and forms of his previous births. This is the first stage of his knowledge; his ignorance [as regards prior births] hath vanished, and his knowledge [as regards prior births] hath arisen: darkness hath departed, and light hath arrived, the result due to one who liveth in meditation, subduing his passions promptly.'[2]

Nowhere, to our knowledge, are there nowadays—as there are said to have been in Buddhaghoṣa's time—*yogīs* among Southern Buddhists who have carried this practice to a successful issue. It is only among Northern Buddhists (as among Hindus) that such *yoga* seems to be, according to trustworthy evidence from well-informed Tibetans and Indians, a practically applied science even until now, producing modern saints, some few of whom are believed worthy to be called perfected saints, or *Arhants*.

As the question, What is and is not the right interpretation of the Rebirth Doctrine? is by no means settled among the Oriental peoples who hold the Doctrine, it is necessary for us frankly to recognize the problem as highly controversial. Consequently in this Section we should try to weigh both interpretations carefully; and, if possible, arrive at a sound conclusion, in order to guide the student aright in what is the most fundamental doctrine underlying the *Bardo Thödol*. In doing so, it seems desirable to invoke the aid of such facts of Western Science as appear to be directly applicable.

As to the esoteric interpretation, the editor has discovered that the initiates who hold to it invariably follow the Buddha's command as contained in the *Kalama Sūtta, Anguttara Nikāya,*

[1] William James, *Varieties of Religious Experiences* (New York, 1902), p. 483.

[2] Cf. translation by E. R. J. Gooneratne, *Anguttara Nikāya, Eka Duka and Tika Nipata* (Galle, Ceylon, 1913), pp. 188–9, 273–4. Passages parallel to these are contained in the *Kandaraka Sūttanta* and *Potaliya Sūttanta* of the *Majjhima Nikāya* (see translations by Bhikkhus Narada and Mahinda in *The Blessing*, Colombo, Ceylon, Jan. and Feb., 1925, vol. i, nos. 1 and 2). Buddhaghosa, in his *Vissudhi Magga* (i.e. 'Path of Purity'), gives in more detail similar *yogic* methods for recovering (from the subconsciousness) memories of past births.

or else the Hindu equivalent in works on *Yoga*, not to accept any doctrine as true until it be tested, and proven true, even though it be 'found written in the Scriptures'; and they hold no Scriptures to be infallible, on this or any doctrine, or free from corruptions, Pali, Sanskrit, Tibetan, or others.

The exoteric interpretation, namely that the human stream of consciousness, that is to say, the human life-flux, not only can, but very often does take re-embodiment in sub-human creatures immediately after having been in human form, is accepted universally by Buddhists, both of the Northern and Southern Schools—as by Hindus—who, referring to Scriptures, invariably regard it as being incontrovertible. Their belief, being based on the authority of written records, and on untested theories of *gurus* and priests who consider the literally interpreted written records to be infallible and who are not adept in *yoga*, is nowadays considered to be the orthodox interpretation.

Over against the exoteric interpretation, which, without any doubt, the *Bardo Thödol*, if read literally, conveys, the esoteric interpretations may be stated—on the authority of the various philosophers, both Hindu and Buddhist, from whom the editor has received instruction—as follows:

The human form (but not the divine nature in man) is a direct inheritance from the sub-human kingdoms; from the lowest forms of life it has evolved, guided by an ever-growing and ever-changing life-flux, potentially conscious-ness, which figuratively may be called the seed of the life-force, connected with or overshadowing each sentient creature, being in its essence psychical. As such, it is the evolving principle, the principle of continuity, the principle capable of acquiring knowledge and understanding of its own nature, the principle whose normal goal is Enlightenment. And, just as the physical seed of a vegetable or animal organism— even man's seed—is seen by the eyes to be capable of pro-ducing after its own kind only, so with that which figuratively may be called the psychical seed of the life-flux which the eyes cannot see—if of a human being it cannot incarnate in, or overshadow, or be intimately bound up with a body foreign to its evolved characteristics, either in this world, in *Bardo*, or in any realm or world of *sangsāric* existence. This is held to be a natural law governing the manifestation of life, as inviolable as the law of *karma*, which sets it into operation.

For a human life-flux to flow into the physical form of a dog, or fowl, or insect, or worm, is, therefore, held to be as impossible as would be—let us say—the transferring of the waters of Lake Michigan into the depression occupied by the waters of Lake Killarney, or—as the Hindu would say—as putting into the bed of the Ganges River the waters of the Indian Ocean.

Degeneration, in a highly developed flowering plant, or apple, or vegetable, or wheat, or animal, is, of course, concomitant with cultural neglect; but within this creation period—at least so far as the physical vision of science has penetrated therein—the flowering plant does not degenerate into the apple, nor into the corn, nor one species of animals into another, nor does man degenerate into anything but the savage man—never into a sub-human creature. As to the processes affecting the life-flux which the human eye cannot see, the esoteric teaching coincides with that of the ancient Greek and Egyptian mystics: 'As below, so above'; which implies that there is one harmonious *karmic* law governing with unwavering and impartial justice the visible as well as the invisible operations of nature.

From this follows the corollary, which the Oriental advocates of the esoteric interpretation give out: Progression or retrogression—never an unchanging neutral state of inactivity—are the alternatives within the *Sangsāra*; and the one or the other, within any of the mansions of existence, cannot lead the life-flux to the threshold of that mansion—neither the sub-human to the human, nor the human to the sub-human—save step by step. And retrogression and progression alike are time-processes: ages pass ere the fire-mist becomes the solidified planet; an Enlightened One is the rare fruit of unknown myriads of embodiments; and man, the highest of the animal-beings, cannot become the lowest of the animal-beings, no matter how heinous his sins, at one bound.

Given ages of continual retrogression, the life-flux which is now human may cease to be human, the human constituents of it becoming atrophied or latent through lack of exercise, in much the same way as atrophy overcomes the activity of a bodily organ or function which is not used. Thereupon, being no longer kinetically, but merely potentially human—just as a dog or horse or elephant are potentially, but not kinetically, human—that life-flux can and ordinarily would fall back into the sub-human kingdoms, whence it may begin anew to rise upwards to the human state or continue to retrograde even below the brute world.

The late Lāma Kazi Dawa-Samdup, the translator, has left on record his own complementary opinion, as follows: ' The forty-nine days of the *Bardo* symbolize ages either of evolution or of degeneration. Intellects able to grasp Truth do not fall into the lower conditions of existence.

' The doctrine of the transmigration of the human to the sub-human may apply solely to the lower or purely brutish constituents of the human principle of consciousness; for the Knower itself neither incarnates nor re-incarnates—it is the Spectator.

' In the *Bardo Thödol*, the deceased is represented as retrograding, step by step, into lower and lower states of consciousness. Each step downwards is preceded by a swooning into unconsciousness; and possibly that which constitutes his mentality on the lower levels of the *Bardo* is some mental element or compound of mental elements formerly a part of his earth-plane consciousness, separated, during the swooning, from higher or more spiritually enlightened elements of that consciousness. Such a mentality ought not to be regarded as on a par with a human mentality; for it seems to be a mere faded and incoherent reflex of the human mentality of the deceased. And perhaps it is some such thing as this which incarnates in sub-human animal bodies—if anything does in a literal sense.'

This theory, coming from the translator, is unusually interesting, for he expressed it while quite unaware of its similarity to the theory held esoterically by the Egyptian priests and exoterically recorded by Herodotus, who, apparently, became their pupil in the monastic college at Heliopolis. Judging from what Herodotus and others of the ancient Greeks, and Romans as well, have written touching thereon, we arrive at the following summary : The human soul was believed to remain in the after-death state during a period of three thousand years. Its human-plane body of the moment of death disintegrating, the constituents went to form the bodies of animals and plants, transmigrating from one to another during the three thousand years. At the end of that period the soul gathers together the identical particles of matter which had thus been continually transmigrating and which had constituted its former earth-plane body of the moment of death, and from them rebuilds, through habit, as a bird its nest, a new body and is reborn in it as a human being.[1]

---

[1] Cf. Herodotus, ii. 123 ; Lucretius, *De Rerum Natura*, iii. 843-61. In common with ancient historians and philosophers, Herodotus (ii. 171) refuses to divulge, in a literal manner, the higher or esoteric teachings of the Mysteries of Antiquity :

' On this lake [within the sacred precinct of the temple at Sais] the Egyptians perform by night the representation of his adventures [i. e. the symbolic adventures touching the birth, life, death, and regeneration of Osiris—' whose name ', writes Herodotus, ' I consider it impious to divulge '], which they call Mysteries. On these matters, however, though accurately acquainted with the particulars of them, I must [as an initiate] observe a discreet silence. So, too, with regard to the Mysteries of Demeter [celebrated at Eleusis, in Greece], which the Greeks term "The Thesmophoria", I know them [as an initiate], but I shall not mention them, except so far as may be done without impiety [or done lawfully].'

It has now been proven by archaeological and other research that the Mysteries consisted of symbolic dramatic performances open only to initiates and neophytes fit for initiation, illustrating the universally diffused esoteric teachings concerning death and resurrection (i. e. rebirth) ; and that the doctrine of transmigration of the human soul into animal bodies—if depicted at all—was not intended to be taken (as it has been taken by the uninitiated) literally, but symbolically as in Plato's *Republic*, detailed reference to which follows herein. (Cf. Herodotus, ii. 122.)

Herodotus in the last-mentioned passage gives a symbolic account of the descent into Hades and the return to the human world of King Rhampsinitus, in whose honour the priests of Egypt therefore instituted what was probably— when rationally interpreted—a rebirth festival. The most ancient recorded parallel now known exists in the *Ṛig Veda* (*Maṇḍala* x, *Sūkta* 135), wherein,

And this theory, when amended with certain necessary modifications, helps to illustrate the symbolical or esoteric interpretation of the *Bardo* Rebirth Doctrine.

In further illustration, applicable to the higher Hinduism as to the higher Buddhism, advocates of this interpretation point out that even before the final dissolution of the human body of the moment of death there is incessant transmigration of the bodily atoms. So long as the body is the receptacle of the consciousness-principle, it is said to renew itself completely every seven years. And even as the constituents of the physical man thus transmigrate throughout all organic and inorganic kingdoms and the mind remains unchangedly human during the brief cycle of one life-time, so, normally, it likewise remains human during the greater evolutionary cycle—i. e. until it reaches the end of all *sangsāric* evolution, namely, *Nirvāṇic* Enlightenment.

The esoteric teaching concerning this may be stated literally: That which is common to the human and to the sub-human worlds alike, namely, matter in its varied aspects as solids, liquids, and gases, eternally transmigrates. That which is specifically human and specifically sub-human remains so, in accordance with the law of nature that like attracts like and produces like, that all forces ever follow the line of least

---

as Sayana in his *Commentary* in the *Atharva Veda* (xix) seems to explain, the boy mentioned is the same as the boy Nachiketas of the [*Taittirīya*] *Brāhmaṇa*, who went to the realm of Yama, the King of the Dead, in *Yama-Loka*, and then returned to the realm of men. That this primeval Hades legend was interpreted esoterically as teaching a rebirth doctrine is confirmed by the ancient *Katha Upanishad*, the story of Nachiketas being used therein as a literary vehicle to convey the highest Vedāntic teachings concerning birth, life, and death. (Cf. *Katha Upanishad*, ii. 5; iii. 8, 15; iv. 10–11; vi. 18.)

Preserved in an Old Javanese MS. of the fourteenth century is a very similar Hades legend in which the Yaksha Kuñjarakarṇa is commanded by the Lord Vairōchana 'to go to Yama's kingdom to see what is prepared for all evil-doers'. Peculiar interest attaches to this version, because it records a doctrine—akin to that referred to by the Greek and Roman writers—of thousand-year periods of transmigration into plants, animals, and defective human beings, prior to rebirth in a human body free from *karmic* blemishes. It mentions, too, that from Yama's kingdom Pûrṇavijaya was recalled to human life. (Cf. *The Legend of Kuñjarakarṇa*, translated from the Dutch of Prof. Kern by Miss L. A. Thomas, in the *Indian Antiquary*, Bombay, 1903, vol. xxxii, pp. 111–27.)

resistance, that such highly evolved mental compounds as are bound up with the complex human consciousness cannot be disintegrated instantaneously, but require due allowance of time for their degeneration and ultimate dissolution and transmigration.[1]

---

[1] Examination of *The Laws of Manu*, the authority of which is unquestioned by orthodox Hindus, seems to confirm the esoteric interpretation, following the translation by Sir William Jones as revised by G. C. Haughton (in *Institutes of Hindu Law or the Ordinances of Menu*, London, 1825), and that by G. Bühler (in *The Sacred Books of the East*, vol. xxv, Oxford, 1886).

Manu at first sets forth the fundamental laws that 'Action, which springs from the mind, from speech, and from the body, produces either good or evil results ; by action are caused the [various] conditions of man, the highest, the middling, and the lowest ' ; and that '[A man] obtains [the results of] a good or evil mental [act] in his mind, [that of] a verbal [act] in his speech, [that of] a bodily [act] in his body '. (Bühler's trans., xii. 3, 8.)

Manu then proceeds to expound how man is not a simple but a complex being :

'That substance, which gives a power of motion to the body, the wise call *kshētrajna* [i. e. 'the knower of the field'—Bühler's trans.], or *jīvātman*, the vital spirit ; and that body, which thence derives active functions, they name *bhūtātman*, or *composed of elements*:

'Another internal spirit, *called mahat*, or *the great soul*, attends the birth of all creatures embodied, and thence in all mortal forms is conveyed a perception either pleasing or painful.

'These two, the vital spirit and reasonable soul, are closely united with *five* elements, but connected with the supreme spirit, or divine essence, which pervades all beings high and low.' (Jones's trans., xii. 12–14.)

From what follows, Manu apparently implies that it is this 'vital spirit', or animal soul, which alone is capable of transmigrating into sub-human forms, and not 'the reasonable soul', or super-animal principle :

'When the vital soul has gathered the fruit of sins, which arise from a love of sensual [i. e. animal or brutish] pleasure, but must produce misery, and, when its taint has thus been removed, it approaches again those two most effulgent essences, *the intellectual soul and the divine spirit*:

'They two, closely conjoined, examine without remission the virtues and vices of that sensitive [or animal] soul, according to its union with which it acquires pleasure or pain in the present and future worlds.

If the vital spirit had practised virtue for the most part, and vice in a small degree, it enjoys delight in celestial abodes, clothed with a body formed of pure elementary [i. e. ethereal] particles ;

'But, if it had generally been addicted to vice, and seldom attended to virtue, then shall it be deserted by those pure elements, and, *having a coarser body of sensible nerves*, it feels the pains to which Yama shall doom it :

'Having endured those torments according to the sentence of Yama, and its taint being almost removed, it again reaches those five pure elements in the order of their natural distribution.' (Jones's trans., xii. 18–22.)

Accordingly, the esotericists hold it to be unscientific to believe that a human life-flux or consciousness-principle could re-incarnate in the body of a sub-human creature within forty-nine days after its extraction from the human form, as the exotericist believes who accepts literally such a rebirth doctrine

After further exposition of the science of rebirth in its esoteric or rational aspect, Manu arrives at the following summary:

'Thus, by indulging the sensual [i.e. animal or brutish] appetites, and by neglecting the performance of duties, the basest of men, ignorant of sacred expiations, assume [in their vital spirit form, but not in their reasonable soul form] the basest forms.

'What particular bodies the vital spirit enters in this world, and in consequence of what sins here committed, now hear at large and in order.' (Jones's trans., xii. 52-3.)

Manu evidently exerts himself apart from the main subject of his treatise, as the whole of *The Laws* suggests, to invest with legal and divine sanction the dogma that the person of a Brāhmin is peculiarly sacred and inviolable, and so gives prominence to the sin of slaying a Brāhmin by mentioning it first; then to the sin of a priest drinking spirituous liquor, and then to the sin of stealing the gold of a priest. In all such instances, as in all which follow them, the implication is, as we have above observed, that the 'vital spirit', or animal soul, separated from the two higher elements of man's complex constitution, which are 'the reasonable soul' and 'the divine essence', suffers the penalty of migrating in sub-human creatures:

'The slayer of a *Brāhmen* [i. e. the vital spirit, or the irrational animal soul, of a *Brāhmen*-slayer] must enter, *according to the circumstances of the crime*, the body of a dog, a boar, an ass, a camel, a bull, a goat, a sheep, a stag, a bird, a *Chandāla*, or a *Puccasa*'; and so on for other crimes (Jones's trans., xii. 55-7).

In this connexion, it is interesting to observe a few of the correspondences between cause and effect which other of *The Laws* suggest. Thus, if a man steal precious things he 'shall be born *in the tribe of goldsmiths* [considered to be of very low caste], *or* among *birds called hēmacāras, or gold-makers.* If a man steal grain in the husk, he shall be born a rat; if a yellow mixed metal, a gander [which is of like mixed colour]; if water, a *plava*, or diver. ... If he steal flesh-meat, a vulture; ... if oil, a *blatta*, or oil-drinking beetle; ... if exquisite perfumes, a musk-rat'. (Jones's trans., xii. 61-5.)

Understanding Manu in the sense which this note aims to set forth, the esotericists disallow such popular and literal interpretation of *Manu's Laws* as the Brāhmins in their own Brāhmin interests promulgate—according to the esotericists—among the common people concerning the doctrines of rebirth and *karma*.

The student should observe that the italicized non-Sanskrit words in the passages quoted in this note from the translation by Sir William Jones mark his interpolations from commentaries on Manu, especially from the *Gloss of Culluca*, and that the bracketed words indicate our own interpolations. Because the italicized interpolations tend to bring out the more obscure meanings of the passages cited, preference has been given to the Jones translation, although that by Bühler, which is more literal and therefore more technical, is, in all essentials, substantially the same.

as the *Bardo Thödol*, when viewed exoterically, or literally, presents.

The *Bardo* rebirth symbols themselves ought now to be considered from the standpoint of the esoteric interpretation; and to elucidate them innumerable parallels could be chosen from widely separated sources, but because of its recognized authority no parallel seems more appropriate than that contained in the tenth book of Plato's *Republic*, describing certain of the Greek Heroes in the *Sidpa Bardo* choosing their bodies for the next incarnations:

The *Bardo* legend as recorded in the *Republic* concerns Er the son of Armenius, a Pamphylian by birth, who, as Plato tells us, 'was slain in battle, and ten days afterwards, when the bodies of the dead were taken up already in a state of corruption, his body was found unaffected by decay, and carried home to be buried. And on the twelfth day, as he was lying on the funeral pile, he returned to life and told them what he had seen in the other world. He said that when his soul left the body he went on a journey with a great company, and they came to a mysterious place at which there were two openings in the earth; they were near together, and over against them were two other openings in the heaven above. In the intermediate space there were judges seated, who commanded the just, after they had given judgement on them and had bound their sentences in front of them, to ascend by the heavenly way on the right hand; and in like manner the unjust were bidden by them to descend by the lower way on the left hand; these also bore the symbols of their deeds, but fastened to their backs.'

Having thus described the otherworld Judgement—which closely resembles the Judgement described in our text—Plato goes on to describe the souls of the Greek Heroes in their *Sidpa Bardo* preparing for reincarnation: 'Most curious, he said, was the spectacle—sad and laughable and strange; for the choice of the souls was in most cases based on their own experience of a previous life. There he saw the soul which had once been Orpheus choosing the life of a swan out of enmity to the race of women, hating to be born of a woman because they had been his murderers; he beheld also the soul of Thamyras choosing the life of a nightingale; birds, on the other hand, like the swan and other musicians, wanting to be men. The soul which obtained the twentieth lot chose the life of a lion, and this was the soul of Ajax the son of Telamon, who would not be a man, remembering the injustice which was done him in the judgement about the arms. The next was Agamemnon, who took the life of an eagle, because, like Ajax, he hated human nature by reason of his sufferings. About the middle came the lot of Atalanta; she, seeing the great fame of an athlete, was unable to resist the temptation: and after her there followed the soul of Epeius the son of Panopeus passing into the nature of a woman cunning in the arts; and far away among the last who chose, the soul of the jester Thersites was putting on the form of a monkey. There came also the soul of Odysseus having yet to make a choice, and his lot happened to be the last of them all. *Now the recollection of former toils had disenchanted him of ambition, and he went about for a considerable time in search of the life of a private man who had no cares; he had some difficulty in finding this, which was lying about and had been neglected by everybody else;* and when he saw it he said that he would have done the same had his lot been first instead of last, and that he was delighted to have it. And not only did men pass into animals, but I must also mention that there were animals tame and wild which changed into one another and into corresponding human natures—the good into the gentle and the evil into the savage, in all sorts of combinations.'

If read superficially, this Platonic account of the rebirth process may be understood literally—even as the *Bardo Thödol* may be; and it is not impossible to imagine that Plato, as an initiate into the Greek Mysteries, who, like Herodotus, never refers to their esoteric teachings openly, but only in figurative and very often intentionally misleading phraseology, intended that it should be understood so by the uninitiated. Nevertheless, when the passage is examined closely, the exoteric doctrine of transmigration of the human into the sub-human, or ·vice versa, is evidently not the meaning underlying it.

The reference to the choice made by Odysseus, as italicized by us, gives the clue to the real meaning intended. Odysseus' choice was last; each of the heroes preceding him in choosing their lot had neglected the lot of 'the life of a private man who had no cares', and Odysseus chooses this lot as the best of all.

If we consider the sort of life chosen by each of the Greeks who preceded Odysseus, we find it to be definitely symbolical of the character of the chooser:

Thus, Orpheus, the founder of the Orphic Mysteries, a divine teacher sent to instruct mankind by the god of song and music, Apollo, and held by the Greeks to have been the greatest of harp-players and the most enlightened of poets and singers, very appropriately chooses 'the life of a swan'; for since immemorial time the swan has symbolized—as it still does—song and music; and Plato's figurative language, correctly interpreted, implies that Orpheus was to reincarnate as a great poet and musician, as was but natural. To assume— as the exotericist may—that such a being as Orpheus could be born as a swan in reality thus appears to the esotericist to be untenable.

Likewise, Thamyras, an ancient Thracian bard, renowned as a harp-player and singer, symbolically chooses the life of the sweet-singing nightingale.

Ajax, the Homeric hero, who, next to Achilles, was the bravest of the Greeks, most fittingly chooses the life of a lion; for the king of beasts is, and has been for unknown ages, the symbol denoting bravery or fearlessness, which almost all nations and races of men have recognized.

Agamemnon, the next to choose, selects the life of an eagle; for among Greek heroes he was the chief, as Zeus was among the gods of Olympus; and, he having been regarded as an incarnation of Zeus and worshipped as one of the divinities, there is assigned to him the symbol of Zeus, which is the eagle.

Atalanta, the most swift-footed of mortals and famous for her foot-races with her many suitors, very naturally is reborn as a great athlete; and, in her case, Plato uses no symbol.

Nor is a symbol used in connexion with Epeius, who, noted for his cunning in constructing the wooden horse at the siege of Troy, and whose cowardice afterwards became proverbial, is seen 'passing into the nature of a woman cunning in the arts'.

As to the jester Thersites, who puts on the form of a monkey, comment is unnecessary.

Accordingly, the expressions concerning the heroes' hatred of being born of woman seem to be purely metaphorical and employed to carry out logically the literary use of the animal-symbols, just as the passages are concerning 'animals tame and wild which changed into one another and into corresponding human natures—*the good into the gentle and the evil into the savage, in all sorts of combinations*', and of 'birds, on the other hand, like the swan and other musicians, wanting to be men'.

Even the ordinary soul, the first seen by Er to make choice—although neither an incarnate divinity like Orpheus or Agamemnon, nor a hero like Ajax—and though possessed of a mind obscured by animal propensities, is not assigned by Plato, as he would be by a believer in the exoteric rebirth doctrine, to birth in sub-human form. In his case, too, no animal-symbol is made use of:

'He who had the first choice came forward and in a moment chose the greatest tyranny; his mind having been darkened by folly and sensuality, he had not thought out the whole matter before he chose, and did not at first perceive that he was fated, among other evils, to devour his own children. . . . Now he was one of those who came from heaven, and in a former life had dwelt in a well-ordered State, but his virtue was a matter of habit only and he had no philosophy.'

And, as the *Bardo Thödol* teaches, in other language, in its insistence on the need of Right Knowledge to the devotee who follows the *Bodhic* Path, so Plato teaches:

'For if a man had always on his arrival in this world dedicated himself from the first to sound philosophy, and had been moderately fortunate in the number of the lot, he might, as the messenger reported, be happy here, and also his journey to another life and return to this, instead of being rough and underground, would be smooth and heavenly.'[1]

With the assistance of symbols and metaphors, Pindar, Empedocles, Pythagoras, and Socrates, like Plato and the Greek Mysteries, also taught the rebirth doctrine.

On a golden funereal tablet dug up near the site of Sybaris there is the following line of an inscription: 'And thus I escaped from the cycle, the painful, the misery-laden.'[2] This, like known Orphic teachings, is purely Buddhistic and Hindu, and suggests that in ancient Greece the rebirth doctrine was widespread, at least among Greeks of culture who had been initiated into the Mysteries.

Symbolism similar to that used by Plato has been used by the recorders of the Buddhist Scriptures as well, as, for example, in the account of the Northern School of the birth of the Buddha Himself. This latter from the Tibetan *Vinaya Pitaka* or *Dulva* (the most trustworthy and probably oldest part of the *Bkah-hgyur*), III, folio 452[a] of the copy in the East India Office, Calcutta, runs thus:

'Now the future Buddha was in the Tushita Heaven, and knowing that his time had come, he made the five preliminary examinations: first, of the proper family [in which to be born]; second, of the country; third, of the time; fourth, of the race; fifth, of the woman. And having decided that Mahāmāyā was the right mother, in the midnight watch he entered her womb under the appearance of an elephant. Then the queen had four dreams: first, she saw a six-tusked white elephant enter her womb; second, she moved in space above; third, she ascended a great rocky mountain; fourth, a great multitude bowed down to her.

'The soothsayers predicted that she would bring forth a son with the thirty-two signs of the great man. "If he stay at home, he will become a universal monarch; but if he shave his hair and beard, and, putting on an orange-coloured robe, leave his home for the homeless state and

---

[1] Cf. B. Jowett, *Dialogues of Plato* (Oxford, 1892), iii. 336–7: Republic, x. 614–20.

[2] *Inscr. gr. Sicil. et Ital. 641*; cf. Waddell, *The Buddhism of Tibet*, p. 109[2].

renounce the world, he will become a Tāthagata, Arhant, a perfectly enlightened Buddha." '

Again, the *Jātaka*,—of the Southern School,—a compilation of folk-lore, folk-belief, and popular mythology touching the Buddha and his many incarnations, which crystallized round about His personality in much the same way as the matter of the Arthurian Legend crystallized round about King Arthur, during the third century after His death [1]—attributes to Him many previous births in sub-human form ; and although the esotericist would concede that in remote aeons of evolution such incarnations could possibly have been really sub-human, he would give to such of them as may have occurred in this world-period a symbolical significance, whereas the orthodox Theravādist interprets all of them literally.

In any case, a literal interpretation of the *Jātaka*—seeing that it is, according to the esotericist, essentially an exoteric treatise designed for the people [2]—appears to be more plausible than that of the *Dulva* account of the Buddha's birth. Furthermore, since there is a parallel account in the Pali Scriptures wherein the same animal symbol, namely, the six-tusked white elephant, is employed, we have here an example of the use of symbolism, definite in purpose, common to both Northern and Southern Buddhism, which even the exotericist could not but interpret symbolically.

Similarly, as the popular interpretation appears to have fundamentally shaped the *Jātaka*, so it may have also affected the compilation of the *Bardo Thödol*; for like all treatises which have had at least a germ-origin in very ancient times and then grown up by the ordinary process of amalgamating congenial material, the *Bardo Thödol*, as a Doctrine of Death and Rebirth, seems to have existed at first unrecorded, like almost all sacred books now recorded in Pali, Sanskrit, or Tibetan, and was a growth of unknown centuries. Then by the time it had fully developed and been set down in writing

---

[1] Theravādists, on the contrary, believe that the *Jātaka* dates from the Buddha's lifetime, and that its verses, but not its prose, are His very words.

[2] Here, again, in opposition to this view, the Southern Buddhists maintain that the *Jātaka*, in its verses, is the most transcendental part of the *Sūtta Pitika*, and is designed for study by Bodhisattvas rather than for the common people.

no doubt it had lost something of its primitive purity. By its very nature and religious usage, the *Bardo Thödol* would have been very susceptible to the influence of the popular or exoteric view; and in our own opinion it did fall under it, in such manner as to attempt the impossible, namely, the harmonizing of the two interpretations. Nevertheless, its original esotericism is still discernible and predominant. Let us take, for example, the animal-thrones of the Five Dhyānī Buddhas as it describes them, in harmony with Northern Buddhist symbolology: the Lion-throne is associated with Vairochana, the Elephant-throne with Vajra-Sattva, the Horse-throne with Ratna-Sambhava, the Peacock-throne with Amitābha, the Harpy-throne with Amogha-Siddhi. And, in interpreting the symbols, we find them to be poetically descriptive of the peculiar attributes of each deity: the Lion symbolizes courage or might, and sovereign power; the Elephant, immutability; the Horse, sagacity and beauty of form; the Peacock, beauty and power of transmutation, because in popular belief it is credited with the power of eating poisons and transforming them into the beauty of its feathers; the Harpy, mightiness and conquest over all the elements. The deities, too, in the last analysis, are symbolical of particular *Bodhic* attributes of the *Dharma-Kāya* and of supramundane forces of Enlightenment emanating thence, upon which the devotee may depend for guidance along the Path to Buddhahood.

In attempting the esoteric interpretation of the animal symbols used in the *Sidpa Bardo*—and this interpretation finds its parallel in the esoteric interpretation obviously intended by the *Sidpa Bardo* episode in Plato, as in the *Dulva* account of the birth of the Buddha—we have sufficient Buddhist rebirth symbols whose esoteric interpretation is clearly known and generally accepted to guide us.

Dr. L. A. Waddell, a well-known authority on Lāmaism, in *Lāmaism in Sikhim*,[1] refers to the symbolism of the famous, but recently ruined, wall-painting of the *Sī-pa-ī-khor-lo* or 'Circle of Existence' in the Tashiding monastery, Sikkim, as follows: 'This picture is one of the purest Buddhist

[1] See *Gazetteer of Sikhim*, ed. by H. H. Risley, p. 266.

emblems that the *lāmas* have preserved for us. And by
its means I have been able to restore the fragment of a
cycle in the verandah of Ajaṇṭā Cave No. XVII, hitherto
uninterpreted, and merely known as "the Zodiac". This
picture portrays in symbolic and concrete form the three
original sins and the recognized causes of rebirth (*Nidānas*),
so as to ensure their being vividly perceived and avoided;
while the evils of existence in its various forms and the
tortures of the damned are intended to intimidate evil-doers.'
In it, the three original sins are depicted as a pig, a cock,
and a snake, and their esoteric significance is given by
Dr. Waddell thus: 'The pig symbolizes the ignorance of
stupidity; the cock, animal desire or lust; and the snake,
anger.'[1] In the accompanying symbolic illustrations of the
Twelve *Nidānas*, only the third is an animal symbol, the
others being human and figurative symbols; and this is
a monkey eating fruit, symbolizing entire knowledge (Tib.
nam-she; Skt. *Vijñāna*) of good and evil fruits, through
tasting every fruit or sensuous experience in the manner
of a roving non-philosophically guided libertine, thus en-
gendering consciousness.[2]

Accordingly, the animal forms and environments named
in the Second Book of the *Bardo Thödol* (see pp. 178-9, 185)
as possible forms and environments to be entered by the
human consciousness-principle upon rebirth in this world may
be interpreted as follows:

(1) The dog-form (like that of the cock in 'The Wheel of
Life') symbolizes excessive sexuality or sensuality.[3] It also
symbolizes, in popular Tibetan lore, jealousy. And the dog-
kennel environment symbolizes abiding in, or living in, a state
of sensuality.

(2) The pig symbolizes (as in 'The Wheel of Life') the
ignorance of stupidity dominated by lust; and selfishness

---

[1] See *Gazetteer of Sikhim*, ed. by H. H. Risley, p. 267.

[2] Ibid., p. 268.

[3] Compare the following passage from the *Yoga Vāshishtha* (*Nirvāṇa Praka-
raṇa, Sarga* 28, verses 78-9): 'Those wise Pandits, learned in the Shāstras,
should be considered Jackals if they relinquish not desire and anger.'

and uncleanliness as well. The pigsty environment symbolizes worldly existence dominated by these characteristics.

(3) The ant symbolizes (as it does amongst the nations of the West) industry, and the lust for worldly possessions; and the ant-hill environment the dwelling under the corresponding conditions of life.

(4) The insect or grub symbolizes an earthly or grovelling disposition, and its hole the dwelling in an environment dominated by such disposition (see text, p. 179).

(5) The calf, kid, lamb, horse, and fowl forms mentioned (see text, pp. 178-9) symbolize, in like manner, corresponding characteristics common to those animals and to the highest of the animal beings, man, such as almost all civilized races have associated therewith, and popularly illustrated in animal mythology like that which Aesop made the basis of his *Fables*. In the *Old Testament* the visions of the prophet Ezekiel and in the *New Testament* the *Revelation* of John show how similar animal symbolism affected even the *Bible*. And, in our view, should the Buddhist and Hindu exotericists re-read their own Scriptures in the light of the Science of Symbols their opposition to Esotericism would probably be given up.

Accordingly, the animal symbols in the *Sidpa Bardo*— despite evident corruptions of the text and of the esoteric rebirth doctrine denoted by these symbols—should rightly be taken to imply that, in accordance with its *karma*, a human principle of consciousness, unless winning Emancipation, will, under the normal *karmic* conditions of gradual progression which govern the majority of mankind, continue to be born in a human form in this creation-period, with the mental traits or characteristics symbolized by animals. Under exceptional or abnormal *karmic* conditions of retrogression, it may, on the other hand, during the course of ages, gradually lose its human nature and fall back into sub-human kingdoms.

As the translator explained, we need but look round us in the human world to find the bloodthirsty tiger-man, the murderer; the lustful swine-man; the deceitful fox-man; the thieving and imitating monkey-man; the grovelling worm-man; the industrious and oft-times miserly ant-man;

the ephemeral—sometimes professedly aesthetic—butterfly-man; the strong ox-man; or the fearless lion-man. Human life is far richer in possibilities for the workings out of evil *karma*—no matter how animal-like the *karma* may be—than any sub-human species could possibly be. The illiterate folk-beliefs so common in Buddhist and Hindu lands, that a human murderer must inevitably be reborn as a ferocious beast of prey, or a sensualist as a pig or dog, or a miser as an ant, are, therefore, like many other popular beliefs, evidently based upon false analogies—some of which have crept into Oriental Scriptures—and upon an unduly limited view of the innumerable conditions offered by human embodiment, from the saint to the criminal, from the King-Emperor to the slum-dweller, or from the man of culture to the lowest savage.

In accordance with our findings, that higher and rational teaching concerning rebirth, which in the *Bardo Thödol* is, perhaps, confused because of corruptions of text, may now be summarized. If, on the Plane of Uncertainty, the in-fluence of innate or *karmic* propensities of desire for the grosser sensations of *sangsāric* existence, such as govern life in a human body, can be dominated through the exercise of the more powerful influence of Right Knowledge, that part of the consciousness-principle capable of realizing Buddhahood triumphs, and the deceased, instead of being obsessed with the frightful hallucinatory spectres of his lower or animal nature, passes the interval between human death and rebirth in one of the paradise realms instead of in the *Bardo*. If such a more enlightened one be very unusually developed spiritually, that is to say if he be a great *yogīc* saint, he may gain even the highest of the paradises and be reborn among mankind under the guiding power of the 'Lords of *Karma*', who, though still *sangsāric* beings, are described by the *lāmas* as being immeasurably higher in evolution than man. When thus directed by the 'Guardians of the Great Law', the earth-returning one is said to reincarnate out of compassion, to assist human kind; he comes as a Teacher, as a Divine Missionary, as a *Nirmāṇa-Kāya*

incarnate. Normally, however, rebirth is of the lower or
ordinary sort, unendowed—because of the lack of enlightenment of the one undergoing it—with consciousness of
the process. Even as a child knowing not the higher
mathematics cannot measure the velocity of light, so the
animal-man cannot profit by the higher law governing the
rebirth of the divine-man; and, drinking of the River of
Forgetfulness, he enters the door of the womb and is reborn,
direct from the desire-world called the *Bardo*. This lower
rebirth, almost brutish in many instances, because controlled chiefly by animal propensities such as sub-human
and human creatures have in common, differs, however, from
that of brutes in virtue of the functional activity of the purely
human element of the consciousness, which in all sub-human
creatures is latent and not active ; and for this element, even
in the lowest of mankind, to become latent instead of active
requires approximately as long a period of cyclic time as it
does for the sub-human consciousnesss to evolve its latent
human element into full human activity. The popular misunderstanding of this aspect of the higher or esoteric Doctrine
of Rebirth thus appears to have assisted in no small measure
to give rise to the obviously irrational belief, found almost
everywhere throughout the Scriptures of both Buddhism and
Hinduism, that the brute principle of consciousness in its
entirety and the human principle of consciousness in its entirety
are capable of alternately exchanging places with one another.

It was the late Dr. E. B. Tylor, father of the modern
science of Anthropology, who after a very careful examination
of the data pronounced the higher doctrine of rebirth to be
the more reasonable :

‘ So it may seem that the original idea of transmigration
was the straightforward and reasonable one of human souls
being reborn in new human bodies. . . . The beast is the very
incarnation of familiar qualities of man ; and such names as
lion, bear, fox, owl, parrot, viper, worm, when we apply them
as epithets to men, condense into a word some leading feature
of a human life.’ [1]

[1] E. B. Tylor, *Primitive Culture* (London, 1891), ii. 17.

That this is the true interpretation is confirmed—so far as Europe is concerned—by the teachings of the Druids, the learned Brahmin-like priests of Europe's scientific pre-Christian religion, held by the Celtic nations.[1]

In *The Fairy-Faith in Celtic Countries*, in the year 1911, I suggested that the rebirth doctrine, in its straightforward, Druidic form, accords, in its essentials, with the psychological science of the West—that the subconscious mind is the storehouse of all latent memories; that these memories are not limited to one lifetime; that these memory-records, being recoverable, prove the doctrine to be based upon demonstrable facts. Since the year 1911 the whole trend of Western psychological research in the realm of the subconscious and in psycho-analysis has tended to confirm that view.

I was unaware when I wrote *The Fairy-Faith* that Huxley held—as he did—the theory of human reincarnation to offer the best explanation of even ordinary physiological and biological phenomena. And since the testimony of Huxley, as one of the greatest biologists, coincides with that, as above given, of the late Dr. Tylor, the foremost of modern anthropologists, and also confirms from the standpoint of our own Western Science the higher or esoteric interpretation of the Rebirth Doctrine as offered by the Occult Sciences of the East, we here record it as a fitting conclusion to this Section :

'Everyday experience familiarizes us with the facts which are grouped under the name of heredity. Every one of us bears upon him obvious marks of his parentage, perhaps of remoter relationships. More particularly, the sum of tendencies to act in a certain way, which we call "character", is often to be traced through a long series of progenitors and collaterals. So we may justly say that this "character"—this moral and intellectual essence of a man—does veritably pass over from one fleshly tabernacle to another, and does really transmigrate

---

[1] Cf. Caesar, *De B. G.* vi. 14. 5; 18. 1; Diodorus Siculus, v. 31. 4; Pomponius Mela, *De Situ Orbis*, iii, c. 2; Lucan, *Pharsalia*, i. 449–62; *Barddas* (Llandovery, 1862), i. 177, 189–91; and W. Y. Evans-Wentz, *The Fairy-Faith in Celtic Countries* (Oxford 1911), Chaps. VII, XII.

from generation to generation. In the new-born infant, the character of the stock lies latent, and the Ego is little more than a bundle of potentialities. But, very early, these become actualities; from childhood to age they manifest themselves in dullness or brightness,—weakness or strength, viciousness or uprightness; and with each feature modified by confluence with another character, if by nothing else, the character passes on to its incarnation in new bodies. The Indian philosophers called character, as thus defined, "*karma*". . . .

'In the theory of evolution, the tendency of a germ to develop according to a certain specific type, e.g. of the kidney-bean seed to grow into a plant having all the characters of *Phaseolus vulgaris*, is its "Karma". It is the "last inheritor and the last result" of all the conditions that have affected a line of ancestry which goes back for many millions of years, to the time when life first appeared on the earth. . . .

'As Prof. Rhys-Davids aptly says [in *Hibbert Lectures*, p. 114], the snowdrop "is a snowdrop and not an oak, and just that kind of snowdrop, because it is the outcome of the *Karma* of an endless series of past existences".'[1]

XI. THE COSMOGRAPHY

Buddhist cosmography as understood by the *lāmas*, and continually referred to throughout our text, more especially in connexion with the Doctrine of Rebirth, is a very vast and complex subject; and to consider it here in any detail would involve the esoteric as well as the exoteric interpretation of an enormous mass of doctrines, more or less of Brahmanic origin, concerning the many states of sentient existence within the *Sangsāra*, or cosmos—some planetary as in this world, some

---

[1] T. H. Huxley, *Evolution and Ethics* (London, 1894), pp. 61-2, 95.
The late William James, the well-known American psychologist, independently arrived at substantially the same conclusion as Huxley; for, after explaining his ' own inability to accept either popular Christianity or scholastic theism', he says, 'I am ignorant of Buddhism and speak under correction, and merely in order the better to describe my general point of view; but, as I apprehend the Buddhist doctrine of *Karma*, I agree in principle with that '.—(*The Varieties of Religious Experiences*, pp. 521-2.)

in the many heavens and paradises, and others in the numerous states of purgation called hells. Generalizing, it may be
said that when the Brahmanic and Buddhist teachings concerning cosmography are carefully examined from the standpoint of the initiated Oriental, and not from the too-oft
prejudiced standpoint of the Christian philologist, it seems to
suggest far-reaching knowledge, handed down from very
ancient times, of astronomy, of the shape and motion of
planetary bodies, and of the interpenetration of worlds and
systems of worlds, some solid and visible (such as are alone
known to Western Science) and some ethereal and invisible
existing in what we may perhaps call a fourth dimension of
space.

Esoterically explained, Mt. Meru (Tib. *Ri-rab*), the central
mountain of Hindu and Buddhist cosmography, round which our
cosmos is disposed in seven concentric circles of oceans separated
by seven intervening concentric circles of golden mountains,
is the universal hub, the support of all the worlds. We may
possibly regard it, like the Central Sun of Western astronomy,
as the gravitational centre of the known universe. Outside
the seven circles of oceans and the intervening seven circles of
golden mountains lies the circle of continents.

In illustration, an onion of fifteen layers may be taken to
represent roughly the *lāmaic* conception of our universe. The
core, to which the fifteen layers cohere, is Mt. Meru. Below,
are the various hells ; above, supported by Mt. Meru, are the
heavens of the gods, the more sensuous, like the thirty-three
heavens ruled by Indra, and those under the sway of Mārā,
being ranged in their own regular gradation beneath the less
sensuous heavens of Brāhma. As apex over all, is the final
heaven, called 'The Supreme' (Tib. *'Og-min*). Being the last
outpost of our universe, *'Og-min*, as the vestibule to *Nirvāṇa*, is the transitional state leading from the mundane to
the supramundane; and thus there presides over it the
divine influence of 'The Best of All' (Tib. *Kuntu-zang-
po*: Skt. *Samanta-Bhadra*), the *lāmaic* personification of
Nirvāṇa.

On a level with Indra's realm dwell, in their own heaven-worlds, the eight Mother Goddesses (Tib. *Hlāmo*), all of whom appear in our text. They are the Mother Goddesses of the early Hindus, called in Sanskrit the *Mātṛis*.

Within Mt. Meru itself, upon which the Heavens rest, there are four realms, one above another. Of these, the three lower are inhabited by various orders of genii; and in the fourth, immediately beneath the Heavens, from which, like the fallen angels of Christian belief, they were expelled on account of their pride, dwell the 'Ungodly Spirits', the *Asuras* (Tib. *Lha-ma-yin*), or Titans, who, as rebels, live and die waging unending war with the gods above.

The innermost layer of the onion is the Ocean surrounding Mt. Meru. The next layer, outwardly expanding, is that of the Golden Mountains; the next beyond is another Ocean; and so on, a circle of Golden Mountains always coming after a circle of Ocean until the fifteenth layer containing the outermost Ocean, in which float the Continents and their satellites. The skin of the onion is a wall of iron enclosing the one universe.

Beyond one such universe there lies another, and so on to infinity.[1] Each universe, like a great cosmic egg, is enclosed within the iron-wall shell, which shuts in the light of the sun and moon and stars, the iron-wall shell being symbolical of the perpetual darkness separating one universe from another. All universes alike are under the domination of natural law, with which *karma* is commonly made synonymous; for, in the Buddhist view, there is no scientific necessity to affirm or to deny the existence of a supreme God-Creator, the *Karmic* Law furnishing a complete explanation of all phenomena and being of itself demonstrable.

Each universe, like our own, rests upon 'a warp and woof' of blue air (i.e. ether), symbolized by crossed *dorjes* (such as are depicted by the emblem on the cover of our book). Upon

---

[1] Could we take the *lāmaic* conception of a universe to be that of a world-system, and of a plurality of universes to be that of a plurality of world-systems forming a universe, we should then be able better to correlate the cosmography of Northern Buddhism (and of Brahmanism, from which it appears to have originated) with the cosmography of Western Science.

this rests 'the body of the waters' of the outer Ocean. Each Ocean symbolizes a stratum of air (or ether), and each of the intervening mountains a stratum of congealed air (or ether), that is to say, material substance; or, from a more occult view-point, the Oceans are the Subtle and the Mountains the Gross, the one alternating with the other as Opposites.

Like the Seven Days of the Mosaic version of Creation, the numerical dimensions which the *lāmas* assign to our universe are more often to be taken as suggestive or symbolical than literal. Mt. Meru, they say, towers 80,000 miles above the Central Enchanted Ocean and extends below the surface of the waters the same distance, the Central Ocean itself being also 80,000 miles deep and 80,000 miles wide. The succeeding girdle of Golden Mountains is just half that number of miles in height and width and depth, and the next Ocean, correspondingly, 40,000 miles deep and 40,000 miles wide. The consecutive circles of alternating pairs composed of Golden Mountains and an Enchanted Ocean gradually diminish as to width, depth, and height, being respectively 20,000, 10,000, 5,000, 2,500, 1,250, and 625 miles. This brings us to the Continents in the Outer Ocean of Space.

Of these Continents, the four chief ones—as described in the Second Book of our *Bardo Thödol*—are situated in the Four Directions. On either side of each of these Four Continents are smaller or satellite Continents, thus making the total number of Continents twelve, which, again, is a symbolical number, like the number seven of the cosmographical arrangement.

The Eastern Continent is called in Tibetan Lü-pah (*Lus-hpags*), or 'Vast Body' (Skt. *Virāt-deha*). Its symbolical shape is like that of a crescent moon; and, accordingly, the colour white is assigned to it, and crescentic faces are ascribed to its inhabitants, who are said to be tranquil-minded and virtuous. Its diameter is given as being 9,000 miles.

The Southern Continent is our Planet Earth, called Jambuling (Skt. *Jambudvīpa*), probably an onomatopoeic word—as the translator held—descriptive of the fruit of a jambu-tree falling into water, *ling* itself meaning 'place', or 'region'.

The name *Jambuling* would thus mean the region or continent wherein jambu-fruit fall into the water. Its symbolic shape is like that of the shoulder-blade of a sheep, that is sub-triangular, or rather pear-shaped, to which the faces of its inhabitants conform. Blue is the colour assigned to it. Riches and plenty abound in it, along with both good and evil. It is said to be the smallest of the Four Continents, being but 7,000 miles in diameter.

The Western Continent is called Balongchöd (*Ba-glang-spyöd*), literally meaning *cow + ox + action* (Skt. *Godhana*, or 'Wealth of Oxen'). In shape it is like the sun, and red of colour. Its inhabitants, whose faces are round like the sun, are believed to be very powerful and to be addicted to eating cattle, as the literal meaning of its name itself may suggest. Its diameter measures 8,000 miles.

The Northern Continent is Daminyan, or Graminyan (*Sgra-mi-snyan*), equivalent to the Sanskrit *Uttara Kuru*, meaning 'Northern Kuru [Race]'. It is of square shape and green colour. Its inhabitants have corresponding faces, square like those of horses. Trees supply all their sustenance and wants, and the Kuru, on dying, haunt the trees as tree-spirits. This is the largest of the Continents, being 10,000 miles in diameter.

Each satellite Continent resembles the Continent to which it is attached, and is one-half its size. The left Satellite of our world (*Jambuling*), called *Ngāyabling*, is, for example, the world of the *Rākṣhasas*, to which Padma Sambhava, the Great *Guru* of Lāmaism, is believed to have gone to teach the *Rākṣhasas* goodness and salvation, and to be there now as their king.[1]

Underlying this *lāmaic* cosmology there is, as research will show, an elaborate symbolism. Take, for instance, the description of Mt. Meru as given by Dr. Waddell : 'Its eastern face is of silver, the south of jasper, the west of ruby, and the north of gold'[2]—which illustrates a use of ancient symbols very similar to that in the *Revelation* of John. The complete rational explanation of all the symbolism connected with

[1] Cf. *Gazetteer of Sikhim*, pp. 320–3.
[2] Cf. ibid., p. 322.

Hindu and in turn Buddhist cosmography would be—even if it were possible for us—quite beyond the scope of an introduction. Suffice it to say that the possession of a key to such explanation is claimed by expert professors of the Occult Sciences in India and in Tibet—compared to which, in the realm of mind and matter, our Western Science is, so they maintain, but at the Threshold of the Temple of Understanding.

XII. THE FUNDAMENTAL TEACHINGS SUMMARIZED

Ere passing on to the final Sections of this Introduction, touching the Manuscript itself, we may now summarize the chief teachings upon which the whole of the *Bardo Thödol* is based, as follows:

1. That all possible conditions, or states, or realms of *sangsāric* existence, heavens, hells, and worlds, are entirely dependent upon phenomena, or, in other words, are nought but phenomena;

2. That all phenomena are transitory, are illusionary, are unreal, and non-existent save in the *sangsāric* mind perceiving them;

3. That in reality there are no such beings anywhere as gods, or demons, or spirits, or sentient creatures—all alike being phenomena dependent upon a cause;

4. That this cause is a yearning or thirsting after sensation, after the unstable *sangsāric* existence;

5. That so long as this cause is not overcome by Enlightenment death follows birth and birth death, unceasingly—even as the wise Socrates believed;

6. That the after-death existence is but a continuation, under changed conditions, of the phenomena-born existence of the human world—both states alike being *karmic*;

7. That the nature of the existence intervening between death and rebirth in this or any other world is determined by antecedent actions;

8. That, psychologically speaking, it is a prolonged dream-like state, in what may be called the fourth dimension of space, filled with hallucinatory visions directly resultant from

the mental-content of the percipient, happy and heaven-like if the *karma* be good, miserable and hell-like if the *karma* be bad ;

9. That, unless Enlightenment be won, rebirth in the human world, directly from the *Bardo*-world or from any other world or from any paradise or hell to which *karma* has led, is inevitable ;

10. That Enlightenment results from realizing the unreality of the *sangsāra*, of existence ;

11. That such realizing is possible in the human world, or at the important moment of death in the human world, or during the whole of the after-death or *Bardo*-state, or in certain of the non-human realms ;

12. That training in *yoga*, i.e. in control of the thinking processes so as to be able to concentrate the mind in an effort to reach Right Knowledge, is essential ;

13. That such training can best be had under a human *guru*, or teacher ;

14. That the Greatest of *Gurus* known to mankind in this cycle of time is Gautama the Buddha ;

15. That His Doctrine is not unique, but is the same Doctrine which has been proclaimed in the human world for the gaining of Salvation, for the Deliverance from the Circle of Rebirth and Death, for the Crossing of the Ocean of *Sangsāra*, for the Realization of *Nirvāṇa*, since immemorial time, by a long and illustrious Dynasty of Buddhas, who were Gautama's Predecessors ;

16. That lesser spiritually enlightened beings, Bodhisattvas and *gurus*, in this world or in other worlds, though still not freed from the Net of Illusion, can, nevertheless, bestow divine grace and power upon the *shishya* (i.e. the *chela*, or disciple) who is less advanced upon the Path than themselves ;

17. That the Goal is and can only be Emancipation from the *Sangsāra* ;

18. That such Emancipation comes from the Realization of *Nirvāṇa* ;

19. That *Nirvāṇa* is non-*sangsāric*, being beyond all paradises, heavens, hells, and worlds ;

20. That it is the Ending of Sorrow;
21. That it is Reality.

He who realized *Nirvāṇa*, the Buddha Gautama Himself, has spoken of it to His own disciples thus:

'There is, disciples, a Realm devoid of earth and water, fire and air. It is not endless space, nor infinite thought, nor nothingness, neither ideas nor non-ideas. Not this world nor that is it. I call it neither a coming nor a departing, nor a standing still, nor death, nor birth; it is without a basis, progress, or a stay; it is the ending of sorrow.

'For that which clingeth to another thing there is a fall; but unto that which clingeth not no fall can come. Where no fall cometh, there is rest, and where rest is, there is no keen desire. Where keen desire is not, naught cometh or goeth; and where naught cometh or goeth there is no death, no birth. Where there is neither death nor birth, there neither is this world nor that, nor in between—it is the ending of sorrow.

'There is, disciples, an Unbecome, Unborn, Unmade, Unformed; if there were not this Unbecome, Unborn, Unmade, Unformed, there would be no way out for that which is become, born, made, and formed; but since there is an Unbecome, Unborn, Unmade, Unformed, there is escape for that which is become, born, made, and formed.'[1]

XIII. THE MANUSCRIPT

Our manuscript copy of the *Bardo Thödol* was procured by the editor early in the year 1919 from a young *lāma* of the Kargyutpa Sect of the Red Hat School attached to the Bhutia Basti Monastery, Darjeeling, who said that it had been handed down in his family for several generations. The manuscript is unlike any other seen by the translator or editor, in that it is illustrated by paintings in colour painted on the folios of the text. All other similarly illustrated Tibetan manuscripts seen by us have had the illustrations made on separate pieces of manuscript paper or else of cotton cloth, pasted to the folios. When procured, the

---

[1] *Udāna*, viii. 1, 4, 3; based on a translation from the original Pali by Mr. Francis J. Payne, London, England.

manuscript was in a very ragged and worn condition, now remedied by each folio being inserted in a protective frame of Tibetan paper of the same sort as that upon which the manuscript is written. Fortunately, all of the illuminated folios, though faded, were in a fair state of preservation. One of the ordinary folios, folio number III, was missing, but this has now been replaced by a faithful copy of the same passage found in a Block-Print version of the *Bardo Thödol* belonging to Dr. Johan Van Manen, Secretary of the Asiatic Society, Calcutta, well known as a Tibetan scholar. Reference to this Block-Print version is made throughout our translation. In all essentials, and, generally, word for word, our manuscript and Dr. Van Manen's Block-Print were found to be identical. In some spellings of proper names of deities of Sanskrit origin there are variations in the two versions, and in both books a number of clerical errors. The manuscript is far older than the modern Block-Print and seems to have been copied from an earlier manuscript.

The manuscript itself is undated, but the translator judged it to be from 150 to 200 years old. It has seen very much service, having been read many times over the dead; its ragged and worn condition is, therefore, no criterion—as it might seem to be—of its age. It is written in an excellent hand on the ordinary paper used for manuscripts among the Tibetans and Himalayan peoples, made from the pulped bark of the *Hdal* (pronounced *Dāā*), otherwise known as Daphne, a kind of laurel of which one species bears a purplish white blossom, another a yellowish white. It is usually by *lāmas* in a monastery that the paper is manufactured. On account of the bark of the *Hdal* being extremely tough, the Sikkimese used it as ropes.

The total number of folios composing the manuscript is 137, each measuring about 9½ by 3¼ inches. Excepting the first folio and the first half of the second, the space actually occupied by the text on each measures on an average 8¼ by 2¼ inches. Most of the folios contain five lines of matter, a few contain four lines. The title-page contains two lines in a space 7 by 1 inches; the second page of the first folio along with the first page of the second folio, which give the Obeisances, consist of three lines, occupying a space $4\frac{1}{2}$ by $2\frac{1}{4}$ inches respectively, and these, like the title-page, are written in gold (now much faded) on a black background. The illustrations are on fourteen of the folios, each illustration being in the centre of the text, on one side of the folio (see Frontispiece), as follows:

On folio 18, Vairochana embraced by his *shakti*, the Mother of the Space of Heaven, seated upon a lion throne, the deities of the First Day;

On folio 20, Vajra-Sattva, embraced by his *shakti*, the Mother Māmakī, surrounded by their four accompanying deities of the Second Day;

On folio 23, Ratna-Sambhava, embraced by his *shakti*, the Mother Sangyay Chanma ('She of the Buddha Eye'), surrounded by their four accompanying deities of the Third Day;

On folio 26, Amitābha, embraced by his *shakti*, the Mother Gökarmo ('She of White Raiment'), surrounded by their four accompanying deities of the Fourth Day;

On folio 31, Amogha-Siddhi, embraced by his *shakti*, the Faithful Dölma (or Skt. *Tārā*), surrounded by their four accompanying deities of the Fifth Day;

On folio 35, the united *maṇḍalas* of the deities that dawn on the Sixth Day;

On folio 44, the *maṇḍala* of the Ten Knowledge-Holding Deities of the Seventh Day;

On folio 55, the Buddha Heruka and *shakti* of the Eighth Day;

On folio 57, the Vajra Heruka and *shakti* of the Ninth Day;

On folio 58, the Ratna Heruka and *shakti* of the Tenth Day;

On folio 59, the Padma Heruka and *shakti* of the Eleventh Day;

On folio 61, the Karma Heruka and *shakti* of the Twelfth Day;

On folio 64, the Eight Kerima and the Eight Htamenma of the Thirteenth Day; and the Four Female Door-keepers of the Fourteenth Day;

On folio 67, the *maṇḍala* of the animal-headed deities of the Fourteenth Day.

Each deity is depicted in conformity with the description given in the text as to colour, position, posture, *mudrā*, and symbols.

All of the illustrations in the manuscript thus belong to the *Chönyid Bardo* of the First Book. In our translation, copious annotations contain the textual name of each deity and the Sanskrit equivalent when, as in most cases, there is one.

No attempt has been made to collate our manuscript with other manuscripts of the same text, none having been available. Such manuscripts are, no doubt, numerous in Tibet, and the production of a standard or uniform text would require years of careful labour—a task remaining for scholars of the future. The only comparison of texts attempted was with Dr. Van Manen's Block-Print, which is probably not more than about twenty to thirty years old. The translator said that, so far as he was aware, Block-Prints of the *Bardo Thödol* have appeared—at least in Sikkim and Darjeeling—rather recently, although probably known in Tibet itself much longer, block-type printing having been carried on for unknown centuries in China, and thence brought to Tibet, long before printing was done in Europe.[1]

---

[1] These Block-Prints are usually composed of separate treatises belonging to the *Bardo Thödol* cycle. One of such Block-Prints—which was purchased in Gyantse, Tibet, during the year 1919, by Major W. L. Campbell, then the British Political Representative in Tibet, Bhutan, and Sikkim, and presented to the editor—contains seventeen treatises, whose Tibetan titles have been rendered, in slightly abbreviated form, by the translator, as follows:

1. 'The Clear Directions on The Divine *Bardo*, called "The Great Liberation by Hearing", from "The Profound Doctrine of the Divine Peaceful and [Wrathful] Self-Liberation"';

2. 'The Exposition of the Wrathful [or Active] Aspect of the *Bardo*';

3. 'The Good Wishes [or Prayers] Invoking the Buddhas and Bodhisattvas for Assistance';

4. 'The Root Verses of the *Bardo*';

5. 'The Prayer to Rescue [One] from the Narrow Places of the *Bardo*';

Each Buddhist Sect in Tibet, according to the opinion of the translator, probably has its own version of the *Bardo Thödol* more or less changed in some details, but not in essentials, from our version, the version used by the reformed Gelugpa, otherwise known as the Yellow-Hat School, being the most altered, with all references to Padma Sambhava, the Founder of the Ñingmapa, the Red-Hat School of Lāmaism, as well as the names of deities peculiar to the Red-Hats, expurgated.

Major W. L. Campbell, who was the British Political Representative in Sikkim during my residence there, wrote to me, from the Residency in Gangtok, under date of the twelfth of July, 1919, concerning the various versions of the *Bardo Thödol*, as follows: 'The Yellow Sect have six, the Red Sect seven, and the *Kar-gyut-pas* five.'

Our text being of the primitive or Red-Hat School and attributed to the Great *Guru* Padma Sambhava himself, who introduced Tantric Buddhism into Tibet, has been deemed by us to be substantially representative of the original version, which, on the basis of internal evidence derived from our

6. 'The Setting-Face-to-Face of the *Sidpa-Bardo*';

7. 'The Salvation by Attaching [whereby] the Body Aggregate is Self-Liberated'—a version of the *Tadhol* Doctrine—(see pp. 136¹, 152³, 194 of our text);

8. 'The Prayer to Protect [One] from the Fears in the *Bardo*';

9. 'The Self-Liberating Diagnosis of the Symptoms of Death'—(cf. pp. 86, 89–97 of our text);

10. 'The Setting-Face-to-Face called "The Naked Vision", and the Self-Liberation [by that]';

11. 'The Special Teaching showing the Forms of Merit or Demerit, while in the *Sidpa Bardo*, called "The Self-Liberating in the *Sidpa-Bardo*"';

12. 'The Addenda [to the above, "The Special Teaching"]';

13. 'Prayer to the Line [of *Gurus*] of the Divine Self-Liberating Doctrine';

14. 'The Ransoming of the Dying';

15. 'Self-Liberation called "Absolution by Confession"';

16. 'The Best Wish-Granting *Tadhol*'—another form of the *Tadhol* Doctrine;

17. 'The Ritual called "The Self-Liberation from Habitual Propensities"'.

Herein, the treatises numbered 1, 2, 3, 4, 5, 6, 8 correspond—in slightly different versions—to the matter contained in our manuscript. The manuscript, moreover, contains much matter in the Appendix not contained in this Block-Print. The Block-Print itself is quite new, but the blocks from which it was printed may be quite old—how old, we have been unable to ascertain.

manuscript text, was probably, at least in essentials, pre-Buddhistic.

As elsewhere noted, our manuscript is arranged as one work in two parts or books, with thirteen folios of texts of *Bardo* prayers as an appendix at the end. The Block-Print is arranged as two distinct books and lacks the appendix of prayers. But at the end of the first book of the Block-Print there comes a very important account of the origin of the *Bardo Thödol*, which is not contained in our manuscript, and this is given in translation in the following Section.

XIV. THE ORIGIN OF THE *BARDO THÖDOL*

Thus, from the Block-Print, and also from other Tibetan sources, we learn that the *Bardo Thödol* text originated, or, what is perhaps more correct, was first committed to writing in the time of Padma Sambhava, in the eighth century A. D.; was subsequently hidden away, and then, when the time came for it to be given to the world, was brought to light by Rigzin Karma Ling-pa. The Block-Print account is as follows :

'This has been brought from the Hill of Gampodar (Tib. *Gampo-dar*), on the bank of the Serdan (Tib. *Gser-ldan*, meaning 'Possessing Gold' or 'Golden') River, by Rigzin Karma Ling-pa (Tib. *Rigs-hdzin Kar-ma Gling-pa*).'

Rigzin, as herein given, is a personal title, and *Karma Ling-pa* the name of a place in Tibet meaning 'Karma Land'. The translator has pointed out that *Rigs* is an erroneous spelling of Rig; for, if *Rigs* were correct, the name *Rigzin* would mean Class-Holder (*Rigs + hZin*). That *Rig* is intended—thus making the name mean Knowledge-Holder (*Rig + hdzin*), a caste or class designation [1]—was confirmed by a small section of a *Bardo Thödol* manuscript in the possession of the translator, in which Rigzin Karma Ling-pa is otherwise called *Tertön* (Tib. *Gter-bstön*), or 'Taker-Out of Treasures'. The *Bardo Thödol* is, therefore, one of the Tibetan Lost

---

[1] *Rig-hdzin*, a translation into Tibetan of the Sanskrit term *Vidyā-Dhara*, used, as herein, of a learned person, such as a pandit, also denotes a class of supernatural beings like certain orders of fairies.

Books recovered by Rigzin of Karma Ling-pa, who is held to be an emanation or incarnation of Padma Sambhava, the Founder of Lāmaism.

It was in the eighth century A. D. that Lāmaism, which we may define as Tantric Buddhism, took firm root in Tibet. A century earlier, under the first king to rule over a united Tibet, King Srong-Tsan-Gampo (who died in A. D. 650), Buddhism itself entered Tibet from two sources: from Nepal, the land of the Buddha's ancestors, through the Tibetan King's marriage with a daughter of the royal family of Nepal; and from China, through his marriage—in the year 641—with a princess of the Chinese Imperial Family. The King had been nurtured in the old Bön faith of Tibet, which, with its primitive doctrine of rebirth, was quite capable of serving as an approach to Buddhism; and under the influence of his two Buddhist wives he accepted Buddhism, making it the state religion; but it made little headway in Tibet until a century later, when his powerful successor, Thī-Srong-Detsan, held the throne from A.D. 740 to 786. It was Thī-Srong-Detsan who invited Padma Sambhava (Tib. *Pēdma Jungnē*, i.e. 'The Lotus-Born'), better known to the Tibetans as *Guru Rin-po-ch'e*, 'The Precious *Guru*', to come to Tibet. The famous *Guru* was at that time a Professor of *Yoga* in the great Buddhist University of Nālanda, India, and far-famed for expert knowledge of the Occult Sciences. He was a native of Udyāna or Swat, in what is now a part of Afghanistan.

The Great *Guru* saw the wonderful opportunity which the King's invitation offered, and promptly accepted the call, passing through Nepal and arriving at Samye (*Sam-yas*), Tibet, in the year 747. It was to Samye that the King had invited him, in order to have exorcized the demons of the locality; for as soon as the walls of a monastery which the King was having erected there were raised they were overthrown by local earthquakes, which the demons opposing Buddhism were believed to have caused. When the Great *Guru* had driven out the demons, all the local earthquakes ceased, much to the wonder of the people; and he himself supervised the completion of the royal monastery, and established therein the first community of Tibetan Buddhist *lāmas*, in the year 749.

During his sojourn in Tibet at that time, and during subsequent visits, Padma Sambhava had many Tantric books translated into Tibetan out of Indian Sanskrit originals—some of which have been preserved in the monasteries of Tibet—and hidden away with appropriate mystic ceremonies in various secret places. He also endowed certain of his disciples with the *yogīc* power of reincarnating at the proper time, as determined by astrology, in order to take them out, along with the treasures hidden away with them and the requisites needed for properly performing the rites described in the texts. This is the generally accepted tradition; but according to another tradition the *Tertons* are to be regarded as various incarnations of the Great *Guru* himself. According to a rough estimate, the religious texts already taken out by such *Tertons*, from century to century, would form an encyclopædia of about sixty-five volumes of block-prints, each, on an average, consisting of about four hundred ordinary-sized folios.

Our text, the *Bardo Thödol*, being one of these recovered apocryphal books, should, therefore, be regarded as having been compiled (for the internal evidence suggests that it was a Tibetan compilation rather than a direct translation from some unknown Sanskrit original) during the first centuries of Lāmaism, either—as it purports to have been—in the time of Padma Sambhava or soon afterwards. Its present general use all over Tibet as a funeral ritual and its acceptance by the different sects, in varying versions, could not have been the outcome of a few generations; it testifies rather convincingly to its antiquity, bears out the pre-Buddhistic and at least partially Bön origin which we attribute to it, and suggests some validity in the claims made for the *Tertons*.

We are well aware of the adverse criticisms passed by European critics on the *Terton* tradition. There is not lacking, nevertheless, sound reason for suspecting that the European critics are not altogether right. Therefore, it seems to us that the only sound attitude to assume towards the *Terton* problem is to keep an open mind until sufficient data accumulate to

pronounce judgement. Though the *Terton* claim be proven
false, the fact that the *Bardo Thödol* is now accepted as
a sacred book in Tibet and has for some considerable time
been used by the *lāmas* for reading over the dead would, of
course, not be affected; only the theory concerning the
textual compilation of what, in its essentials, is apparently
a prehistoric ritual would be subject to revision.

As for Padma Sambhava's own sources, apart from such
congenial traditional teachings as no doubt he incorporated in
some of his Tibetan treatises, we are told, by oral tradition
now current among the *lāmas*, that he had eight *gurus* in
India, each representing one of the eight chief Tantric
doctrines.

In a Tibetan block-print, which belonged to the translator,
purporting to record the history, but much mixed with myth,
of the Great *Guru*, entitled *Orgyan-Padmas-mzad-pahi-bkah-
thang-bsdūd-pa* (pronounced *Ugyan Padmay-zad-pai-ba-thang-
dü-pa*), meaning 'The Abridged Testament made by Ugyan
Padma' (or 'by the Lotus-Born Ugyan'—Padma Sambhava),
consisting of but seventeen folios, there is recorded on the
twelfth folio, sixteenth section, the following passage, confirming the historical tradition touching the origin of the *Bardo
Thödol* text:

'Behold! the Sixteenth Section, showing the Eight Ling-
pas, the Leaders of Religion, is [thus]:

'The Eight Incarnations of the Great Bodhisattvas are:
            'Ugyan-ling-pa, in the centre;
            'Dorje-ling-pa, in the east;
            'Rinchen-ling-pa, in the south;
            'Padma-ling-pa, in the west;
            'Karma-ling-pa, in the north;
            'Samten-ling-pa and Nyinda-ling,
            '[And] Shig-po-ling (or Terdag-ling).
            'These Eight Great *Tertons* shall come;
            'Mine own incarnations alone are they.'

Padma Sambhava himself is herein represented as declaring
that the *Tertons*, or 'Takers-out' of the hidden books, are to

be his own incarnations. According to this account, the *Terton* of our own book, the *Bardo Thödol*, is the fifth, named after the place called Karma Land, thus confirming the Block-Print of the *Bardo Thödol*; and Karma Land is in the northern quarter of Tibet. We have been unable to ascertain the exact time in which this *Terton* lived, although he is a popular figure in the traditional history of Tibet. The name Rigzin, given to him in the Block-Print first above quoted, meaning 'Knowledge-Holder', refers to his character as a religious devotee or *lāma*; *Karma ling-pa*, as given in both accounts, refers also to an ancient Tibetan monastery of primitive Lāmaism in the Kams Province, northern Tibet.

According to our view, the best attitude to take touching the uncertain history and origin of the *Bardo Thödol* is that of a critical truth-seeker who recognizes the anthropological significance of the passing of time, and of the almost inevitable reshaping of ancient teachings handed down at first orally and then, after having crystallized, being recorded in writing. As in the case of the Egyptian *Bardo Thödol*, popularly known as 'The Egyptian Book of the Dead', so in 'The Tibetan Book of the Dead', there is, no doubt, the record of the belief of innumerable generations in a state of existence after death. No one scribe could have been its author and no one genera-tion its creator; its history as a book, if completely known, could only be the history of its compilation and recording; and the question, Whether this compilation and recording were done within comparatively recent times, or in the time of Padma Sambhava or earlier? could not fundamentally affect the ancient teachings upon which it is based.

Although it is remarkably scientific in its essentials, there is no need to consider it as being accurate in all its details; for, undoubtedly, considerable corruption has crept into the text. In its broad outlines, however, it seems to convey a sublime truth, heretofore veiled to many students of religion, a philo-sophy as subtle as that of Plato, and a psychical science far in advance of that, still in its infancy, which forms the study of the Society for Psychical Research. And, as such, it deserves the serious attention of the Western World, now awakening to a New Age, freed, in large measure, from the incrustations of medievalism, and eager to garner wisdom from all the Sacred Books of mankind, be they of one Faith or of another.

XV. THE TRANSLATING AND THE EDITING

Although the translating of this manuscript was done wholly in the presence of the editor in Gangtok, Sikkim, the chief credit should be given to the late Lāma Kazi Dawa-Samdup, the translator. The Lāma himself aptly summarized the editor's part in the work by saying that the editor was his living English dictionary. Indeed the editor could have been little more than this, for his knowledge of Tibetan was almost as nothing.

The aim of both the translator and the editor has been to keep as closely to the sense of the text as the idiomatic structures of the Tibetan and English tongues permit. Sometimes the translator, preferring to render into English the real meaning which a *lāma* would derive from certain more or less technically-worded phrases, has departed from a strictly literal translation.

The Tibetan of Tantric texts, such as ours, is especially difficult to turn into good English; and owing to the terseness of many passages it has been necessary to interpolate words and phrases, which are bracketed.

In years to come, it is quite probable that our rendering—as has been the case with the pioneer translations of the *Bible*—may be subject to revision. A strictly literal render-ing of a work so abstruse in its real meanings as this, and written in symbolical language as well, if attempted by Europeans—who, finding it difficult to get out of their Western mentality, too often are Christians first and scholars second when working with non-Christian sacred texts—would, perhaps, be as misleading as some of their renderings of the ancient Sanskrit *Vedas*. Even to a Tibetan, unless he be a *lāma* and well versed in Tantricism, as the translator was, the *Bardo Thödol* is almost a sealed book.

His profound *lāmaic* training, his fervent faith in the higher *yogic* teachings of The Great Perfectionist School of *Guru*

Padma Sambhava (he being an initiate of the semi-reformed sect known as Kargyutpa, founded by the great *yogīs* Marpa and Milarepa), his practical knowledge of the Occult Sciences as taught to him by his late *Guru* in Bhutan, and his marvellous command both of English and of Tibetan, lead me to think that rarely, if ever again in this century, is there likely to arise a scholar more competent to render the *Bardo Thödol* than the late Lāma Kazi Dawa-Samdup, the actual translator. To him each reader of this book owes a debt of gratitude; for herein he has, in part, opened to the peoples of the West the treasure-house, so long tightly locked, of Tibetan Literature and Northern Buddhism.

As his close disciple for many months, I hereby formally acknowledge that debt of gratitude and respect which is ever due from the disciple to the teacher.

Though the translation was completed and revised by the translator during the year 1919, whilst he was the Head Master of the Maharaja's Bhutia Boarding School, chiefly for Sikkimese boys of good Tibetan ancestry, near Gangtok, Sikkim (formerly a part of Tibet), it is unfortunate for us that he is not now in this world to read the printer's proofs of it as he had hoped to do.

As to the transliterations, it may rightly be objected by philologists that they are in some instances less technically exact than they might be. The editor, however, preferring to preserve the simpler transliterations according to the old-fashioned style—to which ordinary readers are more accustomed—just as the translator dictated them to him, has left them unchanged save for the correcting of a few obvious errors which had crept in.

The editor himself cannot expect, in a book of this nature, that his own interpretations of controversial problems will meet with universal acceptance; nor can he hope to have escaped all error. He trusts, however, that critics, in recognizing the pioneer character of the work, will be prepared to concede to the editor, as to the translator, such measure of indulgence as it may perhaps seem to deserve.

A brief account of the unusual career of the translator will, no doubt, be interesting to all who read this book. The late Lāma Kazi Dawa-Samdup—the honorific term Kazi indicating his superior social standing as a member of a landholding family of Tibetan origin settled in Sikkim—was born on the seventeenth day of June, 1868.

From December of the year 1887 and until October, 1893, as a young man whose learning the British authorities of India had already recognized, he was stationed at Buxaduar, in Bhutan, as Interpreter to the British Government. (In later years he also acted as Interpreter to the Government of Tibet.) It was at Buxaduar that he first met his *guru*, commonly known there as The Hermit *Guru* Norbu (*Slob-dpon-mtshams-pa-Norbu*—pronounced *Lob-on-tsham-pa-Norbu*), a man of vast knowledge and of strict ascetical habits of life; and from him, afterwards, received the mystic initiation.

The late Lāma Kazi Dawa-Samdup once confided to me that at that time he had made all necessary preparations, as a *shishya* on probation, to renounce the world completely; but his father, then an old man, called him home and requested him to perform the usual duties of an eldest son and marry, to perpetuate the family. The son had no option, and he married; two sons and one daughter being born to him.

In the year 1906 the Mahārāja of Sikkim appointed him Head Master of the Gangtok School, where, in the early part of the year 1919, I first met him, through a letter of introduction from Mr. S. W. Laden La, Sardar Bahadur, Chief of Police, Darjeeling, who is a well-known Buddhist Scholar of Tibetan ancestry. About a year later, in 1920, after our work together was finished, the Lāma was appointed Lecturer in Tibetan to the University of Calcutta; but, very unfortunately, as is usual with peoples habituated to the high Himalayan regions, he lost his health completely in the tropical climate of Calcutta, and departed from this world on the twenty-second day of March, 1922.

As records of the Lāma's ripe scholarship, there are his *English-Tibetan Dictionary*, published by the University of Calcutta in 1919, and his edition of the *Shrīchakrasambhāra*

Tantra, with English translation and Tibetan text, published by Sir John Woodroffe (pseudonym, Arthur Avalon) as volume ii of *Tantrik Texts*, London, 1919. In addition to these, and a few small works published by the Asiatic Society of Calcutta, the Lāma left behind him many important translations out of the Tibetan, as yet unpublished, some with the editor, others with Sir E. Denison Ross and with Major W. L. Campbell.

May this book help further to perpetuate the memory of him who revered the teachings of the Great Masters of Tibetan Wisdom and bequeathed this translation of the *Bardo Thödol* to the English-speaking peoples of the world.

'The *Dharma-Kāya* of thine own mind thou shalt see; and seeing That, thou shalt have seen the All—The Vision Infinite, the Round of Death and Birth and the State of Freedom.'—Milarepa.

Jetsün Kahbum, xii (Lāma Kazi Dawa-Samdup's Translation.)

[BOOK I]

[THE *CHIKHAI BARDO* AND THE *CHÖNYID BARDO*]

HEREIN LIETH THE SETTING-FACE-TO-FACE TO THE REALITY IN THE INTERMEDIATE STATE: THE GREAT DELIVERANCE BY HEARING WHILE ON THE AFTER-DEATH PLANE, FROM 'THE PROFOUND DOCTRINE OF THE EMANCIPATING OF THE CONSCIOUSNESS BY MEDITATION UPON THE PEACEFUL AND WRATHFUL DEITIES'[1]

[1] Text: ZAB-CHÖS ZHI-KHRO DGONGS-PA RANG-GRÖL LAS BAR-DOHI THÖS-GROL CHEN-MO CHÖS-NYID BAR-DOHI NGO-SPRÖD BZHUGS-SO (pronounced: ZAB-CHÖ SHI-HTO GONG-PA RANG-DÖL LAY BAR-DOI THÖ-DOL CHEN-MO CHÖ-NYID BAR-DOI NGO-TÖD ZHU-SO).

DEATH'S MESSENGERS

'ALL they who thoughtless are, nor heed,
What time Death's messengers appear,
Must long the pangs of suffering feel
In some base body habiting.
But all those good and holy men,
What time they see Death's messengers,
Behave not thoughtless, but give heed
To what the Noble Doctrine says;
And in attachment frighted see
Of birth and death the fertile source,
And from attachment free themselves,
Thus birth and death extinguishing.
Secure and happy ones are they,
Released from all this fleeting show;
Exempted from all sin and fear,
All misery have they overcome.'

Anguttara-Nikāya, iii. 35[5] (Warren's Translation).

[THE OBEISANCES]

To the Divine Body of Truth,[1] the Incomprehensible, Bound-
    less Light;
To the Divine Body of Perfect Endowment,[2] Who are the
    Lotus and the Peaceful and the Wrathful Deities; [3]
To the Lotus-born Incarnation, Padma Sambhava,[4] Who is
    the Protector of all sentient beings;
To the *Gurus*, the Three Bodies,[5] obeisance.

[THE INTRODUCTION]

This Great Doctrine of Liberation by Hearing, which conferreth spiritual freedom on devotees of ordinary wit while in
the Intermediate State, hath three divisions: the preliminaries,
the subject-matter, and the conclusion.

At first, the preliminaries, *The Guide Series*,[6] for emancipating beings, should be mastered by practice.

[THE TRANSFERENCE OF THE CONSCIOUSNESS-PRINCIPLE [7]]

By *The Guide*, the highest intellects ought most certainly
to be liberated; but should they not be liberated, then while

---

[1], [2] See pp. 10–15.

[3] 'These Deities are in ourselves. They are not something apart from us.
We are one with all that is, in every state of sentient existence, from the
lowest worlds of suffering to the highest states of bliss and Perfect Enlightenment. In this esoteric sense, the Lotus Order of Deities represent the deified
principles of the vocal functions in ourselves; the Peaceful represent the deified
principles of the heart or functions of feeling; the Wrathful represent, in the
same way, the functions of our mentality—such as thinking or reasoning, and
imagination or memory—centred in the brain.'—Lāma Kazi Dawa Samdup.
See p. 131[1].

[4] Padma Sambhava (Tib. *Pĕdma Jungnĕ*), i. e. 'The Lotus-Born ', referring to
birth under pure, or holy, conditions, commonly called by the Tibetans *Guru
Rin-po-ch'e* ('The Precious Guru '), or simply *Guru* (the Sanskrit for ' Teacher '),
is regarded by his followers as an incarnation of the essence of the Buddha
Shakya Muni in its Tantric, or deeply esoteric, aspect.

[5] See pp. 10–15.

[6] ' *The Guide Series* ' refers to various treatises offering practical guidance to
devotees on the *Bodhi* Path through the human world and thence through
Bardo, the After-Death State, and onward to rebirth or else to *Nirvāṇa*.

[7] The Text contains merely the Tibetan word *Hpho* (pron. *Pho*), meaning

in the Intermediate State of the Moments of Death they should practise the Transference, which giveth automatic liberation by one's merely remembering it.

Devotees of ordinary wit ought most certainly to be freed thereby; but should they not be freed, then, while in the Intermediate State [during the experiencing] of Reality, they should persevere in the listening to this Great Doctrine of Liberation by Hearing.

Accordingly, the devotee should at first examine the symptoms of death as they gradually appear [in his dying body], following *Self-Liberation [by Observing the] Characteristics [of the] Symptoms of Death.*[1] Then, when all the symptoms of death are complete [he should] apply the Transference, which conferreth liberation by merely remembering [the process].[2]

'transference' (of the sum-total, or aggregate, of *karmic* propensities, composing, or bound up with, personality and consciousness). The use of the term 'soul' being objectionable, since Buddhism, as a whole, denies the existence of a permanent, unchanging personal-consciousness entity such as the Semitic Faiths and animistic creeds in general understand thereby, the translator has avoided using it. But wherever any similar or equivalent term occurs herein it should be taken to imply something akin to 'consciousness-principle' or 'compound of consciousness' as implied by the Tibetan *Hpho*, or else as synonymous with the term 'life-flux' as used chiefly by Southern Buddhists.

[1] A Tibetan work of the *Bardo* cycle, commonly used by *lāmas* as supplementary to the *Bardo Thödol* (see part 9 of Note 1, p. 71). It treats of the symptoms of death in particular, scientifically and in very great detail. The late Lāma Kazi Dawa-Samdup had planned its translation into English.

[2] Liberation in this context does not necessarily imply, especially in the case of the average devotee, the Liberation of *Nirvāṇa*, but chiefly a liberation of the 'life-flux' from the dying body, in such manner as will afford the greatest possible after-death consciousness and consequent happy rebirth. Yet for the very exceptional and very highly efficient *yogī*, or saint, the same esoteric process of Transference can be, according to the *lāma-gurus*, so employed as to prevent any break in the flow of the stream of consciousness, from the moment of a conscious death to the moment of a conscious rebirth. Judging from a translation, made by the late Lāma Kazi Dawa-Samdup, of an old Tibetan manuscript containing practical directions for performing the Transference, which the editor possesses, the process is essentially *yogic*, and could be employed only by a person trained in mental concentration, or one-pointedness of mind, to such a high degree of proficiency as to have gained control over all the mental and bodily functions. Merely remembering the process at the all-important moment of death—as the text implies—is, for a *yogī*, equivalent to performing the Transference itself; for once the *yogī's* trained mind is directed

[THE READING OF THIS *THÖDOL*]

If the Transference hath been effectually employed, there is no need to read this *Thödol*; but if the Transference hath not been effectually employed, then this *Thödol* is to be read, correctly and distinctly, near the dead body.

If there be no corpse, then the bed or the seat to which the deceased had been accustomed should be occupied [by the reader], who ought to expound the power of the Truth. Then, summoning the spirit [of the deceased], imagine it to be present there listening, and read.[1] During this time no relative or fond mate should be allowed to weep or to wail, as such is not good [for the deceased]; so restrain them.[2]

If the body be present, just when the expiration hath ceased, either a *lāma* [who hath been as a *guru* to the deceased], or a brother in the Faith whom the deceased trusted, or a friend for whom the deceased had great affection, putting the lips close to the ear [of the body] without actually touching it,[3] should read this Great *Thödol*.

to the process, instantaneously, or, as the text explains, automatically, the desired result is achieved.

[1] The *lāma*, or reader, stationed in the house of the deceased as directed, whether the corpse be there or not, is to summon the departed one in the name of Truth, saying, 'As the Trinity is true, and as the Truth proclaimed by the Trinity is true, by the power of that Truth I summon thee'. Although no corpse be at hand (as there would not be when a person had met a violent or accidental death entailing loss or destruction of the human-plane body; or when, to accord with astrological calculations, the body had been removed or disposed of immediately after death, a not uncommon event in Tibet), the spirit of the deceased, in the invisible *Bardo*-plane body, must, nevertheless, be present at the reading, in order to be given the necessary guidance through the Other-world—as the Egyptian *Book of the Dead* also directs (see p. 19).

[2] This prohibition is found in Brāhmanism too.

[3] According to Tibetan and *lāmaic* belief, the body of a dying person should not be touched, that the normal departure of the consciousness-principle, which should take place through the Brāhmanic aperture on the crown of the head, be not interfered with. Otherwise, the departure may be brought about through some other bodily aperture and lead to birth in one of the non-human states. For example, it is held that if the departure is through the aperture of the ear the deceased will be obliged—ere he can return to human birth—to be born in the world of the *Gandharvas* (fairy-like celestial musicians), wherein sound, as in song and music, is the prevailing quality of existence.

[THE PRACTICAL APPLICATION OF THIS *THÖDOL* BY THE
OFFICIANT]

Now for the explaining of the *Thödol* itself:

If thou canst gather together a grand offering, offer it in
worship of the Trinity.   If such cannot be done, then arrange
whatever can be gathered together as objects on which thou
canst concentrate thy thoughts and mentally create as illimitable an offering as possible and worship.

Then the 'Path of Good Wishes Invoking the Aid of the
Buddhas and Bodhisattvas'[1] should be recited seven times
or thrice.

After that, the 'Path of Good Wishes Giving Protection
from Fear in the *Bardo*',[1] and·the 'Path of Good Wishes
for Safe Delivery from the Dangerous Pitfalls of the *Bardo*',[1]
together with the 'Root Words of the *Bardo*',[1] are to be read
distinctly and with the proper intonation.[2]

Then this Great *Thödol* is to be read either seven times or
thrice,[3] according to the occasion.   [First cometh] the setting-
face-to-face [to the symptoms of death] as they occur during
the moments of death ; [second] the application of the great
vivid reminder, the setting-face-to-face to Reality while in the

---

[1] See the Appendix, pp. 197–208, where each of these chief *Bardo* prayers (or
'Paths of Good Wishes') is translated.

[2] Cf. the two following passages, the first from *The Book of the Craft of Dying*,
chap. VI, in *Bodleian MS. 423* (*circa* fifteenth century), Comper's ed. (p. 39),
the second from *The Craft to Know Well to Die* (fifteenth century), chap. IV,
Comper's ed. (p. 74):

'Last of all, it is to be known that the prayers that follow may be conveniently
said upon a sick man that laboureth to his end.   And if it is a religious person,
then when the covent [i.e. convent] is gathered together with smiting of the
table, as the manner is, then shall be said first the litany, with the psalms and
orisons that he used therewith.   Afterward, if he live yet, let some man that is
about him say the orisons that follow hereafter, as the time and opportunity
will suffer.   And they may be often rehearsed again to excite the devotion of
the sick man—if he have reason and understanding with him.'

'And if the sick man or woman may, nor can not, say the orisons and prayers
beforesaid, some of the assistants [i.e. bystanders] ought to say them before him
with a loud voice, in changing the words there as they ought to be changed.'

[3] Cf. the following from *The Craft to Know Well to Die*, chap. IV, Comper's
ed. (p. 73): 'After all these things he [the person dying] ought to say three
times, if he may, these words that follow.'

Intermediate State; and third, the methods of closing the doors of the womb while in the Intermediate State when seeking rebirth.[1]

[PART I]

[THE *BARDO* OF THE MOMENTS OF DEATH]

[INSTRUCTIONS ON THE SYMPTOMS OF DEATH, OR THE FIRST STAGE OF THE *CHIKHAI BARDO*: THE PRIMARY CLEAR LIGHT SEEN AT THE MOMENT OF DEATH]

The first, the setting-face-to-face with the Clear Light, during the Intermediate State of the Moments of Death, is:

Here [some there may be] who have listened much [to religious instructions] yet not recognized; and [some] who, though recognizing, are, nevertheless, weak in familiarity. But all classes of individuals who have received the practical teachings [called] *Guides*[2] will, if this be applied to them, be set face to face with the fundamental Clear Light; and, without any Intermediate State, they will obtain the Unborn *Dharma-Kāya*, by the Great Perpendicular Path.[3]

---

[1] The first *Bardo* is the *Chikhai Bardo*; the second, the *Chönyid Bardo*; the third, the *Sidpa Bardo*. (See p. 102[4-6].)

[2] See p. 85[6].

[3] Text: *Yar-gyi-sang-thal-chen-po*: the 'Great Straight Upward Path'. One of the Doctrines peculiar to Northern Buddhism is that spiritual emancipation, even Buddhahood, may be won instantaneously, without entering upon the *Bardo* Plane and without further suffering on the age-long pathway of normal evolution which traverses the various worlds of *sangsāric* existence. The doctrine underlies the whole of the *Bardo Thödol*. Faith is the first step on the Secret Pathway. Then comes Illumination; and, with it, Certainty; and, when the Goal is won, Emancipation. But here again success implies very unusual proficiency in *yoga*, as well as much accumulated merit, or good *karma*, on the part of the devotee. If the disciple can be made to see and to grasp the Truth as soon as the *guru* reveals it, that is to say, if he has the power to die consciously, and at the supreme moment of quitting the body can recognize the Clear Light which will dawn upon him then, and become one with it, all *sangsāric* bonds of illusion are broken asunder immediately: the

The manner of application is :

It is best if the *guru* from whom the deceased received guiding instructions can be had ; but if the *guru* cannot be obtained, then a brother of the Faith ; or if the latter is also unobtainable, then a learned man of the same Faith ; or, should all these be unobtainable, then a person who can read correctly and distinctly ought to read this many times over. Thereby [the deceased] will be put in mind of what he had [previously] heard of the setting-face-to-face and will at once come to recognize that Fundamental Light and undoubtedly obtain Liberation.

As regards the time for the application [of these instructions] :

When the expiration hath ceased, the vital-force will have sunk into the nerve-centre of Wisdom[1] and the Knower[2] will be experiencing the Clear Light of the natural condition.[3] Then, the vital-force,[4] being thrown backwards and flying downwards through the right and left nerves,[5] the Intermediate State momentarily dawns.

The above [directions] should be applied before [the vital-force hath] rushed into the left nerve [after first having traversed the navel nerve-centre].

The time [ordinarily necessary for this motion of the vital-

Dreamer is awakened into Reality simultaneously with the mighty achievement of recognition.

[1] Here, as elsewhere in our text, 'nerve-centre' refers to a psychic nerve-centre. The psychic nerve-centre of Wisdom is located in the heart. (Cf. pp. 217 ff.)

[2] Text : *Shespa* (pron. *Shepa*) : 'Mind', 'Knower' ; i.e. the mind in its knowing, or cognizing, functions.

[3] Text : *Sprosbral* (pron. *Todal*) : 'devoid of formative activity' ; i.e. the mind in its natural, or primal, state. The mind in its unnatural state, that is to say, when incarnate in a human body, is, because of the driving force of the five senses, continuously in thought-formation activity. Its natural, or discarnate, state is a state of quiescence, comparable to its condition in the highest of *dhyāna* (or deep meditation) when still united to a human body. The conscious recognition of the Clear Light induces an ecstatic condition of consciousness such as saints and mystics of the West have called Illumination.

[4] Text : *rlung* (pron. *lung*) : 'vital-air', or 'vital-force', or 'psychic-force'.

[5] Text : *rtsa-gyas-gyon* (pron. *tsa-yay-yön*) : 'right and left [psychic] nerves' ; Skt. *Pingāla-nādī* (right [psychic] nerve) and *Idā-nādī* (left [psychic] nerve). (Cf. p. 215.)

force] is as long as the inspiration is still present, or about the time required for eating a meal.[1]

Then the manner of the application [of the instructions] is :

When the breathing is about to cease, it is best if the Transference hath been applied efficiently ; if [the application] hath been inefficient, then [address the deceased] thus:

O nobly-born (so and so by name), the time hath now come for thee to seek the Path [in reality]. Thy breathing is about to cease. Thy *guru* hath set thee face to face before with the Clear Light; and now thou art about to experience it in its Reality in the *Bardo* state, wherein all things are like the void and cloudless sky, and the naked, spotless intellect is like unto a transparent vacuum without circumference or centre. At this moment, know thou thyself ; and abide in that state. I, too, at this time, am setting thee face to face.

Having read this, repeat it many times in the ear of the person dying, even before the expiration hath ceased, so as to impress it on the mind [of the dying one].

If the expiration is about to cease, turn the dying one over on the right side, which posture is called the ' Lying Posture of a Lion '. The throbbing of the arteries [on the right and left side of the throat] is to be pressed.

If the person dying be disposed to sleep, or if the sleeping state advances, that should be arrested, and the arteries pressed gently but firmly.[2]   Thereby the vital-force will not be able to return from the median-nerve[3] and will be sure to pass out

---

[1] When this text first took form the reckoning of time was, apparently, yet primitive, mechanical time-keeping appliances being unknown. A similar condition still prevails in many parts of Tibet, where the period of a meal-time is frequently mentioned in old religious books—a period of from twenty minutes to half an hour in duration.

[2] The dying person should die fully awake and keenly conscious of the process of death ; hence the pressing of the arteries. (Cf. p. xxix.)

[3] ' Skt. of text: *dhutih* (pron. *duti*), meaning " median-nerve ", but lit. " tri-junction ". V. S. Apte's *Sanscrit-English Dictionary* (Poona, 1890) gives *dhuti* as the only similar word, defined as " shaking " or " moving ", which, if applied to our text, may refer to the vibratory motion of the psychic force traversing the median-nerve as its channel.'—Lama Kazi Dawa-Samdup.

' *Duti* may also mean " throwing away ", or " throwing out ", with reference

through the Brahmanic aperture.[1]   Now the real setting-face-to-face is to be applied.

At this moment, the first [glimpsing] of the *Bardo* of the Clear Light of Reality, which is the Infallible Mind of the *Dharma-Kāya*, is experienced by all sentient beings.

The interval between the cessation of the expiration and the cessation of the inspiration is the time during which the vital-force remaineth in the median-nerve.[2]

The common people call this the state wherein the consciousness-principle[3] hath fainted away.   The duration of this state is uncertain.   [It dependeth] upon the constitution, good or bad, and [the state of] the nerves and vital-force.   In those who have had even a little practical experience of the firm, tranquil state of *dhyāna*, and in those who have sound nerves, this state continueth for a long time.[4]

---

to the outgoing of the consciousness in the process of death.'—Sj. Atal Bihari Ghosh.

[1] See pp. 18, 87[2], 215. If non-distracted, and alertly conscious, at this psychological moment, the dying person will realize, through the power conferred by the reading of the *Thödol*, the importance of holding the vital-force in the median-nerve till it passes out thence through the Aperture of Brāhma.

[2] After the expiration has ceased, the vital-force (lit. 'inner-breath') is thought to remain in the median-nerve so long as the heart continues to throb.

[3] Text: *rnam-shes* (pron. *nam-she*): Skt. *vijñāna* or, preferably, *chaitanya*: 'conscious-principle' or 'object-knowing principle'.

[4] Sometimes it may continue for seven days, but usually only for four or five days. The consciousness-principle, however, save in certain conditions of trance, such as a *yogī*, for example, can induce, is not necessarily resident in the body all the while ; normally it quits the body at the moment called death, holding a subtle magnetic-like relationship with the body until the state referred to in the text comes to an end. Only for adepts in *yoga* would the departure of the consciousness-principle be accomplished without break in the continuity of the stream of consciousness, that is to say, without the swoon state referred to.

The death process is the reverse of the birth process, birth being the incarnating, death the discarnating of the consciousness-principle ; but, in both alike, there is a passing from one state of consciousness into another. And, just as a babe must wake up in this world and learn by experience the nature of this world, so, likewise, a person at death must wake up in the *Bardo* world and become familiar with its own peculiar conditions. The *Bardo* body, formed of matter in an invisible or ethereal-like state, is an exact duplicate of the human body, from which it is separated in the process of death. Retained in the *Bardo* body are the consciousness-principle and the psychic nerve-system (the counterpart, for the psychic or *Bardo* body, of the physical nerve-system of the human body). (Cf. p. 161[3].)

In the setting-face-to-face, the repetition [of the above address to the deceased] is to be persisted in until a yellowish liquid beginneth to appear from the various apertures of the bodily organs [of the deceased].

In those who have led an evil life, and in those of unsound nerves, the above state endureth only so long as would take to snap a finger. Again, in some, it endureth as long as the time taken for the eating of a meal.

In various *Tantras* it is said that this state of swoon endureth for about three and one-half days. Most other [religious treatises] say for four days; and that this setting-face-to-face with the Clear Light ought to be persevered in [during the whole time].

The manner of applying [these directions] is:

If [when dying] one be by one's own self capable [of diagnosing the symptoms of death], use [of the knowledge] should have been made ere this.[1] If [the dying person be] unable to do so, then either the *guru*, or a *shishya*, or a brother in the Faith with whom the one [dying] was very intimate, should be kept at hand, who will vividly impress upon the one [dying] the symptoms [of death] as they appear in due order [repeatedly saying, at first] thus:[2]

Now the symptoms of earth sinking into water are come.[3]

---

[1] The full meaning implied is that not only should the person about to die diagnose the symptoms of death as they come, one by one, but that he should also, if able, recognize the Clear Light without being set face to face with it by some second person.

[2] Cf. the following instructions, from *Ars Moriendi* (fifteenth century), Comper's ed. (p. 93): 'When any of likelihood shall die [i.e. is likely to die], then it is most necessary to have a special friend, the which will heartily help and pray for him, and therewith counsel the sick for the weal [i.e. health] of his soul.'

[3] The three chief symptoms of death (which the text merely suggests by naming the first of them, it being taken for granted that the reader officiating will know the others and name them as they occur), with their symbolical counterpart, are as follows: (1) a bodily sensation of pressure, 'earth sinking into water'; (2) a bodily sensation of clammy coldness as though the body were immersed in water, which gradually merges into that of feverish heat, 'water sinking into fire'; (3) a feeling as though the body were being blown to atoms, 'fire sinking into air'. Each symptom is accompanied by visible external changes in the body, such as loss of control over facial muscles, loss of hearing, loss of sight,

When all the symptoms [of death] are about to be completed, then enjoin upon [the one dying] this resolution, speaking in a low tone of voice in the ear:

O nobly-born (or, if it be a priest, O Venerable Sir), let not thy mind be distracted.

If it be a brother [in the Faith], or some other person, then call him by name, and [say] thus:

O nobly-born, that which is called death being come to thee now, resolve thus: ' O this now is the hour of death. By taking advantage of this death, I will so act, for the good of all sentient beings, peopling the illimitable expanse of the heavens, as to obtain the Perfect Buddhahood, by resolving on love and compassion towards [them, and by directing my entire effort to] the Sole Perfection.'

Shaping the thoughts thus, especially at this time when the *Dharma-Kāya* of Clear Light [in the state] after death can be realized for the benefit of all sentient beings, know that thou art in that state; [and resolve] that thou wilt obtain the best boon of the State of the Great Symbol,[1] in which thou art, [as follows]:

' Even if I cannot realize it, yet will I know this *Bardo*, and, mastering the Great Body of Union in *Bardo*, will appear in whatever [shape] will benefit [all beings] whomsoever:[2]

the breath coming in gasps just before the loss of consciousness, whereby *lāmas* trained in the science of death detect, one by one, the interdependent psychic phenomena culminating in the release of the *Bardo* body from its human-plane envelope. The translator held that the science of death, as expounded in this treatise, has been arrived at through the actual experiencing of death on the part of learned *lāmas*, who, when dying, have explained to their pupils the very process of death itself, in analytical and elaborate detail. (See p. 162².)

[1] In this state, realization of the Ultimate Truth is possible, providing sufficient advance on the Path has been made by the deceased before death. Otherwise, he cannot benefit now, and must wander on into lower and lower conditions of the *Bardo*, as determined by *karma*, until rebirth. (See p. 135².)

[2] The Tibetan of the text is here unusually concise. Literally rendered it is, ' will appear in whatever will subdue [for beneficial ends] whomsoever '. To subdue in this sense any sentient being of the human world, a form which will appeal religiously to that being is assumed. Thus, to appeal to a Shaivite devotee, the form of Shiva is assumed; to a Buddhist, the form of the Buddha Shakya Muni; to a Christian, the form of Jesus; to a Moslem, the form of the Prophet; and so on for other religious devotees; and for all manners and conditions of mankind a form appropriate to the occasion—for example, for subduing

I will serve all sentient beings, infinite in number as are the limits of the sky.'

Keeping thyself unseparated from this resolution, thou shouldst try to remember whatever devotional practices thou wert accustomed to perform during thy lifetime.[1]

In saying this, the reader shall put his lips close to the ear, and shall repeat it distinctly, clearly impressing it upon the dying person so as to prevent his mind from wandering even for a moment.

After the expiration hath completely ceased, press the nerve of sleep firmly; and, a *lāma*, or a person higher or more learned than thyself, impress in these words, thus:

Reverend Sir, now that thou art experiencing the Fundamental Clear Light, try to abide in that state which now thou art experiencing.

And also in the case of any other person the reader shall set him face-to-face thus:

O nobly-born (so-and-so), listen. Now thou art experiencing the Radiance of the Clear Light of Pure Reality. Recognize it. O nobly-born, thy present intellect,[2] in real nature void, not formed into anything as regards characteristics or colour, naturally void, is the very Reality, the All-Good.[3]

Thine own intellect, which is now voidness, yet not to be children, parents, and vice versa; for *shishyas, gurus,* and vice versa; for common people, kings or rulers; and for kings, ministers of state.

[1] Cf. the following, from *The Book of the Craft of Dying*, chap. V, in *Bodleian MS. 423 (circa* fifteenth century), Comper's ed. (p. 35): 'Also, if he that shall die have long time and space to be-think himself, and be not taken with hasty death, then may be read afore him, of them that be about him, devout histories and devout prayers, in the which he most delighted in when he was in heal [i. e. health].'

[2] Text: *Shes-rig* (pron. *She-rig*) is the intellect, the knowing or cognizing faculty.

[3] Text: *Chös-nyid Kün-tu-bzang-po* (pron. *Chö-nyid Küntu-zang-po*), Skt. *Dharma-Dhātu Samanta-Bhadra,* the embodiment of the *Dharma-Kāya,* the first state of Buddhahood. Our Block-Print text, in error here, gives for the All-Good (*Kuntu-Zang-po,* meaning 'All-Good Father') *Kuntu-Zang-mo,* which means 'All-Good Mother'. According to the Great Perfectionist School, the Father is that which appears, or phenomena, the Mother is that which is conscious of the phenomena. Again, Bliss is the Father, and the Voidness perceiving it, the Mother; the Radiance is the Father, and the Voidness perceiving it, the Mother; and, as in our text here, the intellect is the Father, the Voidness the Mother. The repetition of 'void' is to emphasize the importance of knowing the intellect to be in reality void (or of the nature of voidness), i. e. of the unborn, uncreated, unshaped Primordial.

regarded as of the voidness of nothingness, but as being the intellect itself, unobstructed, shining, thrilling, and blissful, is the very consciousness,[1] the All-good Buddha.[2]

Thine own consciousness, not formed into anything, in reality void, and the intellect, shining and blissful,—these two,—are inseparable. The union of them is the *Dharma-Kāya* state of Perfect Enlightenment.[3]

Thine own consciousness, shining, void, and inseparable from the Great Body of Radiance, hath no birth, nor death, and is the Immutable Light—Buddha Amitābha.[4]

Knowing this is sufficient. Recognizing the voidness of thine own intellect to be Buddhahood, and looking upon it as being thine own consciousness, is to keep thyself in the [state of the] divine mind [5] of the Buddha.[6]

[1] Text: *Rig-pa*, meaning 'consciousness' as distinct from the knowing faculty by which it cognizes or knows itself to be. Ordinarily, *rig-pa* and *shes-rig* are synonymous; but in an abstruse philosophical treatise, as herein, *rig-pa* refers to the consciousness in its purest and most spiritual (i. e. supramundane) aspect, and *shes-rig* to the consciousness in that grosser aspect, not purely spiritual, whereby cognizance of phenomena is present.

In this part of the *Bardo Thödol* the psychological analysis of consciousness or mind is particularly abstruse. Wherever the text contains the word *rig-pa* we have rendered it as 'consciousness', and the word *shes-rig* as 'intellect'; or else, to suit the context, *rig-pa* as 'consciousness' and *shes-rig* as 'consciousness of phenomena', which is 'intellect'.

[2] Text: *Kun-tu-bzang-po*: Skt. *Samanta* ('All' or 'Universal' or 'Complete') *Bhadra* ('Good' or 'Beneficent'). In this state, the experiencer and the thing experienced are inseparably one and the same, as, for example, the yellowness of gold cannot be separated from gold, nor saltness from salt. For the normal human intellect this transcendental state is beyond comprehension.

[3] From the union of the two states of mind, or consciousness, implied by the two terms *rig-pa* and *shes-rig*, and symbolized by the All-Good Father and the All-Good Mother, is born the state of the *Dharma-Kāya*, the state of Perfect Enlightenment, Buddahood. The *Dharma-Kāya* (' Body of Truth') symbolizes the purest and the highest state of being, a state of supramundane consciousness, devoid of all mental limitations or obscurations which arise from the contact of the primordial consciousness with matter.

[4] As the Buddha-Samanta-Bhadra state is the state of the All-Good, so the Buddha-Amitābha state is the state of the Boundless Light; and, as the text implies, both are, in the last analysis, the same state, merely regarded from two viewpoints. In the first, is emphasized the mind of the All-Good, in the second, the enlightening *Bodhi* power, symbolized as Buddha Amitābha (the personification of the Wisdom faculty), Source of Life and Light.

[5] Text: *dgongs-pa* (pron. *gong-pa*): 'thoughts' or 'mind', and, being in the honorific form, 'divine mind'.

[6] Realization of the Non-*Sangsāra*, which is the Voidness, the Unbecome, the

Repeat this distinctly and clearly three or [even] seven times. That will recall to the mind [of the dying one] the former [i.e. when living] setting-face-to-face by the *guru*. Secondly, it will cause the naked consciousness to be recognized as the Clear Light; and, thirdly, recognizing one's own self [thus], one becometh permanently united with the *Dharma-Kāya* and Liberation will be certain.[1]

[INSTRUCTIONS CONCERNING THE SECOND STAGE OF THE *CHIKHAI BARDO*: THE SECONDARY CLEAR LIGHT SEEN IMMEDIATELY AFTER DEATH]

Thus the primary Clear Light is recognized and Liberation attained. But if it be feared that the primary Clear Light hath not been recognized, then [it can certainly be assumed] there is dawning [upon the deceased] that called the secondary

Unborn, the Unmade, the Unformed, implies Buddhahood, Perfect Enlightenment—the state of the Divine Mind of the Buddha. Compare the following passage, from *The Diamond* [or Immutable] *Sūtra*, with its Chinese commentary (trans. by W. Gemmell, London, 1912, pp. 17-18): 'Every form or quality of phenomena is transient and illusive. When the mind realizes that the phenomena of life are not real phenomena, the Lord Buddha may then be clearly perceived.'—(*Chinese Annotation*: 'The spiritual Buddha must be realized within the mind, otherwise there can be no true perception of the Lord Buddha.')

[1] If, when dying, one be familiar with this state, in virtue of previous spiritual (or *yogic*) training in the human world, and have power to win Buddhahood at this all-determining moment, the Wheel of Rebirth is stopped, and Liberation instantaneously achieved. But such spiritual efficiency is so very rare that the normal mental condition of the person dying is unequal to the supreme feat of holding on to the state in which the Clear Light shines; and there follows a progressive descent into lower and lower states of the *Bardo* existence, and then rebirth. The simile of a needle balanced and set rolling on a thread is used by the *lāmas* to elucidate this condition. So long as the needle retains its balance, it remains on the thread. Eventually, however, the law of gravitation affects it, and it falls. In the realm of the Clear Light, similarly, the mentality of a person dying momentarily enjoys a condition of balance, or perfect equilibrium, and of oneness. Owing to unfamiliarity with such a state, which is an ecstatic state of non-ego, of subliminal consciousness, the consciousness-principle of the average human being lacks the power to function in it; *karmic* propensities becloud the consciousness-principle with thoughts of personality, of individualized being, of dualism, and, losing equilibrium, the consciousness-principle falls away from the Clear Light. It is ideation of ego, of self, which prevents the realization of *Nirvāṇa* (which is the 'blowing out of the flame of selfish longing'); and so the Wheel of Life continues to turn.

Clear Light, which dawneth in somewhat more than a meal-time period after that the expiration hath ceased.[1]

According to one's good or bad *karma*, the vital-force floweth down into either the right or left nerve and goeth out through any of the apertures [of the body].[2] Then cometh a lucid condition of the mind.[3]

To say that the state [of the primary Clear Light] endureth for a meal-time period [would depend upon] the good or bad condition of the nerves and also whether there hath been previous practice or not [in the setting-face-to-face].

When the consciousness-principle getteth outside [the body, it sayeth to itself], 'Am I dead, or am I not dead?' It cannot determine. It seeth its relatives and connexions as it had been used to seeing them before. It even heareth the wailings. The terrifying *karmic* illusions have not yet dawned. Nor have the frightful apparitions or experiences caused by the Lords of Death[4] yet come.

During this interval, the directions are to be applied [by the *lāma* or reader]:

There are those [devotees] of the perfected stage and of the

---

[1] Immediately after the passing of the vital-force into the median-nerve, the person dying experiences the Clear Light in its primitive purity, the *Dharma-Kāya* unobscured; and, if unable to hold fast to that experience, next experiences the secondary Clear Light, having fallen to a lower state of the *Bardo*, wherein the *Dharma-Kāya* is dimmed by *karmic* obscurations.

[2] Cf. p. xxx.

[3] Text: *shes-pa*, rendered here as 'mind'. The translator has added the following comment: 'The vital-force, passing from the navel psychic-nerve centre, and the principle of consciousness, passing from the brain psychic-nerve centre, unite in the heart psychic-nerve centre, and in departing thence from the body, normally through the Aperture of Brāhma, produce in the dying person a state of ecstasy of the greatest intensity. The succeeding stage is less intense. In the first, or primary, stage, is experienced the Primary Clear Light, in the second stage, the Secondary Clear Light. A ball set bounding reaches its greatest height at the first bound; the second bound is lower, and each succeeding bound is still lower until the ball comes to rest. Similarly is it with the consciousness-principle at the death of a human body. Its first spiritual bound, directly upon quitting the earth-plane body, is the highest; the next is lower. Finally, the force of *karma* having spent itself in the after-death state, the consciousness-principle comes to rest, a womb is entered, and then comes rebirth in this world.'

[4] Text: *Gshin-rje* (pron. *Shin-je*): 'Lord of Death'; but the plural form is allowable and preferable here.

visualizing stage. If it be one who was in the perfected stage, then call him thrice by name and repeat over and over again the above instructions of setting-face-to-face with the Clear Light. If it be one who was in the visualizing stage, then read out to him the introductory descriptions and the text of the Meditation on his tutelary deity,[1] and then say,

O thou of noble-birth, meditate upon thine own tutelary deity.—[Here the deity's name is to be mentioned by the reader.[2]] Do not be distracted. Earnestly concentrate thy mind upon thy tutelary deity. Meditate upon him as if he were the reflection of the moon in water, apparent yet inexistent [in itself]. Meditate upon him as if he were a being with a physical body.

So saying, [the reader will] impress it.

If [the deceased be] of the common folk, say,

Meditate upon the Great Compassionate Lord.[3]

By thus being set-face-to-face even those who would not be expected to recognize the *Bardo* [unaided] are undoubtedly certain to recognize it.

Persons who while living had been set face to face [with the Reality] by a *guru*, yet who have not made themselves familiar with it, will not be able to recognize the *Bardo* clearly by themselves. Either a *guru* or a brother in the Faith will have to impress vividly such persons.[4]

---

[1] Cf. the following, from *The Craft to Know Well to Die*, chap. IV, Comper's ed. (p. 73): 'And after he [the person dying] ought to require the apostles, the martyrs, the confessors and the virgins, and in special all the saints that he most loved ever.'

[2] The favourite deity of the deceased is the tutelary (Tib. *yi-dam*), usually one of the Buddhas or Bodhisattvas, of whom Chenrazee is the most popular.

[3] Text: *Jo-vo-thugs-rje-chen-po* (pron. *Jo-wo-thu-ji-chen-po*): 'Great Compassionate Lord', synonymous with Tib. *Spyan-ras-gaigs* (pron. *Chen-rä-zi*): Skt. *Avalokiteshvara*.

[4] A person may have heard a detailed description of the art of swimming and yet never have tried to swim. Suddenly thrown into water he finds himself unable to swim. So with those who have been taught the theory of how to act in the time of death and have not applied, through *yogic* practices, the theory: they cannot maintain unbroken continuity of consciousness; they grow bewildered at the changed conditions; and fail to progress or to take advantage of the opportunity offered by death, unless upheld and directed by a living *guru*. Even with all that a *guru* can do, they ordinarily, because of bad *karma*, fail to recognize the *Bardo* as such.

There may be even those who have made themselves familiar with the teachings, yet who, because of the violence of the disease causing death, may be mentally unable to withstand illusions. For such, also, this instruction is absolutely necessary.

Again [there are those] who, although previously familiar with the teachings, have become liable to pass into the miserable states of existence, owing to breach of vows or failure to perform essential obligations honestly. To them, this [instruction] is indispensable.

If the first stage of the *Bardo* hath been taken by the forelock, that is best. But if not, by application of this distinct recalling [to the deceased], while in the second stage of the *Bardo*, his intellect is awakened and attaineth liberation.

While on the second stage of the *Bardo*, one's body is of the nature of that called the shining illusory-body.[1]

Not knowing whether [he be] dead or not, [a state of] lucidity cometh [to the deceased].[2] If the instructions be successfully applied to the deceased while he is in that state, then, by the meeting of the Mother-Reality and the Offspring-Reality,[3] *karma* controlleth not.[4] Like the sun's rays, for example, dispelling the darkness, the Clear Light on the Path dispelleth the power of *karma*.

---

[1] Text : *dag-pahi-sgyu-lus* (pron. *tag-pay-gyu-lü*) : 'pure (or shining) illusory body' : Skt. *māyā-rūpa*. This is the ethereal counterpart of the physical body of the earth-plane, the 'astral-body' of Theosophy.

[2] With the departure of the consciousness-principle from the human body there comes a psychic thrill which gives way to a state of lucidity.

[3] Text : *Chös-nyid-ma-bu* : Skt. *Dharma Mātri Putra* : 'Mother and Offspring Reality (or Truth).' The Offspring-Truth is that realized in this world through practising deep meditation (Skt. *dhyāna*). The Mother-Truth is the Primal or Fundamental Truth, experienced only after death whilst the Knower is in the *Bardo* state of equilibrium, ere *karmic* propensities have erupted into activity. What a photograph is compared to the object photographed, the Offspring-Reality is to the Mother-Reality.

[4] Lit., '*karma* is unable to turn the mouth or head', the figure implied being that of a rider controlling a horse with a bridle and bit. In the *Tantra of the Great Liberation*, there is this similar passage : 'The man blinded by the darkness of ignorance, the fool caught in the meshes of his actions, and the illiterate man, by listening to this Great Tantra, are released from the bonds of *karma*' (cf. *Tantra of the Great Liberation*, line 205, as edited by Arthur Avalon, London, 1913, p. 359).

That which is called the second stage of the *Bardo* dawneth upon the thought-body.[1] The Knower[2] hovereth within those places to which its activities had been limited. If at this time this special teaching be applied efficiently, then the purpose will be fulfilled; for the *karmic* illusions will not have come yet, and, therefore, he [the deceased] cannot be turned hither and thither [from his aim of achieving Enlightenment].

[PART II]

[THE *BARDO* OF THE EXPERIENCING OF REALITY]

[INTRODUCTORY INSTRUCTIONS CONCERNING THE EXPERIENCING OF REALITY DURING THE THIRD STAGE OF THE *BARDO*, CALLED THE *CHÖNYID BARDO*, WHEN THE *KARMIC* APPARITIONS APPEAR]

But even though the Primary Clear Light be not recognized, the Clear Light of the second *Bardo* being recognized, Liberation will be attained. If not liberated even by that, then that called the third *Bardo* or the *Chönyid Bardo* dawneth.

In this third stage of the *Bardo*, the *karmic* illusions come to shine. It is very important that this Great Setting-face-to-face of the *Chönyid Bardo* be read: it hath much power and can do much good.

About this time [the deceased] can see that the share of food is being set aside, that the body is being stripped of its garments, that the place of the sleeping-rug is being swept;[3]

---

[1] Text: *yid-kyi-lüs* (pron. *yid-kyi-lü*), 'mental-body', 'desire-body', or 'thought-body'.

[2] Cf. pp. 92³, 95², 96¹.

[3] The references are (1) to the share of food being set aside for the deceased during the funeral rites; (2) to his corpse being prepared for the shroud; (3) to his bed or sleeping-place.

can hear all the weeping and wailing of his friends and relatives, and, although he can see them and can hear them calling
upon him, they cannot hear him calling upon them, so he
goeth away displeased.

At that time, sounds, lights, and rays—all three—are
experienced. These awe, frighten, and terrify, and cause
much fatigue. At this moment, this setting-face-to-face with
the *Bardo* [during the experiencing] of Reality is to be
applied. Call the deceased by name, and correctly and distinctly explain to him, as follows :

O nobly-born, listen with full attention, without being
distracted : There are six states of *Bardo*, namely : the
natural state of *Bardo* while in the womb ;[1] the *Bardo*
of the dream-state ;[2] the *Bardo* of ecstatic equilibrium,
while in deep meditation ;[3] the *Bardo* of the moment of
death ;[4] the *Bardo* [during the experiencing] of Reality ;[5]
the *Bardo* of the inverse process of *sangsāric* existence.[6]
These are the six.

O nobly-born, thou wilt experience three *Bardos*, the *Bardo*
of the moment of death, the *Bardo* [during the experiencing]
of Reality, and the *Bardo* while seeking rebirth. Of these
three, up to yesterday, thou hadst experienced the *Bardo* of
the moment of death. Although the Clear Light of Reality
dawned upon thee, thou wert unable to hold on, and so thou
hast to wander here. Now henceforth thou art going to
experience the [other] two, the *Chönyid Bardo* and the *Sidpa
Bardo*.

---

[1] Text : *Skye-gnas Bardo* (pron. *Kye-nay Bardo*) : 'Intermediate State', or
'State of Uncertainty, of the place of birth (or while in the womb)'.

[2] Text : *Rmi-lam Bardo* (pron. *Mi-lam Bardo*) : 'Intermediate State', or
'State of Uncertainty, [during the experiencing] of the dream-state'.

[3] Text : *Ting-nge-hzin Bsam-gtam Bardo* (pron. *Tin-ge-zin Sam-tam Bardo*) :
'Intermediate State', or 'State of Uncertainty, [during the experiencing] of
Dyhāna (Meditation) in *Samādhi* (Ecstatic equilibrium)'.

[4] Text : *Hchi-khahi Bardo* (pron. *Chi-khai Bardo*) : 'Intermediate State', or
'State of Uncertainty, of the dying moment (or moment of death)'.

[5] Text : *Chös-nyid Bardo* (pron. *Chö-nyid Bardo*) : 'Intermediate State', or
'State of Uncertainty, [during the experiencing] of Reality'.

[6] Text : *Lugs-hbyung Srid-pahi Bardo* (pron. *Lu-jung Sid-pai Bardo* : 'Intermediate State', or 'State of Uncertainty, in the inverse process of *sangsāric*
(worldly) existence'—the state wherein the Knower is seeking rebirth.

Thou wilt pay undistracted attention to that with which I am about to set thee face to face, and hold on:

O nobly-born, that which is called death hath now come. Thou art departing from this world, but thou art not the only one; [death] cometh to all. Do not cling, in fondness and weakness, to this life. Even though thou clingest out of weakness, thou hast not the power to remain here. Thou wilt gain nothing more than wandering in this *Sangsāra*.[1] Be not attached [to this world]; be not weak. Remember the Precious Trinity.[2]

O nobly-born, whatever fear and terror may come to thee in the *Chönyid Bardo*, forget not these words; and, bearing their meaning at heart, go forwards: in them lieth the vital secret of recognition:

'Alas! when the Uncertain Experiencing of Reality is
        dawning upon me here,[3]
With every thought of fear or terror or awe for all [appari-
        tional appearances] set aside,
May I recognize whatever [visions] appear, as the reflections
        of mine own consciousness;
May I know them to be of the nature of apparitions in the
        Bardo:
When at this all-important moment [of opportunity] of
        achieving a great end,
May I not fear the bands of Peaceful and Wrathful [Deities],
        mine own thought-forms.[4]'

Repeat thou these [verses] clearly, and remembering their significance as thou repeatest them, go forwards, [O nobly-born]. Thereby, whatever visions of awe or terror appear,

[1] Text: *Hkhor-va* (pron. *Khor-wa*): 'a thing whirling round'; 'whirligig': Skt. *Sangsāra* (or *Saṁsāra*).

[2] That is, the Buddha, the Dharma, the Sangha.

[3] Reality is experienced or glimpsed in a state of uncertainty, because the Knower experiences it through the *Bardo* counterpart of the illusory perceptive faculties of the earth-plane body and not through the unobscured supramundane consciousness of the pure *Dharma-Kāya* state, wherein there can be no *Bardo* (i.e 'Uncertain', or 'Intermediate State').

[4] Text: *rang-snang* (pron. *rang-nang*): 'one's own [mental] visions (or thought-forms).'

recognition is certain; and forget not this vital secret art lying therein.

O nobly-born, when thy body and mind were separating, thou must have experienced a glimpse of the Pure Truth, subtle, sparkling, bright, dazzling, glorious, and radiantly awesome, in appearance like a mirage moving across a landscape in spring-time in one continuous stream of vibrations. Be not daunted thereby, nor terrified, nor awed. That is the radiance of thine own true nature. Recognize it.

From the midst of that radiance, the natural sound of Reality, reverberating like a thousand thunders simultaneously sounding, will come. That is the natural sound of thine own real self. Be not daunted thereby, nor terrified, nor awed.

The body which thou hast now is called the thought-body of propensities.[1] Since thou hast not a material body of flesh and blood, whatever may come,—sounds, lights, or rays, —are, all three, unable to harm thee: thou art incapable of dying. It is quite sufficient for thee to know that these apparitions are thine own thought-forms. Recognize this to be the *Bardo*.

O nobly-born, if thou dost not now recognize thine own thought-forms, whatever of meditation or of devotion thou mayst have performed while in the human world—if thou hast not met with this present teaching—the lights will daunt thee, the sounds will awe thee, and the rays will terrify thee. Shouldst thou not know this all-important key to the teachings,—not being able to recognize the sounds, lights, and rays,—thou wilt have to wander in the *Sangsāra*.

[THE DAWNING OF THE PEACEFUL DEITIES, FROM THE FIRST TO THE SEVENTH DAY]

[Assuming that the deceased is *karmically* bound—as the average departed one is—to pass through the forty-nine days of the *Bardo* existence, despite the very frequent settings-face-to-face, the daily trials and dangers which he must meet and

---

[1] Text: *bag-chags yid-lüs* (pron. *bag-chah yid-lü*). *yid-lüs*: 'mind-body' or 'thought-body'; *bag-chags*: 'habit', 'propensities' (born of *sangsāric* or worldly existence).

attempt to triumph over, during the first seven days, wherein
dawn the Peaceful Deities, are next explained to him in
detail; the first day, judging from the text, being reckoned
from the time in which normally he would be expected to wake
up to the fact that he is dead and on the way back to rebirth,
or about three and one-half to four days after death.]

[THE FIRST DAY]

O nobly-born, thou hast been in a swoon during the last three
and one-half days. As soon as thou art recovered from this
swoon, thou wilt have the thought, 'What hath happened!'

Act so that thou wilt recognize the *Bardo*. At that time,
all the *Sangsāra* will be in revolution;[1] and the phenomenal
appearances that thou wilt see then will be the radiances and
deities.[2] The whole heavens will appear deep blue.

Then, from the Central Realm, called the Spreading Forth
of the Seed,[3] the Bhagavān Vairochana,[4] white in colour, and

[1] That is to say, phenomena, or phenomenal experiences as experienced
when in the human world, will be experienced in quite another way in the
Bardo world, so that to one just dead they will seem to be in revolution or
confusion; hence the warning to the deceased, who must accustom himself to
the after-death state as a babe must accustom itself after birth to our world.

[2] At this point, where the marvellous *Bardo* visions begin to dawn, the
student in attempting to rationalize them should ever keep in mind that this
treatise is essentially esoteric, being in most parts, especially from here onwards,
allegorical and symbolical of psychic experiences in the after-death state.

[3] Text: *Thiglé-Brdalva* (pron. *Thigle-Dalwa*): 'Spreading forth the Seed [of
all Things].' Esoterically, this is the *Dharma-Dhātu*.

[4] Text: *Rnam-par-Snang-mzad* (pron. *Nam-par-Nang-zad*); Skt. *Vairochana*,
the Dhyānī Buddha of the Centre (or Central Realm). *Vairochana* literally
means, 'in shapes making visible'; hence he is the Manifester of Phenomena,
or the Noumena. The wheel he holds symbolizes sovereign power. His title
Bhagavān (applied to many other of the deities to follow hereinafter), meaning
'One Possessed of Dominion' (or 'of the Six Powers'), or 'The Victorious',
qualifies him as being a Buddha, i. e. One who has conquered, or has dominion
over, *sangsāric*, or worldly, existence.

As the Central Dhyānī Buddha, Vairochana is the highest path to Enlightenment of the Esoteric School. Like a Central Sun, surrounded by the four
Dhyānī Buddhas of the four cardinal directions, who dawn on the four succeeding days, he symbolizes the One Truth surrounded by its four constituents or
elements. As the source of all organic life, in him all things visible and invisible
have their consummation and absorption.

For general references to the deities of the *Bardo Thödol*, see L. A. Waddell,
The Buddhism of Tibet or Lamaism (London, 1895); and A. Getty, *The Gods of
Northern Buddhism* (Oxford, 1914).

seated upon a lion-throne, bearing an eight-spoked wheel
in his hand, and embraced by the Mother of the Space of
Heaven,[1] will manifest himself to thee.

It is the aggregate of matter resolved into its primordial
state which is the blue light.[2]

The Wisdom of the *Dharma-Dhātu*, blue in colour, shining,
transparent, glorious, dazzling, from the heart of Vairochana
as the Father-Mother,[3] will shoot forth and strike against thee
with a light so radiant that thou wilt scarcely be able to look
at it.

Along with it, there will also shine a dull white light from
the *devas*, which will strike against thee in thy front.

Thereupon, because of the power of bad *karma*, the glorious
blue light of the Wisdom of the *Dharma-Dhātu* will produce
in thee fear and terror, and thou wilt [wish to] flee from it.
Thou wilt beget a fondness for the dull white light of the
devas.

At this stage, thou must not be awed by the divine blue
light which will appear shining, dazzling, and glorious; and
be not startled by it. That is the light of the Tathāgata[4]
called the Light of the Wisdom of the *Dharma-Dhātu*. Put
thy faith in it, believe in it firmly, and pray unto it, thinking
in thy mind that it is the light proceeding from the heart of
the Bhagavān Vairochana coming to receive thee while in the

---

[1] Text : *Nam-mkh-ah-dvyings-kyi-dvang-phyung-ma* (pron. *Nam-kha-ing-kya-wang-chug-ma*) : 'Sovereign Lady of the Space of Heaven' : Skt. *Ākāsa Dhātu Íshvarī*. The Mother is the female principle of the universe ; the Father, Vairochana, the seed of all that is.

[2] Here the Block-Print reads : 'It is the aggregate of consciousness (*Rnam-par Shes-ṭahi*—pro. *Nam-par She-pay*—Skt. *Vijñāna Skandha*) resolved into its primordial state which is the blue light.' In our MS. the aggregate of consciousness shines as a white light in relationship with Vajra-Sattva, on the Second Day (see p. 109).

[3] Here, as in parallel passages following, the chief deity personifies in himself the female as well as the male principle of nature, and hence is called the Father-Mother—depicted, as described by the text, in appropriate symbolic colours, on the corresponding illuminated folio of our MS., as the Divine Father and the Divine Mother in union (i.e. in divine at-one-ment).

[4] Text : *De-bzhing-shegs-pa* (pron. *De-shing-sheg-pa*) : Skt. *Tathāgata*, meaning '[He] who hath gone that same way', i.e. One who hath reached the Goal (*Nirvāṇa*)—a Buddha.

(reading left to right)
THE TRANSLATOR AND THE EDITOR IN GANGTOK,
SIKKIM
Described on page xxvii

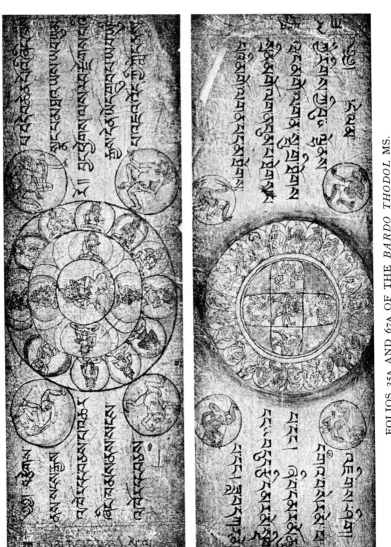

FOLIOS 35A AND 67A OF THE *BARDO THODOL* MS.

THE GREAT *MANDALA* OF THE PEACEFUL DEITIES
Described on pages xxviii–xxix, 118–22, 217–20

THE GREAT *MANDALA* OF THE KNOWLEDGE-HOLDING
AND WRATHFUL DEITIES

Described on pages xxix-xxx, 127-8, 217-20

THE JUDGEMENT

Described on pages xxx–xxxiii, 35-8, 165-7, 240

THE INDIAN WHEEL OF THE LAW

Described on page xxxiii

THE LĀMAIC CROSSED DORJE

Described on page xxxiii

THE TIBETAN WHEEL OF THE LAW

Described on page xxxiii

THE *MANTRA* OF CHENRAZEE

"OM MA-ṆI PAD-ME HŪṂ"

Described on page xxxiv

THE *DORJE*
THE *LĀMAIC* SCEPTRE
Described on page xxxiii

dangerous ambuscade[1] of the *Bardo*. That light is the light of the grace of Vairochana.

Be not fond of the dull white light of the *devas*: Be not attached [to it]; be not weak. If thou be attached to it, thou wilt wander into the abodes of the *devas* and be drawn into the whirl of the Six *Lokas*. That is an interruption to obstruct thee on the Path of Liberation. Look not at it. Look at the bright blue light in deep faith. Put thy whole thought earnestly upon Vairochana and repeat after me this prayer:

'Alas! when wandering in the *Sangsāra*, because of intense
   stupidity,
On the radiant light-path of the *Dharma-Dhātu* Wisdom
May [I] be led by the Bhagavān Vairochana,
May the Divine Mother of Infinite Space be [my] rear-
   guard;
May [I] be led safely across the fearful ambush of the
   Bardo;
May [I] be placed in the state of the All-Perfect Buddha-
   hood.'[2]

Praying thus, in intense humble faith, [thou] wilt merge, in halo of rainbow light, into the heart of Vairochana, and obtain Buddhahood in the *Sambhoga-Kāya*, in the Central Realm of the Densely-Packed.[3]

---

[1] Text: *hphrang* (pron. *htang*): 'narrow passage', 'ambush'.

[2] Cf. the following instructions to the dying person and the prayer from *The Craft to Know Well to Die*, chap. IV, Comper's ed. (p. 73): ' He ought after-wards, if he may, to call on the holy angels, in saying: " Ye spirits of Heaven, Angels much glorious, I beseech you that ye will be assistant [i.e. present] with me that now beginneth to depart, and that ye deliver me mightily from the awaits and fallacies of mine adversaries; and that it please you to receive my soul into your company. The principal, my leader and my good angel, which by our Lord art deputed to be my warder and keeper, I pray and require thee that thou now aid and help me."'

[3] Text: *Stug-po-bkod-pahi shing-khams* (pron. *Tug-po-kod-pai shing-kham*): 'Thickly-formed' or 'Densely-packed Realm', i.e. the seed of all universal forces and things are densely packed together therein; also called in Tibetan *'Og-min*: lit. ' *No-down* ', the realm whence there is no fall, the state leading into *Nirvāṇa*; it is pre-eminently the realm of the Buddhas.

[THE SECOND DAY]

But if, notwithstanding this setting-face-to-face, through
power of anger or obscuring *karma* one should be startled at
the glorious light and flee, or be overcome by illusions, despite
the prayer, on the Second Day, Vajra-Sattva and his attendant
deities, as well as one's evil deeds [meriting] Hell, will come
to receive one.

Thereupon the setting-face-to-face is, calling the deceased
by name, thus:

O nobly-born, listen undistractedly. On the Second Day
the pure form of water will shine as a white light. At that
time, from the deep blue Eastern Realm of Pre-eminent Happiness, the Bhagavān Akṣhobhya [as] Vajra-Sattva,[1] blue in
colour, holding in his hand a five-pronged *dorje*,[2] seated upon
an elephant-throne, and embraced by the Mother Māmakī[3],
will appear to thee, attended by the Bodhisattvas Kṣhitigarbha[4] and Maitreya,[5] with the female Bodhisattvas, Lasema
and Pushpema.[6] These six *Bodhic* deities will appear to thee.

---

[1] Text: *Rdorje-sems-dpah Mi-bskyod-pa* (pron. *Dorje-sems-pa Mi-kyod-pa*): Skt.
Vajra-Sattva Akṣhobhya. Akṣhobhya (the 'Unagitated' or 'Immovable'), the
Dhyānī Buddha of the Eastern Direction, here, as throughout the text, appears
as Vajra-Sattva ('The Divine Heroic-Minded', or 'Indestructible-Minded'), his
Sambhoga-Kāya, or adorned active reflex. Vajra-Dhāra ('The Indestructible
or Steadfast Holder' [see p. 13]) is, also, a reflex of Akṣhobhya; and both
reflexes are very important deities of the Esoteric School.

[2] The *dorje* is the *lāmaic* sceptre, a type of the thunderbolt of Indra (Jupiter).

[3] This is the Sanskrit form as incorporated in our Tibetan text. Here the
Block-Print, evidently in error, contains, in Tibetan, *Sangs-rgyas-spyan-ma*
(pron. *Sang-yay Chan-ma*), meaning 'She of the Buddha Eye', who, in our manuscript text, comes with Ratna-Sambhava on the Third Day. Māmakī is also
one of the 108 names given to Dōlma (Skt. *Tārā*), the national goddess of Tibet.
(See p. 116[3].) In the *Dharma Samgraha* it is said that there are four Devīs,
namely, Rochanī, Māmakī, Pāndurā, and Tārā.

[4] Text: *Sahi-snying-po* (pron. *Sayi-nying-po*): Skt. *Kṣhitigarbha*: 'Womb
(or Matrix) of the Earth.'

[5] Text: *Byams-pa* (pron. *Cham-pa*): Skt. *Maitreya*: 'Love'; the Buddha to
come, who will reform mankind through the power of divine love.

[6] *Lasema* and *Pushpema* are corrupt Sanskrit forms incorporated in our
manuscript. Their Tibetan equivalents are, respectively, *Sgeg-mo-ma* (Skt.
Lāsyā), meaning 'Belle' (or 'Dallying One'), and *Me-tog-ma* (Skt. *Pushpā*),
'She who offers (or holds) Blossoms'. *Pushpā*, depicted holding a blossom
in her hand, is a personification of blossoms. *Lāsyā*, the Belle, depicted
holding a mirror in a coquettish attitude, personifies beauty.

The aggregate of thy principle of consciousness,[1] being in its pure form—which is the Mirror-like Wisdom—will shine as a bright, radiant white light, from the heart of Vajra-Sattva, the Father-Mother,[2] with such dazzling brilliancy and transparency that thou wilt scarcely be able to look at it, [and] will strike against thee.   And a dull, smoke-coloured light from Hell will shine alongside the light of the Mirror-like Wisdom and will [also] strike against thee.

Thereupon, through the power of anger, thou wilt beget fear and be startled at the dazzling white light and wilt [wish to] flee from it; thou wilt beget a feeling of fondness for the dull smoke-coloured light from Hell.   Act then so that thou wilt not fear that bright, dazzling, transparent white light. Know it to be Wisdom.   Put thy humble and earnest faith in it.   That is the light of the grace of the Bhagavān Vajra-Sattva.   Think, with faith, ' I will take refuge in it'; and pray·

That is the Bhagavān Vajra-Sattva coming to receive thee and to save thee from the fear and terror of the *Bardo*. Believe in it; for it is the hook of the rays of grace of Vajra-Sattva.[3]

Be not fond of the dull, smoke-coloured light from Hell. That is the path which openeth out to receive thee because of the power of accumulated evil *karma* from violent anger. If thou be attracted by it, thou wilt fall into the Hell-Worlds; and, falling therein, thou wilt have to endure unbearable misery, whence there is no certain time of getting out.   That being an interruption to obstruct thee on the Path of Liberation, look not at it; and avoid anger.[4]   Be not attracted by

---

[1] Text : *Rnampar-shes-pahi-phung-po* (pron. *Nampar-she-pay-phung-po*), ' aggregate of consciousness-principle', the Knower.   The Block-Print contains, in place of this, *Gzugs-kyi-phung-po* (pron. *Zu-kyi-phung-po*), ' aggregate of the body ' or ' Bodily-aggregate '.

[2] See p. 106³.

[3] The rays of divine grace are a hook of salvation to catch hold of the deceased and drag him away from the dangers of the *Bardo*.   Sometimes each ray is thought of as ending in a hook, just as each ray emanating from the sun-god Ra, and descending as a grace ray upon a devotee, is depicted in ancient temples of Egypt as ending in a hand.   Similarly, the Christian thinks of the saving grace of God.

[4] The deceased is here thought of, perhaps, as being able to see his people

it ; be not weak. Believe in the dazzling bright white light ;
[and] putting thy whole heart earnestly upon the Bhagavān
Vajra-Sattva, pray thus :

> ' Alas ! when wandering in the *Sangsāra* because of the
>   power of violent anger,
> On the radiant light-path of the Mirror-like Wisdom,
> May [I] be led by the Bhagavān Vajra-Sattva,
> May the Divine Mother Māmakī be [my] rear-guard ;
> May [I] be led safely across the fearful ambush of the
>   *Bardo* ;
> And may [I] be placed in the state of the All-perfect
>   Buddhahood.'

Praying thus, in intense humble faith, thou wilt merge, in
rainbow light, into the heart of the Bhagavān Vajra-Sattva
and obtain Buddhahood in the *Sambhoga-Kāya*, in the Eastern
Realm called Pre-eminently Happy.

[THE THIRD DAY]

Yet, even when set face to face in this way, some persons,
because of obscurations from bad *karma*, and from pride,
although the hook of the rays of grace [striketh against them],
flee from it. [If one be one of them], then, on the Third Day,
the Bhagavān Ratna-Sambhava [1] and his accompanying deities,
along with the light-path from the human world, will come to
receive one simultaneously.

Again, calling the deceased by name, the setting-face-to-face
is thus :

O nobly-born, listen undistractedly. On the Third Day
the primal form of the element earth will shine forth as a yellow
light. At that time, from the Southern Realm Endowed with

---

on earth and as liable to anger should he see them disputing over the division
of his property, or if he perceives avarice on the part of the *lāma* conducting
the funeral rites.   But the prohibition touching anger is essentially *yogic*, *yogīs*
of all religions recognizing that anger prevents spiritual progress ; and it
parallels the moral teaching against giving way to anger contained in the ancient
Egyptian *Precepts of Ptah-hotep*.

[1] Text : *Rinchen-hbyung-ldan* (pron. *Rinchen-Jung-dan*) : Skt. *Ratna-Sam-*
bhava, i. e. ' Born of a Jewel '.   He is the Beautifier, whence comes all that is
precious ; a personified attribute of the Buddha.

Glory, the Bhagavān Ratna-Sambhava, yellow in colour, bearing a jewel in his hand, seated upon a horse-throne and embraced by the Divine Mother Sangyay-Chanma,[1] will shine upon thee.

The two Bodhisattvas, Ākāsha-Garbha[2] and Samanta-Bhadra,[3] attended by the two female Bodhisattvas, Mahlaima and Dhupema,[4]—in all, six Bodhic forms,—will come to shine from amidst a rainbow halo of light. The aggregate of touch in its primal form, as the yellow light of the Wisdom of Equality, dazzlingly yellow, glorified with orbs having satellite orbs of radiance, so clear and bright that the eye can scarcely look upon it, will strike against thee. Side by side with it, the dull bluish-yellow light from the human [world] will also strike against thy heart, along with the Wisdom light.

Thereupon, through the power of egotism, thou wilt beget a fear for the dazzling yellow light and wilt [wish to] flee from it. Thou wilt be fondly attracted towards the dull bluish-yellow light from the human [world].

At that time do not fear that bright, dazzling-yellow, transparent light, but know it to be Wisdom; in that state, keeping thy mind resigned, trust in it earnestly and humbly. If thou knowest it to be the radiance of thine own intellect—although thou exertest not thy humility and faith and prayer to it— the Divine Body and Light will merge into thee inseparably, and thou wilt obtain Buddhahood.

If thou dost not recognize the radiance of thine own intellect, think, with faith, ‘ It is the radiance of the grace of the

---

[1] Text: *Sangs-rgyas-spyan-ma* (pron. *Sang-yay Chan-ma*): ‘She of the Buddha Eye (or Eyes).’

[2] Text: *Nam-mkhahi-snying-po* (pron. *Nam-khai-nying-po*): Skt. *Ākāsha-Garbha*, ‘Womb (or Matrix) of the Sky’.

[3] Text: *Kuntu-bzang-po* (pron. *Küntu-zang-po*): Skt. *Samanta-Bhadra*, ‘All-Good’. This is not the Ādi-Buddha Samanta-Bhadra (cf. p. 95[3]), but the spiritual son of the Dhyāni Buddha Vairochana.

[4] Text: *Mahlaima*, ‘She Who Holds (or Bears) the Rosary’; and *Dhupema*, ‘She Who Holds (or Bears) the Incense’. These are corrupt forms, hybrids of Sanskrit and Tibetan, their Sanskrit equivalents being *Mālā* and *Dhūpa*, and their Tibetan equivalents *Hphreng-ba-ma* (pron. *Phreng-ba-ma*) and *Bdug-spös-ma* (pron. *Dug-pö-ma*). The colour of these goddesses, corresponding to that of the earth-light, is yellow.

Bhagavān Ratna-Sambhava; I will take refuge in it'; and pray. It is the hook of the grace-rays of the Bhagavān Ratna-Sambhava; believe in it.

Be not fond of that dull bluish-yellow light from the human [world]. That is the path of thine accumulated propensities of violent egotism come to receive thee. If thou art attracted by it, thou wilt be born in the human world and have to suffer birth, age, sickness, and death; and thou wilt have no chance of getting out of the quagmire of worldly existence. That is an interruption to obstruct thy path of liberation. Therefore, look not upon it, and abandon egotism, abandon propensities; be not attracted towards it; be not weak. Act so as to trust in that bright dazzling light. Put thine earnest thought, one-pointedly, upon the Bhagavān Ratna-Sambhava; and pray thus:

> 'Alas! when wandering in the *Sangsāra* because of the
>   power of violent egotism,
> On the radiant light-path of the Wisdom of Equality,
> May [I] be led by the Bhagavān Ratna-Sambhava;
> May the Divine Mother, She-of-the-Buddha-Eye, be [my]
>   rear-guard;
> May [I] be led safely across the fearful ambush of the
>   *Bardo*;
> And may [I] be placed in the state of the All-Perfect
>   Buddhahood.'

By praying thus, with deep humility and faith, thou wilt merge into the heart of the Bhagavān Ratna-Sambhava, the Divine Father-Mother, in halo of rainbow light, and attain Buddhahood in the *Sambhoga-Kāya*, in the Southern Realm Endowed with Glory.

[THE FOURTH DAY]

By thus being set face to face, however weak the mental faculties may be, there is no doubt of one's gaining Liberation. Yet, though so often set face to face, there are classes of men who, having created much bad *karma*, or having failed in observance of vows, or, their lot [for higher development] being altogether lacking, prove unable to recognize: their obscurations

and evil *karma* from covetousness and miserliness produce
awe of the sounds and radiances, and they flee. [If one be
of these classes], then, on the Fourth Day, the Bhagavān
Amitābha[1] and his attendant deities, together with the light-
path from the *Preta-loka*, proceeding from miserliness and
attachment, will come to receive one simultaneously.

Again the setting-face-to-face is, calling the deceased by
name, thus:

O nobly-born, listen undistractedly. On the Fourth Day
the red light, which is the primal form of the element fire, will
shine. At that time, from the Red Western Realm of Happiness,[2] the Bhagavān Buddha Amitābha, red in colour, bearing
a lotus in his hand, seated upon a peacock-throne and embraced by the Divine Mother Gökarmo,[2] will shine upon thee,
[together with] the Bodhisattvas Chenrazee[3] and Jampal,[4]
attended by the female Bodhisattvas Ghirdhima[5] and Āloke.[5]
The six bodies of Enlightenment will shine upon thee from
amidst a halo of rainbow light.

[1] Text: *Snang-va-mthah-yas* (pron. *Nang-wa-tha-yay*): Skt. *Amitābha*, 'Boundless (or Incomprehensible) Light'. As an embodiment of one of the Buddha-
attributes or Wisdoms, the All-discriminating Wisdom, Amitābha personifies
life eternal.

[2] Text: *Gös-dkar-mo* (pron. *Gö-kar-mo*), 'She-in-White-Raiment'.

[3] Text: *Spyan-ras-gzigs* (pron. *Chen-rä-zī*): Skt. *Avalokiteshvara*, 'Down-
Looking One', the embodiment of mercy or compassion. The Dalai Lāmas are
believed to be his incarnations; Amitābha, with whom he here dawns, is his
spiritual father, whose incarnate representatives are the Tashi Lāmas. He is
often depicted with eleven heads and a thousand arms, each with an eye in the
palm—as 'The Great Pitier'—his thousand arms and eyes appropriately
representing him as ever on the outlook to discover distress and to succour the
troubled. In China, Avalokiteshvara becomes the Great Goddess of Mercy
Kwanyin, represented by a female figure bearing a child in her arms.

[4] Text: *Hgam-dpal* (pron. *Jam-pal*): Skt. *Mañjushrī*, 'Of Gentle Glory'.
A fuller Tibetan form is *Hgam-dpal-dvyangs* (pron. *Jam-pal-yang*): Skt. *Mañjughosha*, 'Glorious Gentle-Voiced One'. He is 'The God of Mystic Wisdom',
the Buddhist Apollo, commonly depicted with the flaming sword of light held
aloft in his right hand and the lotus-supported Book of Wisdom, the *Prajñā-
Pāramitā*, held in his left.

[5] Text: *Ghir-dhi-ma* and *Āloke*, corrupted from Skt. *Gītā*, 'Song', and *Āloka*,
'Light': Tib. *Glu-ma* (pron. *Lu-ma*) and *Snang-gsal-ma* (pron. *Nang-sal-ma*).
Gītā, commonly represented holding a lyre, personifies (or symbolizes) music
and song, and *Āloka*, holding a lamp, personifies (or symbolizes) light. Related
to the element fire, as herein, their colour is red.

The primal form of the aggregate of feelings as the red
light of the All-Discriminating Wisdom, glitteringly red, glorified with orbs and satellite orbs, bright, transparent, glorious
and dazzling, proceeding from the heart of the Divine Father-
Mother Amitābha, will strike against thy heart [so radiantly]
that thou wilt scarcely be able to look upon it.   Fear it not.

Along with it, a dull red light from the *Preta-loka*, coming
side by side with the Light of Wisdom, will also shine upon thee.
Act so that thou shalt not be fond of it.   Abandon attachment [and] weakness [for it].

At that time, through the influence of intense attachment,
thou wilt become terrified by the dazzling red light, and wilt
[wish to] flee from it.   And thou wilt beget a fondness for
that dull red light of the *Preta-loka*.

At that time, be not afraid of the glorious, dazzling, transparent, radiant red light.   Recognizing it as Wisdom, keeping
thine intellect in the state of resignation, thou wilt merge
[into it] inseparably and attain Buddhahood.

If thou dost not recognize it, think, 'It is the rays of the
grace of the Bhagavān Amitābha, and I will take refuge in it';
and, trusting humbly in it, pray unto it.   That is the hook-
rays of the grace of the Bhagavān Amitābha.   Trust in it
humbly; flee not.   Even if thou fleest, it will follow thee
inseparably [from thyself].   Fear it not.   Be not attracted
towards the dull red light of the *Preta-loka*.   That is the light-
path proceeding from the accumulations of thine intense
attachment [to *sangsāric* existence] which hath come to
receive thee.   If thou be attached thereto, thou wilt fall into
the World of Unhappy Spirits and suffer unbearable misery
from hunger and thirst.   Thou wilt have no chance of gaining
Liberation [therein].[1]   That dull red light is an interruption
to obstruct thee on the Path of Liberation.   Be not attached
to it, and abandon habitual propensities.   Be not weak.   Trust
in the bright dazzling red light.   In the Bhagavān Amitābha,

---

[1] Lit. 'Of Liberation there will be no time.'   Once the deceased becomes
a *preta*, or unhappy ghost, the after-death attainment of *Nirvāṇa* is, normally,
no longer possible; he must then wait for the opportunity afforded by rebirth
in the human world, when his *Preta-loka* existence has ended.

the Father-Mother, put thy trust one-pointedly and pray
thus:

'Alas! when wandering in the *Sangsāra* because of the
power of intense attachment,
On the radiant light-path of the Discriminating Wisdom
May [I] be led by the Bhagavān Amitābha;
May the Divine Mother, She-of-White-Raiment, be [my]
rear-guard;
May [I] be safely led across the dangerous ambush of the
Bardo;
And may [I] be placed in the state of the All-Perfect
Buddhahood.'

By praying thus, humbly and earnestly, thou wilt merge
into the heart of the Divine Father-Mother, the Bhagavān
Amitābha, in halo of rainbow-light, and attain Buddhahood in
the *Sambhoga-Kāya*, in the Western Realm named Happy.

[THE FIFTH DAY]

It is impossible that one should not be liberated thereby.
Yet, though thus set face to face, sentient beings, unable
through long association with propensities to abandon propensities, and, through bad *karma* and jealousy, awe and terror
being produced by the sounds and radiances—the hook-rays
of grace failing to catch hold of them—wander down also to
the Fifth Day. [If one be such a sentient being], thereupon
the Bhagavān Amogha-Siddhi,[1] with his attendant deities
and the light and rays of his grace, will come to receive one.
A light proceeding from the *Asura-loka*, produced by the evil
passion of jealousy, will also come to receive one.

The setting-face-to-face at that time is, calling the deceased
by name, thus:

O nobly-born, listen undistractedly. On the Fifth Day, the
green light of the primal form of the element air will shine
upon thee. At that time, from the Green Northern Realm of
Successful Performance of Best Actions, the Bhagavān Buddha
Amogha-Siddhi, green in colour, bearing a crossed-*dorje* in

---

[1] Text: *Don-yod-grub-pa* (pron. *Don-yöd-rub-pa*): Skt. *Amogha-Siddhi*: 'Almighty Conqueror.'

hand,[1] seated upon a sky-traversing Harpy-throne,[2] embraced by the Divine Mother, the Faithful Dölma,[3] will shine upon thee, with his attendants,—the two Bodhisattvas Chag-na-Dorje [4] and Dibpanamsel,[5] attended by two female Bodhisattvas, Gandhema [6] and Nidhema.[7] These six *Bodhic* forms, from amidst a halo of rainbow light, will come to shine.

The primal form of the aggregate of volition, shining as the green light of the All-Performing Wisdom, dazzlingly green, transparent and radiant, glorious and terrifying, beautified with orbs surrounded by satellite orbs of radiance, issuing from the heart of the Divine Father-Mother Amogha-Siddhi, green in colour, will strike against thy heart [so wondrously

---

[1] That is, a dorje with four heads, such as is depicted on the front cover of this volume. It symbolizes equilibrium, immutability, and almighty power.

[2] Text: *shang-shang*, refers to an order of creatures like the fabulous harpies of classical mythology, having human form from the waist upwards, and from the waist downwards the form of a bird ; but whereas the Greek harpies were female, these are of both sexes. That a race of such harpies exists in the world somewhere is a popular belief among Tibetans.

[3] Text: *Sgrol-ma* (pron. *Döl-ma*): *Dölma* (Skt. *Tārā*) = 'Saviouress'. She is the divine consort of Avalokiteshvara. There are now two recognized forms of this goddess : the Green Dölma, as worshipped in Tibet, and the White Dölma, as worshipped chiefly in China and Mongolia. The royal Nepalese princess who became the wife of the first Buddhist king of Tibet is believed to have been an incarnation of the Green Dölma, and his wife from the Imperial House of China an incarnation of the White Dölma. (See p. 74.) The late Lāma Kazi Dawa-Samdup told me that, because Tibetans saw the likeness of Queen Victoria on English coins and recognized it as being that of Dölma, there developed throughout Tibet during the Victorian Era a belief that Dölma had come back to birth again to rule the world in the person of the Great Queen of England ; and that, owing to this belief, the British representatives of the Queen then met with an unusually friendly reception in their negotiations with Lhassa, although probably unaware of the origin of the friendship.

[4] Text: *Phyag-na-rdorje* (pron. *Chag-na-dorje*) : 'Bearing the *Dorje* in hand ': Skt. *Vajra-pāṇi*.

[5] Text: *Sgrib-pa-rnam-sel* (pron. *Ḍib-pa-nam-sel*): 'Clearer of Obscurations': Skt. *Dīpanī*, also *Dīpikā*.

[6] Skt.-Tib. hybrid of text. Corresponding Tib., *Dri-chha-ma* (Skt. *Gandha*), 'She Spraying Perfume ', one of the eight mother goddesses (*Mātṛis*) of the Hindu pantheon. She is depicted holding a shell-vase of perfume (*dri*).

[7] Skt.-Tib. hybrid of text. Corresponding Tib., *Zhal-zas-ma* (pron. *Shal-za-ma*), 'She Holding Sweetmeats '. Although a goddess like Gandhema, Nidhema (Skt. *Naivedya*) cannot be included in the formal list of eight *Mātṛis*, the eight already having been named in our text. Both goddesses are green in colour, like the light of the All-Performing Wisdom.

bright] that thou wilt scarcely be able to look at it. Fear it not. That is the natural power of the wisdom of thine own intellect. Abide in the state of great resignation of impartiality.

Along with it [i. e. the green light of the All-Performing Wisdom], a light of dull green colour from the *Asura-loka*, produced from the cause of the feeling of jealousy, coming side by side with the Wisdom Rays, will shine upon thee. Meditate upon it with impartiality,—with neither repulsion nor attraction. Be not fond of it: if thou art of low mental capacity, be not fond of it.

Thereupon, through the influence of intense jealousy,[1] thou wilt be terrified at the dazzling radiance of the green light and wilt [wish to] flee from it; and thou wilt beget a fondness for that dull green light of the *Asura-loka*. At that time fear not the glorious and transparent, radiant and dazzling green light, but know it to be Wisdom; and in that state allow thine intellect to rest in resignation. Or else [think], 'It is the hook-rays of the light of grace of the Bhagavān Amogha-Siddhi, which is the All-Performing Wisdom'. Believe [thus] on it. Flee not from it.

Even though thou shouldst flee from it, it will follow thee inseparably [from thyself]. Fear it not. Be not fond of that dull green light of the *Asura-loka*. That is the *karmic* path of acquired intense jealousy, which hath come to receive thee. If thou art attracted by it, thou wilt fall into the *Asura-loka* and have to engage in unbearable miseries of quarrelling and warfare.[2] [That is an] interruption to obstruct thy path of liberation. Be not attracted by it. Abandon thy propensities. Be not weak. Trust in the dazzling green radiance, and putting thy whole thought one-pointedly upon the Divine Father-Mother, the Bhagavān Amogha-Siddhi, pray thus:

[1] Here, as in the previous and following paragraph, the jealousy referred to is the *karmic* propensities of jealousy existing as part of the content of the consciousness (or subconsciousness) of the deceased; and, erupting on this the Fifth Day of the *Bardo* existence, they produce their corresponding 'astral' hallucinations.

[2] Quarrelling and warfare are the chief passions of a being born as an *asura* in the *Asura-loka*.

'Alas! when wandering in the *Sangsāra* because of the
power of intense jealousy,

On the radiant light-path of the All-Performing Wisdom

May [I] be led by the Bhagavān Amogha-Siddhi;

May the Divine Mother, the Faithful Tārā, be [my] rear-
guard;

May [I] be led safely across the dangerous ambush of
the *Bardo*;

And may [I] be placed in the state of the All-Perfect
Buddhahood.'

By praying thus with intense faith and humility, thou
wilt merge into the heart of the Divine Father-Mother, the
Bhagavān Amogha-Siddhi, in halo of rainbow light, and attain
Buddhahood in the *Sambhoga-Kāya*, in the Northern Realm of
Heaped-up Good Deeds.[1]

[THE SIXTH DAY]

Being thus set face to face at various stages, however weak
one's *karmic* connexions may be, one should have recognized in
one or the other of them; and where one has recognized in any
of them it is impossible not to be liberated. Yet, although set
face to face so very often in that manner, one long habituated
to strong propensities and lacking in familiarity with, and pure
affection for, Wisdom, may be led backwards by the power of
one's own evil inclinations despite these many introductions.
The hook-rays of the light of grace may not be able to catch
hold of one: one may still wander downwards because of one's
begetting the feeling of awe and terror of the lights and rays.

Thereupon all the Divine Fathers-Mothers of the Five
Orders [of Dhyānī Buddhas] with their attendants will come
to shine upon one simultaneously. At the same time, the
lights proceeding from the Six *Lokas* will likewise come to
shine upon one simultaneously.

The setting-face-to-face for that is, calling the deceased by
name, thus:

O nobly-born, until yesterday each of the Five Orders of

---

[1] The Block-Print has 'Realm of Perfected Good Deeds (or "Actions")';
and this is the more correct form.

Deities had shone upon thee, one by one; and thou hadst been set face to face, but, owing to the influence of thine evil propensities, thou wert awed and terrified by them and hast remained here till now.

If thou hadst recognized the radiances of the Five Orders of Wisdom to be the emanations from thine own thought-forms, ere this thou wouldst have obtained Buddhahood in the *Sambhoga-Kāya*, through having been absorbed into the halo of rainbow light in one or another of the Five Orders of Buddhas. But now look on undistractedly. Now the lights of all Five Orders, called the Lights of the Union of Four Wisdoms,[1] will come to receive thee. Act so as to know them.

O nobly-born, on this the Sixth Day, the four colours of the primal states of the four elements [water, earth, fire, air] will shine upon thee simultaneously. At that time, from the Central Realm of the Spreading Forth of Seed, the Buddha[2] Vairochana, the Divine Father-Mother, with the attendant

---

[1] The philosophically descriptive Tibetan terms (which are not contained in our text) for these Four Wisdoms are: (1) *Snang-Stong* (pron. *Nang-Tong*), 'Phenomena and Voidness'; (2) *Gsal-Stong* (pron. *Sal-Tong*), 'Radiance and Voidness'; (3) *Bde-Stong* (pron. *De-Tong*), 'Bliss and Voidness'; (4) *Rig-Stong* (pron. *Rig-Tong*), 'Consciousness and Voidness'.

They correspond to the four stages of *dhyāna* which arise in the same order. They probably also correspond, but in a less exact manner, to the Four Wisdoms: the Mirror-like Wisdom, the Wisdom of Equality, the All-Discriminating Wisdom, and the All-Performing Wisdom.

'*Dhyāna* consists of progressive mental states: analysis (Skt. *vitarka*), reflection (Skt. *vichāra*), fondness (Skt. *prīti*), bliss (Skt. *ānanda*), and concentration (Skt. *ekāgratā*). In the first stage of *dhyāna*, the devotee asks himself, "What is this body? Is it lasting; is it the thing to be saved?" and decides that to cling to an impermanent, corruptible bodily form, such as he thereby realizes it to be, is not desirable. Similarly, having gained knowledge of the nature of Form, he analyses and reflects upon Touch, Feeling, Volition, Cognition, and Desire; and, finding that Mind is the apparent reality, arrives at ordinary concentration.

'In the second stage of *dhyāna*, reflection only is employed; in other words, reflection transcends the lower mental process called analysis. In the third stage, reflection gives way to a blissful state of consciousness; and this bliss, being at first apparently a physical sensation, merges into pure ecstasy, in the fourth stage. In the fifth stage, the sensation of ecstasy, although always present in a suppressed or secondary condition, gives way to complete concentration.'—Lāma Kazi Dawa-Samdup.

[2] Heretofore each of the chief deities has been called Bhagavān ('The Victorious'), but, herein, Buddha ('The Enlightened') is the designation. The text contains Tib. *Sangs-rgyas* (pron. *Sang-yay*) = Skt. Buddha: *Sangs* =

[deities], will come to shine upon thee. From the Eastern Realm of Pre-eminent Happiness, the Buddha Vajra-Sattva, the Divine Father-Mother, with the attendant [deities] will come to shine upon thee. From the Southern Realm endowed with Glory, the Buddha Ratna-Sambhava, the Divine Father-Mother, with the attendant [deities] will come to shine upon thee. From the Happy Western Realm | [1] of Heaped-up Lotuses, the Buddha Amitābha, the Divine Father-Mother, along with the attendant [deities] will come to shine upon thee. From the Northern Realm of Perfected Good Deeds, the Buddha Amogha-Siddhi, the Divine Father-Mother, along with the attendants will come, amidst a halo of rainbow light, to shine upon | thee at this very moment.

O nobly-born, on the outer circle of these five pair of Dhyānī Buddhas, the [four] Door-Keepers, the Wrathful [Ones]: the Victorious One,[2] the Destroyer of the Lord of Death,[3] the Horse-necked King,[4] the Urn of Nectar;[5] with the four female Door-keepers: the Goad-Bearer,[6] the Noose-Bearer,[7] the Chain-Bearer,[8] and the Bell-Bearer;[9]

'awakened [from sleep of stupidity]' + *rgyas* = 'developed fully [in all attributes of perfection (or moral virtues)]'.

[1] Between this bar and the bar in the sentence following is contained the translation of the Tibetan text on the upper folio (35a) of our Frontispiece.

[2] Text: *Rnam-par-rgyal-va* (pron. *Nam-par-gyal-wa*): Skt. *Vijaya*: 'Victorious [One]', the Door-keeper of the East.

[3] Text: *Gshin-rje-gshed-po* (pron. *Shin-je-shed-po*): Skt. *Yamāntaka*: 'Destroyer of Yama (Death)', the Door-keeper of the South, a form of Shiva, and the wrathful aspect of Avalokiteshvara. He, as a Wrathful Deity, personifies one of the ten forms of Anger (Tib. *K'ro-bo*—pron. *T'o-wo*: Skt. *Krodha*).

[4] Text: *Rta-mgrin-rgyal-po* (pron. *Tam din-gyal-po*): Skt. *Hayagrīva*: 'Horse-necked King', the Door-keeper of the West.

[5] Text: *Bdud-rtsi-hkhyil-va* (pron. *Dü-tsi-khyil-wa*): Skt. *Amṛita-Dhāra*: '[He who is the] Urn of Nectar', whose divine function is to transmute all things into nectar (in the esoteric sense of Tantric *Yoga*), *amṛita* meaning 'nectar' exoterically, and, esoterically, 'voidness'. He is the Door-keeper of the North.

[6] Text: *Chags-kyu-ma* (pron. *Chak-yu-ma*): Skt. *Ankushā*: 'She holding the Goad', the *shakti*, or female counterpart, of Vijaya.

[7] Text: *Zhags-pa-ma* (pron. *Zhag-pa-ma*): Skt. *Pāshadhari*: 'She holding the Noose', the *shakti* of Yamāntaka.

[8] Text: *Lghags-sgrog-ma* (pron. *Cha-dog-ma*): Skt. *Vajra-shṛingkhalā*: 'She holding the Chain', the *shakti* of Hayagrīva.

[9] Text: *Dril-bu-ma* (pron. *Til-bu-ma*): Skt. *Kinkini-Dharī*: 'She holding the Bell', the *shakti* of Amṛita-Dhāra.

All the Door-keepers and their *shaktis* possess occult significance in relation

along with the Buddha of the *Devas*, named the One of
Supreme Power,[1] the Buddha of the *Asuras*, named [He of]
Strong Texture,[2] the Buddha of Mankind, named the Lion
of the Shākyas, the Buddha of the brute kingdom, named
the Unshakable Lion, the Buddha of the *Pretas*, named the
One of Flaming Mouth, and the Buddha of the Lower World,
named the King of Truth:[3]—[these], the Eight Father-
Mother Door-keepers and the Six Teachers, the Victorious
Ones—will come to shine, too.

The All-Good Father, and the All-Good Mother,[4] the
Great Ancestors of all the Buddhas: Samanta-Bhadra [and
Samanta-Bhadrā], the Divine Father and the Divine Mother—
these two, also will come to shine.

These forty-two perfectly endowed deities, issuing from
within thy heart, being the product of thine own pure love,
will come to shine. Know them.

O nobly-born, these realms are not come from somewhere
outside [thyself]. They come from within the four divisions
of thy heart, which, including its centre, make the five directions. They issue from within there, and shine upon thee. The

to the four directions and to the *mandala* (or conclave of deities) to which they
belong. As Tantric faith-guarding deities (Tib. *Ch'os-skyon* : Skt. *Dharmapāla*)
they rank with Bodhisattvas. They symbolize, too, the four tranquil or peaceful methods employed by Divine Beings for the salvation of sentient creatures
(of whom mankind are the highest), which are : Compassion, Fondness, Love,
and Stern Justice.

[1] Text: *Dvang-po-rgya-byin* (pron. *Wang-po-gya-jin*) : 'Powerful One of a
Hundred Sacrifices' : Skt. *Shata-Kratu*, a name of *Indra* ('[One of] Supreme
Power').

[2] Text: *Thag-bzang-ris* (pron. *Thag-zang-ree*) : '[He of] Strong Texture'
(Skt. *Vīrāchāra*) : a name referring either to the bodily strength of, or else to the
coat of mail worn by, this Lord of the *Asura-loka*, the world wherein warfare
is the predominant passion of existence.

[3] Text: *Chos-kyi-rgyal-po* (pron. *Chö-kyi-gyal-po*) : Skt. *Dharma-Rāja*.

[4] Text: *Kūntu-bzang-mo* (pron. *Kūntu-bzang-mo*) : 'All-Good Mother' ; Skt.
Samanta-Bhadrā. The Tantric School holds that every deity, even the Supreme,
has its *shakti*. A few deities are, however, commonly depicted *shakti*-less—for
example, Mañjushrī, or Mañjughosha (see p. 113[4]) ; though there may be, as in
the instance of the *Prajñā-Pāramitā* (often called the Mother) which this deity
holds, some symbolic representation of a *shakti*. This is, apparently, a doctrine
of universal dualism. In the final analysis, however, all pairs of opposites being
viewed as having a Single Source—in the Voidness of the *Dharma-Kāya*—the
apparent dualism becomes monism.

deities, too, are not come from somewhere else: they exist from eternity within the faculties of thine own intellect.[1] Know them to be of that nature.

O nobly-born, the size of all these deities is not large, not small, [but] proportionate. [They have] their ornaments, their colours, their sitting postures, their thrones, and the emblems that each holds.

These deities are formed into groups of five pairs, each group of five being surrounded by a fivefold circle of radiances, the male Bodhisattvas partaking of the nature of the Divine Fathers, and the female Bodhisattvas partaking of the nature of the Divine Mothers. All these divine conclaves will come to shine upon thee in one complete conclave.[2] They are thine own tutelary deities.[3] Know them to be such.

O nobly-born, from the hearts of the Divine Fathers and Mothers of the Five Orders, the rays of light of the Four Wisdoms united, extremely clear and fine, like the rays of the sun spun into threads, will come and shine upon thee and strike against thy heart.

On that path of radiance there will come to shine glorious orbs of light, blue in colour, emitting rays, the *Dharma-Dhātu* Wisdom [itself], each appearing like an inverted turquoise cup, surrounded by similar orbs, smaller in size, glorious and dazzling, radiant and transparent, each made more glorious with five yet smaller [satellite] orbs dotted round about with five starry spots of light of the same nature, leaving neither the centre nor the borders [of the blue light-path] unglorified by the orbs and the smaller [satellite] orbs.

[1] According to the esotericism of Northern Buddhism, man is, in the sense implied by the mystical philosophies of ancient Egypt and Greece, the microcosm of the macrocosm.

[2] Text: *dkyil-hkhor* (pron. *kyil-khor*): Skt. *maṇḍala*, i. e. conclave of deities.

[3] The Tutelary Deities, too, in the last analysis, are the visualizations of the person believing in them. *The Demchok Tantra* says that the ' Devatās are but symbols representing the various things which occur on the Path, such as the helpful impulses and the stages attained by their means'; and that 'should doubts arise as to the divinity of these Devatās, one should say "The Dākinī is only the recollection of the body" and remember that the deities constitute the Path' (cf. A. Avalon, *Tantrik Texts*, London, 1919, vii. 41).

From the heart of Vajra-Sattva, the white light-path of the Mirror-like Wisdom, white and transparent, glorious and dazzling, glorious and terrifying, made more glorious with orbs surrounded by smaller orbs of transparent and radiant light upon it, each like an inverted mirror, will come to shine.

From the heart of Ratna-Sambhava, the yellow light-path of the Wisdom of Equality, [glorified] with yellow orbs [of radiance], each like an inverted gold cup, surrounded by smaller orbs, and these with yet smaller orbs, will come to shine.

From the heart of Amitābha, the transparent, bright red light-path of the Discriminating Wisdom, upon which are orbs, like inverted coral cups, emitting rays of Wisdom, extremely bright and dazzling, each glorified with five [satellite] orbs of the same nature,—leaving neither the centre nor the borders [of the red light-path] unglorified with orbs and smaller satellite orbs,—will come to shine.

These will come to shine against thy heart simultaneously.[1]

O nobly-born, all those are the radiances of thine own intellectual faculties come to shine. They have not come from any other place. Be not attracted towards them; be not weak; be not terrified; but abide in the mood of non- thought-formation.[2] In that state all the forms and radiances will merge into thyself, and Buddhahood will be obtained.

The green light-path of the Wisdom of Perfected Actions will not shine upon thee, because the Wisdom-faculty of thine intellect hath not been perfectly developed.

O nobly-born, those are called the Lights of the Four

---

[1] Each of these mystical radiances symbolizes the particular *Bodhic*, or Wisdom, quality of the Buddha whence it shines. In the Tibetan of our text there is here such fervency in the poetical description of the light-paths that the translator, in order to render something of the beauty of the original language, essayed several renderings, of which the actual rendering is the outcome.

[2] 'The mood of non- thought-formation' is attained in *samādhi-yoga*. This state, regarded as the primordial state of Mind, is illustrated by the following figure: So long as a man afloat on a river passively submits to the current, he is carried along smoothly; but if he attempts to grasp an object fixed in the water the tranquillity of his motion is broken. Similarly, thought-formation arrests the natural flow of the mind.

Wisdoms United, [whence proceeds that] which is called the Inner Path through Vajra-Sattva.[1]

At that time, thou must remember the teachings of the setting-face-to-face which thou hast had from thy *guru*. If thou hast remembered the purport of the settings-face-to-face, thou wilt have recognized all these lights which have shone upon thee, as being the reflection of thine own inner light, and, having recognized them as intimate friends, thou wilt have believed in them and have understood [them at] the meeting, as a son understandeth his mother.

And believing in the unchanging nature of the pure and holy Truth, thou wilt have had produced in thee the tranquil-flowing *Samādhi*; and, having merged into the body of the perfectly evolved intellect, thou wilt have obtained Buddhahood in the *Sambhoga-Kāya*, whence there is no return.

O nobly-born, along with the radiances of Wisdom, the impure illusory lights of the Six *Lokas* will also come to shine. If it be asked, 'What are they?' [they are] a dull white light from the *devas*, a dull green light from the *asuras*, a dull yellow light from human beings, a dull blue light from the brutes, a dull reddish light from the *pretas*, and a dull smoke-coloured light from Hell.[2] These six thus will come to shine, along with the six radiances of Wisdom; whereupon, be not afraid of nor be attracted towards any, but allow thyself to rest in the non-thought condition.

---

[1] In the transcendental state of the Illumination of Buddhahood, on the Inner, or Secret, Path, into Vajra-Sattva merge, in at-one-ment, all the Peaceful and Wrathful Deities of the greater *maṇḍala* described by our text; in all, one-hundred and ten,—forty-two in the heart-centre, ten in the throat-centre, and fifty-eight in the brain-centre. (Cf. pp. 217-8.)

[2] There are irreconcilable differences between the colours assigned to these light-paths in the Block-Print (25b) and in our MS. The Block-Print gives them as follows: white, from the *devas*; red, from the *asuras*; blue, from human beings; green, from the brutes; yellow, from the *pretas*; smoke-coloured from Hell. According to the translator, the colours should correspond to the colour of the Buddha of each *loka*, thus: *deva*, white; *asura*, green; human, yellow; brute, blue; *preta*, red; Hell, smoke-coloured or black. Therefore, the Block-Print is wrong in all save the first and last; and the MS. is wrong in assigning dull blue to the human and black or smoke-coloured to the animal world. On folio 23, the MS. correctly assigns yellow to the human world light-path. The necessary corrections have been made in the translation herein and in the corresponding passages in folio 46 following.

If thou art frightened by the pure radiances of Wisdom and attracted by the impure lights of the Six *Lokas*, then thou wilt assume a body in any of the Six *Lokas* and suffer *sangsāric* miseries; and thou wilt never be emancipated from the Ocean of *Sangsāra*, wherein thou wilt be whirled round and round and made to taste of the sufferings thereof.

O nobly-born, if thou art one who hath not obtained the select words of the *guru*, thou wilt have fear of the pure radiances of Wisdom and of the deities thereof. Being thus frightened, thou wilt be attracted towards the impure *sangsāric* objects. Act not so. Humbly trust in the dazzling pure radiances of Wisdom. Frame thy mind to faith, and think, 'The compassionate radiances of Wisdom of the Five Orders of Buddhas [1] have come to take hold of me out of compassion; I take refuge in them.'

Not yielding to attraction towards the illusory lights of the Six *Lokas*, but devoting thy whole mind one-pointedly towards the Divine Fathers and Mothers, the Buddhas of the Five Orders, pray thus:

'Alas! when wandering in the *Sangsāra* through the power of the five virulent poisons,[2]
On the bright radiance-path of the Four Wisdoms united,
May [I] be led by the Five Victorious Conquerors,
May the Five Orders of Divine Mothers be [my] rear-guard;
May [I] be rescued from the impure light-paths of the Six *Lokas*;
And, being saved from the ambuscades of the dread *Bardo*,
May [I] be placed within the five pure Divine Realms.'

By thus praying, one recognizeth one's own inner light;[3]

[1] Text: *Bde-var-gshegs-pa* (pron. *De-war-sheg-pa*): Skt. *Sugata*: literally meaning 'Those who have passed into Happiness (or attained *Nirvāṇa*)'—i.e. Buddhas.

[2] The five virulent poisons, which, like drugs, enslave and bind mankind to the sufferings of existence within the confines of the Six *Lokas*, are: lust, hatred, stupidity, pride or egoism, and jealousy.

[3] Text: *rang* ('self') + *sNang* ('light'): 'self-light' or 'inner-light', i.e. thoughts or ideas appearing in the radiance of the consciousness-principle. The *Bardo* state is the after-death dream state following the waking or living-on-earth state, as explained in our Introduction (pp. 28 ff.); and the whole

and, merging one's self therein, in at-one-ment, Buddhahood is attained : through humble faith, the ordinary devotee cometh to know himself, and obtaineth Liberation ; even the most lowly, by the power of the pure prayer, can close the doors of the Six *Lokas*, and, in understanding the real meaning of the Four Wisdoms united, obtain Buddhahood by the hollow pathway through Vajra-Sattva.[1]

Thus by being set face to face in that detailed manner, those who are destined to be liberated will come to recognize [the Truth] ;[2] thereby many will attain Liberation.

The worst of the worst, [those] of heavy evil *karma*, having not the least predilection for any religion—and some who have failed in their vows—through the power of *karmic* illusions, not recognizing, although set face to face [with Truth], will stray downwards.

[THE SEVENTH DAY]

On the Seventh Day, the Knowledge-Holding Deities, from the holy paradise realms, come to receive one. Simultaneously, the pathway to the brute world, produced by the obscuring passion, stupidity, also cometh to receive one.[3] The setting-face-to-face at that time is, calling the deceased by name, thus :

aim of the *Bardo Thödol* teaching is to awaken the Dreamer to Reality—to a supramundane state of consciousness, to an annihilation of all bonds of *sangsāric* existence, to Perfect Enlightenment, Buddhahood.

[1] Vajra-Sattva, as a symbolic deity, the reflex of Akṣhobhya, is visualized, in Tibetan occult rituals, as being internally vacuous. As such, he represents the Void, concerning which there are many treatises with elaborate commentaries, essentially esoteric. Through Vajra-Sattva there lies a certain pathway to Liberation, he being the embodiment of all the one-hundred and ten deities constituting the *maṇḍala* of the Peaceful and Wrathful Ones (see p. 124[1]). To tread this Path successfully, the Neophyte must be instructed by the Hierophant.

[2] This Truth is that there is no reality behind any of the phenomena of the *Bardo* plane, save the illusions stored up in one's own mind as accretions from *sangsāric* experiences. Recognition of this automatically gives Liberation.

[3] As the gross physical atoms of a life-deserted human-plane body gradually separate and go to their appropriate places, some as gases, some as fluids, some as solids, so on the after-death plane there comes about a gradual dispersion of the psychic or mental atoms of the *Bardo* thought-body, each propensity—directed by *karmic* affinity—inevitably going to that environment most congenial to it. Hence, as our text suggests, the brute-passion stupidity has a natural tendency to gravitate to the brute kingdom and become embodied therein as a disintegrated part of the mentality of the deceased. (See pp. 44 ff.)

O nobly-born, listen undistractedly. On the Seventh Day the vari-coloured radiance of the purified propensities will come to shine. Simultaneously, the Knowledge-Holding Deities,[1] from the holy paradise realms, will come to receive one.

From the centre of the Circle [or *Maṇḍala*], enhaloed in radiance of rainbow light, the supreme Knowledge-Holding [Deity], the Lotus Lord of Dance, the Supreme Knowledge-Holder Who Ripens *Karmic* Fruits, radiant with all the five colours, embraced by the [Divine] Mother, the Red *Ḍākinī*,[2] [he] holding a crescent knife and a skull [filled] with blood,[3] dancing and making the *mudrā* of fascination,[4] [with his right hand held] aloft, will come to shine.

To the east of that Circle, the deity called the Earth-Abiding Knowledge-Holder, white of colour, with radiant smiling countenance, embraced by the White *Ḍākinī*, the [Divine] Mother, [he] holding a crescent knife and a skull [filled] with blood, dancing and making the *mudrā* of fascination, [with his right hand held] aloft, will come to shine.

To the south of that Circle, the Knowledge-Holding Deity called [He] Having Power Over Duration of Life, yellow in colour, smiling and radiant, embraced by the Yellow *Ḍākinī*, the [Divine] Mother, [he] holding a crescent knife and a skull

---

[1] Text: *Rig-ḥdsin* (pron. *Rig-zin*): 'possessing (or holding) knowledge'. These deities are purely Tantric. (See p. 73[1].)

[2] The Ḍākinīs (Tib. *Mkhaḥ-ḥgro-ma* [or 'Sky-goer']: Skt. *Ḍākinī*), fairy-like goddesses possessing peculiar occult powers for good or for evil, are, also, purely Tantric; and, as such, they are invoked in most of the chief rituals of Northern Buddhism. (See p. 122[3].)

[3] Esoterically, the skull (which is human), and the blood (also human) filling it, signify, in one sense, renunciation of human life, the giving up of the *Sangsāra*, self-immolation on the cross of the world; and in the mass-ritual of Lāmaism there are resemblances between the blood (symbolized by a red fluid) in the skull and the wine (as blood) in the chalice of the Christian Communion.

[4] A *mudrā* is a mystic sign made by posturing the hand and fingers or the body. Some *mudrās* are used as signs of recognition by members of occult fraternities, after the manner of the Masonic hand-clasp. Others, chiefly employed by *yogīs* as bodily postures, short-circuit or otherwise change the magnetic currents of the body. Placing the tip of one finger against the tip of another in *mudrā* controls, likewise, the bodily forces, or life-currents. The *mudrā* of fascination is of this last sort, being made (with the right hand) by the second finger touching the thumb, the index-finger and the little finger held upright, and the third finger folded in the palm of the hand.

[filled] with blood, dancing and making the *mudrā* of fascination, [with his right hand held] aloft, will come to shine.

To the west of that Circle, the deity called the Knowledge-Holding Deity of the Great Symbol,[1] red of colour, smiling and radiant, embraced by the Red *Ḍākinī*, the [Divine] Mother, [he] holding a crescent-knife and a skull [filled] with blood, dancing and making the *mudrā* of fascination, [with his right hand held] aloft, will come to shine.

To the north of that Circle, the deity called the Self-Evolved Knowledge-Holder, green of colour, with a half-angry, half-smiling radiant countenance, embraced by the Green *Ḍākinī*, the [Divine] Mother, [he] holding a crescent-knife and a skull [filled] with blood, dancing and making the *mudrā* of fascination, [with his right hand held] aloft, will come to shine.

In the Outer Circle, round about these Knowledge-Holders, innumerable bands of *ḍākinīs*,—*ḍākinīs* of the eight places of cremation, *ḍākinīs* of the four classes, *ḍākinīs* of the three abodes, *ḍākinīs* of the thirty holy-places and of the twenty-four places of pilgrimage,[2]—heroes, heroines, celestial warriors, and faith-protecting deities, male and female, each bedecked with the six bone-ornaments, having drums and thigh-bone trumpets, skull-timbrels, banners of gigantic human[-like] hides,[3] human-hide canopies, human-hide bannerettes, fumes of human-fat incense, and innumerable [other] kinds of musical instruments, filling [with music] the whole world-systems and causing them to vibrate, to quake and tremble with sounds so mighty as to daze one's brain, and dancing various measures, will come to receive the faithful and punish the unfaithful.[4]

---

[1] See p. 135[2].

[2] Herein the *ḍākinīs* are represented like various orders of fairy-like beings, some dwelling in one place, some in another. The eight places of cremation are the eight known to Hindu mythology ; the three abodes are the heart-centre, the throat-centre, and the brain-centre, over which, esoterically speaking, certain *ḍākinīs* (as the personification of the psychic forces resident in each centre) preside, just as other *ḍākinīs* preside over the holy-places and places of pilgrimage.

[3] That is, hides of *rākṣasas*, an order of giant demoniacal beings having human form and possessed of certain *siddhis* (i. e. supernormal powers).

[4] Tibetan *lāmas*, in chanting their rituals, employ seven (or eight) sorts of

O nobly-born, five-coloured radiances, of the Wisdom of the Simultaneously-Born,[1] which are the purified propensities, vibrating and dazzling like coloured threads, flashing, radiant, and transparent, glorious and awe-inspiring, will issue from the hearts of the five chief Knowledge-Holding Deities and strike against thy heart, so bright that the eye cannot bear to look upon them.

At the same time, a dull blue light from the brute world will come to shine along with the Radiances of Wisdom. Then, through the influence of the illusions of thy propensities, thou wilt feel afraid of the radiance of the five colours; and [wishing to] flee from it, thou wilt feel attracted towards the dull light from the brute-world. Thereupon, be not afraid of that brilliant radiance of five colours, nor terrified; but know the Wisdom to be thine own.

Within those radiances, the natural sound of the Truth will reverberate like a thousand thunders. The sound will come with a rolling reverberation, [amidst which] will be heard, 'Slay! Slay!' and awe-inspiring *mantras*.[2] Fear not. Flee not. Be not terrified. Know them [i. e. these sounds] to be [of] the intellectual faculties of thine own [inner] light.

musical instruments: big drums, cymbals (commonly of brass), conch-shells, bells (like the handbells used in the Christian Mass Service), timbrels, small clarionets (sounding like Highland bagpipes), big trumpets, and human thigh-bone trumpets. Although the combined sounds of these instruments are far from being melodious, the *lāmas* maintain that they psychically produce in the devotee an attitude of deep veneration and faith, because they are the counterparts of the natural sounds which one's own body is heard producing when the fingers are put in the ears to shut out external sounds. Stopping the ears thus, there are heard a thudding sound, like that of a big drum being beaten; a clashing sound, as of cymbals; a soughing sound, as of a wind moving through a forest—as when a conch-shell is blown; a ringing as of bells; a sharp tapping sound, as when a timbrel is used; a moaning sound, like that of a clarionet; a bass moaning sound, as if made with a big trumpet; and a shriller sound, as of a thigh-bone trumpet.

Not only is this interesting as a theory of Tibetan sacred music, but it gives the clue to the esoteric interpretation of the symbolical natural sounds of Truth (referred to in the second paragraph following, and elsewhere in our text), which are said to be, or to proceed from, the intellectual faculties within the human mentality.

[1] That is, the Wisdom which is born simultaneously with the achievement of Recognition: the Simultaneously-Born Wisdom.

[2] See Addenda, pp. 220–2.

Be not attracted towards the dull blue light of the brute-world; be not weak. If thou art attracted, thou wilt fall into the brute-world, wherein stupidity predominates, and suffer the illimitable miseries of slavery and dumbness and stupidness; [1] and it will be a very long time ere thou canst get out. Be not attracted towards it. Put thy faith in the bright, dazzling, five-coloured radiance. Direct thy mind one-pointedly towards the deities, the Knowledge-Holding Conquerors. Think, one-pointedly, thus: 'These Knowledge-Holding Deities, the Heroes, and the *Ḍākinīs* have come from the holy paradise realms to receive me; I supplicate them all: up to this day, although the Five Orders of the Buddhas of the Three Times have all exerted the rays of their grace and compassion, yet have I not been rescued by them. Alas, for a being like me! May the Knowledge-Holding Deities not let me go downwards further than this, but hold me with the hook of their compassion, and lead me to the holy paradises.'

Thinking in that manner, one-pointedly, pray thus:

'O ye Knowledge-Holding Deities, pray hearken unto me;
Lead me on the Path, out of your great love.
When [I am] wandering in the *Sangsāra*, because of intensi-
    fied propensities,
On the bright light-path of the Simultaneously-born
    Wisdom
May the bands of Heroes, the Knowledge-Holders, lead me;
May the bands of the Mothers, the *Ḍākinīs*, be [my] rear-
    guard;
May they save me from the fearful ambuscades of the *Bardo*,
And place me in the pure Paradise Realms.'

Praying thus, in deep faith and humility, there is no doubt that one will be born within the pure Paradise Realms, [2] after

---

[1] Cf. p. 126³.

[2] The deceased, having by now fallen to lower and lower stages of the *Bardo*, looks to the heaven-worlds (which are worlds of embodiment within the *Sangsāra*) rather than to *Nirvāṇa* (which is non-*Sangsāric*) as a place of refuge. Although, theoretically, *Nirvāṇa* is ever realizable from any stage of the *Bardo*, practically, for the ordinary devotee, it is not, meritorious *karma* being inadequate; hence the *lāma* or reader officiating aims at making the best of the situation in which, it is assumed, the deceased inevitably finds himself.

being merged, in rainbow-light, into the heart of the Knowledge-Holding Deities.

All the pandit classes, too, coming to recognize at this
stage, obtain liberation ; even those of evil propensities being
sure to be liberated here.

Here endeth the part of the Great *Thödol* concerned with
the setting-face-to-face of the Peaceful [Deities] of the *Chönyid
Bardo* and the setting-face-to-face of the Clear Light of the
Chikhai Bardo.

[THE DAWNING OF THE WRATHFUL DEITIES, FROM THE EIGHTH TO THE FOURTEENTH DAY]

[INTRODUCTION]

Now the manner of the dawning of the Wrathful Deities is
to be shown.

In the above *Bardo* of the Peaceful [Deities] there were
seven stages of ambuscade.   The setting-face-to-face at each
stage should have [caused the deceased] to recognize either
at one or another [stage] and to have been liberated.

Multitudes will be liberated by that recognition ; [and]
although multitudes obtain liberation in that manner, the
number of sentient beings being great, evil *karma* powerful, obscurations dense, propensities of too long standing,
the Wheel of Ignorance and Illusion becometh neither exhausted nor accelerated.   Although [all be] set face-to-face
in such detail, there is a vast preponderance of those who
wander downwards unliberated.

Therefore, after the cessation [of the dawning] of the Peaceful and the Knowledge-Holding Deities, who come to welcome
one, the fifty-eight flame-enhaloed, wrathful, blood-drinking
deities come to dawn, who are only the former Peaceful
Deities in changed aspect—according to the place [or psychic-
centre of the *Bardo*-body of the deceased whence they
proceed] ; nevertheless, they will not resemble them.[1]

---

[1] Up to this time, the fifty-two Peaceful and Knowledge-Holding Deities,
emanations from the heart and throat psychic-centres of the *Bardo*-body of the
deceased, have dawned.   The Wrathful Deities now about to dawn issue from

This is the *Bardo* of the Wrathful Deities; and, they being influenced by fear, terror, and awe,[1] recognition becometh more difficult. The intellect, gaining not in independence, passeth from one fainting state to a round of fainting states. [Yet], if one but recognize a little, it is easier to be liberated [at this stage]. If it be asked why? [the answer is]: Because of the dawning of the radiances—[which produce] fear, terror, and awe—the intellect is undistractedly alert in one-pointedness; that is why.[2]

If at this stage one do not meet with this kind of teaching, one's hearing [of religious lore]—although it be like an ocean [in its vastness]—is of no avail. There are even discipline-holding abbots [or *bhikkhus*] and doctors in metaphysical discourses who err at this stage, and, not recognizing, wander into the *Sangsāra*.

As for the common worldly folk, what need is there to mention them! By fleeing, through fear, terror, and awe, they fall over the precipices into the unhappy worlds and suffer. But the least of the least of the devotees of the mystic *mantrayāna* doctrines, as soon as he sees these blood-drinking deities, will recognize them to be his tutelary deities, and the meeting will be like that of human acquaintances. He will trust them; and becoming merged into them, in at-one-ment, will obtain Buddhahood.[3]

the brain psychic-centre; they are the excited, or wrathful, reflex forms of the Peaceful Deities (who, when contrasted with their wrathful aspects, include the Knowledge-Holding Deities). (See p. 85[3] and Addenda, pp. 217-9.)

[1] The fear, terror, and awe (or fascination)—on the part of the deceased on beholding the deities—arise only in the case of the ordinary devotee, who, as the text explains, has not had adequate *yogic* training, ere death, to enable him to recognize the *Bardo* as such, immediately upon dying, and pass beyond it. For the adept in *yoga*, who can take the *Bardo* 'by the forelock', as the text puts it (p. 100), mastering Death, and who knows that all apparitional appearances are unreal and powerless, both in this world and in all other worlds, there is no *Bardo* to experience; his goal is either an immediate and conscious rebirth among men or in one of the paradise realms, or, if he be really ripened—which would be an exceedingly rare circumstance—*Nirvāna*.

[2] No sooner does one radiance cease than another dawns; the deceased not having a moment of distraction, his intellect becomes concentratedly (i.e. one-pointedly) alert.

[3] The blood symbolizes *sangsāric* existence; the blood-drinking, the thirsting for, the drinking of, and the quenching of the thirst for, *sangsāric* existence.

By having meditated on the description of these blood-drinking deities, while in the human world, and by having performed some worship or praise of them; or, at least, by having seen their painted likenesses and their images, upon witnessing the dawning of the deities at this stage, recognition of them will result, and liberation. In this lieth the art.

Again, at the death of those discipline-holding abbots and doctors in metaphysical discourses [who remain uninstructed in these *Bardo* teachings], however assiduously they may have devoted themselves to religious practices, and however clever they may have been in expounding doctrines while in the human world, there will not come any phenomenal signs such as rainbow-halo [at the funeral-pyre] nor bone-reliques [from the ashes]. This is because when they lived the mystic [or esoteric] doctrines were never held within their heart, and because they had spoken contemptuously of them, and because they were never acquainted [through initiation] with the deities of the mystic [or esoteric] doctrines; thus, when these dawn on the *Bardo*, they do not recognize them. Suddenly [seeing] what they had never seen before, they view it as inimical; and, an antagonistic feeling being engendered, they pass into the miserable states because of that. Therefore, if the observers of the disciplines, and the metaphysicians, have not in them the practices of the mystic [or esoteric] doctrines, such signs as the rainbow-halo come not, nor are bone-reliques and seed-like bones ever produced [from the bones of their funeral-pyre]: [1] these are the reasons for it.

For the devotee who—even at this stage—can be made to realize that these deities are thus but the *karmic* personifications of his own propensities, born from having lived and drunken life, and who has, in addition, the supreme power to face them unwaveringly (as in Bulwer Lytton's *Zanoni* the Neophyte to succeed must face the ' Dweller on the Threshold '), meeting them like old acquaintances, and then losing his personality in them, enlightenment as to the true nature of *sangsāric* existence dawns, and, with it, the All-Perfect Illumination called Buddhahood.

[1] The belief, prevalent among almost all peoples since immemorial time, that unusual phenomena commonly mark the death (as the birth) and funeral of a great hero or saint, also prevails among the Tibetans; and the *lāmas* hold that such phenomena have a purely rational explanation, such as our text herein suggests. Furthermore, the *lāmas* maintain that, if a reputed saint be

The least of the least of *mantrayānic* [devotees],—who may seem to be of very unrefined manners, unindustrious, untactful, and who may not live in accordance with his vows, and who in every way may be inelegant in his habits, and even unable, perhaps, to carry the practices of his teachings to a successful issue,—let no one feel disrespect for nor doubt him, but pay reverence to the esoteric [or mystic] doctrines [which he holdeth]. By that, alone, one obtaineth liberation at this stage.

Even though the deeds [of one paying such reverence] may not have been very elegant while in the human world, at his death there will come at least one kind of sign, such as rainbow-radiance, bone-images, and bone-reliques. This is because the esoteric [or mystic] doctrines possess great gift-waves.[1]

[Those of, and] above, the mystic *mantrayānic* devotees of ordinary [psychic development], who have meditated upon the visualization and perfection processes and practised the essences [or essence *mantras*],[2] need not wander down this far on the *Chönyid Bardo*. As soon as they cease to breathe, they will be led into the pure paradise realms by the Heroes and Heroines and the Knowledge-Holders.[3] As a sign of

really a saint, among the charred bones from his funeral pyre there will be found some shaped into beautiful forms like images, and that small pearl-like (or, as the text has it, seed-like) nodules will appear in the ashes of the bones cremated.

[1] That is to say, the esoteric doctrines being realizable—because based on Truth itself—one who follows or even reverences them is, thereby, automatically brought into rapport with very definite psychic forces.

[2] That is to say, those devotees who have practised, in a thoroughly scientific manner, under a competent *guru*, the intonation of certain sacred *mantras* called essence *mantras*. Examples of such *mantras* are : *Ōm Maṇi Padme Hūṃ* ('Hail to the Jewel in the Lotus !' or 'Hail to Him Who is the Jewel in the Lotus !') ; *Ōm Wagi Shori Mūm* ('Hail to the Lord of Speech ! *Mūm*') ; *Ōm Vajra Pāni Hūṃ* ('Hail to the Holder of the Dorje !') : the three essence *mantras* of 'The Three Protectors' of Lāmaism ; the first being the essence *mantra* of the Bodhisattva Chenrazee (Skt. *Avalokita*), 'The Seer with keen eyes', The Great Pitier ; the second, that of the Bodhisattva Jampalyang (Skt. *Mañjughosha*), 'The God of Mystic Wisdom' ; and the third, that of the Bodhisattva Chakdor (Skt. *Vajra-Pāni*), 'The Wielder of the Thunderbolt '.

[3] Cf. the following passage, from a prayer on behalf of the dying person, in *The Book of the Craft of Dying*, Chap. VI, Cómper's ed. (p. 45) : 'When thy soul passeth out of thy body, [may] glorious companies of angels come against thee : the victorious host, worthy judges, and senators of the holy apostles meet

this, the sky will be cloudless; they will merge into rainbow radiance; there will be sun-showers, sweet scent of incense [in the air], music in the skies, radiances; bone-reliques and images [from their funeral-pyre].

Therefore, to the abbots [or discipline-holders], to the doctors, and to those mystics who have failed in their vows, and to all the common people, this *Thödol* is indispensable.[1] But those who have meditated upon the Great Perfection and the Great Symbol[2] will recognize the Clear Light at the moment of death; and, obtaining the *Dharma-Kāya*, all of them will be such as not to need the reading of this *Thödol*. By recognizing the Clear Light at the moment of death, they also will recognize the visions of the Peaceful and the Wrathful during the *Chönyid Bardo*, and obtain the *Sambhoga-Kāya*; or, recognizing during the *Sidpa Bardo*, obtain the *Nirmāṇa-Kāya*; and, taking birth on the higher planes, will, in the next rebirth, meet with this Doctrine, and then enjoy the continuity of *karma*.[3]

---

with thee: the fair, white, shining company of holy confessors, with the victorious number of glorious martyrs, come about thee: the joyful company of holy virgins receive thee: and the worthy fellowship of holy patriarchs open to thee the place of rest and joy, and deem thee to be among them that they be among, everlastingly.'

[1] The *lāmas* maintain that, while mere goodness and book knowledge are desirable in devotees seeking Liberation, spiritual wisdom coupled with unshakable faith, and the setting aside of all intellectualisms, are indispensable. One of the precepts of the great Tibetan *yogīs*, taught to all neophytes, is: ' Difficult indeed is it to obtain Liberation through intellectual knowledge alone ; through faith, Liberation is easily obtained.'

[2] ' The Great Perfection ' refers to the fundamental doctrine concerning the gaining of Perfection or Buddhahood as taught by the School of *Guru* Padma Sambhava. ' The Great Symbol (Tib. *Chhag-chhen*: Skt. *Mahā Mudrā*) ' refers to an ancient Indian system of *yoga*, related to the same School, but more especially practised nowadays by the followers of the semi-reformed Kargyutpa sect, founded in the latter half of the eleventh century A. D. by the learned Tibetan *yogī* Marpa, who, having sojourned in India as the disciple of the *pandit* Atīsha and of Naropa, Atīsha's disciple, introduced the Great Symbol into Tibet. Milarepa, the most beloved of all Tibetan *yogīs*, who was Marpa's successor, developed the practice of the Great Symbol and made it the foundation teaching of the Sect. (See pp. 78–9.)

[3] If there be recognition of Reality when it first dawns, i. e. if the Dreamer in *sangsāric* existence be awakened into the divine state of the *Sambhoga-Kāya* during the *Chönyid Bardo*, the normal cycle of rebirth is broken ; and the Awakened One returns voluntarily and fully conscious to the human world as

Therefore, this *Thödol* is the doctrine by which Buddhahood
may be attained without meditation; the doctrine liberating
by the hearing [of it] alone; the doctrine which leadeth
beings of great evil *karma* on the Secret Path; the doctrine
which produceth differentiation instantaneously [between
those who are initiated into it and those who are not]:
being the profound doctrine which conferreth Perfect Enlightenment instantaneously. Those sentient beings who have
been reached by it cannot go to the unhappy states.

This [doctrine] and the *Tahdol* [doctrine] [1], when joined together being like unto a *maṇḍala* of gold inset with turquoise,
combine them.

Thus, the indispensable nature of the *Thödol* being shown,
there now cometh the setting-face-to-face with the dawning of
the Wrathful [Deities] in the *Bardo*.

[THE EIGHTH DAY]

Again, calling the deceased by name, [address him] thus:

O nobly-born, listen undistractedly. Not having been able
to recognize when the Peaceful [Deities] shone upon thee in
the *Bardo* above, thou hast come wandering thus far. Now,
on the Eighth Day, the blood-drinking Wrathful Deities will
come to shine. Act so as to recognize them without being
distracted.

a Divine Incarnation, to work for the uplifting of mankind. If recognition be
delayed till the *Sidpa Bardo*, and the *Nirmāṇa-Kāya* be attained, that is but
a partial awakening, not an unclouded realization of Reality, the *Sidpa Bardo*
being a much lower plane than the *Chönyid Bardo*; but even then there will be
won the great boon of spiritually enlightened birth on one of the higher planes—
deva-loka, *asura-loka*, or the human-*loka*—and, upon being born anew in the
human world, the devotee will take up, in virtue of acquired propensities gained
in the previous earth-life, the study of the mystic *mantrayāna* doctrines and
yogīc practices from the point where it was broken off by death—this being the
continuity of *karma*.

[1] Text: *Btags-grol* (pron. *Tah-dol*), a small Tibetan work, consisting wholly
of *mantras*, used as an accompaniment to the *Bardo Thödol*. If the deceased
dies knowing the *Tahdol mantras*, they, being powerful talismans, give him safe
passage through the *Bardo* and a happy rebirth. Very often a copy of the
Tahdol (or perhaps merely some of its *mantras* copied on small strips of paper
and wound together in a tiny roll) is tied to the corpse and burned or buried
with it—just as a copy of the Egyptian *Book of the Dead* was ordinarily interred
with a mummy.

O nobly-born, the Great Glorious Buddha-Heruka,[1] dark-brown of colour; with three heads, six hands, and four feet firmly postured; the right [face] being white, the left, red, the central, dark-brown; the body emitting flames of radiance; the nine eyes widely opened, in terrifying gaze; the eyebrows quivering like lightning; the protruding teeth glistening and set over one another; giving vent to sonorous utterances of 'a-la-la' and 'ha-ha', and piercing whistling sounds; the hair of a reddish-yellow colour, standing on end, and emitting radiance; the heads adorned with dried [human] skulls, and the [symbols of the] sun and moon; black serpents and raw [human] heads forming a garland for the body; the first of the right hands holding a wheel, the middle one, a sword, the last one, a battle-axe; the first of the left hands, a bell, the middle one, a [human] scalp, the last one, a plough-share; his body embraced by the Mother, Buddha-Kroti-shaurima,[2] her right hand clinging to his neck and her left putting to his mouth a red shell [filled with blood], [making] a palatal sound like a crackling [and] a clashing sound, and a rumbling sound as loud as thunder; [emanating from the two deities] radiant flames of wisdom, blazing from every hair-pore [of the body] and each containing a flaming *dorje*; [the two deities together thus], standing with [one] leg bent and [the other] straight and tense, on a dais supported by horned eagles,[3] will come forth from within thine own brain and shine vividly upon thee. Fear that not. Be not awed. Know it to be the embodiment of thine own intellect. As it is thine own tutelary deity, be not terrified. Be not afraid, for in reality it is the Bhagavān Vairochana, the Father-Mother. Simultaneously with the recognition, liberation will be obtained: if they be recognized, merging [thyself], in at-one-

---

[1] Text: *Dpal-chen-po Bud-dha Heruka* (pron. *Pal-chen-po Bud-dha Heruka*): 'Great Glorious Buddha-Heruka.'

[2] Text: *Bud-dha Kro-ti-shva-ri-ma* (pron. *Buddha Kroti-shau-ri-ma*), i.e. the [female] Buddha, the Mighty Wrathful Mother.

[3] These are the *Garudas* of Indian and Tibetan mythology. They are depicted with eagle head, and human-bird body, having two human-like arms, two eagle wings, and two eagle feet. Symbolically, they personify energy and aspiration. (Cf. p. 116[2].)

ment, into the tutelary deity, Buddhahood in the *Sambhoga-Kāya* will be won.

[THE NINTH DAY]

But if one flee from them, through awe and terror being begotten, then, on the Ninth Day, the blood-drinking [deities] of the Vajra Order will come to receive one. Thereupon, the setting-face-to-face is, calling the deceased by name, thus:

O nobly-born, listen undistractedly. [He] of the blood-drinking Vajra Order named the Bhagavān Vajra-Heruka, dark-blue in colour; with three faces, six hands, and four feet firmly postured; in the first right hand [holding] a *dorje*, in the middle [one], a [human] scalp, in the last [one], a battle-axe; in the first of the left, a bell, in the middle [one], a [human] scalp, in the last [one], a ploughshare; his body embraced by the Mother Vajra-Krotishaurima, her right [hand] clinging to his neck, her left offering to his mouth a red shell [filled with blood], will issue from the eastern quarter of thy brain and come to shine upon thee. Fear it not. Be not terrified. Be not awed. Know it to be the embodiment of thine own intellect. As it is thine own tutelary deity, be not terrified. In reality [they are] the Bhagavān Vajra-Sattva, the Father and Mother. Believe in them. Recognizing them, liberation will be obtained at once. By so proclaiming [them], knowing them to be tutelary deities, merging [in them] in at-one-ment, Buddhahood will be obtained.

[THE TENTH DAY]

Yet, if one do not recognize them, the obscurations of evil deeds being too great, and flee from them through terror and awe, then, on the Tenth Day, the blood-drinking [deities] of the [Precious]-Gem Order will come to receive one. Thereupon the setting-face-to-face is, calling the deceased by name, thus:

O nobly-born, listen. On the Tenth Day, the blood-drinking [deity] of the [Precious]-Gem Order named Ratna-Heruka, yellow of colour; [having] three faces, six hands, four feet firmly postured; the right [face] white, the left, red, the central, darkish yellow; enhaloed in flames; in the first of the six hands holding a gem, in the middle [one], a trident-staff, in the last [one], a baton; in the first of the left [hands], a bell, in the middle [one], a [human] scalp, in the last [one], a trident-staff; his body embraced by the Mother Ratna-Krotishaurima, her right [hand] clinging to his neck, her left offering to his mouth a red shell [filled with blood], will issue from the southern quarter of thy brain and come to shine upon thee. Fear not. Be not terrified. Be not awed. Know them to be the embodiment of thine own intellect. [They] being thine own tutelary deity, be not terrified. In reality [they are] the Father-Mother Bhagavān Ratna-Sambhava. Believe in them. Recognition [of them] and the obtaining of liberation will be simultaneous.

By so proclaiming [them], knowing them to be tutelary deities, merging in them in at-one-ment, Buddhahood will be obtained.

[THE ELEVENTH DAY]

Yet, though set face-to-face thus, if, through power of evil propensities, terror and awe being produced, not recognizing them to be tutelary deities, one flee from them, then, on the Eleventh Day, the blood-drinking Lotus Order will come to receive one. Thereupon the setting-face-to-face is, calling the deceased by name, thus:

O nobly-born, on the Eleventh Day, the blood-drinking [deity] of the Lotus Order, called the Bhagavān Padma-Heruka, of reddish-black colour; [having] three faces, six hands, and four feet firmly postured; the right [face] white, the left, blue, the central, darkish red; in the first of the right of the six hands holding a lotus, in the middle [one], a trident-staff, in the last, a club; in the first of the left [hands], a bell, in the middle [one], a [human] scalp filled with blood,[1] in the last, a small drum; his body embraced by the Mother Padma-Krotishaurima, her right hand clinging to his neck, her left offering to his mouth a red shell [full of blood]; the Father

---

[1] Lit., 'filled with red substance'; and likewise for parallel passages following. In *lāmaic* rituals a fluid red pigment is commonly used to represent blood (symbolical of renunciation of life, or of *sangsāric* existence), as red wine is by Christians in the Eucharist.

and Mother in union; will issue from the western quarter of thy brain and come to shine upon thee. Fear that not. Be not terrified. Be not awed. Rejoice. Recognize [them] to be the product of thine own intellect; as [they are] thine own tutelary deity, be not afraid. In reality they are the Father-Mother Bhagavān Amitābha. Believe in them. Concomitantly with recognition, liberation will come. Through such acknowledging, recognizing them to be tutelary deities, in at-one-ment thou wilt merge [into them], and obtain Buddhahood.

[THE TWELFTH DAY]

Despite such setting-face-to-face, being still led backwards by evil propensities, terror and awe arising, it may be that one recognize not and flee. Thereupon, on the Twelfth Day, the blood-drinking deities of the Karmic Order, accompanied by the Kerima, Htamenma, and Wang-chugma,[1] will come to receive one. Not recognizing, terror may be produced. Whereupon, the setting-face-to-face is, calling the deceased by name, thus:

O nobly-born, on the Twelfth Day, the blood-drinking deity of the Karmic Order, named Karma-Heruka, dark green of colour; [having] three faces, six hands, [and] four feet firmly postured; the right [face] white, the left, red, the middle, dark green; majestic [of appearance]; in the first of the right of the six hands, holding a sword, in the middle [one], a trident-staff, in the last, a club; in the first of the left [hands], a bell, in the middle [one], a [human] scalp, in the last, a plough-share; his body embraced by the Mother Karma-Kroti-

---

[1] These three orders of deities are goddesses, Indian and Tibetan in origin, the *Kerima* having human shape, the *Htamenma* and the *Wang-chugma*, like Egyptian deities (more or less totemistic), having human-like bodies and animal heads; and each deity symbolizes some particular *karmic* impulse or propensity appearing as a hallucination in the *Bardo* consciousness of the deceased. *Kerima* seems to be a hybrid Sanskrit-Tibetan word (from Skt. *Keyūrī*), which, having become current in Tibet—like so many similar words—was incorporated into our text unchanged. *Htamenma* (as pronounced from Tib. *Phra-men-ma*) is probably the name of an order of pre-Buddhistic deities belonging to the ancient Bön religion of Tibet. *Wang-chugma* (as pronounced from Tib. *Dvang-phyug-ma*) is the Tibetan rendering of the Sanskrit *Īshvarī*, meaning 'Mighty Goddesses'.

shaurima, her right [hand] clinging to his neck, the left offering to his mouth a red shell; the Father and Mother in union, issuing from the northern quarter of thy brain, will come to shine upon thee. Fear that not. Be not terrified. Be not awed. Recognize them to be the embodiment of thine own intellect. [They] being thine own tutelary deity, be not afraid. In reality they are the Father-Mother Bhagavān Amogha-Siddhi. Believe; and be humble; and be fond [of them]. Concomitantly with recognition, liberation will come. Through such acknowledging, recognizing them to be tutelary deities, in at-one-ment thou wilt merge [into them], and obtain Buddhahood. Through the *guru's* select teaching, one cometh to recognize them to be the thought-forms issuing from one's own intellectual faculties. For instance, a person, upon recognizing a lion-skin [to be a lion-skin], is freed [from fear]; for though it be only a stuffed lion-skin, if one do not know it to be so actually, fear ariseth, but, upon being told by some person that it is a lion-skin only, one is freed from fear. Similarly here, too, when the bands of blood-drinking deities, huge of proportions, with very thick-set limbs, dawn as big as the skies, awe and terror are naturally produced in one. [But] as soon as the setting-face-to-face is heard [one] recognizeth them to be one's own tutelary deities and one's own thought-forms. Then, when upon the Mother Clear-Light—which one had been accustomed to formerly—a secondary Clear-Light, the Offspring Clear-Light, is produced, and the Mother and Offspring Clear-Light, coming together like two intimate acquaintances, blend inseparably, and [therefrom] a self-emancipating radiance dawneth upon one, through self-enlightenment and self-knowledge one is liberated.

[THE THIRTEENTH DAY]

If this setting-face-to-face be not obtained, good persons on the Path,[1] too, fall back from here and wander into the *Sangsāra*. Then the Eight Wrathful Ones, the Kerimas, and the Htamenmas, having various [animal] heads, issue from within

---

[1] Or 'undergoing psychical development'.

one's own brain and come to shine upon one's self. Thereupon the setting-face-to-face is, calling the deceased by name,
thus:

O nobly-born, listen undistractedly. On the Thirteenth
Day, from the eastern quarter of thy brain, the Eight Kerimas
will emanate and come to shine upon thee. Fear that not.

From the east of thy brain, the White Kerima,[1] holding a
human corpse, as a club, in the right [hand]; in the left,
holding a [human] scalp filled with blood, will come to shine
upon thee. Fear not.

From the south, the Yellow Tseurima,[2] holding a bow and
arrow, ready to shoot; from the west, the Red Pramoha,[3]
holding a *makara*[4]-banner; from the north, the Black Petali,[5]
holding a *dorje* and a scalp filled with blood; from the south-
east, the Red Pukkase,[6] holding intestines in the right [hand]
and [with] the left putting them to her mouth; from the
south-west, the Dark-Green Ghasmarī,[7] the left [hand] holding
a scalp filled with blood, [with] the right stirring it with a
dorje, and [she then] drinking it with majestic relish; from the
north-west, the Yellowish-White Tsandhalī,[8] tearing asunder
a head from a corpse, the right [hand] holding a heart, the
left putting the corpse to the mouth and [she then] eating
[thereof]; from the north-east, the Dark-Blue Smasha,[9] tearing
asunder a head from a corpse and eating [thereof]: these,

---

[1] Text: *Kerima*, corrupted from Skt. *Keyūrī*, name of an Indian cemetery
goddess.

[2] The corrupted Skt. form in text, name of another Indian cemetery goddess.

[3] Tib.-Skt. of text.

[4] Text: *chu-srin* (pron. *chu-sin*): 'water-lion', or 'leviathan' (Skt. *Makara*),
a mythological monster.

[5, 6, 7] Tib.-Skt. of text.

[8] Textual form, from Skt. *Chaṇḍālī*, referring, apparently, to the spirit of
a female of low caste (i.e. *Chaṇḍālī*), who, like each of the goddesses of our
text herein, haunts cemeteries or cremation grounds. All such goddesses, here
appearing, seem intended as symbols—each in its own way—to impress upon
the deceased, as in an initiatory drama, the nature of *sangsāric* existence—its
impermanence, its unsatisfactoriness—and the need to rise above it, conquering
it through world-renunciation: all the goddesses emanating, as the text
repeatedly teaches, from the mental content which the percipient's *sangsāric*
existence has bequeathed to him.

[9] In place of this Tib.-Skt. form of our text, the Block-Print gives *Smashalī*,
which is a more correct form.

the Eight Kerimas of the Abodes [or Eight Directions], also come to shine upon thee, surrounding the Five Blood-drinking Fathers. Yet be not afraid.

O nobly-born, from the Circle outside of them, the Eight Htamenmas of the [eight] regions [of the brain] will come to shine upon thee : from the east, the Dark-Brown Lion-Headed One, the hands crossed on the breast, and in the mouth holding a corpse, and shaking the mane ; from the south, the Red Tiger-Headed One, the hands crossed downwards, grinning and showing the fangs and looking on with protruding eyes ; from the west, the Black Fox-Headed One, the right [hand] holding a shaving-knife, the left holding an intestine, and [she] eating and licking the blood [therefrom] ; from the north, the Dark-Blue Wolf-Headed One, the two hands tearing open a corpse and looking on with protruding eyes ; from the south-east, the Yellowish-White Vulture-Headed One, bearing a gigantic [human-shaped] corpse on the shoulder and holding a skeleton in the hand ; from the south-west, the Dark-Red Cemetery-Bird-Headed One, carrying a gigantic corpse on the shoulder ; from the north-west, the Black Crow-Headed One, the left [hand] holding a scalp, the right holding a sword, and [she] eating heart and lungs ; from the north-east, the Dark-Blue Owl-Headed One, holding a *dorje* in the right [hand], and holding a sword in the left, and eating.

These Eight Htamenmas of the [eight] regions, likewise surrounding the Blood-Drinking Fathers, and issuing from within thy brain, come to shine upon thee. Fear that not. Know them to be the thought-forms of thine own intellectual faculties.

[THE FOURTEENTH DAY]

O nobly-born on the Fourteenth Day, the Four Female Door-Keepers, also issuing from within thine own brain, will come to shine upon thee. Again recognize. From the east [quarter] of thy brain will come to shine the White Tiger-Headed Goad-Holding Goddess, bearing a scalp filled with blood in her left [hand] ; from the south, the Yellow Sow-Headed Noose-Holding Goddess ; from the west, the Red

Lion-Headed Iron-Chain-Holding Goddess; and from the
north, the Green Serpent-Headed Bell-Holding Goddess.
Thus issue the Four Female Door-Keepers also from within
thine own brain and come to shine upon thee; as tutelary
deities, recognize them.

O nobly-born, on the outer Circle of these thirty wrathful
deities, Herukas, the twenty-eight various-headed mighty
goddesses, bearing various weapons, issuing from within
thine own brain, will come to shine upon thee. Fear that
not. Recognize whatever shineth to be the thought-forms
of thine own intellectual faculties. At this vitally important
time, recollect the select teachings of the *guru*.

O nobly-born, [there will dawn] from the east the Dark-
Brown Yak-Headed Rākṣhasa-Goddess, holding a *dorje* and
a skull; and the Reddish-Yellow Serpent-Headed Brāhma-
Goddess, holding a lotus in her hand; and the Greenish-
Black Leopard-Headed Great-Goddess, holding a trident in
her hand; and the Blue Monkey-Headed Goddess of In-
quisitiveness, holding a wheel; and the Red Snow-Bear-Headed
Virgin-Goddess, bearing a short spear in the hand; and the
White Bear-Headed Indra-Goddess, holding an intestine-noose
in the hand: [these], the Six Yoginīs of the East, issuing from
within the [eastern quarter of thine own]¹ brain, will come to
shine upon thee; | ² fear that not.

O nobly-born, from the south [will dawn] the Yellow Bat-
Headed Delight-Goddess, holding a shaving-knife in the hand;
and the Red Makara-Headed Peaceful-[Goddess], holding an
urn in the hand; and the Red Scorpion-Headed Amṛitā-Goddess,
holding a lotus in the hand; and the White Kite-Headed Moon-
Goddess, | holding a *dorje* in the hand; and the Dark-Green
Fox-Headed Baton-Goddess, flourishing a club in the hand;
and the Yellowish-Black Tiger-Headed Rākṣhasī, holding
a skull [filled with] blood in the hand: [these] the Six

---

¹ This bracketed phrase here (and in the three corresponding passages
following in this section) is incorporated from the text of the Block-Print, our
MS. text omitting it.

² Between this bar and the bar after 'Moon-goddess' in the sentence following
is contained the translation of the Tibetan text of the lower folio (67ᵃ) of our
Frontispiece.

Yoginīs of the South, issuing from within the [southern quarter of thine own] brain, will come to shine upon thee; fear that not.

O nobly-born, from the west [will dawn] the Greenish-Black Vulture-Headed Eater-Goddess, holding a baton in the hand; and the Red Horse-Headed Delight-Goddess, holding a huge trunk of a corpse; and the White Eagle-Headed Mighty-Goddess, holding a club in the hand; and the Yellow Dog-Headed Rākshasī, holding a *dorje* in the hand and a shaving-knife and cutting [with this]; and the Red Hoopoo-Headed Desire-Goddess, holding a bow and arrow in the hand aimed; and the Green Stag-Headed Wealth-Guardian Goddess, holding an urn in the hand: [these], the Six Yoginīs of the West, issuing from within the [western quarter of thine own] brain, will come to shine upon thee; fear that not.

O nobly-born, from the north [will dawn] the Blue Wolf-Headed Wind-Goddess, waving a pennant in the hand; and the Red Ibex-Headed Woman-Goddess, holding a pointed stake in the hand; and the Black Sow-Headed Sow-Goddess, holding a noose of fangs in the hand; and the Red Crow-Headed Thunderbolt-Goddess, holding an infant corpse in the hand; and the Greenish-Black Elephant-Headed Big-Nosed Goddess,[1] holding in the hand a big corpse and drinking blood from a skull; and the Blue Serpent-Headed Water-Goddess, holding in the hand a serpent noose: [these], the Six Yoginīs of the North, issuing from within [the northern quarter of] thine own brain, will come to shine upon thee; fear that not.

O nobly-born, the Four Yoginīs of the Door, issuing from within the brain, will come to shine upon thee: from the east, the Black Cuckoo-Headed Mystic Goddess,[2] holding an iron hook in the hand; from the south, the Yellow Goat-Headed Mystic Goddess, holding a noose in the hand; from the west, the Red Lion-Headed Mystic Goddess, holding an iron chain

---

[1] Here the Block-Print gives only 'the Big Elephant-Headed Goddess'.

[2] Text: *Rdor-je-ma* (pron. *Dor-je-ma*): 'She [called] the Dorje', or 'She [called] the Mystic One'; hence 'Mystic Goddess'. The Block-Print gives 'White Cuckoo-Headed Mystic Goddess'.

in the hand; and from the north, the Greenish-Black Serpent-Headed Mystic Goddess: [these], the Four Door-Keeping Yoginīs, issuing from within the brain, will come to shine upon thee.

Since these Twenty-eight Mighty Goddesses emanate from the bodily powers of Ratna-Sambhava, [He] of the Six Heruka Deities, recognize them.[1]

O nobly-born, the Peaceful Deities emanate from the Voidness of the *Dharma-Kāya*;[2] recognize them.   From the Radiance of the *Dharma-Kāya*[3] emanate the Wrathful Deities; recognize them.

At this time when the Fifty-eight Blood-Drinking Deities[4] emanating from thine own brain come to shine upon thee, if thou knowest them to be the radiances of thine own intellect, thou wilt merge, in the state of at-one-ment, into the body of the Blood-Drinking Ones there and then, and obtain Buddhahood.

O nobly-born, by not recognizing now, and by fleeing from the deities out of fear, again sufferings will come to overpower thee. If this be not known, fear being begotten of the Blood-Drinking Deities, [one is] awed and terrified and fainteth away: one's own thought-forms turn into illusory appearances, and one wandereth into the *Sangsāra*; if one be not awed and terrified, one will not wander into the *Sangsāra*.

Furthermore, the bodies of the largest of the Peaceful and Wrathful Deities are equal [in vastness] to the limits of the heavens; the intermediate, as big as Mt. Meru;[5] the smallest,

---

[1] In place of this, the Block-Print gives the following synonymous sentence: ‘Since these Twenty-eight Mighty Goddesses also are emanations from the power of the self-produced Wrathful Deities, recognize them.’

[2] They are the emanations from the void, or primordial, tranquil, unshaped aspect of the *Dharma-Kāya* state, viewing man as the microcosm of the macrocosm.

[3] They are the emanations from the active radiant aspect of the *Dharma-Kāya* state,—the Clear Light shining in the primordial Voidness,—man, as the microcosm of the macrocosm, being inseparable therefrom.

[4] The symbolism of the blood-drinking should here be kept in mind. (See p. 132[3].)

[5] Mt. Meru (Tib. *Ri-rab*) is the central mystical mountain of Buddhist cosmography. (See pp. 62 ff.) The spinal column, the central support of the human bodily structure, is, analogously, symbolized in the *Tantras* and in works on *Yoga* as the Mt. Meru of man the microcosm.

equal to eighteen bodies such as thine own body, set one upon another. Be not terrified at that; be not awed. If all existing phenomena shining forth as divine shapes and radiances be recognized to be the emanations of one's own intellect, Buddhahood will be obtained at that very instant of recognition. The saying, 'Buddhahood will be obtained in a moment [of time]' is that which applieth now. Bearing this in mind, one will obtain Buddhahood by merging, in at-one-ment, into the Radiances and the *Kāyas*.

O nobly-born, whatever fearful and terrifying visions thou mayst see, recognize them to be thine own thought-forms.

O nobly-born, if thou recognize not, and be frightened, then all the Peaceful Deities will shine forth in the shape of Mahā-Kāla;[1] and all the Wrathful Deities will shine [forth] in the form of Dharma-Rāja, the Lord of Death;[2] and thine own thought-forms becoming Illusions [or *Māras*], thou wilt wander into the *Sangsāra*.

O nobly-born, if one recognize not one's own thought-forms, however learned one may be in the Scriptures—both *Sūtras* and *Tantras*—although practising religion for a *kalpa*, one obtaineth not Buddhahood. If one recognize one's own thought-forms, by one important art and by one word, Buddhahood is obtained.

If one's thought-forms be not recognized as soon as one dieth, the shapes of Dharma-Rāja, the Lord of Death, will shine forth on the *Chönyid Bardo*. The largest of the bodies of Dharma-Rāja, the Lord of Death, equalling the heavens [in vastness]; the intermediate, Mt. Meru; the smallest, eighteen times one's own body, will come filling the world-systems. They will come having their upper teeth biting the nether lip; their eyes glassy; their hairs tied up on the top of the head; big-bellied, narrow-waisted; holding a [*karmic*] record-

---

[1] Text: *Mgon-po-Nag-po* (pron. *Gon-po-Nag-po*): Skt. *Kāla-Nāth*, commonly known in India as Mahā-Kāla. At this stage, all the illusory forms of the Peaceful Deities blend and appear as this one deity.

[2] Text: *Gshin-rje-hi-chös-kyi-rgyal-po* (pron. *Shin-jei-chö-kyi-gyal-po*): Skt. *Dharma-Rāja* + *Yama-Rāja*. As described here and in the Second Book of the *Bardo Thödol* (see p. 167[1]) this illusory deity commonly assumes many and varied forms capable of merging into a single form.

board[1] in the hand; giving utterance from their mouth to sounds of 'Strike! Slay!', licking [human] brain, drinking blood, tearing heads from corpses, tearing out [the] hearts: thus will [they] come, filling the worlds.

O nobly-born, when such thought-forms emanate, be thou not afraid, nor terrified; the body which now thou possessest being a mental-body of [*karmic*] propensities, though slain and chopped [to bits], cannot die. Because thy body is, in reality, one of voidness, thou needest not fear. The [bodies of the] Lord of Death, too, are emanations from the radiances of thine own intellect; they are not constituted of matter; voidness cannot injure voidness. Beyond the emanations of thine own intellectual faculties, externally, the Peaceful and the Wrathful Ones, the Blood-Drinking Ones, the Various-Headed Ones, the rainbow lights, the terrifying forms of the Lord of Death, exist not in reality: of this, there is no doubt. Thus, knowing this, all the fear and terror is self-dissipated; and, merging in the state of at-one-ment, Buddhahood is obtained.

If thou recognizest in that manner, exerting thy faith and affection towards the tutelary deities and believing that they have come to receive thee amidst the ambuscades of the *Bardo*, think, '[I] take refuge [in them]'; and remember the Precious Trinity, exerting towards them [the Trinity] fondness and faith. Whosoever thine own tutelary deity may be, recollect now; [and] calling him by name, pray thus:

---

[1] Text: *khram-shing* (pron. *htam-shing*), referring to a board—either a flogging-board such as that on which culprits are stretched and flogged in Tibet, or else, as here, a board written over with *karmic* records of the deceased's life. *Khram* is the name given to a scroll of records or an inventory like a rent-roll; *shing* alone means 'wood'. Hence we may render the two words as 'wood-register' or 'record-board'. In the great Tibetan Arthurian-like saga called in Tibetan *Ge-sar-bsgrungs* (pron. *Ke-sar-doong*), or Kesar Saga (of unknown author, but probably dating from the eighth or ninth century A.D.), which is so much the popular saga of Tibet that many Tibetans know it by heart, a boy, thirteen years of age, who, when wishing to join in a battle, is held back by fond relatives, brushes them aside, saying, 'The place of illness, the place of death, and the place of cremation are in accordance with the [*karmic*] register of the Lords of Death'; and here the Tibetan word for register is *khram*.

The verification of our rendering of this passage is important because, like other passages in the *Bardo Thödol*, particularly the closely-related passage describing the Judgement, coming in the Second Book (pp. 165-9), it has striking correspondence with parts of the Egyptian *Book of the Dead*.

'[Alas!], wandering am I in the *Bardo*; run to my rescue;
Uphold me by thy grace, O Precious Tutelary!'

Calling upon the name of thine own *guru*, pray thus:

'[Alas!] wandering am I in the *Bardo*; rescue me!
[O] let not thy grace forsake me!'

Have faith in the Blood-Drinking Deities, too, and offer up
this prayer:

'Alas! when [I am] wandering in the *Sangsāra*, through
    force of overpowering illusions,
On the light-path of the abandonment of fright, fear, and awe,
May the bands of the Bhagavāns, the Peaceful and Wrathful
    Ones, lead [me];
May the bands of the Wrathful Goddesses Rich in Space
    be [my] rear-guard,
And save me from the fearful ambuscades of the *Bardo*,
And place me in the state of the Perfectly-Enlightened
    Buddhas.
When wandering alone, separated from dear friends,
When the void forms of one's own thoughts are shining here,
May the Buddhas, exerting the force of their grace,
Cause not to come the fear, awe, and terror in the *Bardo*.
When the five bright Wisdom-Lights are shining here,
May recognition come without dread and without awe;
When the divine bodies of the Peaceful and the Wrathful
    are shining here,
May the assurance of fearlessness be obtained and the
    Bardo be recognized.
When, by the power of evil *karma*, misery is being tasted,
May the tutelary deities dissipate the misery;
When the natural sound of Reality is reverberating [like]
    a thousand thunders,
May they be transmuted into the sounds of the Six
    Syllables.[1]

---

[1] These are of the essence *mantra* of Chenrazee (Avalokiteshvara), being *Om-Ma-ṇi-Pad-me-Hūṃ* (pron. *Ōm-Mă-ṇi-Pāy-mē-Hūng*). (See p. 134[1].) Chenrazee being the patron-god, or national tutelary deity, of Tibet, and this being his *mantra*, its repetition, both in the human world and on the *Bardo* plane, is credited with bringing to an end the cycle of rebirth and thereby giving entrance

When unprotected, *karma* having to be followed here,
I beseech the Gracious Compassionate [One][1] to protect me;
When suffering miseries of *karmic* propensities here,
May the blissfulness of the Clear Light dawn;
May the Five Elements[2] not rise up as enemies;
But may I behold the realms of the Five Orders of the
    Enlightened Ones.'

Thus, in earnest faith and humility, offer up the prayer;
whereby all fears will vanish and Buddhahood in the *Sambhoga-
Kāya* will undoubtedly be won: important is this. Being undistracted, repeat it in that manner, three or [even] seven times.

into *Nirvāṇa*; hence its importance in the *Bardo* prayer. In the Tibetan work
called *Mani-bkah-hbum* (pron. *Ma-ni-kah-boom*), i. e. 'History of the *Māṇi* (or
Mantra of Chenrazee)' this *mantra* is said to be 'the essence of all happiness,
prosperity, and knowledge, and the great means of liberation'; also it is said
that the *ōm* closes the door of rebirth among the gods, *mā*, among the *asuras*
(or titans), *ṇĭ*, among mankind, *pāy*, among sub-human creatures, *mĕ*, among
pretas (or unhappy ghosts), and *hūng*, among the inhabitants of Hell. Accordingly, each of the six syllables is given the colour of the light-path corresponding
to the six states of existence, thus : *ōm*, the white light-path of the *deva-loka* (or
world of the gods); *mā*, the green light-path of the *asura-loka* (or world of the
titans); *ṇĭ*, the yellow light-path of the *manaka-loka* (or human world); *pāy*,
the blue light-path of the *tiryaka-loka* (or brute world); *mĕ*, the red light-path
of the *preta-loka* (or ghost world); and *hūng*, the smoke-coloured or black light-
path of the *naraka-loka* (or Hell world).

There is an old Tibetan folk-tale concerning a religious devotee who tried to
incline his irreligious mother to devotional observances and merely succeeded in
habituating her to the recitation of this *mantra*. Her bad *karma* predominating
over her good *karma*, at death she passed into the Hell-world, whereupon her
son, being proficient in *yoga*, went to her rescue; and she, upon seeing him,
was able, in virtue of having recited the *mantra* on earth, to recite it in Hell,
and instantaneously she and all who heard it were liberated from Hell: for, as
the tale at its end teaches, 'Such is the power of the *mantra*'.

The origin of this *mantra* is traceable through *terton* works concerning the
introduction (during the eighth century) of Tantric Buddhism into Tibet. Dr.
Waddell is inclined to doubt that these *terton* works were hidden away then
(i. e. in the time of Padma Sambhava) and in later centuries recovered, as the
tertons (i. e. 'takers-out' of such lost books) claim, and suggests that their
compilation dates from the fourteenth to the sixteenth century—a tentative and
possibly unsound theory (cf. L. A. Waddell, *Lamaism in Sikhim*, in the *Gazetteer of Sikhim*, ed. by H. H. Risley, Calcutta, 1894, p. 289; also our Introduction,
pp. 73-7). In any case, the *mantra*, at least by tradition (which ordinarily
is as reliable as recorded history), seems to have come into, or been originated
in, Tibet contemporaneously with the introduction of Buddhism into Tibet.

[1] That is, Chenrazee.

[2] These are: Earth, Air, Water, Fire, and Ether.

However heavy the evil *karma* may be and however weak the remaining *karma* may be, it is not possible that liberation will not be obtained [if one but recognize]. If, nevertheless, despite everything done in these [stages of the *Bardo*], recognition is still not brought about, then—there being danger of one's wandering further, into the third *Bardo*, called the *Sidpa Bardo*—the setting-face-to-face for that will be shown in detail hereinafter.

[THE CONCLUSION, SHOWING THE FUNDAMENTAL IMPORTANCE OF THE *BARDO* TEACHINGS]

Whatever the religious practices of any one may have been, —whether extensive or limited,—during the moments of death various misleading illusions occur; and hence this *Thödol* is indispensable. To those who have meditated much, the real Truth dawneth as soon as the body and consciousness-principle part. The acquiring of experience while living is important: they who have [then] recognized [the true nature of] their own being,[1] and thus have had some experience, obtain great power during the *Bardo* of the Moments of Death, when the Clear Light dawneth.

Again, the meditation on the deities of the Mystic Path of the *Mantra*, [both in the] visualizing and the perfecting stages, while living, will be of great influence when the peaceful and wrathful visions dawn on the *Chönyid Bardo*. Thus the training in this *Bardo* being of particular importance even while living,[2] hold to it, read it, commit it to memory, bear it in mind properly, read it regularly thrice; let the words and the meanings be very clear; it should be so that the words and the meanings will not be forgotten even though a hundred executioners were pursuing [thee].

---

[1] Lit., 'intellect' or 'consciousness-principle'.

[2] Cf. the following passage from *The Book of the Craft of Dying*, chap. V, Comper's ed. (p. 37): ' That what man that lusteth, and will gladly die well and surely and meritorily, without peril, he must take heed visibly, and study and learn diligently this craft of dying, and the dispositions thereof abovesaid, while he is in heal [i. e. health]; and not abide till the death entereth in him.'

It is called the Great Liberation by Hearing, because even those who have committed the five boundless sins[1] are sure to be liberated if they hear it by the path of the ear. Therefore read it in the midst of vast congregations. Disseminate it. Through having heard it once, even though one do not comprehend it, it will be remembered in the Intermediate State without a word being omitted, for the intellect becometh ninefold more lucid [there]. Hence it should be proclaimed in the ears of all living persons; it should be read over the pillows of all persons who are ill; it should be read at the side of all corpses: it should be spread broadcast.

Those who meet with this [doctrine] are indeed fortunate. Save for them who have accumulated much merit and absolved many obscurations, difficult is it to meet with it. Even when met with, difficult is it to comprehend it. Liberation will be won through simply not disbelieving it upon hearing it. Therefore treat this [doctrine] very dearly: it is the essence of all doctrines.[2]

The Setting-Face-to-Face while experiencing Reality in the Intermediate State, called 'The Teaching Which Liberateth By Merely Being Heard And That Which Liberateth By Merely Being Attached',[3] is finished.[4]

---

[1] These are : patricide, matricide, setting two religious bodies at war, killing a saint, and causing blood to flow from the body of a Tathāgata (i. e. a Buddha).

[2] Here the Block-Print has : 'This is the *Tantra* of all doctrines.'

[3] This refers to the *Thadol*. (See p. 192[4].)

[4] The Block-Print text, corresponding in all essentials, and in almost every important detail, word for word with the text of our Manuscript, contains (on folio 48b), as the parallel concluding sentence of the *Chönyid Bardo*, the following, which differs from our own: 'The Teaching for the Intermediate State, the Setting-Face-to-Face while experiencing Reality, from *The Great Liberation by Hearing While in the Intermediate State, Liberating by Merely Being Heard, And Liberating By Merely Being Seen*, is finished.'

[BOOK II]

[THE *SIDPA BARDO*]

THIS IS KNOWN AS THE GOOD HEAD-PART OF THAT CALLED 'THE PROFOUND ESSENCE OF THE LIBERATION BY HEARING',—THE REMINDER, THE CLEAR SETTING-FACE-TO-FACE IN THE INTERMEDIATE STATE WHEN SEEKING REBIRTH[1]

[1] Text: SRID-PA BAR-DOHI NGO-SPRÖD GSAL-HDEBS THÖS-GROL ZHES-BYA-VA ZAB-PAHI NYING-KHU ZHES-BYA-VAHI DVU-PHYOGS LEGS (pronounced: SID-PA BAR-DOI NGO-TÖD SAL-DEB THÖ-DOL SHAY-CHA-WA ZAB-PAI NYING-KHU SHAY-CHA-WAI U-CHŌ LAY).

In the Block-Print, the *Bardo Thödol* being divided into two distinctly separate books—whereas in our MS. Book II is an unbroken continuation of Book I—the first four folios of its second book contain—unlike our MS.—a summary of the introductory parts of the first book; and the title of Book II of the Block-Print is as follows: *Bar-do Thös-grol Chen-mo Las Srid-pa Bar-dohi Ngo-Spröd Bzhugs-so* (pronounced: *Bar-do Thö-dol Chen-mo Lay Sid-pa Bar-doi Ngo-Töd Zhu-so*), which means, 'Herein Lieth the Setting-Face-to-Face in the Intermediate State of [or when seeking] Worldly Existence (i. e. Rebirth), from "The Great Liberation by Hearing on the After-Death Plane"'.

'The essence of all things is one and the same, perfectly calm and tranquil, and shows no sign of "becoming"; ignorance, however, is in its blindness and delusion oblivious of Enlightenment, and, on that account, cannot recognize truthfully all those conditions, differences, and activities which characterize the phenomena of the Universe.' — Ashvaghosha. *The Awakening of Faith* (Suzuki's Translation).

[THE OBEISANCES]

To the assembled Deities, to the Tutelaries, to the *Gurus*,
Humbly is obeisance paid:
May Liberation in the Intermediate State be vouchsafed by
Them.[1]

[INTRODUCTORY VERSES]

Above, in the Great *Bardo-Thödol*,
The *Bardo* called *Chönyid* was taught;
And now, of the *Bardo* called *Sidpa*,
The vivid reminder is brought.

[PART I]

[THE AFTER-DEATH WORLD]

[Introductory Instructions to the Officiant]: Although,
heretofore, while in the *Chönyid Bardo*, many vivid re-
mindings have been given,—setting aside those who have
had great familiarity with the real Truth and those who
have good *karma*,—for them of evil *karma* who have had
no familiarity, and for them of evil *karma* who because
of the influence thereof become stricken with fear and terror,
recognition is difficult. These go down to the Fourteenth
Day; and, to reimpress them vividly, that which follows is
to be read.

[THE *BARDO* BODY: ITS BIRTH AND ITS SUPERNORMAL FACULTIES]

Worship having been offered to the Trinity, and the prayer
invoking the aid of the Buddhas and Bodhisattvas having been
recited, then, calling the deceased by name, three or seven
times, speak thus:
O nobly-born, listen thou well, and bear at heart that birth

---

[1] Lit., ' Act so as to liberate in the Intermediate State '—a direct supplication
to the Deities, Tutelaries, and *Gurus*, rendered by us in the third person to fit
the context better.

in the Hell-world, in the *Deva*-world, and in this *Bardo*-body
is of the kind called supernormal birth.[1]

Indeed, when thou wert experiencing the radiances of the
Peaceful and the Wrathful, in the *Chönyid Bardo*, being unable
to recognize, thou didst faint away, through fear, about three[2]
and one-half days [after thy decease] ; and, then, when thou
wert recovered from the swoon, thy Knower must have risen
up in its primordial condition and a radiant body, resembling
the former body, must have sprung forth[3]—as the *Tantra* says,

'Having a body [seemingly] fleshly [resembling] the former
        and that to be produced,
Endowed with all sense-faculties and power of unimpeded
        motion,
Possessing *karmic* miraculous powers,
Visible to pure celestial eyes [of *Bardo* beings] of like
        nature.'

Such, then, is the teaching.

That [radiant body]—thus referred to as [resembling] 'the
former and that to be produced' (meaning that one will have
a body just like the body of flesh and blood, the former human,
propensity body)—will also be endowed with certain signs and
beauties of perfection such as beings of high destiny possess.

This body, [born] of desire, is a thought-form hallucination
in the Intermediate State, and it is called desire-body.

At that time—if thou art to be born as a *deva*—visions
of the *Deva*-world will appear to thee ; similarly—wherever
thou art to be born—if as an *asura*, or a human being, or

---

[1] Text: *rdzüs-skyes* (pron. *zü-kye*), meaning 'to be born in disguise'—*rdzüs* =
'to disguise' + *skyes* = 'to be born'—or 'to be born in a supernormal manner',
i. e. 'supernormal birth'. As the text will proceed to explain, the birth-process
in the after-death states is quite unlike that known on earth.

[2] In error, probably in transcribing, the text here has 'four' instead of
'three'.

[3] This springing forth, or birth of the *Bardo*-body, about three and one-half
days after death, i. e. upon the expiration of the three and one-half (or four)
days (comparable to the pre-natal period, normally passed in sleep, or dream,
or unconsciousness, on the human-plane), mentioned on pages 93 and 105, is
said to occur instantaneously. 'Like a trout leaping forth from water' is the
simile used by Tibetan *gurus* to explain it ; it is the actual process of being born
in the Intermediate State, paralleling birth in our world.

a brute,[1] or a *preta*, or a being in Hell, a vision of the place will appear to thee.

Accordingly, the word 'former' [in the quotation] implieth that prior to the three and one-half days thou wilt have been thinking thou hadst the same sort of a body as the former body of flesh and blood, possessed by thee in thy former existence because of habitual propensities;[2] and the word 'produced' is so used because, afterwards, the vision of thy future place of birth will appear to thee. Hence, the expression as a whole, 'former and that to be produced', referreth to these [i.e. the fleshly body just discarded and the fleshly body to be assumed at rebirth].

At that time, follow not the visions which appear to thee. Be not attracted; be not weak: if, through weakness, thou be fond of them, thou wilt have to wander amidst the Six *Lokas* and suffer pain.

Up to the other day thou wert unable to recognize the *Chönyid Bardo*, and hast had to wander down this far. Now, if thou art to hold fast to the real Truth, thou must allow thy mind to rest undistractedly in the nothing-to-do, nothing-to-hold condition of the unobscured, primordial, bright, void state of thine intellect, to which thou hast been introduced by thy *guru*.[3] [Thereby] thou wilt obtain Liberation without having to enter the door of the womb. But if thou art unable to know thyself, then, whosoever may be thy tutelary deity and thy *guru*, meditate on them, in a state of intense fondness

---

[1] That is to say, esoterically, a human brute-like being (cf. pp. 126, 129; and 39–61).

[2] That is to say, the habitual (or *karmic*) predilection for *sangsāric* existence arising from the thirst for life, from the wish to be born, is the sole cause of one's possessing a body, human or any other. The Goal which the devotee must gain is 'the Unbecome, the Unborn, the Unmade, the Unformed'—*Nirvāṇa*.

[3] It is herein assumed that the deceased has had, when in the human world, some elementary teachings, at least, concerning mental concentration, or control of the thinking processes, sufficient to have realized the state of non-thought formation described as that of 'the nothing-to-do, nothing-to-hold condition' of the unmodified, primordial mind, which is the state of *Yoga* defined by Patanjali (in his *Yoga Aphorisms*, i. 2) as 'the suppression of the transformations of the thinking principle'. Another rendering of the same passage is, '*Yoga* is the restraint of mental modifications' (Rama Prasad, *Patanjali's Yoga Sūtras* in *The Sacred Books of the Hindus*, Allahabad, 1912, iv. 5).

and humble trust, as overshadowing the crown of thy head.[1]
This is of great importance. Be not distracted.

[Instructions to the Officiant]: Thus speak, and, if recognition result from that, Liberation will be obtained, without
need of the wandering in the Six *Lokas*. If, however, through
influence of bad *karma*, recognition is made difficult, thereupon
say as follows:

O nobly-born, again listen. 'Endowed with all sense-
faculties and power of unimpeded motion' implieth [that
although] thou mayst have been, when living, blind of the
eye, or deaf, or lame, yet on this After-Death Plane thine
eyes will see forms, and thine ears will hear sounds, and all
other sense-organs of thine will be unimpaired and very keen
and complete. Wherefore the *Bardo*-body hath been spoken
of as 'endowed with all sense-faculties'. That [condition of
existence, in which thou thyself now art] is an indication that
thou art deceased and wandering in the *Bardo*. Act so as to
know this. Remember the teachings; remember the teachings.

O nobly-born, 'unimpeded motion' implieth that thy present
body being a desire-body—thine intellect having been separated
from its seat [2]—is not a body of gross matter, so that now thou
hast the power to go right through any rock-masses, hills,
boulders, earth, houses, and Mt. Meru itself without being im-
peded.[3] Excepting Budh-Gayā and the mother's womb,[4] even

---

[1] Or 'directly above'; or lit., 'as being upon the crown of thy head'. The
significance herein is occult: the Brāhmanic Aperture, through which the
consciousness-principle normally departs from the human body, either tem-
porarily in *yogic* trance or permanently at death, is upon the crown of the head;
and if the visualization be centred directly over that aperture very definite
psychic or spiritual benefit accrues to the visualizer. (Cf. p. 92[1].)

[2] The 'seat' is the human body which has been left behind.

[3] This power, supernormal in the human world, is normal in the fourth-
dimensional after-death state. In the human world, such powers, innate in all
persons, can be developed and exercised through proficiency in *yoga*. The
Buddha describes some of them thus: 'In this case suppose that a being
enjoyeth the possession, in various ways, of mystic power: from being one, he
becometh multiform; from being multiform, he becometh one; from being visible,
he becometh invisible; he passeth without hindrance to the further side of
a wall or battlement, or a mountain, as if through air; he walketh on water
without dividing it, as if on solid ground; he travelleth cross-legged through
the sky, like the birds on the wing'—(*Brāhmaṇa Vagga, Anguttara Nikāya*).

[4] Unless previously endowed with a very high degree of spiritual enlighten-

the King of Mountains, Mt. Meru itself, can be passed through
by thee, straight forwards and backwards unimpededly. That,
too, is an indication that thou art wandering in the *Sidpa
Bardo*. Remember thy *guru's* teachings, and pray to the
Compassionate Lord.

O nobly-born, thou art actually endowed with the power
of miraculous action,[1] which is not, however, the fruit of any
samādhi, but a power come to thee naturally; and, therefore, it is of the nature of *karmic* power.[2] Thou art able
in a moment to traverse the four continents round about
Mt. Meru.[3] Or thou canst instantaneously arrive in whatever
place thou wishest; thou hast the power of reaching there
within the time which a man taketh to bend, or to stretch
forth his hand. These various powers of illusion and of
shape-shifting desire not, desire not.[4]

None is there [of such powers] which thou mayst desire
which thou canst not exhibit. The ability to exercise them
unimpededly existeth in thee now. Know this, and pray to
the *guru*.

O nobly-born, 'Visible to pure celestial eyes of like nature'

ment, the deceased cannot consciously go to these two places at will; for from
Budh-Gayā (as a great psychic-centre) and from the mother's womb (as being
the destined path to rebirth) radiate such psychically-blinding radiances that
the ordinary mentality would be overcome with fear in the same manner as
when in the *Bardo* various radiances dawn, and so would avoid them. (Cf.
stanza 6, 'The Path of Good Wishes Which Protecteth from Fear in the
Bardo', p. 206.)

   [1] Text: *rdzu-hphrul* (pron. *zu-tül*); *rdzu* meaning 'power to change one's
shape'; and *hphrul* meaning 'power to change one's size and number', by
appearing or disappearing at will, as one or as many, large or small. If
developed on the earth-plane, through *yogic* practices, such miraculous power
becomes a permanent endowment, and can be employed in the body or out of
the body (as when in the *Bardo*).

   [2] The text implies that the deceased is possessed of the miraculous power as
a result of his being—through the workings of *karma*—in the Intermediate
State, wherein such power is natural, and not because of merit acquired through
the practice of *yoga* when in the human body.

   [3] See pp. 62–5, concerning Cosmography.

   [4] The most advanced of the *lāmas* teach the disciple not to strive after psychic
powers of this nature for their own sake; for until the disciple is morally fit to use
them wisely they become a serious impediment to his higher spiritual development: not until the lower or passional nature of man is completely mastered is
he safe in using them.

implieth that those [beings] of like nature, being those of similar constitution [or level of knowledge] in the Intermediate State, will individually see each other.¹ For example, those beings who are destined to be born amongst *devas* will see each other [and so on]. Dote not on them [seen by thee], but meditate upon the Compassionate One.

'Visible to pure celestial eyes' [also] implieth that the *devas*, being born [pure] in virtue of merit, are visible to the pure celestial eyes of those who practise *dhyāna*. These will not see them at all times: when mentally concentrated [upon them] they see [them], when not, they see [them] not. Sometimes, even when practising *dhyāna*, they are liable to become distracted [and not see them].²

[CHARACTERISTICS OF EXISTENCE IN THE INTERMEDIATE STATE]

O nobly-born, the possessor of that sort of body will see places [familiarly known on the earth-plane] and relatives [there] as one seeth another in dreams.

Thou seest thy relatives and connexions and speakest to them, but receivest no reply. Then, seeing them and thy family weeping, thou thinkest, 'I am dead! What shall I do?' and feelest great misery, just like a fish cast out

---

¹ In addition to the normal human eyes with their limited vision, *lāmas* say that there are five sorts of eyes : (1) Eyes of Instinct (or Eyes of the Flesh), like those of birds and beasts of prey, which, in most cases, possess a greater range of vision than human eyes ; (2) Celestial Eyes, like the eyes of the *devas*, capable of seeing the human world as well as their own, and the past and future births of beings in both worlds throughout many lifetimes ; (3) Eyes of Truth, like the eyes of Bodhisattvas and Arhants, capable of seeing throughout hundreds of world-periods (or *kalpas*) backwards and in the future ; (4) Divine Eyes, of the most highly advanced Bodhisattvas, capable of seeing throughout millions of world-periods that which has been and that which will be ; and (5) Eyes of Wisdom of the Buddhas, capable of seeing, in like manner, throughout eternity.

² Ordinarily it is only when clairvoyant vision is induced by *dhyāna*, or exists naturally in certain specially gifted clairvoyants, and directed to the *deva*-world, that the *devas* are seen ; sometimes, however, the *devas* appear unexpectedly. The *Tri-Pitaka*, like the canonical literature of Northern Buddhism, is replete with visions and unexpected visitations of *devas*, as Christian and Moslem sacred literature is replete with lore concerning angels.

[of water] on red-hot embers. Such misery thou wilt be experiencing at present. But feeling miserable will avail thee nothing now. If thou hast a divine *guru*,[1] pray to him. Pray to the Tutelary Deity, the Compassionate One. Even though thou feelest attachment for thy relatives and connexions, it will do thee no good. So be not attached. Pray to the Compassionate Lord; thou shalt have nought of sorrow, or of terror, or of awe.

O nobly-born, when thou art driven [hither and thither] by the ever-moving wind of *karma*, thine intellect, having no object upon which to rest, will be like a feather tossed about by the wind, riding on the horse of breath.[2] Ceaselessly and involuntarily wilt thou be wandering about. To all those who are weeping [thou wilt say], 'Here I am; weep not.' But they not hearing thee, thou wilt think, 'I am dead!' And again, at that time, thou wilt be feeling very miserable. Be not miserable in that way.

There will be a grey twilight-like light, both by night and by day, and at all times.[3] In that kind of Intermediate State thou wilt be either for one, two, three, four, five, six, or seven weeks, until the forty-ninth day.[4] It hath been said that ordinarily the miseries of the *Sidpa Bardo* are experienced for about twenty-two days; but, because of the determining influence of *karma*, a fixed period is not assured.

O nobly-born, at about that time, the fierce wind of *karma*, terrific and hard to endure, will drive thee [onwards], from behind, in dreadful gusts. Fear it not. That is thine own

---

[1] This refers to a superhuman *guru* of the Divyaugha Order. (See Addenda, p. 222.)

[2] Like the restless wind, *karma* is ever in motion, and the intellect, when without the support of the human body, is its plaything.

[3] *Yogīs* explain this by saying that in the *Bardo*-body, which is a mind-born desire-body, the nervous system of the earth-plane body being lacking, the light of the sun and moon and stars is not visible to the deceased. Only the natural light of nature (referred to by medieval alchemists and mystics as the 'astral light') is to be seen in the after-death state; and this 'astral light' is said to be universally diffused throughout the ether, like an earth twilight, yet quite bright enough for the eyes of the ethereally constituted beings in the *Bardo*. (Cf. p. 92⁴.)

[4] See our Introduction, pp. 6–7.

illusion. Thick awesome darkness will appear in front of thee continually, from the midst of which there will come such terror-producing utterances as 'Strike! Slay!' and similar threats,[1] Fear these not.

In other cases, of persons of much evil *karma*, *karmically*-produced flesh-eating *rākṣhasas* [or demons] bearing various weapons will utter, 'Strike! Slay!' and so on, making a frightful tumult. They will come upon one as if competing amongst themselves as to which [of them] should get hold of one. Apparitional illusions, too, of being pursued by various terrible beasts of prey will dawn. Snow, rain, darkness, fierce blasts [of wind], and hallucinations of being pursued by many people likewise will come; [and] sounds as of mountains crumbling down, and of angry overflowing seas, and of the roaring of fire, and of fierce winds springing up.[2]

When these sounds come one, being terrified by them, will flee before them in every direction, not caring whither one fleeth. But the way will be obstructed by three awful precipices—white, and black, and red. They will be terror-inspiring and deep, and one will feel as if one were about to fall down them. O nobly-born, they are not really precipices; they are Anger, Lust, and Stupidity.[3]

[1] The dweller in the *Bardo*, because of the *karmic* effects of selfishness when living in the human world, is obsessed with the belief that all other *Bardo* beings are at enmity with him; hence he has these frightful hallucinations, as in a nightmare. (Cf. p. 148.)

[2] In *The Six Doctrines*, a treatise on the practical application of various *yogas*, which we have translated out of the original Tibetan, there is a parallel passage which amplifies this, as follows: 'If one findeth not the Path during the Second *Bardo* (i.e. during the *Chönyid Bardo*), then four sounds called "awe-inspiring sounds" [are heard]: from the vital-force of the earth-element, a sound like the crumbling down of a mountain; from the vital-force of the water-element, a sound like the breaking of [storm-tossed] ocean-waves; from the vital-force of the fire-element, a sound as of a jungle afire; from the vital-force of the air-element, a sound like a thousand thunders reverberating simultaneously.' Herein are described the psychic resultants of the disintegrating process called death as affecting the four grosser elements composing the human body aggregate; the ether-element is not named, because in that element alone—i.e. in the ethereal, or *Bardo*-body—the consciousness-principle continues to exist. (Cf. page 93[3].)

[3] The precipices are *karmic* illusions, symbolical of the three evil passions; and the falling down them symbolizes the entrance into a womb prior to rebirth. (See page 125[2].)

Know at that time that it is the *Sidpa Bardo* [in which thou art]. Invoking, by name, the Compassionate One, pray earnestly, thus: ' O Compassionate Lord, and my *Guru*, and the Precious Trinity, suffer it not that I (so-and-so by name) fall into the unhappy worlds.' Act so as to forget this not.

Others who have accumulated merit, and devoted themselves sincerely to religion, will experience various delightful pleasures and happiness and ease in full measure. But that class of neutral beings who have neither earned merit nor created bad *karma* will experience neither pleasure nor pain, but a sort of colourless stupidity of indifference. O nobly-born, whatever cometh in that manner—whatever delightful pleasures thou mayst experience—be not attracted by them; dote not [on them]: think, 'May the *Guru* and the Trinity be worshipped [with these merit-given delights]'. Abandon all dotings and hankerings.

Even though thou dost not experience pleasure, or pain, but only indifference, keep thine intellect in the undistracted state of the [meditation upon the] Great Symbol, without thinking that thou art meditating.[1] This is of vast importance.

O nobly-born, at that time, at bridge-heads, in temples, by *stūpas* of eight kinds,[2] thou wilt rest a little while, but thou wilt not be able to remain there very long, for thine

---

[1] Text : *bsgom-med-yengs-med* (pron. *yom-med-yeng-med*) = ' non-meditation + non-distraction '; referring to a state of mental concentration in which no thought of meditation itself is allowed to intrude. This is the state of *Samādhi*. If one thinks one is meditating, the thought alone inhibits the meditation; hence the warning to the deceased.

[2] This refers to the eight purposes for which a *stūpa* (or pagoda) is built. Two such instances may be cited in elucidation : (1) *rnam-rgyal-mchod-rten* (pron. *ram-gyal-chöd-ten*) : *mchod-rten* (or *chorten = stūpa*) is here translatable as ' object of worship ', and *rnam-rgyal* as ' victory '; hence this sort of pagoda is one for marking a victory, i. e. a monument ; (2) *myang-hdas-mchod-rten* (pron. *nyang-day-chöd-ten*) refers to a *stūpa* used as a monument for marking the spot where a saint or sage died, or the place of burial of the urn containing such a one's ashes. Other pagodas are purely symbolical structures erected—as Christian crosses are—as objects of worship or veneration. In Ceylon many *stūpas* are erected solely to enshrine sacred books or reliques. The great *stūpas* of North-west India, near Peshawar and at Taxila, lately opened, contained bone-reliques and other objects. Two of them contained authentic bits of the bones of the Buddha.

intellect hath been separated from thine [earth-plane] body.[1]
Because of this inability to loiter, thou oft-times wilt feel per-
turbed and vexed and panic-stricken. At times, thy Knower
will be dim ; at times, fleeting and incoherent. Thereupon this
thought will occur to thee, 'Alas! I am dead! What shall
I do?' and because of such thought the Knower will become
saddened and the heart chilled, and thou wilt experience
infinite misery of sorrow.[2] Since thou canst not rest in
any one place, and feel impelled to go on, think not of
various things, but allow the intellect to abide in its own
[unmodified] state.

As to food, only that which hath been dedicated to thee
can be partaken of by thee, and no other food.[3] As to
friends at this time, there will be no certainty.[4]

These are the indications of the wandering about on the
Sidpa Barāo of the mental-body. At the time, happiness
and misery will depend upon *karma*.

Thou wilt see thine own home, the attendants, relatives,
and the corpse, and think, 'Now I am dead! What shall
I do?' and being oppressed with intense sorrow, the thought

---

[1] Like a person travelling alone at night along a highway, having his attention
arrested by prominent landmarks, great isolated trees, houses, bridge-heads,
temples, *stupas*, and so on, the dead, in their own way, have similar experiences
when earth-wandering. They are attracted, by *karmic* propensities, to familiar
haunts in the human world, but being possessed of a mental or desire body
cannot remain long at any one place. As our text explains, they are driven
hither and thither by the winds of *karmic* desires—like a feather before a gale.

[2] It should be remembered here that all the terrifying phenomena and the
unhappiness are entirely *karmic*. Had the deceased been developed spiritually,
his *Bardo* existence would have been peaceful and happy from the first, and he
would not have wandered down so far as this. The *Bardo Thödol* is concerned
chiefly with the normal individual, and not with highly developed human beings
whom death sets free into Reality.

[3] Like fairies and spirits of the dead according to Celtic belief, or the daemons
of ancient Greek belief, the dwellers in the *Bardo* are said to live on invisible
ethereal essences, which they extract either from food offered to them on the
human plane or else from the general store-house of nature. In *The Six
Doctrines*, already referred to above (p. 162[2]), there is this reference to the
inhabitants of the *Bardo*: 'They live on odours [or the spiritual essences of
material things].'

[4] Friends may or may not exist in the Intermediate State, as on earth ; but
even if they do, they are powerless to counteract any bad *karma* of the deceased.
He must follow his own path, as marked out by *karma*.

will occur to thee, 'O what would I not give to possess a body!' And so thinking, thou wilt be wandering hither and thither seeking a body.

Even though thou couldst enter thy dead body nine times over—owing to the long interval which thou hast passed in the *Chönyid Bardo*—it will have been frozen if in winter, been decomposed if in summer, or, otherwise, thy relatives will have cremated it, or interred it, or thrown it into the water, or given it to the birds and beasts of prey.[1] Wherefore finding no place for thyself to enter into, thou wilt be dissatisfied and have the sensation of being squeezed into cracks and crevices amidst rocks and boulders.[2] The experiencing of this sort of misery occurs in the Intermediate State when seeking rebirth. Even though thou seekest a body, thou wilt gain nothing but trouble. Put aside the desire for a body; and permit thy mind to abide in the state of resignation, and act so as to abide therein.

By thus being set face to face, one obtaineth liberation from the *Bardo*.

[THE JUDGEMENT]

[Instructions to the Officiant]: Yet, again, it may be possible that because of the influence of bad *karma* one will not recognize even thus. Therefore, call the deceased by name, and speak as follows:

O nobly-born, (so-and-so), listen. That thou art suffering so cometh from thine own *karma*; it is not due to any one else's: it is by thine own *karma*. Accordingly, pray earnestly to the Precious Trinity; that will protect thee. If thou neither prayest nor knowest how to meditate upon the Great Symbol nor upon any tutelary deity, the Good Genius,[3] who

---

[1] All known forms of disposal of a corpse are practised in Tibet, including mummification. (See pp. 25-8.)

[2] This symbolizes the getting into undesirable wombs, such as those of human beings of animal-like nature.

[3] Text: *Lhan-chig-skyes-pahi-lha* (pron. *Lhan-chig-kye-pai-lha*) = 'simultaneously-born god (or good spirit, or genius)', the personification of a human being's higher, or divine, nature; popularly known in Sikkimese as *Lha-kar-chung*, 'Little white god'.

was born simultaneously with thee, will come now and count out thy good deeds [with] white pebbles, and the Evil Genius,[1] who was born simultaneously with thee, will come and count out thy evil deeds [with] black pebbles. Thereupon, thou wilt be greatly frightened, awed, and terrified, and wilt tremble; and thou wilt attempt to tell lies, saying, 'I have not committed any evil deed'.

Then the Lord of Death will say, 'I will consult the Mirror of *Karma*'.

So saying, he will look in the Mirror, wherein every good and evil act is vividly reflected. Lying will be of no avail.

Then [one of the Executive Furies of] the Lord of Death will place round thy neck a rope and drag thee along; he will cut off thy head, extract thy heart, pull out thy intestines, lick up thy brain, drink thy blood, eat thy flesh, and gnaw thy bones;[2] but thou wilt be incapable of dying. Although thy body be hacked to pieces, it will revive again. The repeated hacking will cause intense pain and torture.

Even at the time that the pebbles are being counted out, be not frightened, nor terrified; tell no lies; and fear not the Lord of Death.

Thy body being a mental body is incapable of dying even though beheaded and quartered. In reality, thy body is of the nature of voidness;[3] thou needst not be afraid. The

---

[1] Text: *Lhan-chig-skyes-pahi-hdre* (pron. *Lhan-chig-kye-pai-de*) = 'simultaneously-born demon (or evil spirit, or genius)', the personification of a human being's lower, or carnal, nature; popularly known in Sikkimese as *Bdud-nag-chung* (pron. *Düd-nag-chung*), 'Little black *māra* (or demon)'.

[2] These tortures symbolize the pangs of the deceased's conscience; for the Judgement, as herein described, symbolizes the rising up of the Good Genius in judgement against the Evil Genius, the Judge being the conscience itself in its stern aspect of impartiality and love of righteousness; the Mirror is memory. One element—the purely human element—of the consciousness-content of the deceased, comes forward, and, by offering lame excuses, tries to meet accusations against it, saying, 'Owing to such-and-such circumstances I had to do so-and-so'. Another element of the consciousness-content comes forward and says, 'You were guided by such-and-such motives; your deeds partake of the black colour'. Then some more friendly one of such elements arises and protests, 'But I have such-and-such justification; and the deceased deserves pardon on these grounds'. And so—as the *lāmas* explain—the Judgement proceeds. (Cf. pp. 35-7.)

[3] Meaning that the 'astral' or desire-body is incapable of ordinary physical

Lords of Death[1] are thine own hallucinations. Thy desire-body is a body of propensities, and void. Voidness cannot injure voidness; the qualityless cannot injure the qualityless.

Apart from one's own hallucinations, in reality there are no such things existing outside oneself as Lord of Death, or god, or demon, or the Bull-headed Spirit of Death.[2] Act so as to recognize this.

At this time, act so as to recognize that thou art in the *Bardo*. Meditate upon the *Samādhi* of the Great Symbol. If thou dost not know how to meditate, then merely analyse with care the real nature of that which is frightening thee. In reality it is not formed into anything, but is a Voidness which is the *Dharma-Kāya*.[3]

That Voidness is not of the nature of the voidness of nothingness, but a Voidness at the true nature of which thou feelest awed, and before which thine intellect shineth clearly and more lucidly: that is the [state of] mind of the *Sambhoga-Kāya*.

In that state wherein thou art existing, there is being experienced by thee, in an unbearable intensity, Voidness and Brightness inseparable,—the Voidness bright by nature and the Brightness by nature void, and the Brightness inseparable from the Voidness,—a state of the primordial [or unmodified] intellect, which is the *Ādi-Kāya*.[4] And the

injury. 'As through a cloud, a sword can be plunged through the *Bardo*-body without harming it'—the *lāmas* explain; or it is like the forms seen in materializing seances of necromancers and spirit-mediums.

[1] These Lords of Death are Yama-Rāja and his Court of Associates, including, perhaps, the Executive Furies. These last are, as Tormenting Furies, comparable to the Eumenides of Aeschylus' great drama—elements of one's own consciousness-content. Following the *Abhidhamma*, of Southern Buddhism, there are mind (Skt. *chit*, Tib. *sems*—pron. *sem*) and impulses of mind (Skt. *chittavritti*, Tib. *sems-hbyung*—pron. *sem-jung*); and the impulses of mind are the Furies. (Cf. pp. 147-8.)

[2] Text: *Ragsha-glang-mgo* (pron. *Ragsha-lang-go*): 'Bull-headed Spirit of Death', commonly depicted as having a buffalo-head. The chief tutelary deity of the Gelugpa or Yellow Hat Sect, called *Jampal Shinjeshed* (Tib. *Hjam-dpal Gshin-rje-gshed*), meaning '*Jampal* (Skt. *Mañjusrhī*), the Destroyer of the Lord of Death (Skt. *Yamāntaka*)', is often represented as a blue buffalo-headed deity.

[3] See pp. 10-15.

[4] Tib. *Gowo-nyidku*: Skt. *Ādi-Kāya* ('First Body'), which is synonymous with the *Dharma-Kāya*.

power of this, shining unobstructedly, will radiate everywhere; it is the *Nirmāṇa-Kāya*.

O nobly-born, listen unto me undistractedly. By merely
recognizing the Four *Kāyas*, thou art certain to obtain perfect
Emancipation in any of Them. Be not distracted. The line
of demarcation between Buddhas and sentient beings lieth
herein.[1] This moment is one of great importance; if thou
shouldst be distracted now, it will require innumerable aeons
of time for thee to come out [2] of the Quagmire of Misery.

A saying, the truth of which is applicable, is:

'In a moment of time, a marked differentiation is created;
In a moment of time, Perfect Enlightenment is obtained.'

Till the moment which hath just passed, all this *Bardo*
hath been dawning upon thee and yet thou hast not recognized, because of being distracted. On this account, thou
hast experienced all the fear and terror. Shouldst thou become distracted now, the chords of divine compassion of the
Compassionate Eyes will break,[3] and thou wilt go into the
place from which there is no [immediate] liberation. Therefore, be careful. Even though thou hast not recognized ere
this—despite thus being set face to face—thou wilt recognize
and obtain liberation here.

[Instructions to the Officiant]: If it be an illiterate boor
who knoweth not how to meditate, then say this:

O nobly-born, if thou knowest not how thus to meditate,
act so as to remember the Compassionate One, and the Saṅgha,
the Dharma, and the Buddha, and pray. Think of all these
fears and terrifying apparitions as being thine own tutelary
deity, or as the Compassionate One.[4] Bring to thy recollection the mystic name that hath been given thee at the time

---

[1] In virtue of knowing the true nature of *saṅgsānc* existence—that all phenomena are unreal—Buddhas, or Perfectly Enlightened Ones, are beings quite apart
from unenlightened sentient beings.

[2] Lit., 'there will be no time when thou canst get out'.

[3] This is a literal rendering, meaning that the rays of grace or compassion of
Chenrazee will cease to dawn.

[4] The idea meant to be conveyed is that trials and tribulations, although
karmic, act as divine tests, and so, being for the good of the deceased, ought
even to be visualized as such, i. e. as the tutelary deity, or as Chenrazee.

of thy sacred initiation when thou wert a human being, and
the name of thy *guru*, and tell them to the Righteous King
of the Lord[s] of Death.[1] Even though thou fallest down precipices, thou wilt not be hurt. Avoid awe and terror.

[THE ALL-DETERMINING INFLUENCE OF THOUGHT]

[Instructions to the Officiant]: Say that; for by such setting-face-to-face, despite the previous non-liberation, liberation ought surely to be obtained [2] here. Possibly, [however,]
liberation may not be obtained even after that setting-face-
to-face ; and earnest and continued application being essential,
again calling the deceased by name, speak as follows:

O nobly-born, thy immediate experiences will be of momentary joys followed by momentary sorrows, of great intensity,
like the [taut and relaxed] mechanical actions of catapults.[3]
Be not in the least attached [to the joys] nor displeased
[by the sorrows] of that.

If thou art to be born on a higher plane, the vision of that
higher plane will be dawning upon thee.

Thy living relatives may—by way of dedication for the
benefit of thee deceased—be sacrificing many animals,[4] and
performing religious ceremonies, and giving alms. Thou,

[1] This revealing of the initiatory name is for the purpose of establishing
occult connexion between the deceased and the King of Death—i. e. between
the human and the divine in man—in much the same way as a Freemason will
make himself known to another Freemason by giving some secret password.

[2] Lit., ' will be obtained '.

[3] That is to say, at one time good *karma* will be operative and raise the
deceased to a spiritual state of mind, and at another time, bad *karma* becoming
predominant, the deceased will be pulled down in mental depression. The
operator of the catapult is *karma*, who stretches out the catapult to its limit and
then relaxes it, alternately.

[4] Each time an animal is sacrificed—presumably to be prepared for food
afterwards—the deceased is said to be unable to escape the *karmic* result, the
sacrifice being done in his name, so that horrors come upon him directly. He
calls to the living to cease, but, they not hearing him, he is inclined to grow
angry ; and anger he must avoid at all costs, for if allowed to arise on the
Bardo-plane, like a heavy weight, it forces him down to the lowest mental state
called Hell.

Animal sacrifice to the dead, in Tibet as in India, originated in ancient times,
far prior to the rise of Buddhism, which, of course, prohibits it. Survivals of it

because of thy vision not being purified, mayst be inclined to grow very angry at their actions and bring about, at this moment, thy birth in Hell: whatever those left behind thee may be doing, act thou so that no angry thought can arise in thee, and meditate upon love for them.

Furthermore, even if thou feelest attached to the worldly goods thou hast left behind, or, because of seeing such worldly goods of thine in the possession of other people and being enjoyed by them, thou shouldst feel attached to them through weakness, or feel angry with thy successors, that feeling will affect the psychological moment in such a way that, even though thou wert destined to be born on higher and happier planes, thou wilt be obliged to be born in Hell, or in the world of *pretas* [or unhappy ghosts]. On the other hand, even if thou art attached to worldly goods left behind, thou wilt not be able to possess them, and they will be of no use to thee. Therefore, abandon weakness and attachment for them; cast them away wholly; renounce them from thy heart. No matter who may be enjoying thy worldly goods, have no feeling of miserliness, but be prepared to renounce them willingly. Think that thou art offering them to the Precious Trinity and to thy *guru*, and abide in the feeling of unattachment, devoid of weakness [of desire].

have persisted in Tibet, but without the approval of the *lāmas*, as our text clearly proves; and, if practised nowadays, it is only rarely, and by the rude folk of remote districts, who are Buddhist merely in name.

Save for the *yogī* or *lāma* eager for the highest spiritual development—with which flesh-eating is said to be incompatible—Tibetans, being confirmed eaters of animal corpses, like the Brāhmins of Kashmir (who are, consequently, not recognized as Brāhmins by the pure-living Brāhmins of India), excuse their meat-eating on the grounds of climatic and economic necessity. Although Tibet is poor in cereals and vegetables and fruits, this seems to be chiefly an unconscious attempt to cover up a racial predisposition, inherited from nomadic and pastoral ancestors, for a flesh diet. Even in Ceylon, where there can be no such excuse for Buddhists to disobey the precept prohibiting the taking of life, flesh-eating has already made rapid progress since the advent of Christianity, which, unlike Buddhism, does not, unfortunately, teach kindness to animals as a religious tenet, St. Paul himself being of opinion that God cares not for oxen (see *1 Cor.* ix. 9). And yet on Ceylon's Sacred Mount of Mihintale still stands, as witness of a purer Buddhism, the ancient edict, cut on a stone slab, prohibiting—as the Edicts of Aṣoka prohibit—the slaying of any animal, either in sacrifice or for food.

Again, when any recitation of the *Kamkanī Mantra*[1] is
being made on thy behalf as a funeral rite, or when any
rite for the absolving of bad *karma* liable to bring about
thy birth in lower regions is being performed for thee, the
sight of their being conducted in an incorrect way, mixed
up with sleep and distraction and non-observance of the
vows and lack of purity [on the part of any officiant], and
such things indicating levity—all of which thou wilt be able
to see because thou art endowed with limited *karmic* power
of prescience[2]—thou mayst feel lack of faith and entire disbelief [in thy religion].   Thou wilt be able to apprehend
any fear and fright, any black actions, irreligious conduct,
and incorrectly recited rituals.[3]   In thy mind thou mayst
think, 'Alas! they are, indeed, playing me false'.   Thinking
thus, thou wilt be extremely depressed, and, through great
resentment, thou wilt acquire disbelief and loss of faith,
instead of affection and humble trustfulness.   This affecting
the psychological moment, thou wilt be certain to be born
in one of the miserable states.

Such [thought] will not only be of no use to thee, but will
do thee great harm.   However incorrect the ritual and im-
proper the conduct of the priests performing thy funeral
rites, [think], 'What! mine own thoughts must be impure!
How can it be possible that the words of the Buddha should
be incorrect?   It is like the reflection of the blemishes on mine
own face which I see in a mirror; mine own thoughts must
[indeed] be impure.   As for these [i.e. the priests], the Saṅgha
is their body, the Dharma their utterance, and in their mind
they are the Buddha in reality: I will take refuge in them'.

[1] This *mantra* is believed to have the magical power of so transmuting food
sacrificed to the dead as to make it acceptable to them.

[2] In its fullness, this power of prescience includes knowledge of the past,
present, and future, the ability to read others' thoughts, and the unobscured
knowing of one's own capabilities and limitations.   Only highly developed
beings, such, for example, as adepts in *yoga*, enjoy such complete power of
prescience.   On the *Bardo* plane—unlike the human world—every being
possesses, in virtue of freedom from the impeding gross physical body, a certain
degree of the power, as the text makes clear.

[3] That is, fear and fright, or impropriety, or carelessness on the part of any
person conducting the funeral rites.

Thus thinking, put thy trust in them and exercise sincere love towards them. Then whatever is done for thee [by those] left behind will truly tend to thy benefit. Therefore the exercise of that love is of much importance; do not forget this.

Again, even if thou wert to be born in one of the miserable states and the light of that miserable state shone upon thee, yet by thy successors and relatives performing white [1] religious rites unmixed with evil actions, and the abbots and learned priests devoting themselves, body, speech, and mind, to the performance of the correct meritorious rituals, the delight from thy feeling greatly cheered at seeing them will, by its own virtue, so affect the psychological moment that, even though thou deservest a birth in the unhappy states, there will be brought about thy birth on a higher and happier plane. [Therefore] thou shouldst not create impious thoughts, but exercise pure affection and humble faith towards all impartially. This is highly important. Hence be extremely careful.

O nobly-born, to sum up: thy present intellect in the Intermediate State having no firm object whereon to depend, being of little weight and continuously in motion, whatever thought occurs to thee now—be it pious or impious—will wield great power; therefore think not in thy mind of impious things, but recall any devotional exercises; or, if thou wert unaccustomed to any such exercises, [show forth] pure affection and humble faith; pray to the Compassionate One, or to thy tutelary deities; with full resolve, utter this prayer:

' Alas! while wandering alone, separated from loving friends, [2]
When the vacuous, reflected body of mine own mental ideas dawneth upon me,
May the Buddhas, vouchsafing their power of compassion,
Grant that there shall be no fear, awe, or terror in the *Bardo*.
When experiencing miseries, through the power of evil *karma*,
May the tutelary deities dispel the miseries.

---

[1] ' White ' as opposed to ' black ' (as in black magic or sorcery).
[2] Cf. the following from the *Orologium Sapientiae*, Comper's ed. (p. 119): ' Where is now the help of my friends? Where be now the good behests of our kinsmen and others?'

When the thousand thunders of the Sound of Reality re-
verberate,
May they all be sounds of the Six Syllables.[1]
When *Karma* follows, without there being any protector,
May the Compassionate One protect me, I pray.
When experiencing the sorrows of *karmic* propensities here,
May the radiance of the happy clear light of *Samādhi*
shine upon me.'

Earnest prayer in this form will be sure to guide thee
along; thou mayst rest assured that thou wilt not be deceived.
Of great importance is this: through that being recited, again
recollection cometh; and recognition and liberation will be
achieved.

[THE DAWNING OF THE LIGHTS OF THE SIX *LOKAS*]

[Instructions to the Officiant]: Yet—though this [instruction]
be so oft repeated—if recognition be difficult, because of the
influence of evil *karma*, much benefit will come from repeating
these settings-face-to-face many times over. Once more, [then,]
call the deceased by name, and speak as follows:

O nobly-born, if thou hast been unable to apprehend the
above, henceforth the body of the past life will become more
and more dim and the body of the future life will become
more and more clear. Saddened at this [thou wilt think],
'O what misery I am undergoing! Now, whatever body
I am to get, I shall go and seek [it]'. So thinking, thou wilt
be going hither and thither, ceaselessly and distractedly.
Then there will shine upon thee the lights of the Six *Sangsāric
Lokas*. The light of that place wherein thou art to be born,
through power of *karma*, will shine most prominently.

O nobly-born, listen. If thou desirest to know what those
six lights are: there will shine upon thee a dull white light
from the *Deva*-world, a dull green light from the *Asura*-
world, a dull yellow light from the Human-world, a dull blue

[1] See p. 149[1].

light from the Brute-world, a dull red light from the *Preta*-world, and a smoke-coloured light from the Hell-world.[1]   At that time, by the power of *karma*, thine own body will partake of the colour of the light of the place wherein thou art to be born.

O nobly-born, the special art of these teachings is especially important at this moment: whichever light shineth upon thee now, meditate upon it as being the Compassionate One; from whatever place the light cometh, consider that [place] to be [or to exist in] the Compassionate One.   This is an exceedingly profound art; it will prevent birth.   Or whosoever thy tutelary deity may be, meditate upon the form for much time,— as being apparent yet non-existent in reality, like a form produced by a magician.   That is called the pure illusory form.   Then let the [visualization of the] tutelary deity melt away from the extremities, till nothing at all remaineth visible of it; and put thyself in the state of the Clearness and the Voidness [2]—which thou canst not conceive as something— and abide in that state for a little while.   Again meditate upon the tutelary deity; again meditate upon the Clear Light: do this alternately.   Afterwards, allow thine own intellect also to melt away gradually,[3] [beginning] from the extremities.

Wherever the ether [4] pervadeth, consciousness pervadeth; wherever consciousness pervadeth, the *Dharma-Kāya* pervadeth.   Abide tranquilly in the uncreated state of the *Dharma-Kāya*.   In that state, birth will be obstructed and Perfect Enlightenment gained.

---

[1] Here as before (see p. 124[2]) the MS. is faulty.   It gives the lights as follows: white for the *Deva*-world, red for the *Asura*-world, blue for the Human-world, green for the Brute-world, yellow for the *Preta*-world, smoke-coloured for the Hell-world.   This error, apparently on the part of the copyist of the MS., has been corrected by the translator.

[2] This expression, 'the Clearness and the Voidness', from the instructions following, seems to be synonymous with 'the Clear Light', or 'the Clear Light and the Voidness'.

[3] This process corresponds to the two stages of *Samādhi*: the visualization stage, and the perfected stage.   (See p. 119[1].)

[4] Text: *nam-mkhah* (pron. *nam-kha*): Skt. *Ākāsha*: 'ether', or 'sky'.

[PART II]

[THE PROCESS OF REBIRTH]

[THE CLOSING OF THE DOOR OF THE WOMB]

[Instructions to the Officiant]: Again, if through great weakness in devotions and lack of familiarity one be not able to understand, illusion may overcome one, and one will wander to the doors of wombs. The instruction for the closing of the womb-doors becometh very important: call the deceased by name and say this:

O nobly-born, if thou hast not understood the above, at this moment, through the influence of *karma*, thou wilt have the impression that thou art either ascending, or moving along on a level, or going downwards. Thereupon, meditate upon the Compassionate One. Remember. Then, as said above, gusts of wind, and icy blasts, hail-storms, and darkness, and impression of being pursued by many people will come upon thee. On fleeing from these [hallucinations], those who are unendowed with meritorious *karma* will have the impression of fleeing into places of misery; those who are endowed with meritorious *karma* will have the impression of arriving in places of happiness. Thereupon, O nobly-born, in whatever continent or place thou art to be born, the signs of that birth-place will shine upon thee then.

For this moment there are several vital profound teachings. Listen undistractedly. Even though thou hast not apprehended by the above settings-face-to-face, here [thou wilt, because] even those who are very weak in devotions will recognize the signs. Therefore listen.

[Instructions to the Officiant]: Now it is very important to employ the methods of closing the womb-door. Wherefore it is necessary to exercise the utmost care. There are two [chief] ways of closing: preventing the being who would enter from entering, and closing the womb-door which might be entered.

[METHOD OF PREVENTING ENTRY INTO A WOMB]

The instructions for preventing the being from entering are thus:

O nobly-born, (so-and-so by name,) whosoever may have been thy tutelary deity, tranquilly meditate upon him,—as upon the reflection of the moon in water, apparent yet non-existent [as a moon], like a magically-produced illusion. If thou hast no special tutelary, meditate either upon the Compassionate Lord or upon me; and, with this in mind, meditate tranquilly.

Then, causing the [visualized form of the] tutelary deity to melt away from the extremities, meditate, without any thought-forming, upon the vacuous Clear Light. This is a very profound art; in virtue of it, a womb is not entered.

[THE FIRST METHOD OF CLOSING THE WOMB-DOOR]

In that manner meditate; but even though this be found inadequate to prevent thee from entering into a womb, and if thou findest thyself ready to enter into one, then there is the profound teaching for closing the womb-door. Listen thou unto it:

'When, at this time, alas! the *Sidpa Bardo* is dawning
  upon oneself,
Holding in mind one single resolution,
Persist in joining up the chain of good *karma*;[1]
Close up the womb-door, and remember the opposition.[2]
This is a time when earnestness and pure love are
  necessary;
Abandon jealousy, and meditate upon the *Guru* Father-
  Mother.'

Repeat this, from thine own mouth, distinctly; and re-

---

[1] To obtain results, the accumulated merit, born of good actions done in the earth-life, must be made operative, that is, it must be linked with the *Bardo* existence of the deceased.

[2] Normally, existence in the *Bardo* ever tends to lead the deceased back to birth; and this is due to *karmic* propensities, which are the opposition, the forces opposing the Enlightenment of Buddhahood. Hence the deceased must oppose this innate tendency with every help available.

member its meaning vividly, and meditate upon it. The putting of this into practice is essential.

The significance of the above teaching, 'When, at this time, the *Sidpa Bardo* is dawning upon me [or upon oneself]', is that now thou art wandering in the *Sidpa Bardo*. As a sign of this, if thou lookest into water, or into mirrors, thou wilt see no reflection of thy face or body; nor doth thy body cast any shadow. Thou hast discarded now thy gross material body of flesh and blood. These are the indications that thou art wandering about in the *Sidpa Bardo*.

At this time, thou must form, without distraction, one single resolve in thy mind. The forming of one single resolve is very important now. It is like directing the course of a horse by the use of the reins.

Whatever thou desirest will come to pass. Think not upon evil actions which might turn the course [of thy mind]. Remember thy [spiritual] relationship with the Reader of this *Bardo Thödol*, or with any one from whom thou hast received teachings, initiation, or spiritual authorization for reading religious texts while in the human world; and persevere in going on with good acts: this is very essential. Be not distracted. The boundary line between going upwards or going downwards is here now. If thou givest way to indecision for even a second, thou wilt have to suffer misery for a long, long time. This is the moment. Hold fast to one single purpose. Persistently join up the chain of good acts.

Thou hast come now to the time of closing the womb-door. 'This is a time when earnestness and pure love are necessary', which implieth that now the time hath come when, first of all, the womb-door should be closed, there being five methods of closing. Bear this well at heart.

[THE SECOND METHOD OF CLOSING THE WOMB-DOOR]

O nobly-born, at this time thou wilt see visions of males and females in union. When thou seest them, remember to withhold thyself from going between them. Regarding the father and mother as thy *Guru* and the Divine Mother,[1] meditate upon them and bow down; humbly exercise thy faith; offer up mental worship with great fervency; and resolve that thou wilt request [of them] religious guidance.

By that resolution alone, the womb ought certainly to be closed; but if it is not closed even by that, and thou findest thyself ready to enter into it, meditate upon the Divine *Guru* Father-Mother,[2] as upon any tutelary deity, or upon the Compassionate Tutelary and *Shakti*; and meditating upon them, worship them with mental offerings. Resolve earnestly that thou wilt request [of them] a boon. By this, the womb-door ought to be closed.

[THE THIRD METHOD OF CLOSING THE WOMB-DOOR]

Still, if it be not closed even by that, and thou findest thyself ready to enter the womb, the third method of re-pelling attachment and repulsion is hereby shown unto thee:

There are four kinds of birth: birth by egg, birth by womb, supernormal birth,[3] and birth by heat and moisture.[4] Amongst these four,[5] birth by egg and birth by womb agree in character.

As above said, the visions of males and females in union will appear. If, at that time, one entereth into the womb through the feelings of attachment and repulsion, one may be born either as a horse, a fowl, a dog, or a human being.[6]

---

[1] 'The father and mother' are the male and female seen in union; the *Guru* is the celestial or spiritual *Guru*, not the human *guru*; and the Divine Mother is the *Guru's Shakti.*

[2] That is, the *Guru* with the *Shakti*, as above directed.

[3] Text: *brzus-skyes* (pron. *zu-kye*): Skt. *Svayambhū*: 'supernormal (or mira-culous) birth', by translation or transference of the consciousness-principle from one *loka* to another. (See pp. 85-6.)

[4] This refers to the germination of seeds and spores, or the processes of birth in the vegetable kingdom.

[5] 'Brāhmanism, likewise, recognizes four kinds of birth: *svedaja* (sweat-born, or moisture-born), *aṇḍaja* (egg-born), *jarāyuja* (womb-born), and *udbhijja* (vegetation).'—Sj. Atal Behari Ghosh.

[6] Esoterically, this passage implies that, in accordance with *karma*, one may be reborn with the peculiar propensities which the various animals named symbolize. Plato in *The Republic* has employed animal symbols in the same way. (See p. 179[1].)

If [about] to be born as a male, the feeling of itself being a male dawneth upon the Knower, and a feeling of intense hatred towards the father and of jealousy and attraction towards the mother is begotten. If [about] to be born as a female, the feeling of itself being a female dawneth upon the Knower, and a feeling of intense hatred towards the mother and of intense attraction and fondness towards the father is begotten. Through this secondary cause—[when] entering upon the path of ether, just at the moment when the sperm and the ovum are about to unite—the Knower experienceth the bliss of the simultaneously-born state, during which state it fainteth away into unconsciousness. [Afterwards] it findeth itself encased in oval form, in the embryonic state, and upon emerging from the womb and opening its eyes it may find itself transformed into a young dog. Formerly it had been a human being, but now if it have become a dog it findeth itself undergoing sufferings in a dog's kennel; or [perhaps] as a young pig in a pigsty, or as an ant in an ant-hill, or as an insect, or a grub in a hole, or as a calf, or a kid, or a lamb,[1] from which shape there is no [immediate] returning. Dumbness, stupidity, and miserable intellectual obscurity are suffered, and a variety of sufferings experienced. In like manner, one may wander into hell, or into the world of unhappy ghosts, or throughout the Six *Lokas*, and endure inconceivable miseries.

Those who are voraciously inclined towards this [i.e. *sangsaric* existence], or those who do not at heart fear it,—O dreadful! O dreadful! Alas!—and those who have not received a *guru's*

---

[1] Herein we see the animal symbolism expanded in such manner as quite to parallel the passage in Plato's *Republic* describing the choosing of animal bodies for the next incarnation. (See p. 178[6]; also pp. 49–53.) The popular or exoteric interpretation of such passages in our text as this passage (cf. pp. 126, 129, 156–7 herein) would seem to be as reasonable as it would if applied to similar passages in Plato; and, furthermore, the copyist, and possibly the composer or composers of the *Bardo Thödol*, may have been exotericists, or at least intended their text to emphasize the exoteric interpretation, holding as priests often have held, and as some hold even nowadays, that fear-producing doctrines (e. g. the Christian doctrine that hell is an eternal condition), although literally untrue, are, nevertheless, like whips to keep the lower mentalities alert and possibly more virtuous. Nevertheless, for our own (more or less corrupted) text, as for Plato's, there does exist the esoteric key to the real meaning, such as we have given in our Introduction, pp. 55–9.

teachings, will fall down into the precipitous depths of the *Sangsāra* in this manner, and suffer interminably and unbearably. Rather than meet with a like fate, listen thou unto my words and bear these teachings of mine at heart.

Reject the feelings of attraction or repulsion, and remember one method of closing the womb-door which I am going to show to thee. Close the womb-door and remember the opposition. This is the time when earnestness and pure love are necessary. As hath been said, 'Abandon jealousy, and meditate upon the *Guru* Father-Mother.'

As above explained, if to be born as a male, attraction towards the mother and repulsion towards the father, and if to be born as a female, attraction towards the father and repulsion towards the mother, together with a feeling of jealousy [for one or the other] which ariseth, will dawn upon thee.

For that time there is a profound teaching. O nobly-born, when the attraction and repulsion arise, meditate as follows:

'Alas! what a being of evil *karma* am I! That I have wandered in the *Sangsāra* hitherto, hath been owing to attraction and repulsion. If I still go on feeling attraction and repulsion, then I shall wander in endless *Sangsāra* and suffer in the Ocean of Misery for a long, long time, by sinking therein. Now I must not act through attraction and repulsion. Alas, for me! Henceforth I will never act through attraction and repulsion.'

Meditating thus, resolve firmly that thou wilt hold on to that [resolution]. It hath been said, in the *Tantras*, 'The door of the womb will be closed up by that alone.'

O nobly-born, be not distracted. Hold thy mind one-pointedly upon that resolution.

[THE FOURTH METHOD OF CLOSING THE WOMB-DOOR]

Again, even if that doth not close the womb, and one findeth [oneself] ready to enter the womb, then by means of the teaching [called] 'The Untrue and the Illusory'[1]

---

[1] Text: *Bden-ned-sgyu-ma-llabu* (pron. *Den-ned-gyu-ma-tabu*): 'Non-true [and] Illusion-like', the title of a Tibetan treatise on the unreality of phenomena.

the womb should be closed. That is to be meditated as follows:

'O, the pair, the father and the mother, the black rain, the storm-blasts, the clashing sounds, the terrifying apparitions, and all the phenomena, are, in their true nature, illusions. Howsoever they may appear, no truth is there [in them]; all substances are unreal and false. Like dreams and like apparitions are they; they are non-permanent; they have no fixity. What advantage is there in being attached [to them]! What advantage is there in having fear and terror of them! It is the seeing of the non-existent as the existent. All these are hallucinations of one's own mind. The illusory mind itself doth not exist from eternity; therefore where should these external [phenomena] exist?

'I, by not having understood these [things] in that way hitherto, have held the non-existent to be the existent, the unreal to be the real, the illusory to be the actual, and have wandered in the *Sangsāra* so long. And even now if I do not recognize them to be illusions, then, wandering in the *Sangsāra* for long ages, [I shall be] certain to fall into the morass of various miseries.

'Indeed, all these are like dreams, like hallucinations, like echoes, like the cities of the Odour-eaters,[1] like mirage, like mirrored forms, like phantasmagoria, like the moon seen in water—not real even for a moment. In truth, they are unreal; they are false.'

By holding one-pointedly to that train of thought, the belief that they are real is dissipated; and, that being impressed upon the inner continuity [of consciousness], one turneth backwards: if the knowledge of the unreality be impressed deeply in that way, the womb-door will be closed.

[THE FIFTH METHOD OF CLOSING THE WOMB-DOOR]

Still, even when this is done, if the holding [phenomena] as real remaineth undissolved, the womb-door is not closed; and, if one be ready to enter into the womb, thereupon one

---

[1] Text: *Dri-za* (pron. *Di-za*): 'Odour-eaters'; Skt. *Gandharva*, the Fairies of Indian and Buddhist mythology. Their cities are fantastically-shaped clouds, which dissolve in rain and vanish. (Cf. p. 164³.)

should close the womb-door by meditating upon the Clear Light, this being the fifth [method]. The meditation is performed as follows:

'Lo! all substances are mine own mind;[1] and this mind is vacuousness, is unborn, and unceasing.'

Thus meditating, allow the mind to rest in the uncreated [state]—like, for example, the pouring of water into water. The mind should be allowed its own easy mental posture, in its natural [or unmodified] condition, clear and vibrant. By maintaining this relaxed, uncreated [state of mind], the womb-doors of the four kinds of birth[2] are sure to be closed. Meditate thus until the closing is successfully accomplished.

[Instructions to the Officiant]: Many very profound teachings for closing the womb-door have been given above. It is impossible that they should not liberate people of the highest, the average, and the lowest intellectual capacity. If it be asked why this should be so, it is because, firstly, the consciousness in the *Bardo* possessing supernormal power of perception[3] of a limited kind, whatever is spoken to one then is apprehended. Secondly, because—although [formerly] deaf or blind—here, at this time, all one's faculties are perfect, and one can hear whatever is addressed to one. Thirdly, being continually pursued by awe and terror, one thinketh, 'What is best?' and, being alertly conscious, one is always coming to hear whatever may be told to one. Since the consciousness is without a prop,[4] it immediately goeth to whatever place the mind directeth. Fourthly, it is easy

---

[1] Text: *rNam-shes* (pron. *Nam-she*): 'consciousness-principle': Skt. *Vijñāna Skandha*. The translator preferred to follow the context here and rendered this as 'mind', as synonymous with 'consciousness'.

[2] As mentioned above, on p. 178.

[3] Text: *mngon-shes* (pron. *ngon-she*), referring to certain gifts of supernormal perception (Skt. *Abhijñā*), of which six are commonly enumerated: (1) supernormal vision and (2) hearing; (3) thought-reading; (4) knowledge of miraculous power; (5) recollection of former existences; (6) knowledge of the destruction of the passions. For the ordinary deceased person such 'supernormal power of perception' is limited (or exhaustible), and only operative in the after-death state; whereas for a Buddha, or a devotee perfected in *yoga*, it is a permanent and unlimited possession on all planes of consciousness.

[4] That is, without the human-plane body to depend upon.

to direct it.[1]   The memory[2] is ninefold more lucid than before.   Even though stupid [before], at this time, by the workings of *karma*, the intellect becometh exceedingly clear and capable of meditating whatever is taught to it.   [Hence the answer is], it is because it [i.e. the Knower] possesseth these virtues.

That the performance of funeral rites should be efficacious, is, likewise, because of that reason.   Therefore, the perseverance in the reading of the Great *Bardo Thödol* for forty-nine days is of the utmost importance.   Even if not liberated at one setting-face-to-face, one ought to be liberated at another: this is why so many different settings-face-to-face are necessary.

[THE CHOOSING OF THE WOMB-DOOR]

[Instructions to the Officiant]: There are, nevertheless, many classes of those who—though reminded, and instructed to direct their thoughts one-pointedly—are not liberated, owing to the great force of evil *karmic* obscurations, and because of being unaccustomed to pious deeds, and of being much accustomed to impious deeds throughout the aeons.   Therefore, if the womb-door hath not been closed ere this, a teaching also for the selection of a womb-door is going to be given hereinafter.   Now, invoking the aid of all the Buddhas and Bodhisattvas, repeat the Refuge; and, once more calling the deceased by name thrice, speak as follows:

O nobly-born, (so-and-so), listen.   Although the above setting-face-to-face teachings have been given one-pointedly, yet thou hast not understood them.   Therefore, if the womb-door hath not been closed, it is almost time to assume a body.   Make thy selection of the womb [according to] this best teaching.   Listen attentively, and hold it in mind.

[THE PREMONITORY VISIONS OF THE PLACE OF REBIRTH]

O nobly-born, now the signs and characteristics of the

---

[1] Lit., 'Fourthly, turning the mouth [of the consciousness-principle or Knower, as of a horse with a bit] is easy.'

[2] Text: *dranpa* (pron. *tanpa*), lit. 'train (or stream) of consciousness'; usually meaning 'consciousness', or 'recollection', or 'memory': Skt. *smṛiti*.

place of birth will come. Recognize them. In observing
the place of birth, choose the continent too.[1]

If to be born in the Eastern Continent of Lüpah, a lake
adorned with swans, male and female, [floating thereon], will
be seen. Go not there. Recollect the revulsion [against
going there].[2] If one goeth there, [that] Continent—though
endowed with bliss and ease—is one wherein religion doth
not predominate. Therefore, enter not therein.

If to be born in the Southern Continent of Jambu, grand
delightful mansions will be seen. Enter therein, if one is to
enter.

If to be born in the Western Continent of Balang-Chöd,
a lake adorned with horses, male and female, [grazing on its
shores], will be seen. Go not even there, but return here.
Although wealth and abundance are there, that being a land
wherein religion doth not prevail, enter not therein.

If to be born in the Northern Continent of Daminyan,
a lake adorned with male and female cattle, [grazing on its
shores], or trees, [round about it], will be seen. Although
duration of life, and merits are there, yet that Continent,
too, is one wherein religion doth not predominate. Therefore
enter not.

These are the premonitory signs [or visions] of the taking
rebirth in those [Continents]. Recognize them. Enter not.[3]

If one is to be born as a *deva*, delightful temples [or
mansions] built of various precious metals also will be seen.[4]
One may enter therein ; so enter therein.

---

[1] In the description of these Continents which follows, Tibetan names are
given ; in our Introduction (pp. 64–5) the Sanskrit names are given along with
complementary description.

[2] Text: *rulog*: 'rebellion' or 'revulsion'. By recollecting the revulsion,
i. e. the mental attitude which will oppose entering there, the deceased is put on
his guard.

[3] This paragraph is misplaced in the MS., having been copied as coming after
'will be seen' in the paragraph immediately above, following our rendering.

[4] The Christian conception of Heaven, as a definite place, having streets of
gold and walls of precious stones, probably owes its origin to pre-Christian
beliefs parallel to the Hindu and Buddhist beliefs concerning the Heaven of the
Devas. *Nirvāṇa* misleadingly has been called the Buddhist Heaven : a Heaven
implies a place and *sangsāric* phenomena, whereas *Nirvāṇa* is non-*sangsāric*, is
beyond all phenomena, being 'the Unbecome, the Unborn, the Unmade, the

If to be born as an *asura*, either a charming forest will be seen or else circles of fire revolving in opposite directions. Recollect the revulsion; and do not enter therein by any means.

If to be born amongst beasts,[1] rock-caverns and deep holes in the earth and mists will appear. Enter not therein.

If to be born amongst *pretas*, desolate treeless plains and shallow caverns, jungle glades and forest wastes will be seen. If one goeth there, taking birth as a *preta*, one will suffer various pangs of hunger and thirst. Recollect the revulsion; and do not go there by any means. Exert great energy [not to enter therein].

If to be born in Hell, songs [like wailings], due to evil *karma*, will be heard. [One will be] compelled to enter therein unresistingly. Lands of gloom, black houses and white houses, and black holes in the earth, and black roads along which one hath to go, will appear. If one goeth there, one will enter into Hell; and, suffering unbearable pains of heat and cold, one will be very long in getting out of it.[2] Go not there into the midst of that. It hath been said, ' Exert thine energy to the utmost': this is needed now.

[THE PROTECTION AGAINST THE TORMENTING FURIES]

O nobly-born, although one liketh it not, nevertheless, being pursued from behind by *karmic* tormenting furies,[3] one feeleth compelled involuntarily to go on; [and with] tormenting furies in the front, and life-cutters as a vanguard leading one, and darkness and *karmic* tornadoes, and noises and snow and rain

Unformed'—a concept altogether foreign to popular, or exoteric, Christianity and found only in esoteric Christianity, i. e. Gnosticism, which, very unwisely, the councils of exoteric Christianity have officially repudiated as being 'heretical'.

[1] Or, as in the text on p. 194 (wherein the clue to the esotericism underlying the references to birth 'amongst beasts' is given), amongst human beings 're-sembling the brute order'.

[2] Lit., 'there will be no time [soon] when one can get out of it'. Buddhism (and Hinduism, too,) does not postulate eternal condemnation to a state of hell, and is, in this respect, more logical than Christian theology which has in the past postulated it.

[3] Text: *gshed-ma* (pron. *shed-ma*): 'tormentors' or 'life-takers', used here to mean 'tormenting furies'. (Cf. p. 167[1].)

and terrifying hail-storms and whirlwinds of icy blasts occurring, there will arise the thought of fleeing from them.

Thereupon, by going to seek refuge because of fear, [one beholdeth] the aforesaid visions of great mansions, rock-caverns, earth-caverns, jungles, and lotus blossoms which close [on entering them]; and one escapeth by hiding inside [one of such places] and fearing to come out therefrom, and thinking, 'To go out is not good now'. And fearing to depart therefrom, one will feel greatly attracted to one's place of refuge [which is the womb]. Fearful lest, by going out, the awe and terror of the *Bardo* will meet one, and afraid to encounter them, if one hide oneself within [the place or womb chosen], one will thereby assume a very undesirable body and suffer various sufferings.

That [condition] is an indication that evil spirits and *rākshasas* [or demons] are interfering with one.[1] For this time there is a profound teaching. Listen; and heed it:

At that time—when the tormenting furies will be in pursuit of thee, and when awe and terror will be occurring—instantaneously [visualize] either the Supreme Heruka, or Hayagrīva, or Vajra-Pāni,[2] or [any other] tutelary deity if thou hast such, perfect of form, huge of body, of massive limbs, wrathful and terrifying in appearance, capable of reducing to dust all mischievous spirits. Visualize it instantaneously. The gift-waves and the power of its grace will separate thee from the tormenting furies and thou wilt obtain the power to select the womb-door. This is the vital art of the very profound teaching; therefore bear it thoroughly well in mind.

O nobly-born, the *dhyānī* and other deities are born of the power of *Samādhi* [or meditation]. *Pretas* [or unhappy spirits or shades] and malignant spirits of certain orders are those who by changing their feeling [or mental attitude] while in the Intermediate State assumed that very shape which they thereafter retained, and became *pretas*, evil spirits, and *rākshasas*, possessed of the power of shape-shifting. All

---

[1] That is to say, interfering in such a way as to prevent birth or a good birth.

[2] Each of these three deities, who dawn in the *Chönyid Bardo* (see pp. 116⁴, 120⁴, 137¹), is held to be particularly potent as an exorcizer of evil spirits.

pretas, who exist in space, who traverse the sky, and the eighty thousand species of mischievous sprites, have become so by changing their feelings [while] in the mental-body [on the *Bardo*-plane].[1]

[1] Owing to having arrived at the false concept that the Intermediate State is a desirable or fixed state of existence, all dwellers therein,—sprites, *pretas*, demons, and deceased human entities,—becoming thereby habituated to the *Bardo*, their normal evolution is retarded. According to the most enlightened of the *lāmas*, whenever a spirit is called up, as in such spirit-evocations as are nowadays common throughout the West, that spirit, through contact with this world and the prevailing traditional animistic beliefs concerning the hereafter, being strengthened in the illusion that the *Bardo* is a state wherein real spiritual progress is possible, makes no attempt to quit it. The spirit called up ordinarily describes the *Bardo* (which is pre-eminently the realm of illusion), in which it is a dweller, more or less after what it had believed whilst in the fleshly body concerning the hereafter; for just as a dreamer in the human world lives over again in the dream-state the experience of the waking state, so the inhabitant of the *Bardo* experiences hallucinations in *karmic* accord with the content of his consciousness created by the human world. His symbolic visions, as the *Bardo Thödol* repeatedly emphasizes, are but the psychic reflexes of thought-forms carried over from earth-life as mental deposits or seeds of *karma*. (See pp. 31-5.) This is said to explain why none but very exceptional spirits when evoked have any rational philosophy to offer concerning the world in which they exist; they are regarded as being merely the playthings of *karma*, lacking in mental coherence and stability of personality—more often than not, as being senseless ghosts, or psychic 'shells' which have been cast off by the consciousness-principle, and which, when coming into rapport with a human ' medium ', are galvanized into automaton-like life.

It is true that spirit-evocation of a kind is practised in Tibet, as throughout Mongolia and China, by *lāmas* who form a class of oracular priests, consulted on important problems of political policy even by the Dalai Lāma himself. But the spirits called up are tutelary deities of a low order called the 'executive-order' (Tib. *bkah-dod*—pron. *ka-döt*, meaning ' one awaiting orders') and never intentionally the spirits or ghosts of men or women recently deceased. Some of these *bkahdods* are, so the Tibetans believe, the spirits of *lāmas* and devotees who have failed—often through practising black magic—to obtain spiritual enlightenment when in the human world, or who otherwise, in the manner described in the text here, have been diverted from the normal path of progress. Thus, in many instances, they have become demoniacal and malignant spirits, whose progress has been arrested not by being bound to the earth-plane through having been called up by ' mediums ' soon after their decease, but naturally through very evil *karma*. Such *bkahdods*, thus often presenting themselves with ordinary spirits of the dead, are, as obsessing demons, said to do much harm mentally and psychically to the untrained 'medium' and clients, insanity and moral irresponsibility not infrequently resulting. For these reasons, the *lāmas* maintain that psychic research should be conducted only by masters of the occult, or magical, sciences, and not indiscriminately by the *guru*-less multitude.

In Sikkim, where our translation was made, necromancy precisely like that now practised in the West has been practised for unknown centuries, as it still

At this time, if one can recollect the Great Symbol [teachings] concerning the Voidness, that will be best. If one be not trained in that, train the [mental] powers [1] into [regarding] all things as illusion [or *māyā*]. Even if this be impossible, be not attracted by anything. By meditating upon the Tutelary Deity, the Great Compassionate [One], Buddhahood will be obtained in the *Sambhoga-Kāya*.

[THE ALTERNATIVE CHOOSING: SUPERNORMAL BIRTH; OR WOMB-BIRTH]

If, however, O nobly-born, thou hast, because of the influence of *karma*, to enter into a womb, the teaching for the selection of the womb-door will be explained now. Listen.

Do not enter into any sort of womb which may be come by. If compelled by tormenting furies to enter, meditate upon Hayagrīva.

Since thou now possessest a slender supernormal power of foreknowledge, all the places [of birth] will be known to thee, one after another.[2] Choose accordingly.

There are two alternatives: the transference [of the consciousness-principle] to a pure Buddha realm, and the selection of the impure *sangsàric* womb-door, to be accomplished as follows:

is. The Lepchas, descendants of the primitive races of Sikkim, who still form a large part of the rural population, are as thoroughly animistic in their worships as the American Red Men; and, largely through their influence, the evocation of the dead has become rather widespread among the Sikkimese Buddhist layfolk, many of whom are of both Tibetan and Lepcha blood. Similarly, in Buddhist Bhutan, such spirit-evocation is common. In both countries, however, the *lāmas* strenuously, though rather ineffectually, oppose it.

It is said that the retardation of a *Bardo*-bound spirit may be for any time from five hundred to one thousand years; and, in exceptional cases, for ages. All the while, escape from the *Bardo* being prevented, the deceased can neither pass on to a paradise realm nor be reborn in the human world. Ultimately, however, the womb will be entered and the *Bardo* come to an end.

[1] Text: *rtsal* (pron. *sal*): 'powers'; elsewhere in our text *dvang-po* (pron. *wang-po*) being rendered as 'faculties'.

[2] In a series of visions, the Knower will become aware of the lot or destiny associated with each womb or place of birth seen. Here again we are reminded of the episode in the tenth book of Plato's *Republic*, describing a band of Greek heroes in the Otherworld choosing their bodies for the next incarnation.

[SUPERNORMAL BIRTH BY TRANSFERENCE TO A PARADISE REALM]

In the first—the transference to a pure paradise—the projection is directed [by thinking or meditating] thus:

'Alas! how sorrowful it is that I, during all the innumerable *kalpas* since illimitable, beginningless time, until now, have been wandering in the Quagmire of *Sangsāra*! O how painful that I have not been liberated into Buddhahood by knowing the consciousness to be the self[1] hitherto ere this! Now doth this *Sangsāra* disgust me, horrify me, sicken me; now hath the hour come to prepare to flee from it. I myself will so act as to be born in The Happy Western Realm, at the feet of the Buddha Amitābha,[2] miraculously from amidst a lotus blossom.'[3]

Thinking thus, direct the resolution [or wish] earnestly [to that Realm]; or, likewise, to any Realm thou mayst desire,—The Pre-eminently Happy Realm, or The Thickly-Formed Realm, or The Realm [of Those] of Long Hair,[4]

---

[1] Text: *rig-pa* ('consciousness') + *bdag* (pro. *dag*, meaning 'self': Skt. *ātmā*). Should we consider 'consciousness' in this context to be the essential or true consciousness, i. e. the subconsciousness—and this meaning is implied— the passage would be in direct accord with the psychology of the West, which, on the basis of much accumulated data, might very well postulate that the subconsciousness, being the storehouse of all memory-records, from this life or from hypothetical past lives, is the real self—the bed in which flows on unbrokenly the 'life-flux', from one state of existence to another, and which, when transmuted by the alchemy of Perfect Enlightenment, becomes the supramundane consciousness, i. e. the Buddha consciousness. (Cf. W. Y. Evans-Wentz, *The Fairy-Faith in Celtic Countries*, Oxford University Press, 1911, chap. XII.)

That this view is in keeping with the recorded teachings of the Buddha Himself is evident from the *Lonaphala Vagga* of the *Anguttara Nikāya*, wherein He expounds the *yogīc* method of recovering memories, innate in the subconsciousness (see our Introduction, pp. 40–1). Sobhita, one of the Buddha's disciples, was declared, by the Buddha Himself, to be pre-eminent in 'ability to remember former existences' (cf. *Etaddagga Vagga*, *Anguttara Nikāya*), being credited with ability to recall systematically his former existences throughout 500 *kalpas*; and, in the same *Vagga*, the Buddha names, from among His female disciples, *Bhaddā Kapilānī* as being pre-eminent 'in ability to trace lineage of prior *skandhas* (or human bodies)'.

[2] Here, as elsewhere through this treatise, the Buddha Amitābha is to be regarded not as a personal deity, but as a divine power or principle inherent in or emanating from The Happy Western Realm.

[3] See p. 190[3].

[4] This is the Paradise of Vajra-Pāni (see p. 116[4]), and is not a Buddha Realm.

or The Illimitable Vihāra of the Lotus Radiance,[1] in Urgyan's presence; or direct thy wish to any Realm which thou desirest most, in undistracted one-pointedness [of mind]. By doing so, birth will take place in that Realm instantaneously.

Or, if thou desirest to go to the presence of Maitreya, in the Tushita Heavens,[2] by directing an earnest wish in like manner and thinking, 'I will go to the presence of Maitreya in the Tushita Heavens, for the hour hath struck for me here in the Intermediate State', birth will be obtained miraculously inside a lotus blossom[3] in the presence of Maitreya.

[WOMB-BIRTH: THE RETURN TO THE HUMAN WORLD]

If, however, such [a supernormal birth] be not possible, and one delighteth in entering a womb or hath to enter, there is a teaching for the selection of the womb-door of impure *Sangsāra*. Listen:

Looking with thy supernormal power of foresight over the Continents, as above, choose that in which religion prevaileth and enter therein.

If birth is to be obtained over a heap of impurities,[4] a sensation that it is sweet-smelling will attract one towards that impure mass, and birth will be obtained thereby.

Whatsoever they [the wombs or visions] may appear to be, do not regard them as they are [or seem]; and by not being attracted or repelled a good womb should be chosen. In this, too, since it is important to direct the wish, direct it thus:

'Ah! I ought to take birth as a Universal Emperor;

If, as seems probable, the 'long hair' refers to wearing the hair in 'pigtails' after the Chinese fashion, that would provide further internal evidence of our text having taken form in Tibet rather than in India.

[1] This is the Realm wherein the Great *Guru* Padma Sambhava (here called Urgyan) now reigns.

[2] Maitreya, the next *Bodhic* World-Teacher, now bides his time in the Tushita Heavens, where He reigns as King. (See p. 108⁵.)

[3] Birth from within a lotus blossom, in the Tushita Heavens, as in the *Deva*-world, esoterically implies pure birth, that is, birth without entrance into a womb, womb-birth being considered impure.

[4] That is, the sperm and the ovum in the impregnated womb.

or as a Brāhmin, like a great sal-tree;[1] or as the son of an adept in *siddhic* powers;[2] or in a spotless hierarchical line; or in the caste of a man who is filled with [religious] faith; and, being born so, be endowed with great merit so as to be able to serve all sentient beings.'

Thinking thus, direct thy wish, and enter into the womb. At the same time, emit thy gift-waves [of grace, or good-will] upon the womb which thou art entering, [transforming it thereby] into a celestial mansion.[3] And believing that the Conquerors and their Sons [or Bodhisattvas] of the Ten Directions,[4] and the tutelary deities, especially the Great Compassionate [One], are conferring power thereon, pray unto Them, and enter the womb.

In selecting the womb-door thus, there is a possibility of error: through the influence of *karma*, good wombs may appear bad and bad wombs may appear good; such error is possible. At that time, too, the art of the teaching being important, thereupon do as follows:

Even though a womb may appear good, do not be attracted; if it appear bad, have no repulsion towards it. To be free from repulsion and attraction, or from the wish to take or to avoid, —to enter in the mood of complete impartiality,—is the most profound of arts. Excepting only for the few who have had some practical experience [in psychical development], it is difficult to get rid of the remnants of the disease of evil propensities.

[Instructions to the Officiant]: Therefore, if unable to part with the attraction and repulsion, those of the least mentality

---

[1] Text: *sala*: Skt. *shāla* (the *shorea robusta*), one of the hardwood forest-trees of India, growing to great size; the Tibetan word for Brāhmin is *Brāmze* (pron. *Tāmze*). The ancient Indians regarded the sal-tree, with its splendid foliage and beautiful blossoms, as the best of trees; and for the Buddhists it is sanctified by the birth and death of the Enlightened One which took place under its protecting shade.

[2] Text: *grub-pa-thob-pa* (pron. *dub-pa-thob-pa*): Skt. *Siddha-purusha*: 'adept in *siddhic* (or *yogic*) powers.'

[3] The meaning may otherwise be put thus: By exercise of thy supernormal powers, visualize, as a celestial mansion, the womb thou art entering.

[4] These are: the four cardinal points, the four midway points, and the nadir and zenith.

and of evil *karma* will be liable to take refuge amongst brutes.[1]
The way to repel therefrom is to call the deceased by name
again, thus:

O nobly-born, if thou art not able to rid thyself of attraction and repulsion, and know not the [art of] selecting the
womb-door, whichever of the above visions may appear, call
upon the Precious Trinity and take refuge [therein]. Pray
unto the Great Compassionate One. Walk with thy head
erect. Know thyself in the *Bardo*. Cast away all weakness
and attraction towards thy sons and daughters or any relations
left behind thee; they can be of no use to thee. Enter upon
the White Light-[Path] of the *devas*, or upon the Yellow
Light-[Path][2] of human beings; enter into the great mansions
of precious metals and into the delightful gardens.

[Instructions to the Officiant]: Repeat that [address to the
deceased] seven times over. Then there should be offered
'The Invocation of the Buddhas and Bodhisattvas'; 'The
Path of Good Wishes Giving Protection from Fears in the
Bardo'; 'The Root Words [or Verses] of the *Bardo*'; and
'The Rescuer [or Path of Good Wishes for Saving] from
the Ambuscades [or Dangerous Narrow Passage-Way] of
the *Bardo*'.[3] These are to be read over thrice. 'The *Tahdol*',
which liberateth the body-aggregate,[4] should also be read out.

---

[1] Or, esoterically, amongst wombs of brute-like human beings. (Cf. p. 185[1].)

[2] The text here contains, instead of Yellow Light, 'Blue Light', evidently, as
in like instances above, through error in copying.

[3] These four Prayers (or 'Paths of Good Wishes') are given in the Appendix,
pp. 197-208.

[4] The aggregate of a living human body, according to some Tibetan systems
of *yoga*, is composed of twenty-seven parts: (1) the five elements (earth, water,
fire, air, ether); (2) the five *skandhas* (body-aggregate, sensation-aggregate,
feelings-aggregate, volition-aggregate, consciousness-aggregate); (3) the five airs
(downward-air, warmth-equalizing-air, the pervader, upward-moving-air, life-
holding air); (4) the five sense-organs (nose, ears, eyes, tongue, skin); (5) the
six faculties (sight, smell, hearing, tasting, perception, reasoning); and (6) the
mentality. These twenty-seven parts constitute the impermanent personality.
Behind them all stands the subconsciousness, the Knower, which, unlike the
personality, is the principle capable of realizing *Nirvāṇa*.

Some portions of the text of the *Tahdol* are made into *Yantras* (or talismans—
see p. 136[1]) and attached to the body, both of the living and dead; and at the
time of a person's death are either cremated or interred with the corpse, the
popular belief being that thus liberation is conferred upon the body-aggregate.

Then ' The Rite which Conferreth of Itself Liberation in [Virtue of] Propensity '[1] should be read too.

[THE GENERAL CONCLUSION]

By the reading of these properly, those devotees [or *yogīs*] who are advanced in understanding can make the best use of the Transference[2] at the moment of death. They need not traverse the Intermediate State, but will depart by the Great Straight-Upward [Path].[3] Others who are a little less practised [in things spiritual], recognizing the Clear Light in the *Chönyid Bardo*, at the moment of death, will go by the upward [course]. Those lower than these will be liberated—in accordance with their particular abilities and *karmic* connexions—when one or other of the Peaceful and Wrathful Deities dawneth upon them, during the succeeding [two] weeks, while in the *Chönyid Bardo*.

There being several turning-points,[4] liberation should be obtained at one or other of them through recognizing. But those of very weak *karmic* connexion, whose mass of obscurations is great [because of] evil actions, have to wander downwards and downwards to the *Sidpa Bardo*. Yet since there are, like the rungs of a ladder, many kinds of settings-face-to-face [or remindings], liberation should have been obtained at one or at another by recognizing. But those of the weakest *karmic* connexions, by not recognizing, fall under the influence of awe and terror. [For them] there are various graded

---

The Astrology for the Dead—a Tibetan work, in many versions, for determining (by using the moment of death as a basis for astrological calculations) the appropriate time, place, and method for the disposal of the corpse, and the after-death realm to which the deceased is destined and the land and condition in which he will be reborn on earth—prescribes such use of the *Tahdol*.

[1] Text : *Chös-spyod-bag-chags-rang-grol* (pron. *Chö-chod-bag-chah-rang-dol*), the title of a metrical version, in brief form, of the *Bardo Thödol*, which, being easy to memorize and thereafter recite as a matter of habit, is referred to as liberating because of such acquired habit or propensity on the part of the deceased, it being supposed that the deceased knows the ritual by heart and that its reading will remind him of it and thereby bring about his liberation.

[2] See pp. 85-6, above.

[3] See p. 89[3], above.

[4] Or ' narrow passages ', or ' ambuscades '.

teachings for closing the womb-door and for selecting the womb-door; and, at one or other of these, they should have apprehended the method of visualization and [applied] the illimitable virtues [thereof] for exalting one's own condition.   Even the lowest of them, resembling the brute order, will have been able—in virtue of the application of the Refuge—to turn from entering into misery; and, [obtaining] the great [boon] of a perfectly endowed and freed human body,[1] will, in the next birth, meeting with a *guru* who is a virtuous friend, obtain the [saving] vows.

If this Doctrine arrive [while one is] in the *Sidpa Bardo*, it will be like the connecting up of good actions, resembling [thus] the placing of a trough in [the break of] a broken drain: such is this Teaching.[2]

Those of heavy evil *karma* cannot possibly fail to be liberated by hearing this Doctrine [and recognizing].   If it be asked, why? it is because, at that time, all the Peaceful and Wrathful Deities being present to receive [one], and the *Māras* and the Interrupters likewise coming to receive [one] along with them, the mere hearing of this Doctrine then turneth one's views, and liberation is obtained; for there

---

[1] Text: *dal-hbyor-phun-sum-tshogs-pahi-mi-lüs* (pron. *tal-jor-phün-sum-tsho-pai-mi-lü*): 'a perfectly endowed and freed human body'; 'freed' implying freedom from the eight thraldoms: (1) the ever-recurring round of pleasure concomitant with existence as a *deva*; (2) the incessant warfare concomitant with existence as an *asura*; (3) the helplessness and slavery concomitant with existence under conditions like those prevailing in the world of brutes; (4) the torments of hunger and thirst concomitant with existence as a *preta*; (5) the extremes of heat and cold concomitant with existence in Hell; (6) the irreligion or perverted religion concomitant with existence amongst certain races of mankind, or (7) the physical or (8) other impediments concomitant with certain sorts of human birth.

To win a perfectly endowed human body, one must inherently possess faith, perseverance, intellect, sincerity, and humility as a religious devotee, and be born at a time when religion prevails (i.e. when an Enlightened One shall be incarnate or when His teachings are the driving force of the world) and meet ther a great, spiritually developed *guru*.

[2] If a drain be broken, the continuity in the flow of the water is broken. The Teaching is, in its effects, like repairing the drain by insertion of a trough to conduct the water across the break (which is symbolical of the break in the stream of consciousness caused by death).   Thereby is the merit of good deeds done in the human world made to carry the deceased forward: the continuity is re-established.

is no flesh and blood body to depend upon, but a mental body, which is [easily] affected. At whatever distance one may be wandering in the *Bardo*, one heareth and cometh, for one possesseth the slender sense of supernormal perception and foreknowledge; and, recollecting and apprehending instantaneously, the mind is capable of being changed [or influenced]. Therefore is it [i.e. the Teaching] of great use here. It is like the mechanism of a catapult.[1] It is like the moving of a big wooden beam [or log] which a hundred men cannot carry, but which by being floated upon water can be towed wherever desired in a moment.[2] It is like the controlling of a horse's mouth by means of a bridle.[3]

Therefore, going near [the body of] one who hath passed out of this life,—if the body be there,—impress this [upon the spirit of the deceased] vividly, again and again, until blood and the yellowish water-secretion begin to issue from the nostrils. At that time the corpse should not be disturbed. The rules to be observed for this [impressing to be efficacious] are: no animal should be slain on account of the deceased;[4] nor should relatives weep or make mournful wailings near the dead body;[5] [let the family] perform virtuous deeds as far as possible.[6]

---

[1] As a catapult enables one to direct a great stone at a definite target or goal, so this Doctrine enables the deceased to direct himself to the Goal of Liberation.

[2] As water makes the moving of the beam possible, so this doctrine makes possible the conducting of the deceased to the place or state of existence most appropriate, or even to Buddhahood.

[3] As with a bridle, controlling the bit and the course of the horse, so with this Doctrine the deceased can be directed or turned in his after-death progression.

[4] This does not refer to animal-sacrifice for the dead, but to the non-Buddhist habit of slaying animals to provide meat for the *lāmas* and the guests at the house of death while the funeral rites are being conducted. Unfortunately, this prohibition is often overlooked; and, though no killing of animals may take place there, slaughtered animals may be brought from a distance—an observance after the letter, but not in the spirit of this Buddhist precept of non-killing. (See p. 169[4].)

[5] Wailings and lamentations have been customary amongst Tibetans and related Himalayan peoples, as amongst the peoples of India and of Egypt, since immemorial times; but Buddhism, like the Islamic Faith, discountenances them.

[6] Such deeds are, for example, the feeding of *lāmas* and of the poor, almsgiving, the presentation of religious texts or images to monasteries, and the endowment of monasteries if the deceased left much wealth.

In other ways, too, this Great Doctrine of the *Bardo Thödol*, as well as any other religious texts, may be expounded [to the dead or dying]. If this [Doctrine] be joined to the end of *The Guide*[1] and recited [along with *The Guide*] it becometh very efficacious. In yet other ways it should be recited as often as possible.[2] The words and meanings should be committed to memory [by every one]; and, when death is inevitable and the death-symptoms are recognized,—strength permitting—one should recite it oneself, and reflect upon the meanings. If strength doth not permit, then a friend should read the Book and impress it vividly. There is no doubt as to its liberating.

The Doctrine is one which liberateth by being seen, without need of meditation or of *sādhanā*;[3] this Profound Teaching liberateth by being heard or by being seen. This Profound Teaching liberateth those of great evil *karma* through the Secret Pathway. One should not forget its meaning and the words, even though pursued by seven mastiffs.[4]

By this Select Teaching, one obtaineth Buddhahood at the moment of death. Were the Buddhas of the Three Times [the Past, the Present, and the Future] to seek, They could not find any doctrine transcending this.

Thus is completed the Profound Heart-Drops of the *Bardo* Doctrine, called *The Bardo Thödol*, which liberateth embodied beings.

[Here endeth the Tibetan Book of the Dead]

---

[1] See p. 85[6].

[2] Lit., ' be recited always '.

[3] Text: *Bsgrub* (pron. *Dub*): Skt. *Sādhanā*, 'perfected devotion', which ordinarily requires the very careful performance of a ritual more or less technical and elaborate.

[4] Fierce mastiffs are numerous in most Tibetan villages, and travellers protect themselves by special charms against them. This reference to seven mastiffs is purely Tibetan, and is additional internal evidence that the *Bardo Thödol* took form in Tibet itself, deriving much of its matter from Indian mythology and systems of *Yoga* philosophy.

[THE APPENDIX]

[In our Manuscript (but not in the Block-Print), directly following the text of the *Bardo Thödol*, there are thirteen folios of rituals and prayers (lit., 'paths of good wishes'), which all professional readers of the *Bardo Thödol* must know, usually from memory, and apply as needed;[1] and they are here rendered into English as follows:]

[I: THE INVOCATION OF THE BUDDHAS AND BODHISATTVAS]

[Instructions to the Officiant] : The invoking of the Buddhas and Bodhisattvas for assistance, when [any one is] dying, is [thus] :

Offer up to the Trinity whatever actual offerings can be offered [by the dying person, or by his family], together with mentally-created offerings ; and, holding in the hand sweet-smelling incense, repeat, with great fervency, the following :

O ye Buddhas and Bodhisattvas, abiding in the Ten Directions,[2] endowed with great compassion, endowed with fore-knowledge, endowed with the divine eye, endowed with love, affording protection to sentient beings, condescend through the power of your great compassion to come hither ; condescend to accept these offerings actually laid out and mentally created.

O ye Compassionate Ones, ye possess the wisdom of under-standing, the love of compassion, the power of [doing] divine deeds and of protecting, in incomprehensible measure. Ye Compassionate Ones, (such-and-such a person) is passing from this world to the world beyond. He is leaving this world. He is taking a great leap. No friends [hath he]. Misery is great. [He is without] defenders, without protectors, without forces and kinsmen. The light of this world hath set. He

---

[1] The directions for employing these rituals and prayers are contained in the *Bardo Thödol* above (pp. 88, 192).

[2] Cf. p. 191[4].

goeth to another place. He entereth thick darkness. He falleth down a steep precipice. He entereth into a jungle solitude. He is pursued by *Karmic* Forces. He goeth into the Vast Silence. He is borne away by the Great Ocean. He is wafted on the Wind of *Karma*. He goeth in the direction where stability existeth not. He is caught by the Great Conflict. He is obsessed by the Great Afflicting Spirit. He is awed and terrified by the Messengers of the Lord of Death. Existing *Karma* putteth him into repeated existence. No strength hath he. He hath come upon a time when he hath to go alone.

O ye Compassionate Ones, defend (so-and-so) who is defenceless. Protect him who is unprotected. Be his forces and his kinsmen. Protect [him] from the great gloom of the *Bardo*. Turn him from the red [or storm] wind of *Karma*. Turn him from the great awe and terror of the Lords of Death. Save him from the long narrow passage-way of the *Bardo*.

O ye Compassionate Ones, let not the force of your compassion be weak; but aid him. Let him not go into misery [or the miserable states of existence]. Forget not your ancient vows; and let not the force of your compassion be weak.

O ye Buddhas and Bodhisattvas, let not the might of the method of your compassion be weak towards this one. Catch hold of him with [the hook of] your grace.[1] Let not the sentient being fall under the power of evil *karma*.

O ye Trinity, protect him from the miseries of the *Bardo*.[2]

Saying this with great humility and faith, let thyself and [all] others [present] repeat it thrice.

---

[1] See p. 109[8].

[2] It is interesting to compare with this Northern Buddhist prayer the following medieval Christian prayer, to Saint Michael, from *The Craft to Know Well to Die*, chap. VI, Comper's ed. (pp. 84–5): 'Saint Michael Archangel of God, succour us now before the right high Judge. O champion invincible, be thou present now and assist thou this (Name), our brother, which strongly laboureth towards his end, and defend him mightily from the dragon infernal, and from all the frauds of the evil spirits. O yet furthermore, we pray thee, which art the right clear and much fair shower of the divinity, to the end that in this last hour of the life of this (Name), our brother, thou wilt benignly and sweetly receive his soul into thy right holy bosom; and that thou wilt bring him in the place of refreshing, of peace and rest. Amen.'

[II:] 'THE PATH OF GOOD WISHES FOR SAVING
    FROM THE DANGEROUS NARROW PASSAGE-
    WAY OF THE *BARDO*'
is [as follows]:

[1]

O ye Conquerors and your Sons, abiding in the Ten
    Directions,
O ye ocean-like Congregation of the All-Good Conquerors,
    the Peaceful and the Wrathful,
O ye *Gurus* and *Devas*, and ye *Ḍākinīs*, the Faithful Ones,
Hearken now out of [your] great love and compassion:
Obeisance, O ye assemblage of *Gurus* and *Ḍākinīs*;
Out of your great love, lead us along the Path.

[2]

When, through illusion, I and others are wandering in the
    Sangsāra,
Along the bright light-path of undistracted listening, reflection,
    and meditation,
May the *Gurus* of the Inspired Line lead us,
May the bands of Mothers be our rear-guard,
May we be saved from the fearful narrow passage-way of
    the *Bardo*,
May we be placed in the state of the perfect Buddhahood.

[3]

When, through violent anger, [we are] wandering in the
    Sangsāra,
Along the bright light-path of the Mirror-like Wisdom,
May the Bhagavān Vajra-Sattva lead us,
May the Mother Māmakī be our rear-guard,
May we be saved from the fearful narrow passage-way of
    the *Bardo*,
May we be placed in the state of the perfect Buddhahood.

[4]

When, through intense pride, [we are] wandering in the
    Sangsāra,
Along the bright light-path of the Wisdom of Equality,
May the Bhagavān Ratna-Sambhava lead us,
May the Mother, She-of-the-Buddha-Eye, be our rear-guard,
May we be saved from the fearful narrow passage-way of the
    Bardo,
May we be placed in the state of the perfect Buddhahood.

[5]

When, through great attachment, [we are] wandering in the
    Sangsāra,
Along the bright light-path of the Discriminating Wisdom,
May the Bhagavān Amitābha lead us,
May the Mother, [She]-of-White-Raiment, be our rear-guard,
May we be saved from the fearful narrow passage-way of the
    Bardo,
May we be placed in the state of the perfect Buddhahood.

[6]

When, through intense jealousy, [we are] wandering in the
    Sangsāra,
Along the bright light-path of the All-Performing Wisdom,
May the Bhagavān Amogha-Siddhi lead us,
May the Mother, the Faithful Tārā, be our rear-guard,
May we be saved from the fearful narrow passage-way of the
    Bardo,
May we be placed in the state of the perfect Buddhahood.

[7]

When, through intense stupidity, [we are] wandering in the
    Sangsāra,
Along the bright light-path of the Wisdom of Reality,
May the Bhagavān Vairochana lead us,
May the Mother of Great Space be our rear-guard,
May we be saved from the fearful narrow passage-way of the
    Bardo,
May we be placed in the state of the perfect Buddhahood.

[8]

When, through intense illusion, [we are] wandering in the
  Sangsāra,

Along the bright light-path of the abandonment of hallucinatory fear, awe, and terror,

May the bands of the Bhagavāns of the Wrathful Ones
  lead us,

May the bands of the Wrathful Goddesses Rich-in-Space be
  our rear-guard,

May we be saved from the fearful narrow passage-way of the
  Bardo,

May we be placed in the state of the perfect Buddhahood.

[9]

When, through intense propensities, [we are] wandering in
  the *Sangsāra*,

Along the bright light-path of the Simultaneously-born
  Wisdom,

May the heroic Knowledge-Holders lead us,

May the bands of the Mothers, the *Dākinīs*, be our rear-guard,

May we be saved from the fearful narrow passage-way of the
  Bardo,

May we be placed in the state of the perfect Buddhahood.

[10]

May the ethereal elements not rise up as enemies;

May it come that we shall see the Realm of the Blue Buddha.

May the watery elements not rise up as enemies;

May it come that we shall see the Realm of the White
  Buddha.

May the earthy elements not rise up as enemies;

May it come that we shall see the Realm of the Yellow
  Buddha.

May the fiery elements not rise up as enemies;

May it come that we shall see the Realm of the Red Buddha.

May the airy elements not rise up as enemies;

May it come that we shall see the Realm of the Green Buddha.[1]

May the elements of the rainbow colours not rise up as enemies;

May it come that all the Realms of the Buddhas will be seen.

May it come that all the Sounds [in the *Bardo*] will be known as one's own sounds;

May it come that all the Radiances will be known as one's own radiances;

May it come that the *Tri-Kāya* will be realized in the *Bardo*.

[III:] Here beginneth

'THE ROOT VERSES OF THE SIX *BARDOS*':

[1]

O now, when the Birthplace *Bardo* upon me is dawning!

Abandoning idleness—there being no idleness in [a devotee's] life—

Entering into the Reality undistractedly, listening, reflecting, and meditating,

Carrying on to the Path [knowledge of the true nature of] appearances and of mind, may the *Tri-Kāya* be realized:

Once that the human form hath been attained,

May there be no time [or opportunity] in which to idle it [or human life] away.

[2]

O now, when the Dream *Bardo* upon me is dawning!

Abandoning the inordinate corpse-like sleeping of the sleep of stupidity,

May the consciousness undistractedly be kept in its natural state;

---

[1] The Blue Buddha is Samanta-Bhadra; the White Buddha, Vajra-Sattva; the Yellow Buddha, Ratna-Sambhava; the Red Buddha, Amitābha; the Green Buddha, Amogha-Siddhi. Herein Samanta-Bhadra occupies the position often given to Vairochana, both deities being in essence the same, although sometimes Vairochana is depicted as being white in colour instead of blue. (Cf. the *Bardo Thödol*, the First to the Fifth Day.)

Grasping the [true nature of] dreams, [may I] train [myself]
    in the Clear Light of Miraculous Transformation:
Acting not like the brutes in slothfulness,
May the blending of the practising of the sleep [state] and
    actual [or waking] experience be highly valued [by me].[1]

[3]

O now, when the *Dhyāna Bardo* upon me is dawning!
Abandoning the whole mass of distractions and illusions,
May [the mind] be kept in the mood of endless undistracted
    Samādhi,
May firmness both in the visualizing and in the perfected
    [stages] be obtained:
At this time, when meditating one-pointedly, with [all other]
    actions put aside,
May I not fall under the power of misleading, stupefying
    passions.

[4]

O now, when the *Bardo* of the Moment of Death upon
    me is dawning!
Abandoning attraction and craving, and weakness for all
    [worldly things],
May I be undistracted in the space of the bright [enlightening]
    teachings,[2]
May I [be able to] transfuse myself into the heavenly space
    of the Unborn:
The hour hath come to part with this body composed of flesh
    and blood;
May I know the body to be impermanent and illusory.

[5]

O now, when the *Bardo* of the Reality upon me is dawning,
Abandoning all awe, fear, and terror of all [phenomena],

---

[1] There is a very profound system of *yoga* in which the devotee's aim is to
enter the dream-state at will and carry on experiments therein in full consciousness of being in the dream-state, and then return to the waking-state with complete memory of the experience; thereby is realized the unreality of both states—
that both are merely illusory, being based wholly upon phenomena.

[2] Or, 'May I enter into the bright space of undistractedness [and enlightening]
teachings'.

May I recognize whatever appeareth as being mine own
thought-forms,

May I know them to be apparitions in the Intermediate
State;

[It hath been said], 'There arriveth a time when the chief
turning-point is reached;

Fear not the bands of the Peaceful and Wrathful, Who are
thine own thought-forms'.

[6]

O now, when the *Bardo* of [taking] Rebirth upon me is
dawning!

One-pointedly holding fast to a single wish,

[May I be able to] continue the course of good deeds through
repeated efforts; [1]

May the womb-door be closed and the revulsion recollected:

The hour hath come when energy and pure love are needed;

[May I] cast off jealousy and meditate upon the *Guru*, the
Father-Mother.

[7]

['O] procrastinating one, who thinketh not of the coming of
death,

Devoting thyself to the useless doings of this life,

Improvident art thou in dissipating thy great opportunity;

Mistaken, indeed, will thy purpose be now if thou returnest
empty-handed [from this life]:

Since the Holy Dharma is known to be thy true need,

Wilt thou not devote [thyself] to the Holy Dharma even
now?'

[EPILOGUE]

Thus say the Great Adepts [2] in devotion.

If the chosen teaching of the *guru* be not borne in mind,

Wilt thou not [O *shishya*] be acting even as a traitor to
thyself?

---

[1] Lit., '[May I be able to] join with the remnants of good deeds by repeated effort'. (Cf. p. 135³.)

[2] Text: *Grub-chen* (pron. *Dub-chen*): Skt. *Mahā-siddhas*.

It is of great importance that these Root Words be known.

[IV:] Here beginneth
'THE PATH OF GOOD WISHES WHICH PRO-
    TECTETH FROM FEAR IN THE *BARDO*':

[1]

When the cast [of the dice] of my life hath become exhausted,
The relatives in this world avail me not;
When I wander alone by myself in the *Bardo*,
[O] ye Conquerors, Peaceful and Wrathful, exercising the
    power of your compassion,
Let it come that the Gloom of Ignorance be dispelled.

[2]

When wandering alone, parted from loving friends,
When the shapes of mine empty thought-forms dawn upon
    me here,
[May the] Buddhas, exerting the power of their divine com-
    passion,
Cause it to come that there be neither awe nor terror in the
    Bardo.

[3]

When the bright radiances of the Five Wisdoms shine upon
    me now,
Let it come that I, neither awed nor terrified, may recognize
    them to be of myself;
When the apparitions of the Peaceful and Wrathful forms are
    dawning upon me here,
Let it come that I, obtaining the assurance of fearlessness,
    may recognize the *Bardo*.

[4]

When experiencing miseries, because of the force of evil
    karma,
Let it come that the Conquerors, the Peaceful and Wrathful,
    may dispel the miseries;

When the self-existing Sound of Reality reverberates [like]
a thousand thunders,
Let it come that they be transmuted into the sounds of the
Mahāyāna Doctrines.[1]

[5]

When [I am] unprotected, [and] *karmic* influences have to be
followed here,
I beseech the Conquerors, the Peaceful and the Wrathful, to
protect me;
When suffering miseries, because of the *karmic* influence of
propensities,
Let it come that the blissful *Samādhi* of the Clear Light
may dawn [upon me].

[6]

When assuming supernormal rebirth in the *Sidpa Bardo*,
Let it come that the perverting revelations of *Mārā* occur not
therein;
When I arrive wheresoever I wish to,
Let it come that I experience not the illusory fright and awe
from evil *karma*.

[7]

When the roarings of savage beasts are uttered,
Let it come that they be changed into the sacred sounds of
the Six Syllables;[2]
When pursued by snow, rain, wind, and darkness,
Let it come that I see with the celestial eyes of bright
Wisdom.

[8]

Let it come that all sentient beings of the same harmonious
order in the *Bardo*,
Without jealousy [towards one another],[3] obtain birth on the
higher planes;

---

[1] That is, into the sounds of the *mantra Ōm-mă-ṇi-pāy-mē-Hūng*! and of
other *mantras* of the *Mahāyāna* and *Mantrayāna* Doctrines; (cf. stanza 7
below; also pp. 149[1], 134[2]).

[2] These are: *Ōm-mă-ṇi-pāy-mē-Hūng*! (Cf. p. 149[1].)

[3] This may also refer to the jealousy arising when one is taking rebirth either
as a male or a female. (See p. 179.)

When [destined to] suffering from intense miseries of hunger
and thirst,

Let it come that I experience not the pangs of hunger and
thirst, heat and cold.[1]

[9]

When I behold the future parents in union,

Let it come that I behold them as the [Divine] Pair, the
Conquerors, the Peaceful and the Wrathful Father and
Mother;

Obtaining the power of being born anywhere, for the good of
others,

Let it come that I obtain the perfect body, adorned with the
signs and the graces.[2]

[10]

Obtaining for myself the body of a male [which is] the
better,

Let it come that I liberate all who see or hear me;

Allowing not the evil *karma* to follow me,

Let it come that whatever merits [be mine] follow me and be
multiplied.

[11]

Wherever I be born, there and then,

Let it come that I meet the Conquerors, the Peaceful and the
Wrathful Deities;

Being able to walk and to talk as soon as [I am] born,[3]

Let it come that I obtain the non-forgetting intellect and
remember my past life[4] [or lives].

[1] 'Hunger and thirst' refer to the sufferings concomitant with existence as
a *preta* (or unhappy ghost); 'heat and cold', to existence in the hot and cold
Hells.

[2] This refers to the body of a Buddha, in which appear various supernormal
signs and powers.

[3] This is a reference to the Buddha, Who when born is said to have taken
fifty-six steps, seven forwards and seven backwards in each of the four cardinal
directions, and to have uttered a divine premonitory sentence at the end of
each fourteen steps. After that supernormal performance He, like an ordinary
babe, was unable to walk or to talk until normally old enough.

[4] In the *Samgīti Sūtta*, *Dīgha Nikāya*, of the Pali Canon of Southern

[12]

In all the various lores, great, small, and intermediate,
Let it come that I be able to obtain mastery merely upon
    hearing, reflecting, and seeing;
In whatever place I be born, let it be auspicious;
Let it come that all sentient beings be endowed with happiness.

[13]

Ye Conquerors, Peaceful and Wrathful, in likeness to your
    bodies,
[Number of your] followers, duration of your life-period, limit
    of your realms,
And [in likeness to the] goodness of your divine name,
Let it come that I, and others, equal your very selves in all these.

[14]

By the divine grace of the innumerable All-Good Peaceful
    and Wrathful [Ones],
And by the gift-waves of the wholly pure Reality,
[And] by the gift-waves of the one-pointed devotion of the
    mystic devotees,
Let it come that whatsoever be wished for be fulfilled here
    and now.

'The Path of Good Wishes Affording Protection from Fears
in the *Bardo*' is finished.

Buddhism, there is the following explanation from the Buddha Himself as to
the non-forgetting (and the forgetting) of past incarnations:

'There are four conditions of entrance of the embryo into the womb:

'Brethren, in this world, one cometh into existence in the mother's womb
without knowing, remaineth in it without knowing, and cometh out from the
mother's womb without knowing; this is the first.

'Brethren, one cometh into existence in the mother's womb knowingly,
remaineth in it without knowing, and cometh out from it without knowing;
this is the second.

'Brethren, one cometh into existence in the mother's womb knowingly,
remaineth in it knowingly, and cometh out from it without knowing; this is the
third.

'Brethren, in this world, one cometh into existence in the mother's womb
knowingly, remaineth in it knowingly, and cometh out from it knowingly; this
is the fourth.'

(Cf. the method, taught by the Buddha, of remembering past lives, pp. 40–1.)

[V: THE COLOPHON]

[The Manuscript concludes with the following seven verses by the *lāma* or scribe who compiled it, but he—faithful to the old *lāmaic* teaching that the human personality should be self-abased and the Scriptures alone exalted before the gaze of sentient creatures—has not recorded his name:]

Through the perfectly pure intention of mine
In the making of this, through the root of the merits
    thereof,
[May] those protectorless sentient beings, Mothers,
[Be] placed in the State of the Buddha:[1]
Let the radiant glory of auspiciousness come to illuminate
    the world;[2]
Let this Book be auspicious;[3]
Let virtue and goodness be perfected in every way.

[Here endeth the Manuscript of the *Bardo Thödol*.]

---

[1] In dedicating the whole of the spiritual merit, derived from the task of transcribing our copy of the *Bardo Thödol*, to mothers, irrespective of race or religion, to the end that they may be helped to attain Buddhahood, the scribe testifies to the position of respect and honour which the democracy of Buddhism has always assigned to woman.

[2] Lit. ' Jambudvīpa ', the proper Sanskrit name given to the realm of human beings.

[3] The text of this verse is *Mangalam*: *dGeho* (pron. *Gewo*), the Sanskrit and the Tibetan term (each meaning 'Let it [i.e. this Book] be auspicious'), in apposition, suggesting that the scribe possessed at least a limited knowledge of Sanskrit.

'Fill up, Puṇṇā, the orb of holy life,
E'en as on fifteenth day the full-orb'd moon.
Fill full the perfect knowledge of the Path,
And scatter all the gloom of ignorance.'—

Puṇṇā, a *Bhikkhunī*.

Psalms of the Early Buddhists, I. iii
(Mrs. Rhys Davids' Translation).

ADDENDA

These Addenda consist of seven sections, complementary to our Introduction and Commentary, concerning (1) Yoga, (2) Tantricism, (3) *Mantras*, or Words of Power, (4) the *Guru* and *Shishya* (or *Chela*) and Initiations, (5) Reality, (6) Northern and Southern Buddhism and Christianity, and (7) the Medieval Christian Judgement.

I. YOGA

The word *Yoga* (frequently appearing in our annotations to the *Bardo Thödol* text), derived from the Sanskrit root *yuj*, meaning 'to join', closely allied with the English verb *to yoke*, implies a joining or yoking of the lower human nature to the higher or divine nature in such manner as to allow the higher to direct the lower;[1] and this condition—essential to the successful application of the *Bardo* doctrines—is to be brought about by control of the mental process. So long as the field of the mind is occupied by such thought-forms and thought-processes as arise from the false concept, universally dominating mankind, that phenomena and phenomenal appearances are real, a state of mental obscuration called ignorance, which prevents true knowledge, exists. It is only when all obscuring and erroneous concepts are totally inhibited and the field of the mind is swept clean of them that the primordial or unmodified condition of mind, which is ever devoid of these thought-formations and thought-processes arising from ignorance, is realizable; and, in its realization, there dawns Illumination, symbolized in the *Bardo Thödol* as the Primal Clear Light of the *Dharma-Kāya*.

A mirror covered with a thick deposit of dust, or a crystal vase filled with muddied water, symbolize the mind of the normal human being darkened with the nescience arising from

[1] Some scholars question this generally accepted explanation and think that the term *yoga* probably means 'practice' as opposed to theory in religion. If so, it would then imply *yogic* practice such as will produce indomitable control over the mental processes and lead to realization of Reality. In this sense, *yoga* may be regarded as a system of applied psychology far more highly developed than any known to Western Science.

heresies and false knowledge. *Yoga* is a scientific method of removing the dust from the mirror and the earthy particles from the water. It is only when the mind is thus made clear and limpid that it can reflect the Light of Reality and man can come to know himself. *Māyā*, or Illusion, is the Veil of Isis hiding from man the Unsullied and Unsulliable Reality; the piercing of this Veil and the seeing of that which it hides is accomplished through methods as definite and certain in psychical results as those employed in a European or American chemical laboratory are in physical results. As gold can be separated from impurities by methods of chemistry, so can Truth be divorced from Error by methods of *Yoga*.

Like the root teachings of Buddhism, the root teachings of the *Bardo Thödol* are incapable of being practically applied without Right Knowledge; Right Knowledge to be at all effective in a devotee's life should not depend merely upon belief or theory, but upon realization; and realization of Right Knowledge is impossible without such mind control as *Yoga* implies. That this is so, the canonical scriptures of all schools of Buddhism confirm.[1]

It is not our purpose to discuss here the intricacies of the various aspects and schools of *Yoga*; for, though technical terms and some of the purely philosophical or theoretical parts of the Hindu, Buddhist, and other systems of the science of mind-control often differ widely, we are convinced, after much research carried on while living among *yogīs* of various schools, that the goal for all *yogīs* is, in the last analysis of esotericism, identical, namely, emancipation from the thraldom of *sangsāric*, or phenomenal, existence, the Hindus calling it *Mukti* and the Buddhists *Nirvāṇa*.[2]

Intellectual understanding of much of the *Bardo Thödol* is,

[1] *Yoga* practice was introduced into *Mahāyāna* Buddhism by Asaṅga, a monk of Gāndhāra (Peshawar, India). He is said to have been inspired directly by the Bodhisat Maitreya, the coming Buddha, and so produced the Scriptures of the Yogā-cārya (i. e. 'Contemplative') School called *The Five Books of Maitreya* (cf. Waddell, *The Buddhism of Tibet*, p. 128).

[2] The editor possesses a number of very important translations, by the late Lāma Kazi Dawa-Samdup, of Tibetan treatises on *Yoga*, one of them having originated in ancient India. If there should be encouragement to publish them, the editor hopes then to put on record in more detail the results of his own researches in *Yoga*.

therefore, obviously dependent upon at least some elementary explanation of *Yoga*, such as we have herein given. The Clear Light, so often referred to in our text—to take but one of the outstanding *yogic* doctrines—is best interpreted from the standpoint of the devotee of *Yoga*, though for all mankind alike it dawns at the all-determining moment of death. As such, the Clear Light symbolizes the visual condition in which one finds oneself at the moment of death and afterwards in the Intermediate State. If the vision be unclouded by *karmic* propensities, which are the source of all phenomena and apparitional appearances in the *Bardo*, the deceased sees Reality as the Primordial Clear Light, and, if he so wills, can renounce the *Sangsāra* and pass into *Nirvāṇa*, beyond the Circle of Death and Rebirth.

Such clarity of spiritual insight is, of course, extremely rare, being the fruit of innumerable lifetimes of right living; nevertheless, the aim of the *Bardo Thödol* teachings is to attempt to place every one, when dying or deceased, in the Path leading to its realization. Unless, through the practice of mental-concentration, complete control over the thinking process be achieved, so as to arrive at Right Knowledge ere death, in virtue of having experienced Illumination (i.e. recognition of the Clear Light in an ecstatic condition while still in the human body), the *lāmas* maintain that comprehension of the nature of the Clear Light is quite impossible for the unilluminated.

II. TANTRICISM [1]

The *Bardo Thödol* being itself a work more or less Tantric,[2] and consequently largely based upon the *Yoga* Philosophy, some general acquaintance with Tantricism, as with *Yoga*, is

---

[1] General references (also for Sections III and IV following): A. Avalon (Sir John Woodroffe), *Tantra of the Great Liberation* (London, 1913), Introduction; and *The Six Centres and the Serpent Power* (London, 1919), *passim*; Sir John Woodroffe, *Shakti and Shâkta* (London, 1920), *passim*; also Rama Prasad, *Nature's Finer Forces* (London, 1890), *passim*.

[2] To define what is and is not a *Tantra* is not easy. According to its Tibetan etymology, *Tantra* (Tib. *Rgyud*—pron. *Gyud*) literally means 'treatise', or 'dissertation', of a religious nature, usually belonging to the School of *Yoga* called *Yogā-cārya Mahāyāna* (see p. 212[1]). Religiously considered, there are two

desirable for all readers of this book. So we record here—in mere outline, and, therefore, more often than not undetailed and incomplete—the following complementary matter concerning Tantricism.

In the preliminary instructions, the *Bardo Thödol* makes reference to the vital-force or vital-airs, which, following the *Tantras*, may be described as follows:

The Vital-Force (Skt. *Prāna*).—The human principle of consciousness, the Knower, clothes itself, when incarnate, in five sheaths (Skt. *Kosha*), which are: (1) the physical-sheath (*Anna-maya-kosha*); (2) the vital-sheath (*Prāna-maya-kosha*); (3) the sheath in which resides the ordinary human consciousness (*Mano-maya-kosha*); (4) that of the subconsciousness (*Vijñāna-maya-kosha*); and (5) that of the all-transcending blissful consciousness of Reality (*Ānanda-maya-kosha*).

In the vital-sheath resides the vital-force (Skt. *prāna*) divided into ten vital-airs (*vāyu*, derived from the root *va*, 'to breathe'

chief groups of *Tantras*, one Hindu, the other Buddhist. The Hindu *Tantra* is generally cast in the form of a dialogue between the god Shiva, as the Divine *Guru*, and his *Shakti* Pàrvatì, often in their wrathful forms as Bhairava and Bhairavì. In the Buddhist *Tantra*, these purely Hindu deities are replaced by Buddhist deities, Buddhas and their *Shaktis*, or by gods and goddesses. One characteristic of both classes of *Tantras* is that usually they are based upon the *Yoga* Philosophy. Which of the two classes is older is a disputed question; but the oldest *Tantras* are probably far older than European critics (who have placed their origin well within the Christian era) have thought. Some *Tantras* are indisputably quite modern. According to orthodox Hindus, the *Tantras* are of Vedic origin, and designed to serve as the chief Scriptures for this age, the Kali Yuga. Some Buddhists claim a purely Buddhist origin for the *Tantras*. The Hindu view is, however, the commonly accepted view.

As encyclopaedias of the knowledge of their times, the *Tantras* are very numerous. Some are concerned with the nature of the cosmos, its evolution and dissolution; the classification of sentient beings and of the various heavens, hells, and worlds; the divinely instituted rules governing human relations and conduct; the numerous forms of worship and spiritual training, ceremonial rites, meditation, *yoga*, duties of kings, law, custom, medicine, astrology, astronomy, magic; and, in short, the whole cycle of the sciences of the East.

In so far as the *Bardo Thödol* is a ritual based upon *Yoga*, and has for its chief matter the science of birth, death, and rebirth, interwoven with descriptions of the various states of existence and beings peopling the universe, and teaches of the ways of obtaining salvation, it is a Tantric work, although, strictly speaking, not a *Tantra*.

For detailed knowledge concerning the *Tantras*, the student is referred to *Principles of Tantra*, Part I, by Arthur Avalon (London, 1914).

or 'to blow', refers to the motive power of *prāṇa*). As the daemons of Plato's occultism are said to control the operations of the Cosmic Body, so these *vāyu*, composed of negative *prāṇa*, control the operations of the human body. Five are fundamental: (1) the *prāṇa*, controlling inspiration; (2) the *udāna*, controlling the ascending vital-force (or vital-air); (3) the *apāna*, controlling the downward vital-force, which expels wind, excrement, urine, and semen; (4) the *samāna*, as the collective force of the *vāyu*, kindles the fire of the body whereby food is digested and then distributed by the blood; and (5) the *vyāna*, controlling division and diffusion in all metabolic processes. The five minor airs are the *Nāga*, *kūrmma*, *kṛikara*, *deva-datta*, and *dhananjaya*, which produce, respectively, hiccuping, opening and closing of the eyes, assistance to digestion, yawning, and distension.

The Psychic Nerves or Channels (Skt. *Nāḍī*).—There are next mentioned in our text the Psychic Nerves. Sanskrit works on *Yoga* say that there are fourteen principal *nāḍī* and hundreds of thousands of minor *nāḍī* in the human body, just as Western physiologists say that there are so many chief nerves and minor nerves. But the *nāḍī* of the East and the nerves of the West, although literally the same in name, are not synonymous. The *nāḍī* are invisible channels for the flow of psychic forces whose conducting agents are the vital-airs (*vāyu*).

Of the fourteen principal *nāḍī*, there are three which are of fundamental importance. These are, to follow our text, the median-nerve (Skt. *suṣhumnā-nāḍī*), the left nerve (*iḍā-nāḍī*), and the right nerve (*pingalā-nāḍī*). The *suṣhumnā-nāḍī* is the chief or median-nerve, situated in the hollow of the spinal column (Skt. *Brāhma-daṇḍa*), the Mt. Meru of the human body, man being regarded as the microcosm of the macrocosm. The *iḍā-nāḍī*, to the left, and the *pingalā-nāḍī*, to the right, coil round it as the two serpents coil round the caduceus carried by the messenger-god Hermes. It is believed that this ancient herald's wand symbolizes the *suṣhumnā-nāḍī*, and the twining serpents the *iḍā-nāḍī* and the *pingalā-nāḍī*. If so, we see again how the esoteric symbol-code of the West corresponds to that of the East.

The Psychic-Nerve Centres (Skt. *Chakra*).—The *suṣhumnā-nāḍī* forms the great highway for the passage of the psychic forces of the human body. These forces are concentrated in centres, or *chakra*, like dynamos, ranged along the *suṣhumnā-nāḍi* and interconnected by it, wherein are stored the vital-force or vital-fluid upon which all psycho-physical processes ultimately depend. Of these, six are of fundamental importance. The first is known as the Root-support (*Mūlādhārā*) of the *suṣhumnā-nāḍī*, situated in the perineum ; and in the *Mūlādhārā* is the secret Fountain of Vital-Force, presided over by the Goddess *Kuṇḍalinī*. Next above, lies the second *chakra*, or lotus, called the *Svādhiṣhṭhāna*, which is the centre of the sex-organs. The navel nerve-centre is above, and called in Sanskrit *Maṇi-pūra-chakra*. The next is the heart nerve-centre, the *Anāhata-chakra*. In the throat is located the fifth, called the *Vishuddhā-chakra*. In the *Ājnā-chakra*, which is the sixth, situated between the eyebrows, as depicted by the 'third eye' on images of the Buddha and of Hindu deities, the three chief psychic nerves (*nāḍī*), *suṣhumnā*, *iḍā*, and *pingalā*, come together and then separate. Above all, in the causal region of psychic man, as the sun of the body, sending its rays downwards over the human-body cosmos, is the Supreme or Seventh *Chakra*, the thousand-petalled lotus (or *chakra*) called *Sahasrāra Padma*; through it the *suṣhumnā-nāḍī* has its exit, the Aperture of Brāhma (Skt. *Brāhma-randhra*) referred to in our text, through which the consciousness-principle normally goes out from the body at death.

The initial aim of the practitioner of *Yoga* is to awaken what in the *Tantras* is called the Serpent Power, personified as the Goddess Kuṇḍalinī. It is in the *Mūlādhāra-chakra*, at the base of the spinal column, containing the root of the *suṣhumnā-nāḍī*, that this mighty occult power lies coiled, like a serpent asleep. Once the Serpent Power is aroused into activity, it is made to penetrate, one by one, the psychic-nerve centres, until, rising like mercury in a magic tube, it reaches the thousand-petalled lotus in the brain-centre. Spreading out in a fountain-like crest, it falls thence as a shower of heavenly ambrosia to feed all parts of the psychic body. Thus becom-

ing filled with supreme spiritual power, the *yogī* experiences
Illumination.

Maṇḍalas.—Of the Psychic-Centres, or *Chakra*, the *Bardo
Thödol* is concerned chiefly with three : (1) the Heart-centre
(*Anāhata-chakra*); (2) the Throat-centre (*Vishuddha-chakra*);
and (3) the Brain-centre (*Sahasrāra Padma*). Of these, two
are of chief importance : the Brain-centre, sometimes called
the Northern Centre, and the Heart-centre, or Southern
Centre. These two constitute the two poles of the human
organism. They are said to be the first centres to form
in the embryo, and the terrestrial *prāṇa*, derived from the
central *prāṇic* reservoir in the sun of our planetary system, is
said to direct their formation.

Related to these three principal *chakra*, there are three
chief *maṇḍalas* or mystic groupings of deities divided into
fourteen subsidiary *maṇḍalas* corresponding to the first
Fourteen (7 + 7) Days of the *Bardo* as described in our text.

The first of these three chief *maṇḍalas* contains 42 deities,
distributed in six subordinate *maṇḍalas* corresponding to the
first Six Days of the *Chönyid Bardo* ; and they emanate from
the Heart-centre. The second *maṇḍala* contains 10 principal
deities, which dawn on the Seventh Day; and these emanate
from the Throat-centre. The third *maṇḍala* contains 58
principal deities, distributed in seven subordinate *maṇḍalas*,
corresponding to the last Seven Days of the *Chönyid Bardo*,
and emanating from the Brain-centre. The first 42 and the
last 58 comprise the Great *Maṇḍala* of the 100 superior
deities, the 42 being called peaceful and the 58 wrathful
deities. The other 10 deities, related to the Throat-centre,
which dawn intermediately between the 42 of the Heart-
centre and the 58 of the Brain-centre, are classed with the
42 peaceful deities. Thus, when united in the Greater
Maṇḍala of the whole of the *Chönyid Bardo*, there are
110 principal deities.

It will be observed, too, that there is definite orientation in
all the *maṇḍalas*.

The Five Dhyānī Buddhas with their *shaktis*[1] are the chief

---

[1] The Sanskrit term *Shakti* (literally '[Divine] Power') refers to the female,

deities dawning on the first Five Days. On the First Day, Vairochana and his *shakti* alone dawn. Then on each of the four succeeding days, along with one of the remaining four of the Dhyānī Buddhas and the *shakti*, there dawn two Bodhisattvas and their *shaktis*. Then, on the Sixth Day, all of these deities, dawning in one *maṇḍala*, are joined by 16 additional deities: 8 Door-keepers, the 6 Buddhas of the Six *Lokas*, and the Ādi-Buddha and *shakti*; and all these deities together compose the 42 deities of the Heart-centre.

Then, after the dawning of the 10 Knowledge-Holding Deities (called, in the Obeisances, p. 85, the Lotus Deities) of the Throat-centre, on the intervening Seventh Day, there dawn during the remaining Seven Days the 58 deities of the Brain-centre, as follows: on each of the first five days, or from the Eighth to the Twelfth Day, one of the Herukas with his *shakti*, in all 10 deities; on the Thirteenth Day, the 8 Kerima and the 8 Htamenma; on the Fourteenth Day, 4 Door-keepers and the 28 animal-headed Deities. Behind the symbolism of deities and *maṇḍalas* and psychic-centres there lies the rational explanation, namely, that each deity, as it dawns from its appropriate psychic-centre, represents the coming into after-death *karmic* activity of some corresponding impulse or

or negative, phase of that divine force or power concentrated in or personified by the consort of a god, the god representing the positive phase; the Tantric worshipper of *Shakti* (Power), or divine universal forces, personified as a Mother-Goddess, being called a *shākta*. The Tantrics—like the ancient Egyptians—exalt right knowledge of the reproductive processes, as no doubt it should be exalted, to the level of a religious science; and in this science, as illustrated in the *Bardo Thödol*, the union of the male and female principles of nature, in what is called in Tibetan the *yab* (Skt. *deva*) -*yum* (Skt. *shakti*) attitude, symbolizes completeness, or at-one-ment. Power, symbolized by the male (*yab*, or *deva*), and Wisdom, symbolized by the female (*yum*, or *shakti*), are said, esoterically, to be ever in union.

It is much to be regretted that actual abuse of Tantric doctrine, due either to wilful perversion or, as is commonly the case, to misunderstanding, resulting in practices (like those of certain decadent sects or individuals in India) improperly called Tantric, by non-initiates in America and in Europe, in some instances under the aegis of organized societies, has brought upon Tantricism undeserved odium. Such unfortunate outcome of lack of guidance under properly trained *gurus* tends to justify the high initiate of Oriental occultism in his stern refusal to divulge the inner teachings of his cult to any save carefully prepared pupils who have been long on probation and found worthy; this was the view both of the late Lāma Kazi Dawa-Samdup and of his late *guru* in Bhutan.

passion of the complex consciousness. As though in an
initiatory mystery-play, the actors for each day of the *Bardo*
come on the mind-stage of the deceased, who is their sole
spectator; and their director is *Karma*. The higher or more
divine elements of the consciousness-principle of the deceased
dawn first in the full glory of the primal Clear Light; and
then, in ever diminishing glory, the visions grow less and less
happy—the Peaceful Deities of the Heart-centre, and then of
the Throat-centre, merge into the Wrathful Deities of the
Brain-centre. Finally, as the purely human and brutish propensities, personified, in the fiercest of the Wrathful Deities,[1]
as horror-producing and threatening spectral hallucinations,
come into the field of mental vision, the percipient flees in
dismay from them—his own thought-forms—to the refuge
of the womb, thereby making himself to be the plaything
of *Māyā* and the slave of Ignorance. In other words, in
a manner similar to that in which the earth-plane body
grows to maturity and then withers and after its death
disintegrates, the after-death body, called the mental-body,
grows from the heavenly days of its *Bardo* childhood to
the less idealist days of its *Bardo* maturity, then fades and
dies in the Intermediate State, as the Knower, abandoning
it, is reborn.

Some clue to the separable elements of consciousness as
they manifest themselves in the Intermediate State is gained
from the significance of the Tantric divisions into petals
of the lotuses, or *chakras*. For example, the Heart-centre
Lotus, or *Anāhata-chakra*, is described as a red-coloured lotus
of twelve petals, each petal representing one of the chief
elements of personality (*vṛitti*) as follows: (1) hope (*āshā*);
(2) care or anxiety (*chintā*); (3) endeavour (*cheshṭā*); (4) feeling
of mineness (*mamatā*); (5) arrogance or hypocrisy (*dambha*);
(6) languor (*vikalatā*); (7) conceit (*ahangkāra*); (8) discrimination (*viveka*); (9) covetousness (*lolatā*); (10) duplicity (*kapa-
ṭatā*); (11) indecision (*vitarka*); (12) regret (*anutāpa*).

The Throat-centre Lotus, or *Vishuddha-chakra*, also called

---

[1] Of the Wrathful Deities there are two classes, the less wrathful (Tib. *To'-wo*) and the more wrathful (Tib. *Drag-po*). See Waddell, op. cit., pp. 332-3.

Bhāratīsthāna, consists of sixteen petals. The first seven symbolize the seven Sanskrit musical notes. The eighth symbolizes the 'venom' of mortality. The next seven represent the seven seed *mantras,* and the sixteenth is the symbol for the nectar of immortality (*amṛitā*).

To each of the thousand petals of the Brain-centre Lotus variously coloured letters of the Sanskrit or Tibetan alphabet, and other symbols, are esoterically assigned; and this *chakra* is said to contain in potential state all that exists in the other *chakras* (of which it is the originator) or in the universe.

Each of the Dhyānī Buddhas, likewise, as elsewhere explained from a different view-point, symbolizes definite spiritual attributes of the cosmos. Thus, Vairochana is appealed to by the Tantrics of Northern Buddhism as the universal force producing or giving form to everything both physical and spiritual; Vajra-Sattva (as the reflex of Akṣhobhya) is the universal force invoked for neutralizing by merit evil *karma*; Ratna-Sambhava, for the reproduction of all things desired; Amitābha, for long life and wisdom; Amogha-Siddhi, for success in arts and crafts. In Vajra-Sattva, in his purely esoteric aspect, all the other Peaceful and Wrathful Deities of the *Maṇḍala* of the *Bardo Thödol* are said to merge or be contained.

III. *MANTRAS,* OR WORDS OF POWER

A clue to the power of *mantras,* as referred to throughout the *Bardo Thödol,* lies in the ancient Greek theory of music; namely, that, if the key-note of any particular body or substance be known, by its use the particular body or substance can be disintegrated. Scientifically, the whole problem may be understood through understanding the law of vibration. Each organism exhibits its own vibratory rate, and so does every inanimate object from the grain of sand to the mountain and even to each planet and sun. When this rate of vibration is known, the organism or form can, by occult use of it, be disintegrated.

For the adept in occultism, to know the *mantra* of any deity is to know how to set up psychic or gift-wave communication similar to, but transcending, wireless or telepathic communication with that deity. For example, if the adept be of the left-hand path, that is to say, a black magician, he can, by *mantras*, call up and command elementals and inferior orders of spiritual beings, because to each belongs a particular rate of vibration, and this being known and formulated as sound in a *mantra* gives the magician power even to annihilate by dissolution the particular elemental or spirit to whom it belongs. As a highwayman at the point of a gun compels a traveller to give up money, so a black magician with a *mantra* compels a spirit to act as he wills.

On account of this supreme power of sound, when formulated in *mantras* corresponding to the particular rate of vibration of spiritual beings and of spiritual and physical forces, the *mantras* are jealously guarded. And, for the purpose of maintaining this guardianship, lines of *gurus* (i.e. religious teachers) are established in whose keeping the words of power are placed. Candidates for initiation into this Brotherhood of Guardians of the Mysteries must necessarily be well tested before the Treasures can be entrusted to them, and they themselves, in turn, be made Guardians.

Unto the *shishya*, after he has been well tested, the *mantra* which confers power over the sleeping Goddess Kuṇḍalinī is transmitted; and when he utters it the Goddess awakens and comes to him to be commanded. Then is the need of the *guru* great; for the awakened Goddess can destroy as well as save—according as the *mantra* is wisely or unwisely used.

As the outer air vibrates to gross sounds, the inner vital-airs (*prāna-vāyu*) are set in motion and utilized by the use of the sounds of *mantras*: the Goddess first catches up the subtle occult sound, and, in tones of divine music, she causes it to ascend from her throne in the Root-Support Psychic-Centre to one after another of the Centres above, until its music fills the Lotus of a Thousand Petals and is there heard and responded to by the Supreme *Guru*.

The visualization of a deity, as frequently directed in our text, is often but another way of thinking of the essential characteristics of that deity. A like *yogic* effect comes from visualizing or else audibly pronouncing the *mantra* corresponding to that deity; for, by speaking forth as sound the *mantra* of any deity, that deity is made to appear.

Unless the *mantras* are properly intoned they are without effect; and when printed and seen by the eye of the uninitiated they appear utterly meaningless—and so they are without the guidance of the human *guru*.

Furthermore, the correct pronunciation of the *mantra* of a deity depends upon bodily purity as well as upon knowledge of its proper intonation. Therefore it is necessary for the devotee first to purify, by purificatory *mantras*, the mouth, the tongue, and then the *mantra* itself, by a process called giving life to or awakening the sleeping power of the *mantra*.

The occult ability to employ a *mantra* properly confers supernormal powers called *Siddhi*,[1] and these can be used, according to the character of the adept, either as white magic for good ends or as black magic for evil ends: the right- and left-hand paths being the same up to this point of practical application of the fruits obtained through psychic development. One path leads upward to Emancipation, the other downward to Enslavement.

IV. THE *GURU* AND *SHISHYA* (OR *CHELA*) AND INITIATIONS

Very frequently the *Bardo Thödol* directs the dying or the deceased to concentrate mentally upon, or to visualize, his tutelary deity or else his spiritual *guru*, and, at other times, to recollect the teachings conveyed to him by his human *guru*, more especially at the time of the mystic initiation. *Yogīs* and Tantrics ordinarily comment upon such ritualistic directions by saying that there exist three lines of *gurus* to whom reverence and worship are to be paid. The first and highest is purely superhuman, called in Sanskrit *divyaugha*, meaning 'heavenly (or "divine") line'; the second is of the most highly developed human beings, possessed of supernormal

---

[1] *Siddhi* here means 'Powers' arrived at through *yogic* practices. Literally, *Siddhi* is the attainment of any aim.

or *siddhic* powers, and hence called *siddhaugha*; the third is of ordinary religious teachers and hence called *mānavaugha*, 'human line'.[1]

Women as well as men, if qualified, may be *gurus*. The *shishya* is, as a rule, put on probation for one year before receiving the first initiation. If at the end of that time he proves to be an unworthy receptacle for the higher teachings, he is rejected. Otherwise, he is taken in hand by the *guru* and carefully prepared for psychical development. A *shishya* when on probation is merely commanded to perform such and such exercises as are deemed suitable to his or her particular needs. Then, when the probation ends, the *shishya* is told by the *guru* the why of the exercises, and the final results which are certain to come from the exercises when successfully carried out. Ordinarily, once a *guru* is chosen, the *shishya* has no right to disobey the *guru*, or to take another *guru* until it is proven that the first *guru* can guide the *shishya* no further. If the *shishya* develops rapidly, because of good *karma*, and arrives at a stage of development equal to that of the *guru*, the *guru*, if unable to guide the *shishya* further, will probably himself direct the *shishya* to a more advanced *guru*.

For initiating a *shishya*, the *guru* must first prepare himself, usually during a course of special ritual exercises occupying several days, whereby the *guru*, by invoking the gift-waves of the divine line of *gurus*, sets up direct communication with the spiritual plane on which the divine *gurus* exist. If the human *guru* be possessed of *siddhic* powers, this communion is believed to be as real as wireless or telepathic communication between two human beings on the earth-plane.

The actual initiation, which follows, consists of giving to the *shishya* the secret *mantra*, or Word of Power, whereby at-one-ment is brought about between the *shishya*, as the new member of the secret brotherhood, and the Supreme *Guru*

---

[1] The three lines of *gurus* are so called not because of any difference in their respective powers, but because of their different places of abode. In the *Tantra-rāja* (ch. I) it is said that the *Gurus* of the Divya Order always abide in Shiva's Heaven, those of the Siddha Order both in the Human-World and in the Heaven-Worlds, and those of the Mānava Order on Earth only.

who stands to all *gurus* and *shishyas* under him as the Divine Father. The vital-force, or vital-airs (*prāṇa-vāyu*), serve as a psycho-physical link uniting the human with the divine; and the vital-force, having been centred in the Seventh Psychic-Centre, or Thousand-petalled Lotus, by exercise of the awakened Serpent-Power, through that Centre, as through a wireless receiving station, are received the spiritual gift-waves of the Supreme *Guru*. Thus is the divine grace received into the human organism and made to glow, as electricity is made to glow when conducted to the vacuum of an electric bulb; and the true initiation is thereby conferred and the *shishya* Illuminated.

In the occult language of the Indian and Tibetan Mysteries, the Supreme *Guru* sits enthroned in the pericarp of the Thousand-petalled Lotus. Thither, by the power of the Serpent Power of the awakened Goddess Kuṇḍalinī, the *shishya*, guided by the human *guru*, is led, and bows down at the feet of the Divine Father, and receives the blessing and the benediction. The Veil of *Māyā* has been lifted, and the Clear Light shines into the heart of the *shishya* unobstructedly. As one Lamp is lit by the Flame of another Lamp, so the Divine Power is communicated from the Divine Father, the Supreme *Guru*, to the newly-born one, the human *shishya*.

The secret *mantra* conferred at the initiation, like the Egyptian Word of Power, is the Password necessary for a conscious passing from the embodied state into the disembodied state. If the initiate is sufficiently developed spiritually before the time comes for the giving up of the gross physical body at death, and can at the moment of quitting the earth-plane remember the mystic *mantra*, or Word of Power, the change will take place without loss of consciousness; nor will the *shishya* of full development suffer any break in the continuity of consciousness from incarnation to incarnation.

V. REALITY

In denying the soul hypothesis, Buddhism of all Schools maintains that personal immortality is impossible, because all personal existence is but a mere flux of instability and continual change *karmically* dependent upon the false concept that phenomena, or phenomenal appearances, or phenomenal states and beings, are real. In other words, Buddhism holds that individualized mind or consciousness cannot realize Reality.

The essence of the *Bardo Thödol* teachings is, likewise, that so long as the mind is human, so long as it is individualized, so long as it regards itself as separate and apart from all other minds, it is but the plaything of *Māyā*, of Ignorance, which causes it to look upon the hallucinatory panorama of existences within the *Sangsāra* as real, and thence leads it to lose itself in the Quagmire of Phenomena.

Followers of the Semitic Faiths are hereditarily so completely dominated by the theory of soul and of personal immortality after death, in a phenomenal paradise or hell, that in their view there can be no alternative; and to them the Buddhist denial of the theory erroneously appears to imply a doctrine of the absolute negation of being.

The realization of Reality, according to the *Bardo Thödol*, is wholly dependent upon expurgating from the mind all error, all false belief, and arriving at a state in which *Māyā* no longer controls. Once the mind becomes freed from all *karmic* obscurations, from the supreme heresy that phenomenal appearances—in heavens, hells, or worlds—are real, then there dawns Right Knowledge; all forms merge into that which is non-form, all phenomena into that which is beyond phenomena, all Ignorance is dissipated by the Light of Truth, personality ceases, individualized being and sorrow are at an end, mind and matter are known to be identical, the mundane consciousness becomes the supramundane, and, one with the *Dharma-Kāya*, the pilgrim reaches the Goal.

The great Patriarch Ashvaghosha, who set down in writing during the first century A.D.[1] the essential teachings of *Mahāyāna* Buddhism as at first handed down orally by

[1] The exact date of Ashvaghosha (or Açvaghosha) is uncertain. According to Suzuki, who has investigated the question with great care, Ashvaghosha 'lived at the time extending from the latter half of the first century before Christ to about 50 or 80 A.D. . . . At the very most, his time cannot be placed later than the first century of the Christian era' (T. Suzuki, *The Awakening of Faith*, Chicago, 1900, p. 17).

initiates direct from the time of the Buddha, has otherwise stated the doctrines touching Reality as follows, in his remarkable treatise called *The Awakening of Faith*: [1]

Of Ignorance : 'The True Reality is originally only one, but the degrees of ignorance are infinite ; therefore the natures of men differ in character accordingly. There are unruly thoughts more numerous than the sands of the Ganges, some arising from ignorant conceptions and others arising from ignorance of senses and desires. Thus all kinds of wild thoughts arise from ignorance and have first and last infinite differences which Ju Lai [i. e. the Tathāgata] alone knows.' [2]

'As from the True Reality man knows that there is no objective world, then the various means of following and obeying this True Reality arise spontaneously [i. e. without thought and without action], and, when influenced by this power for a long time, ignorance disappears. As ignorance disappears, then false ideas cease to arise. As these false ideas do not arise, the former objective world also ends. As the forces cease to exist, then the false powers of the finite mind cease to exist, and this is called *Nirvāṇa*, when the natural forces of the True Reality alone work.' [3]

[1] There are two English translations of *The Awakening of Faith*, from the Chinese, one by a Christian missionary to China, the late Rev. Timothy Richard, made in 1894 and published, in Shanghai, in 1907, the other by the learned Japanese Buddhist Mr. Teitaro Suzuki, published in 1900, in Chicago. We give herein, in parallel, extracts from both. There are, likewise, two Chinese versions, each based upon the original Sanskrit version, which is now lost : one made in A. D. 554, by Paramartha (otherwise called Kulanātha), an Indian Buddhist missionary, who reached China in A. D. 546 and died in A. D. 569, at the age of 71 years ; the other was begun in A. D. 700 by Çikshānanda, also an Indian Buddhist missionary, who died in China, in A. D. 710, at the age of 59. Richard's translation is from Paramartha's version, and Suzuki's from Çikshānanda's.

[2] Richard's trans. (p. 18). Cf. Suzuki's trans. (p. 89) : 'Though all beings are uniformly in possession of suchness, the intensity [of the influence] of ignorance, the principle of individuation, that works from all eternity, varies in such manifold grades as to outnumber the sands of the Ganges. And it is even so with such entangling prejudices (*kleça* or *āçrava*) as the ego-conception, intellectual and affectional prejudices, &c. [whose perfuming efficiency varies according to the karma previously accumulated by each individual],—all these things being comprehended only by the Tathāgata. Hence such immeasurable degrees of difference as regards belief, &c.'

[3] Richard's trans. (p. 17). Cf. Suzuki's trans. (pp. 86–7) : 'On account of this perfuming influence [i. e. through suchness perfuming ignorance] we are

Of Phenomena: 'All phenomena are originally in the mind and have really no outward form; therefore, as there is no form, it is an error to think that anything is there. All phenomena merely arise from false notions in the mind. If the mind is independent of these false ideas, then all phenomena disappear. . . .'[1]

'Therefore the phenomena of the three worlds [of desire, of form, and of non-form] are mind-made. Without mind, then, there is practically no objective existence. Thus all existence arises from imperfect notions in our mind. All differences are differences of the mind. But the mind cannot see itself, for it has no form. We should know that all phenomena are created by the imperfect notions in the finite mind; therefore all existence is like a reflection in a mirror, without substance, only a phantom of the mind. When the finite mind acts, then all kinds of things arise; when the finite mind ceases to act, then all kinds of things cease.'[2]

enabled to believe that we are in possession within ourselves of suchness whose essential nature is pure and immaculate; and we also recognize that all phenomena in the world are nothing but the illusory manifestation of the mind (*ālaya-vijñāna*) and have no reality of their own. Since we thus rightly understand the truth, we can practise the means of liberation, can perform those actions which are in accordance [with the Dharma]. Neither do we particularize, nor cling to. By virtue of this discipline and habituation during the lapse of innumerable *asamkhyeyakalpas* [lit. countless ages], we have ignorance annihilated. As ignorance is thus annihilated, the mind [i.e. *ālaya-vijñāna*] is no more disturbed so as to be subject to individuation. As the mind is no more disturbed, the particularization of the surrounding world is annihilated. When in this wise the principle and the condition of defilement, their products, and the mental disturbances are all annihilated, it is said that we attain to *Nirvāṇa* and that various spontaneous displays of activity are accomplished.'

[1] Richard's trans. (p. 26). Cf. Suzuki's trans. (p. 107): 'In a word, all modes of relative existence, our phenomenal world as a whole, are created simply by the particularization of the confused mind. If we become dissociated from the latter, then all modes of relative existence vanish away by themselves.'

[2] Richard's trans. (p. 12). Cf. Suzuki's trans. (pp. 77-8): 'Therefore the three domains [or *triloka*, i. e. domain of feeling (*kāmaloka*), domain of bodily existence (*rūpaloka*), domain of incorporeality (*arūpāloka*)] are nothing but the self-manifestation of the mind [i. e. *ālaya-vijñāna*, which is practically identical with suchness, *bhūtatathatā*]. Separated from the mind, there would be no such things as the six objects of sense. Why? Since all things, owing the principle of their existence to the mind (*ālaya-vijñāna*), are produced by subjectivity (*smṛti*), all the modes of particularization are the self-particularization of the mind. The mind in itself being, however, free from all attributes, is

Of Space: ' Men are to understand that space is nothing. It has no existence and is not a reality. It is a term in opposition to reality. We only say this or that is visible in order that we might distinguish between things.' [1]

Of Mind and Matter: ' Mind and matter are eternally the same. As the essence of matter is wisdom, the essence of matter is without form and is called the embodiment of wisdom. As the manifested essence of wisdom is matter, it is called the all-pervading embodiment of wisdom. The unmanifested matter is without magnitude; according to the will it can show itself throughout all the universe as the immeasurable *Pusas* [i.e. intelligent devout men, or Bodhisattvas], immeasurable inspired spirits, immeasurable glories, all different without magnitude and without interference with one another. This is what ordinary senses cannot comprehend, as it is the work of Absolute Reality. . . .' [2]

' According to the Absolute Reality there is no distinction between mind and matter; it is on account of the defilement

not differentiated. Therefore, we come to the conclusion that all things and conditions in the phenomenal world, hypostatized and established only through ignorance (*avidya*) and subjectivity (*smrti*) on the part of all beings, have no more reality than the images in a mirror. They evolve simply from the ideality of a particularizing mind. When the mind is disturbed, the multiplicity of things is produced ; but when the mind is quieted, the multiplicity of things disappears.'

[1] Richard's trans. (pp. 25-6). Cf. Suzuki's trans. (p. 107) : ' Be it clearly understood that space is nothing but a mode of particularization and that it has no real existence of its own. Where there is a perception of space, there is side by side a perception of a variety of things, in contradistinction to which space is spoken of as if existing independently. Space therefore exists only in relation to our particularizing consciousness.'

[2] Richard's trans. (pp. 24-5). Cf. Suzuki's trans. (pp. 103-4): ' Matter (*rūpa*) and mind (*citta*) from the very beginning are not a duality. So we speak of [the universe as] a system of rationality (*prajñakāya*), seeing that the real nature of matter just constitutes the norm of mind. Again we speak of [the universe as] a system of materiality (*dharmakāya*), seeing that the true nature of mind just constitutes the norm of matter. Now depending on the *Dharmakāya*, all Tathāgatas manifest themselves in bodily forms and are incessantly present at all points of space. And Bodhisattvas in the ten quarters, according to their capabilities and wishes, are able to manifest infinite Bodies of Bliss and infinite lands of ornamentation, each one of which, though stamped with the marks of individuality, does not hinder the others from being fused into it, and this [mutual fusion] has no interruption. But the manifestation of the *Dharmakāya* in [infinite] bodily forms is not comprehensible to the thought and understanding of common people ; because it is the free and subtlest activity of suchness.'

of the finite in the round of life and death that these distinctions appear. . . .'[1]

'As to the defilements of the world, they are all false; they have no reality behind them. . . .'[2]

'Finally, to leave false concepts, one should know that purity and defilement are both relative terms, and have no independent existence. Although all things from eternity are neither mind nor matter, neither infinite wisdom nor finite knowledge, neither existing nor non-existing, but are after all inexpressible, we nevertheless use words, yet should know that the Buddha's skilful use of words to lead men aright lay in this—to get men to cease conjecturing and to return to the Absolute Reality, for the best human thought of all things is only temporary and is not Truth Absolute.[3]

Of the Nature of the Primordial Mind: 'The mind from the beginning is of a pure nature, but since there is the finite aspect of it which is sullied by finite views, there is the sullied aspect of it. Although there is this defilement, yet the original pure nature is eternally unchanged. This mystery the Enlightened One alone understands.'[4]

---

[1] Richard's trans. (p. 26). Cf. Suzuki's trans. (pp. 108–9): 'Be it clearly understood that suchness (*bhūtatathatā*) has nothing to do with any form of distinction produced by defilement, and that even in case we speak of its possessing innumerable meritorious characteristics they are free from the traces of defilement.'

[2] Richard's trans. (p. 27). Cf. Suzuki's trans. (p. 109): '. . . defiled objects . . . are nothing but non-entity, have from the first no self-existence (*svabhāva*), . . .'

[3] Richard's trans. (pp. 27–8). Cf. Suzuki's trans. (pp. 112–13): 'If one be absolutely freed from particularization and attachment, one will understand that all things both pure and defiled have only relative existence. Be it therefore known that all things in the world from the beginning are neither matter (*rūpa*), nor mind (*citta*), nor intelligence (*prajña*), nor consciousness (*vijñāna*), nor non-being (*abhāva*), nor being (*bhāva*); they are after all inexplicable. The reason why the Tathāgata nevertheless endeavours to instruct by means of words and definitions is through his good and excellent skilfulness [or expediency, *upāya-kauçalya*]. He only provisionally makes use of words and definitions to lead all beings, while his real object is to make men abandon symbolism and directly enter into the real reality (*tattva*). Because if they indulge themselves in reasonings, attach themselves to sophistry, and thus foster their subjective particularization, how could they have the true wisdom (*tattvajñāna*) and attain *Nirvāṇa*?'

[4] Richard's trans. (p. 13). Cf. Suzuki's trans. (pp. 79–80): 'While the essence of the mind is eternally clean and pure, the influence of ignorance makes

'If there were no True Real Nature of the mind, then all existence would not exist; there would be nothing to show it. If the True Real Nature of the mind remains, then finite mind continues. Only when the madness of finite mind ceases will the finite mind cease. It is not the wisdom of the True Reality that ceases.'[1]

'Just as a man having lost his way calls the east west, although the east and west have not really changed, so is mankind lost in ignorance, calling the mind of the universe his thoughts! But the Mind is what it ever was, all unchanged by men's thought. When men consider and realize that the Absolute Mind has no need of thoughts like men's, they will be following the right way to reach the Boundless.'[2]

Of the Nature of the Absolute: 'It is neither that which had an origin some time, nor that which will end at some time; it is really eternal. In its nature it is always full of all possibilities, and is described as of great light and wisdom, giving light to all things, real and knowing. Its true nature is that of a pure mind, eternally joyful, the true being of things, pure, quiet, unchanged; therefore free, with fullness of virtues and *Bodhic* attributes more numerous than

---

possible the existence of a defiled mind. But in spite of the defiled mind the mind [itself] is eternal, clear, pure, and not subject to transformation. Further, as its original nature is free from particularization, it knows in itself no change whatever, though it produces everywhere the various modes of existence. When the oneness of the totality of things (*dharmadhātu*) is not recognized, then ignorance as well as particularization arises, and all phases of the defiled mind are thus developed. But the significance of this doctrine is so extremely deep and unfathomable that it can be fully comprehended by Buddhas and by no others.'

[1] Richard's trans. (p. 15). Cf. Suzuki's trans. (p. 84): 'Let ignorance be annihilated, and the symptom of disturbance [in the mind] will also be annihilated, while the essence of the mind [i.e. suchness] remains the same. Only if the mind itself were annihilated, then all beings would cease to exist, because there would be nothing there by which they could manifest themselves. But so long as the mind be not annihilated its disturbance may continue.'

[2] Richard's trans. (p. 25). Cf. Suzuki's trans. (pp. 105-6): 'As a lost man who takes the east for the west, while the quarter is not changed on account of his confusion, so all beings, because of their misleading ignorance, imagine that the mind is being disturbed, while in reality it is not. But when they understand that the disturbance of the mind [i.e. birth-and-death] is [at the same time] immortality [viz. suchness] they would then enter into the gate of suchness.'

the sands of the Ganges, divine, unending, unchanged and
unspeakable.'¹

'As the nature behind all experience has no beginning, so
it has no end—this is the true *Nirvāṇa*. . . .'²

'Behind all existence there is naturally the Supreme *Nirvāṇa*
[or Supreme Rest].'³

---

¹ Richard's trans. (p. 21). Cf. Suzuki's trans. (pp. 95-6): 'It was not
created in the past, nor is it to be annihilated in the future; it is eternal,
permanent, absolute; and from all eternity it sufficingly embraces in its essence
all possible merits (*punya*). That is to say, suchness has such characteristics as
follows: the effulgence of great wisdom; the universal illumination of the
dharmadhātu [universe]; the true and adequate knowledge; the mind pure and
clean in its self-nature; the eternal, the blessed, the self-regulating, and the
pure; the tranquil, the immutable, and the free. And there is no heterogeneity
in all those *Buddha-dharmas* which, outnumbering the sands of the Ganges, can
be neither identical (*ekārtha*) nor not-identical (*nānārtha*) [with the essence of
suchness], and which therefore are out of the range of our comprehension.'

This description of the Absolute is also a description of the *Dharma-Kāya*, for
the two terms are synonymous. A modern student of Buddhism, Mr. P.
Lakshmi Narasu, in *The Essence of Buddhism* (Madras, 1912), pp. 352-3,
describes the *Summum Bonum* thus: 'Buddhism denies an Ishvara [i.e.
a Supreme Deity, for even the Primordial Buddha is not such, but merely the
lāma's hypothetical First Buddha]; and the latter cannot, therefore, be its goal
and resting-point. The Buddhist's goal is Buddhahood, and the essence of
Buddhahood is *Dharmakāya*, the totality of all those laws which pervade the
facts of life, and whose living recognition constitutes enlightenment. *Dharma-
kāya* is the most comprehensive name by which the Buddhist sums up his
understanding and also his feeling about the universe. *Dharmakāya* signifies
that the universe does not appear to the Buddhist as a mere mechanism, but as
pulsating with life. Further, it means that the most striking fact about the universe
is its intellectual aspect and its ethical order, especially in its higher reaches.
Nay more, it implies that the universe is one in essence, and nowhere chaotic or
dualistic. . . . *Dharmakāya* is no pitiable abstraction, but that aspect of existence
which makes the world intelligible, which shows itself in cause and effect. . . .
Dharmakāya is that ideal tendency in things which reveals itself most completely
in man's rational will and moral aspirations. . . . It is the impersonated inspiring
type of every perfected rational mind. Without *Dharmakāya* there would be
nothing that constitutes personality, no reason, no science, no moral aspiration,
no ideal, no aim and purpose in man's life. . . . *Dharmakāya* is the norm of all
existence, the standard of truth, the measure of righteousness, the good law; it
is that in the constitution of things which makes certain modes of conduct
beneficial and certain other modes detrimental.'

² Richard's trans. (p. 27). Cf. Suzuki's trans. (p. 112): 'Be it clearly understood that the essence of the five *skandhas* is uncreate, there is no annihilation
of them; that, since there is no annihilation of them, they are in their [meta-
physical] origin *Nirvāṇa* itself.'

³ Richard's trans. (p. 31). Cf. Suzuki's trans. (p. 121): '. . . . all things
(*sarvadharma*) from the beginning are in their nature *Nirvāṇa* itself.'

Thus does Ashvaghosha bear witness to the soundness of the supreme philosophy of the Mahāyāna School underlying the *Bardo Thödol*; and, as an independent commentator, confirms our own interpretations.

VI. NORTHERN AND SOUTHERN BUDDHISM AND CHRISTIANITY

Very much matter might also be incorporated herein to show the differences which exist between the two great Schools of Buddhism, the Northern and the Southern School, sometimes known as the *Mahāyāna* (meaning the 'Greater Path') and the *Hīnayāna* (meaning the 'Lesser Path'—a rather belittling name never used by Southern Buddhists of themselves).[1]

Northern Buddhism is chiefly distinguished by its hierarchical and more highly organized priesthood, its emphasis upon rituals, its elaborate doctrine of divine emanations, its Christian-like worships and masses, its Tantricism, its Dhyānī Buddhas, Bodhisattvas and extensive pantheon, its belief in a Primordial Buddha, its greater insistence on *Yoga*, its subtle philosophy, and its transcendental teachings concerning the *Tri-Kāya*.

In Southern Buddhism, on the contrary, there is a very loosely organized priesthood with no recognized heads like the Dalai Lāma, who is the God-King, and the Tashi Lāma, who is the Higher Spiritual Head of Lāmaism. There are no recognized rituals comparable to the rituals of the Northern School, little or nothing clearly Tantric, and no worship of Dhyānī Buddhas or of a Primordial Buddha, but a limited belief in *devas* and demons. The only Bodhisattva appealed to and imaged in temples is the coming Buddha, Maitreya. Although theoretically *Yoga* is insisted upon, it appears to have been but little practised among Southern Buddhists since the times of Buddhagosa and his immediate suc-

[1] Here Sj. Atal Behari Ghosh has contributed the following note : ' *Mahāyāna* may, and possibly does, mean the "Greater" or "Higher Path" (or "Voyage"), and *Hīnayāna* the "Lesser" or "Lower Path" (or "Voyage"). *Yā* (of *Yāna*) means "to go", and *Yāna* "that by which one goes". Western Orientalists have adopted "Vehicle" as an equivalent of *Yāna*, as that is the common meaning given in school-books, but " Path " is preferable.'

cessors, when Buddhist Ceylon is said to have been famous—
as Buddhist Tibet is now—for its great saints, or *yogīs*.
That there exists a transcendental Buddhism, based chiefly
upon Tantric teachings and applied *Yoga*, such as the *lāmas*
claim to possess through oral transmission direct from the
time of the Buddha, Southern Buddhism denies, for it holds
that the Buddha taught no higher or other doctrines than
those recorded in the *Tri-Pitaka* or Pali Canon. Similarly,
the doctrine of the Esoteric Trinity, or *Tri-Kāya*, Southern
Buddhism does not propound, although there are clear
references to the *Dharma-Kāya* in the *Aggañña Sūttānta*
of the *Dīgha Nikāya*, wherein the Buddha speaks of the
Dharma-Kāya to a Brāhmin priest named Vasetta (Skt.
Vashishtha) ; and the Sinhalese work known as the *Dharma-
Pradīpikā* contains elaborated expositions of *Rūpa-Kāya* and
Dharma-Kāya.[1]

The hypothesis of Christian apologists that Northern
Buddhism in its differentiation from Southern Buddhism was
primarily affected by early Christian missionaries seems to
be disproved—in so far as really fundamental doctrines are concerned—by the far-reaching fact (but recently made known to
Western scholars through the recovery of some of the writings
of the greatest of the Fathers of the Northern Buddhist Church,
namely, the Patriarch Ashvagosha) that Northern Buddhism
was fundamentally the same in the first century A. D. as it is now
and was prior to the Christian era. If there were Christian influences, as claimed, brought in by the Nestorians, or St. Thomas,
or later missionaries, it appears that they could only have
been superficial at most.[2] In our own view—which is, of

---

[1] Cf. P. Lakshmi Narasu, *The Essence of Buddhism* (Madras, 1912), p. 352 n.

[2] Huc, in his *Travels in Tartary* (Hazlett's trans., ii. 84), notes that Tson
Khapa, the founder of the Gelugpa, or Established Reformed Church of Tibet,
was acquainted with Christianity through Roman priests who seem to have had
a mission near the place of his birth, in the Province of Amdo, China. But
Tson Khapa having been born during the latter half of the fourteenth century
and having founded the Gelugpa during the early fifteenth, such probable
Christian influence would be of no importance in relation to the primitive.
unreformed Ñingmapa Church founded by Padma Sambhava in the eighth century,
whence our Manuscript had its origin. The semi-reformed Kargyütpa Sect, too,
antedates the Gelugpa, having been founded in the last half of the eleventh

course, merely hypothetical, seeing how little is at present known of the interdependent influences of Hinduism, Buddhism, and other Oriental religions and Christianity—it is Christianity which probably has been shaped, not only in its pre-Christian symbololology and in its rituals, but in its beliefs, by the Faiths preceding it, and out of which it evolved. For example, Christian monasticism, as best studied in the first centuries of the Christian era in Egypt, with its *yoga*-like practices, has had, apparently, direct relationship with the more ancient monastic systems such as those of Hinduism, Buddhism, Jainism, and Taoism. The two great doctrines of Christianity, namely, those of the Trinity and of the Incarnation, are not, as formerly believed, unique; not only did both develop in pre-Christian times in India, but were principal doctrines in the Osirian Faith of Egypt at least six thousand years ago. The primitive Christian Gnostic Church, as the exponent of an esoteric Christianity,[1] was also in general accord with the old Oriental teachings touching Rebirth and *Karma*, which the later or exoteric Christian Church eventually repudiated, the Second Council of Constantinople, in A.D. 553, decreeing that 'Whosoever shall support the mythical doctrine of the pre-existence of the soul and the consequent wonderful opinion of its return, let him be anathema'. The Sermon on the Mount

century by Marpa (see p. 135[2]), whose chief *guru* was the Indian Pandit Atīsha (cf. Waddell, *The Buddhism of Tibet*, pp. 54–75).

[1] Origen, the pupil of St. Clement of Alexandria, and the best-informed and most learned of the Church Fathers, who held the doctrine of rebirth and *karma* to be Christian, and against whom, two hundred and ninety-nine years after he was dead, excommunication was decreed by the exoteric Church, on account of his beliefs, has said: 'But that there should be certain doctrines not made known to the multitude, which are [revealed] after the exoteric ones have been taught, is not a peculiarity of Christianity alone, but also of philosophic systems, in which certain truths are exoteric and others esoteric' (*Origen Contra Celsum*, Book I, c. vii). That Origen was a sound Christian in this view—despite his condemnation as a 'heretic' by the corrupt Second Council of Constantinople, held by the exoteric Church—is clear from sayings attributed to the Founder of Christianity Himself: 'Unto you [the chosen disciples] it is given to know the mystery of the Kingdom of God; but unto them that are without [i. e. the multitude] all these things are done in parable: that seeing they may see, and not perceive; and hearing they may hear, and not understand' (*Mark*, iv. 11–12); cf. St. Paul in *1 Corinthians*, ii. 7; iii. 1–2; and *Pistis Sophia*, i. 9, 12, 15, and *passim*, translation by G. R. S. Mead (London, 1896).

itself, as a study of the pre-Christian Pali Canon indicates, might very well be regarded, as many Buddhist scholars do regard it, as a Christian restating of doctrines which the Buddha, too, formulated as an inheritance from prehistoric Buddhas.[1] It is chiefly the doctrines of the modern Christian Churches that pride themselves in having no esoteric teachings, and not those of primitive, or Gnostic, Christianity, that did propound an elaborate esotericism, which differ widely from the doctrines of Buddhism and other Oriental religions ; and among these doctrines the more outstanding are: (1) the doctrine of the one life on earth to be followed by a never-ending paradise or else an eternal hell ; (2) of the forgiveness of sins through the blood sacrifice of a Saviour ; and (3) of the uniqueness of the Divine Incarnation as exemplified in the Founder of Christianity.

For the student of the West, whose outlook has been more or less affected by this theology of Church-council Christianity, rather than by primitive, or Gnostic, Christianity, there is need to realize exactly how Buddhism differs in fundamentals from modern Christianity.

Thus, unlike modern, or Church-council, Christianity which teaches dependence upon an outside power or Saviour, Buddhism teaches dependence on self-exertion alone if one is to gain salvation. In practice, and to a limited degree in theory, this fundamental doctrine of self-dependence is modified in Lāmaism—as illustrated in the *Bardo Thödol*—and direct appeal is made by the devotee to the Dhyānī Buddhas and tutelary deities, very much as to Jesus and saints and angels by Christians. Similarly, Northern Buddhism and Church-council Christianity, unlike Southern Buddhism, have their masses and their eucharistical ceremonies.

Secondly, as pointed out above, Church-council Christianity condemns the doctrines of Rebirth and *Karma* (which primitive, or Gnostic, Christianity upheld), and Buddhism champions them.

Thirdly, the two Faiths hold divergent views concerning

[1] Cf. A. J. Edmunds, *Buddhist Texts in John* (Philadelphia, 1911); also *Buddhist and Christian Gospels* (Philadelphia, 1908).

the existence or non-existence of a Supreme Deity. 'The Fatherhood of God' as a personal and anthropomorphic deity is the corner-stone of Christian Theology, but in Buddhism—although the Buddha neither denied nor affirmed the existence of a Supreme Deity—it has no place, because, as the Buddha maintained, neither believing nor not believing in a Supreme God, but self-exertion in right-doing, is essential to comprehending the true nature of life.

The Buddha 'argued not that Ishvara was cause, nor did He advocate some cause heretical, nor yet again did He affirm there was no cause for the beginning of the world'. He argued: 'If the world was made by Ishvara deva, ... there should be no such thing as sorrow or calamity, nor doing wrong nor doing right; for all, both pure and impure deeds, these must come from Ishvara deva. ... Again, if Ishvara be the maker, all living things should silently submit, patient beneath the maker's power, and then what use to practise virtue? 'Twere equal, then, the doing right or wrong, ... Thus, you see, the thought of Ishvara is overthrown in this discussion (*shâstra*).'[1]

Although the Great Teacher has set aside, as being nonessential to mankind's spiritual enlightenment, the belief and the non-belief in a Supreme Deity—more especially in an anthropomorphic Supreme Deity—He has, however, made the corner-stone of Buddhism (as it is of Hinduism) the belief in a Supreme Power or Universal Law, called the Law of Cause and Effect by the Science of the West and, by the Science of the East, *Karma*. 'What ye sow, that shall ye reap', saith the Buddha; even as St. Paul wrote long afterward, 'Whatsoever a man soweth, that shall he also reap'.

Again, as elsewhere stated, Buddhism denies that there can be a permanent, unchanging, personal entity such as Christian Theology calls 'soul'. It also denies the possibility of reaching a state of eternal felicity within the *Sangsāra* (i.e. the universe of phenomena); for Reality, or *Nirvāna*, is for all

[1] Ct. the *Fo-sho-hing-tsan-king* (vv. 1455–68), a professed Chinese version of Ashvaghosha's *Buddhakarita*, made by an Indian Buddhist priest named Dharmaraksha about the year A.D. 420, trans. by S. Beal in *The Sacred Books of the East*, xix (Oxford, 1883), pp. 206–8.

Schools of Buddhism non-*sangsāric*, being beyond all heavens, hells, and worlds, in a state only capable of being understood through personal realization of it.

The Buddha has, therefore, not taught of any Father in Heaven, nor of any Only Begotten Son, nor of any method of salvation for mankind save that won by self-exertion leading to Right Knowledge. He, as all Buddhists believe, found the way as a result of innumerable lifetimes of spiritual evolution, and became the Fully Awakened, the Enlightened One, exhausting completely the *Sangsāra* of Impermanency and of Sorrow. Through His own exertions alone He reached the Goal of all existence—Supramundaneness. Buddhists venerate Him, not as Christians do a Saviour, but as a Guide, in whose footsteps each must tread if Truth is to be realized and Salvation attained.

Although, as in the *Bardo Thödol*, there are prayers addressed to higher than human powers, and although all Buddhists pay what is really a sort of worship to the Buddha, the doctrine of Right Knowledge through self-development is never quite lost sight of; there is never that almost complete dependence upon outside forces which Christianity inculcates, nor is there anywhere a parallel to the Christian belief in the forgiveness of sins through repentance, or faith in a Saviour, or through vicarious atonement. Some of the rituals of Northern Buddhism may seem to suggest a Christianlike theory of the forgiveness or absolution of sins, which, more than any other subsidiary doctrine peculiar to Northern Buddhism, may possibly yet be shown to have been shaped—if any of the *Mahāyāna* doctrines have been—by Christianity. But in their last analysis these rituals really imply,—setting aside any possible transformation due to Christianity,—as the whole of Southern Buddhism more clearly teaches, that it is only merit, or an equal amount of good *karma*, which can neutralize the same amount of evil *karma*, as, in physics, two equally balanced opposing forces neutralize one another.

But as in all religions, so in Buddhism, there is apt to be very wide divergency between original teachings and actual doctrines and practices ; and, accordingly, the *Bardo Thödol* as a ritual treatise is no exception. Nevertheless, underneath the symbolism of the *Bardo Thödol* there are to be discovered, by those that have eyes to see, the essential teachings of Northern Buddhism, sometimes called, in contrast with Southern Buddhism, the Higher Buddhism.

VII. THE MEDIEVAL CHRISTIAN JUDGEMENT.

In connexion with the difficult problem of origins, referred to in that part of our Introduction concerning the Judgement (pp. 35-9), and of the probable influences of Buddhism and other Oriental Faiths, including the Osirian Faith, on Christianity, it is interesting to compare with the *Bardo Thödol* version of the Judgement (pp. 165-9) the similar version in the medieval treatise entitled *The Lamentation of the Dying Creature* (date uncertain, but probably of 14th to 15th cent.) contained in the British Museum MS. Harl. 1706 (fol. 96), Comper's ed. (pp. 137-68):

'*The Dying Creature enset with Sickness incurable sorrowfully Complaineth him thus :* "Alas that ever I sinned in my life. To me is come this day the dreadfullest tidings that ever I heard. Here hath been with me a sergeant of arms whose name is Cruelty, from the King of all Kings, Lord of all Lords, and Judge of all Judges; laying on me the mace of His office, saying unto me: 'I arrest thee and warn thee to make ready. . . . The Judge that shall sit upon thee, He will not be partial, nor He will not be corrupt with goods, but He will minister to thee justice and equity. . . ."

'*The Lamentation of the Dying Creature:* "Alas! alas! Excuse me I can not, and whom I might desire to speak for me I wot (i.e. know) not. The day and time is so dreadful; the Judge is so rightful; mine enimies be so evil; my kin, my neighbours, my friends, my servants, be not favourable to me; and I wot well they shall not be heard there."

'*The Complaint of the Dying Creature to the Good Angel:* "O my Good Angel, to whom our Lord took me to keep, where be thee now? Me thinketh ye should be here, and answer for me; for the dread of death distroubleth me, so that I cannot answer for myself. Here is my bad angel ready, and is one of my chief accusers, with legions of fiends with him. I have no creature to answer for me. Alas it is an heavy case!"

' *The Answer of the Good Angel to the Dying Creature:* " As to your bad deeds, I was never consenting. I saw your natural inclination more disposed to be ruled by your bad angel than by me. Howbeit, ye cannot excuse you, but when ye were purposed to do anything that was contrary to the commandments of God I failed not to remember (i.e. remind) you that it was not well; and counselled thee to flee the place of peril, and the company that should stir or move you thereto. Can ye say nay thereto? How can you think that I should answer for you?"'

Though the Dying Creature appeals for assistance to Reason, to Dread, to Conscience, and to the Five Wits—very much after the manner of *Everyman*, probably the best known of the medieval Christian mystery plays (which seem to be the outcome of the spread of Orientalism into Europe)—none can succour him. Thence, in his final appeal to the Virgin, through Faith, Hope, and Charity as mediators, and in the Virgin's resulting appeal to the Son, there is introduced the Christian doctrine of the forgiveness of sins, in opposition to the doctrine of *karma* as expounded by the *Bardo Thödol*. Such introduction suggests that this curious Christian version of the Judgement may possibly have had a pre-Christian and non-Jewish Oriental source, wherein the doctrine of *karma* (and the correlated doctrine of rebirth) remained unmodified by the European medievalism which shaped *The Lamentation of the Dying Creature* (see p. 3²). The ancient doctrine of *karma* (to which the primitive, or Gnostic, Christians adhered, ere Church-council Christianity took shape), being taught in the following answers to the Dying Creature, gives some plausibility, even from internal evidence, to this purely tentative view:

Conscience: 'Ye must sorrowfully and meekly suffer the judgements that ye have deserved.'

The Five Wits: 'Therefore of your necessity your defaults

must be laid upon you. . . . Wherefore of right the peril must
be yours.'

Also compare the similar account of the Judgement in the
Orologium Sapientiæ (14th cent.), chap. V, in *Douce MS.* 322
(fol. 20), Comper's ed., from which the following passage
(p. 118) is taken:

'O thou most righteous Doomsman, how strait and hard be
thy dooms ; charging [i. e. accusing] and hard deeming me,
wretched, in those things the which few folk charge or dread,
forasmuch as they seem small and little. O the dreadful sight
of the righteous Justice, that is now present to me by dread,
and suddenly to come in deed.'

Reference might also be made to the wall-painting of the
Judgement in Chaldon Church, Surrey, England, dating from
about A.D. 1200 and discovered in 1870, which parallels in
a very striking manner our Tibetan painting of the Judgement.[1]
Thus, in both paintings there is the judging of the dead in an
intermediate or *bardo* state, the heaven-world being above
and the hell-world below. In the Chaldon Christianized
version, St. Michael, in place of Shinje, holds the scales ;
instead of *karmic* actions, souls are being weighed ; the Six
Karmic Pathways leading to the Six *Lokas* have become
a single ladder leading to a single heaven ; at the top of the
ladder, in place of the Six Buddhas of the Six *Lokas*, there is
the Christ waiting to welcome the righteous, the sun being
shown on His right hand and the moon on His left—as though
He were a Buddha. In the Hell-world, in both versions, there
is the cauldron in which evil-doers are being cooked under the
supervision of demons ; and, in the Christianized version, the
'Hill of Spikes' of the Buddhist version is represented by
a 'Bridge of Spikes', which the condemned souls are compelled to traverse.

[1] Cf. G. Clinch, *Old English Churches* (London, 1900), pp. 162–4, where
a photograph of the Chaldon wall-painting is reproduced ; also E. S. Bouchier,
Notes on the Stained Glass of the Oxford District (Oxford, 1918), pp. 66–7, concerning a stained glass window in Brightwell Baldwin Church, depicting the
soul-weighing episode of the Judgement : 'Below, the hand of St. Michael in
white glass supports a yellow balance, in the left tray of which a half-length soul
with yellow hair is praying, while beneath the right a small devil, with horns,
tail, claws, and yellow wings, is trying to pull it down.'

All such parallels as these tend to strengthen our opinion that the greater part of the symbolism nowadays regarded as being peculiarly Christian or Jewish seems to be due to adaptations from Egyptian and Eastern religions. They suggest, too, that the thought-forms and thought-processes of Orient and of Occident are, fundamentally, much alike—that, despite differences of race and creed and of physical and social environment, the nations of mankind are, and have been since time immemorial, mentally and spiritually one.

INDEX

Black-type figures indicate the chief references, most of which may be used as a Glossary.

Death, that must come, cometh nobly when we give
Our wealth, and life, and all, to make men live.

The Book of Good Counsels, from the *Hitopadesha*
(Sir Edwin Arnold's Translation)